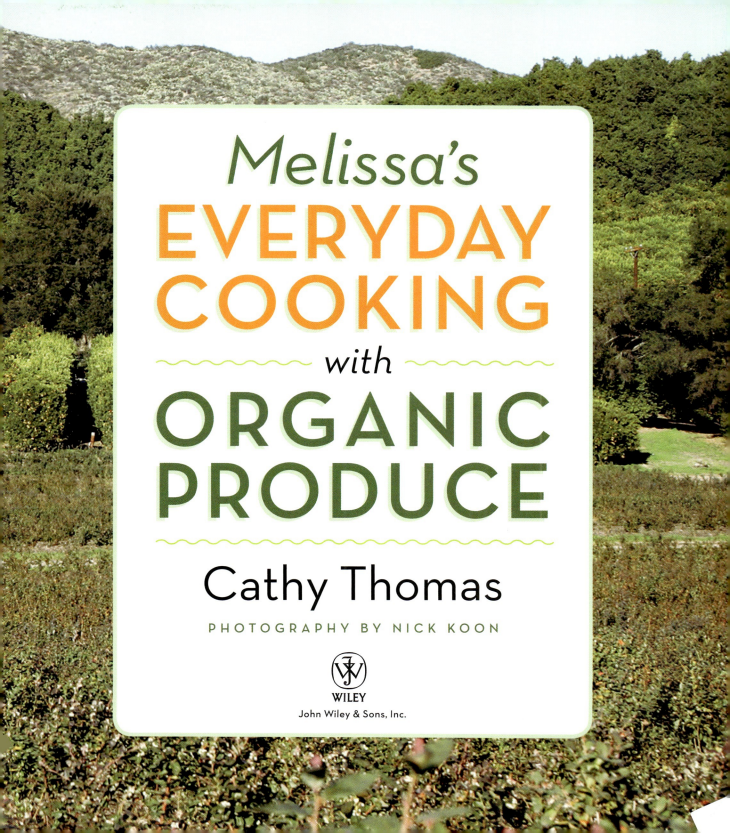

Melissa's
EVERYDAY
COOKING
with
ORGANIC
PRODUCE

Cathy Thomas

PHOTOGRAPHY BY NICK KOON

WILEY

John Wiley & Sons, Inc.

Library of Congress Cataloging-in-Publication Data:

Thomas, Cathy.
Melissa's everyday cooking with organic produce / Cathy Thomas ;
photography by Nick Koon.
p. cm.
Includes index.
ISBN 978-0-470-37105-3 (cloth)
1. Cookery (Natural foods) 2. Cookery (Fruit) 3. Cookery (Vegetables)
I. Melissa's World Variety Produce (Firm) II. Title.
TX741.T52 2010
641.5'636—dc22ISBN: 978-0-470-37105-3

Printed in the United States of America

10 9 8 7 6 5 4 3 2 1

Acknowledgments

Without the team of organic produce gurus at Melissa's/World Variety Produce, this book would have been impossible to create. Enormous thanks go to Sharon and Joe Hernandez and their daughter Melissa for giving me the opportunity to write it.

Imagine my joy at figuring out what to cook with a crate of oh-so-sweet organic plums with 5 percent higher Brix readings than the conventionally grown fruit; or a case of organic strawberries, smaller than their conventional counterparts, but so flavorful that they made me sing; and organic potatoes that tasted so delectable, they could be served for dessert.

Special thanks to Ida Rodriguez, executive chef of Melissa's corporate kitchen, along with her very talented team, Chef Tom Fraker and Chef Miki Hackney. They created many of the recipes, tested recipes, and provided helpful tips.

Heartfelt thanks go to Robert Schueller, Melissa's Director of Public Relations, the knowledgeable "go-to guy" for produce information, and nationally recognized expert on fruits and vegetables. He interviewed organic growers and gathered farming facts for this book. Thanks also to Debra Cohen, Director of Special Projects, for her prompt and accurate fact-checking and guidance. And thanks to registered dietician Cheryl Forberg for her steadfast, accurate nutritional analyses on all the recipes.

Also, I am extremely grateful to the following:

Photographer Nick Koon, who has a rare gift for making food look irresistible.

Editor Anne Ficklen, whose vision and devotion to this project are greatly appreciated.

Assistant Editor Charleen Barila for her constant support, and designers Joel Avirom and Jason Snyder for another irresistible and accessible design.

Finally, I would like to thank my children and husband, Phil McCullough, for their unfailing support, love, and wisdom. And much gratitude goes to my late parents, Harriett and Loren Young, for planting the seeds that nourished my love of fruits, vegetables, cooking, and storytelling.

—*Cathy Thomas*

Contents

Introduction

The Organic Farm

Turn over a spade full of soil from an organic farm. More than likely, it will look as rich and deeply hued as devil's food cake. It's healthy, resilient composted earth, teeming with beneficial micronutrients.

Expect to see some weeds flourishing in that lush soil, and some hand-digging going on to root them out. Clover may thrive between the rows, a cover crop planted to nourish the soil and diminish weed growth.

Get in close and take a look at the beneficial insects that are employed to eliminate unwanted pest infestations: ladybugs and green lacewings, for example, have ravenous appetites for pesky aphids, mites, and whiteflies.

You may find some homespun devices rigged to deter hungry birds, perhaps fluttering ribbons of old cassette tapes tied to poles, or spin-and-whistle whirligigs.

In an organic orchard, there may be rings of white tree paint or copper bands on tree trunks, designed to deter snails and insects. Geese may roam the rows, patrolling for snails. Emus may be enlisted to protect geese from predators. Now, that's creativity.

Organic, sustainable methods of farming provide fruits and vegetables that many think have more flavor. Increased Brix levels for many organically grown produce confirm an increase in sweetness. Brix levels (measured with a refractometer device) are used to measure the specific amount of sugar in fruits, vegetables, and wines (see page 323).

Organic crops mature naturally rather than being manipulated by growth-regulating chemicals, so harvesting is more time consuming because everything cannot be picked at the same time.

Handling Organics   Strict guidelines don't end with the grower. Retailers, food handlers, and retailers are required to adhere to strict policies when handling organic produce. The NOP (National Organic Programs) does not permit the use of packaging materials, storage containers, or bins that contain a "synthetic fungicide, preservative, or fumigant." It does not permit the use or reuse of any bag or container that has been in contact with any such synthetic substances in a manner that compromises the organic integrity of an organically produced product, unless the reusable bag or container has been thoroughly cleaned and poses no risk of contact with synthetic substances.

In the marketplace, organic and conventional produce cannot be commingled; a barrier between the two must be present to prevent direct contact.

BEST BUYS

Yields of organic fruits and vegetables are often smaller than those of crops that are grown conventionally, a reality that often results in higher organic produce prices. The following lists showcase organic produce that are most widely grown. They have vibrant flavor profiles and are often the most competitively priced when compared to conventionally grown counterparts.

FRUITS

Organic Avocados
Organic Fuji Apples
Organic Gala Apples
Organic Grapefruit
Organic Lemons
Organic Limes
Organic Mangoes
Organic Navel Oranges (seasonal)
Organic Tomatoes
Organic Valencia Oranges (seasonal)

VEGETABLES

Organic Broccoli
Organic Carrots
Organic Celery
Organic Cucumbers
Organic Green Bell Peppers
Organic Red Bell Peppers
Organic Romaine Lettuce
Organic Russet Potatoes
Organic Yellow Onions
Organic Zucchini Squash

Recipes for Success

The organic fruits and vegetables showcased in this book were selected based on availability, the organic produce that is most accessible from coast to coast. Specific varieties are also those that are most readily obtainable.

Arranged alphabetically from apples to turnips, this cookbook is formatted to help readers quickly locate information about specific organic fruits and vegetables. Bold headings will guide you to information about availability, plus how to buy, store, prep, and use. With each topic there are four fast serving suggestions in addition to four easy-to-prepare recipes.

The recipes use *all* organic ingredients. Some recipes include meat, but offer meatless tips for preparing the dish meat-free. No fish recipes are included because fish cannot be labeled organic. There are many issues that surround the debate about the criteria that should be used to qualify seafood with the USDA stamp of approval. The National Organic Standards Board of the USDA is in the process of developing those standards.

Melissa's-World Variety Produce

In 1984, produce pioneers Sharon and Joe Hernandez created Melissa's/World Variety Produce, Inc., a family-run business that is now the nation's largest distributor of specialty and organic fruits and vegetables.

The Melissa's brand is named after Joe and Sharon's daughter, Melissa, who takes an active role in the company. Melissa fondly recalls being the only child in grade school with lychees in her lunchbox.

The Los Angeles–based company has a long history of commitment to consumer education. Product tags include recipes, serving suggestions, and nutritional information. The company's Web site, www.melissas.com, provides a wealth of useful guidelines, recipes, and instructional videos.

Melissa's was one of the first nationally recognized brands to bring certified organic produce into mainstream supermarkets. Melissa's Organic Produce started in 1998 with over 100 varieties of produce, a figure that has grown to over 400 year-round and seasonal favorites.

The Integrity of Organic Produce

Creativity runs high among organic growers because they are required to follow very strict guidelines. They are prevented from using synthetically compounded or manufactured fertilizers, pesticides, herbicides, or growth regulators. Companies that handle or process organic food before it gets to your local supermarket or restaurant must follow strict regulations to be certified organic as well.

The USDA National Organic Program (NOP) defines organic as follows:

> Organic food is produced by farmers who emphasize the use of renewable resources and the conservation of soil and water to enhance environmental quality for future generations. Organic food is produced without using most conventional pesticides; fertilizers made with synthetic ingredients or sewage sludge; bioengineering; or ionizing radiation. Before a product can be labeled "organic," a Government-approved certifier inspects the farm where the food is grown to make sure the farmer is following all the rules necessary to meet USDA organic standards.

Nutritional analyses Data is from the USDA National Nutrient Database for Standard Reference, Release 18, and the Food Processor software program, ESHA Research, Inc., in Salem, Oregon. Analyses include: Calories, fat calories, total fat, saturated fat, cholesterol, sodium, total carbohydrates, fiber, sugars, protein, vitamins A and C, calcium, and iron. In recipes that say to add salt and pepper to taste, ½ teaspoon salt and ½ teaspoon ground pepper are used in the analysis. If milk is used in a recipe, 2 percent fat milk is used in the analysis, unless recipe specifies whole milk. If store-bought chicken or vegetable broth is used in a recipe, it is assumed that it is the low-fat, low-sodium version.

SEASONAL ORGANIC PRODUCE CHART

OUT OF SEASON: ▢ AVAILABLE: ●

Produce	J	F	M	A	M	J	J	A	S	O	N	D
APPLE												
Ambrosia	●	●								●	●	●
Braeburn	●	●	●	●	●	●	●			●	●	●
Crimson Gold	●									●	●	●
Fuji	●	●	●	●	●					●	●	●
Gala	●	●	●					●	●	●	●	●
Golden Delicious	●	●					●	●	●	●	●	●
Granny Smith	●	●	●	●	●	●			●	●	●	●
Pink Lady	●									●	●	●
Red Delicious	●	●	●	●					●	●	●	●
APRICOT					●	●	●					
ARTICHOKE	●	●	●	●	●	●			●	●	●	●
ASIAN PEAR	●								●	●	●	●
ASPARAGUS	●	●	●	●	●	●						●
AVOCADO	●	●	●	●	●	●	●	●	●	●	●	●
BANANA	●	●	●	●	●	●	●	●	●	●	●	●
BEAN												
Fava Bean			●	●	●	●						
Green Bean	●	●	●	●	●	●	●	●	●	●	●	●
Soybean	●	●	●	●	●	●	●	●	●	●	●	●
BEET	●	●	●	●	●	●	●	●	●	●	●	●
BELL PEPPER	●	●	●	●	●	●	●	●	●	●	●	●
BERRY												
Blackberry	●	●	●	●	●	●	●	●	●	●	●	●
Blueberry	●	●	●	●	●	●	●	●	●	●	●	●
Cranberry									●	●	●	
Raspberry			●	●	●	●	●	●	●	●		
Strawberry			●	●	●	●	●	●				
BROCCOLI	●	●	●	●	●	●	●	●	●	●	●	●
BRUSSELS SPROUT	●	●	●	●					●	●	●	●

Produce	J	F	M	A	M	J	J	A	S	O	N	D
CABBAGE	●	●	●	●	●	●	●	●	●	●	●	●
CARROT	●	●	●	●	●	●	●	●	●	●	●	●
CAULIFLOWER	●	●	●	●	●	●	●	●	●	●	●	●
CELERY	●	●	●	●	●	●	●	●	●	●	●	●
CHERRY					●	●	●					
CORN	●	●	●	●	●	●	●	●	●	●	●	●
CUCUMBER	●	●	●	●	●	●	●	●	●	●	●	●
EGGPLANT	●	●	●	●	●	●	●	●	●	●	●	●
FENNEL	●	●	●	●	●	●	●	●	●	●	●	●
FIG												
Black Mission							●	●	●			
Brown Turkey							●	●	●			
Kadota								●	●			
GARLIC	●	●	●	●	●	●	●	●	●	●	●	●
GINGER	●	●	●	●	●	●	●	●	●	●	●	●
GRAPE	●	●	●	●	●	●	●	●	●	●	●	●
GRAPEFRUIT	●	●	●	●	●	●	●	●	●	●	●	●
GREENS	●	●	●	●	●	●	●	●	●	●	●	●
HERBS	●	●	●	●	●	●	●	●	●	●	●	●
JICAMA	●	●										
KIWI	●	●	●	●	●	●	●	●	●	●	●	●
KUMQUAT	●	●	●	●								●
LEEK	●	●	●	●	●	●	●	●	●	●	●	●
LEMON	●	●	●	●	●	●	●	●	●	●	●	●
LETTUCE	●	●	●	●	●	●	●	●	●	●	●	●
LIME	●	●	●	●	●	●	●	●	●	●	●	●
MANGO												
Ataulfo			●	●	●	●	●					
Haden	●	●	●	●	●	●						
Kent	●	●	●	●	●	●	●	●	●	●	●	●

	J	F	M	A	M	J	J	A	S	O	N	D
Tommy Atkins	●	●	●	●	●	●	●	●	●	●	●	●
MELON												
Cantaloupe	▢	●	●	●	●	●	●	●	●	●	●	▢
Honeydew	▢	●	●	●	●	●	●	●	●	●	●	▢
Watermelon	▢	▢	▢	●	●	●	●	●	●	●	▢	▢
MUSHROOM	▢	●	●	●	●	●	●	●	●	●	●	●
NECTARINE	▢	▢	▢	▢	●	●	●	●	●	●	▢	▢
ONION												
Cipolline	▢	▢	▢	▢	▢	▢	▢	▢	▢	●	●	●
Green (Scallion)	●	●	●	●	●	●	●	●	●	●	●	●
Red, White	●	●	●	●	●	●	●	●	●	●	●	●
Sweet	▢	▢	▢	●	●	●	●	●	▢	▢	▢	▢
Yellow	●	●	●	●	●	●	●	●	●	●	●	●
ORANGE												
Blood Orange	●	●	▢	▢	▢	▢	▢	▢	▢	▢	▢	●
Cara Cara	●	●	●	▢	▢	▢	▢	▢	▢	▢	▢	▢
Navel	●	●	●	▢	▢	▢	▢	▢	▢	▢	●	●
Valencia	▢	▢	●	●	●	●	●	●	●	▢	▢	▢
PEACH												
Saturn	▢	▢	▢	▢	●	●	●	●	▢	▢	▢	▢
White Flesh	▢	▢	▢	▢	▢	●	●	●	●	▢	▢	▢
Yellow Flesh	▢	▢	▢	▢	●	●	●	●	▢	▢	▢	▢
PEAR												
Bartlett	●	●	●	●	▢	▢	▢	▢	●	●	●	●
Bosc	●	●	●	●	▢	▢	▢	▢	●	●	●	●
D'Anjou	●	●	●	▢	▢	▢	▢	●	●	●	●	●
Red Bartlett	●	●	▢	▢	▢	▢	▢	●	●	●	●	●
Starkrimson	●	▢	▢	▢	▢	▢	▢	●	●	●	●	●
PEAS												
Sno	●	●	●	●	●	●	●	●	●	●	●	●
Sugar Snap	▢	●	●	●	●	●	●	●	●	●	●	●

	J	F	M	A	M	J	J	A	S	O	N	D
PERSIMMON	▢	▢	▢	▢	▢	▢	▢	▢	▢	●	●	●
PINEAPPLE	▢	●	●	●	●	●	●	●	●	●	●	▢
PLUM	▢	▢	▢	●	●	●	●	●	●	●	▢	▢
PLUMCOT	▢	▢	▢	▢	●	●	●	●	▢	▢	▢	▢
POMEGRANATE	▢	▢	▢	▢	▢	▢	▢	▢	●	●	●	▢
POTATO												
Baby, Creamer	▢	●	●	●	●	●	●	●	●	●	●	▢
Fingerling	▢	●	●	▢	▢	▢	▢	▢	▢	▢	●	●
Red, Russet, Yukon Gold	●	●	●	●	●	●	●	●	●	●	●	●
RADISH	●	●	●	●	●	●	●	●	●	●	●	●
SHALLOT	●	●	●	●	●	●	▢	▢	●	●	●	●
SQUASH	●	●	●	●	●	●	●	●	●	●	●	●
SWEET POTATO	●	●	●	●	●	●	●	●	●	●	●	●
TANGERINE, MANDARIN												
Clementine	●	▢	▢	▢	▢	▢	▢	▢	▢	▢	●	●
Honey	●	●	▢	▢	▢	▢	▢	▢	▢	▢	▢	▢
Lee	●	●	▢	▢	▢	▢	▢	▢	▢	▢	▢	▢
Minneola Tangelo	●	●	▢	▢	▢	▢	▢	▢	▢	▢	▢	▢
Orlando Tangelo	●	●	▢	▢	▢	▢	▢	▢	▢	▢	●	●
Page	●	●	▢	▢	▢	▢	▢	▢	▢	▢	▢	▢
Satsuma	●	▢	▢	▢	▢	▢	▢	▢	▢	▢	●	●
TOMATO												
Baby Heirloom	▢	▢	▢	▢	▢	▢	▢	●	●	▢	▢	▢
Cherry	●	●	●	●	●	●	●	●	●	●	●	●
Common Red (Beefsteak)	●	●	●	●	●	●	●	●	●	●	●	●
Grape	●	●	●	●	●	●	●	●	●	●	●	●
Heirloom	●	●	●	●	●	●	●	●	●	●	●	●
Red (Cluster, On-the-Vine)	●	●	●	●	●	●	●	●	●	●	●	●
Roma (Plum)	●	●	●	●	●	●	●	●	●	●	●	●
Teardrop (Red or Yellow)	●	●	●	●	●	●	●	●	●	●	●	●
TURNIP	●	●	●	●	●	●	●	●	●	●	●	●

Year-Round

Best Buy

Apple

Ambrosia

Braeburn

Crimson Gold

Fuji

Gala

Golden Delicious

Granny Smith

Pink Lady

Red Delicious

Braeburn

Fuji

Granny Smith

Golden Delicious

Gala

Ambrosia

Crimson Gold

It's the no-snooze sound that is the first delight as teeth break through apple skin into juicy interior. But there is so much more than just the crunch. Each apple variety has its own unique taste, texture, fragrance, and appearance. Cooking traits vary, too. Some are best cooked, while others are best eaten out of hand. Some are delectable either way.

Many apples in the marketplace are coated with wax to extend their shelf life. But organically grown apples are wax-free and have a lovely natural sheen (but a shorter shelf life).

BUYING AND STORING: Look for firm fruit with smooth skin without bruises or cuts. Store unwashed and dry at room temperature up to one week, or for prolonged storage, refrigerate in plastic bag in crisper drawer up to 3 weeks.

PREP AND USE: Wash. If removing peel, use a small paring knife or swivel-bladed vegetable peeler to remove a thin ribbon of peel. In many dishes, such as fruit salads or grain dishes, it is eye-appealing to leave apples unpeeled. If coring, cut in half or quarters lengthwise; use paring knife to cut away core and seeds (or use an apple corer, a tool that often looks like a metal tube with a handle). With most apples, the flesh discolors when exposed to air. To prevent browning, place in cold water with a little lemon juice.

Eat raw or cooked, peeled or unpeeled. Bake, sauté, braise, or cook in a slow cooker. Use in sweet or savory dishes.

VARIETIES

Ambrosia: Juicy-sweet with crisp, crunchy texture and honeyed, low-acid flavor profile. Unlike other varieties, the flesh doesn't discolor when exposed to air. Especially delicious in salads and applesauce.

Braeburn: Aromatic, firm-crisp, and sweet-spicy flavor with a hint of tartness. Use for cooking or snacking.

Crimson Gold: Petite, generally about the size of a golf ball. Crisp; sweetness balanced with gentle tartness and hint of vanilla. Great no-waste snack for children.

Fuji: Super sweet and spicy, juicy and crisp texture. Use for cooking or snacking.

Gala: Very crunchy with high sugar content. It is the most popular apple in America. Use for cooking and snacking.

Golden Delicious: Very sweet with softer texture. Although it is delicious eaten raw, it is generally used in cooked dishes. Great in cakes, pies, tarts, and galettes.

Granny Smith: Pucker-up tartness and crisp texture makes this a great snack for those who prefer a not-too-sweet flavor burst. It is great for baking into crisps, tarts, and pies.

Pink Lady: Mild, sweet taste with a hint of tartness. Firm, crisp flesh. Use for cooking or snacking. Delicious thinly sliced and used inside a grilled cheese sandwich.

Red Delicious: Crunchy with mild, subtle sweetness. Good for snacking, not for cooking.

AVAILABLE

Ambrosia: October to February

Braeburn: October to August

Crimson Gold: October to February

Fuji: October to August

Gala: Year-round

Golden Delicious: September to April

Granny Smith: Year-round

Pink Lady: September to January

Red Delicious: Year-round

NUTRITIONAL INFORMATION (per 1 cup chopped raw): Calories 65, fat calories 2; total fat 0 grams, sat fat 0 grams, cholesterol 0 milligrams; sodium 1 milligram; total carbohydrates 17 grams, fiber 3 grams, sugars 13 grams; protein 0 grams; vitamin A IUs 1%; vitamin C 10%; calcium 1%; iron 1%.

SERVING SUGGESTIONS

Quickie Pork Chops with Apples

Season ½ cup flour with salt and pepper. Dredge 8 very thin pork chops with seasoned flour. Heat 2 tablespoons unsalted butter and 2 tablespoons extra-virgin olive oil in large, deep skillet. Brown chops and cook on both sides, about 3 minutes on each side, or until thoroughly cooked. Remove pork and add 2 tart apples such as Granny

Smiths (peeled, cored, thinly sliced) and 1 tablespoon fresh thyme leaves; cook, tossing occasionally, until apples start to soften, about 4 minutes. Spoon apples over chops and serve.

Crimson Gold 'n' Chocolate

These petite apples are delectable dipped in chocolate. Wash and thoroughly dry several Crimson Gold apples. Place a sheet of waxed paper on baking sheet. Melt semisweet chocolate in top of double boiler over barely simmering water, stirring frequently, until melted but not hot. Holding apple by the stem, dip bottom half of apple in chocolate (if apple doesn't have stem, insert a bamboo skewer in stem end and use that to hold apple while dipping). Place on waxed paper chocolate-side down. If necessary, harden chocolate by chilling in refrigerator.

Apple Coleslaw

Shred or cut cored apples into thin matchsticks; add along with cabbage to coleslaw.

Fast Spiced Apple Topping

Peel medium apple, core, and cut into thin slices. Place in microwave-safe bowl. Sprinkle with ⅛ teaspoon ground cinnamon and pinch of ground nutmeg. Top with 2 teaspoons butter cut into several pieces. Cover and microwave on high power until apple is softened, about 1 to 2 minutes. Cautiously remove cover, opening it on the side opposite you. Enjoy as is, or spoon over pancakes, French toast, ice cream, or pudding.

Ambrosia Applesauce

YIELD: ABOUT 6 CUPS

Ambrosia apples lend an irresistible honey-like sweetness to applesauce. Serve applesauce with pork or game. Or for dessert, serve it topped with a dollop of whipped cream or vanilla yogurt and garnish with a sprig of fresh mint. If you like, accompany with crisp cookies. This applesauce also is a great topping for pancakes, waffles, or French toast.

> 3 pounds Ambrosia apples, peeled, cored, cut into eighths
>
> 1 cup water or ½ cup water plus ½ cup apple juice
>
> 1 tablespoon fresh lemon juice, Meyer lemon juice preferred

1   Place all ingredients in large saucepan; bring to boil on high heat. Reduce heat to medium-low, cover, and simmer until apples are soft, about 30 minutes.

2   Use slotted spoon to cautiously lift hot apples into food processor or blender. Process until smooth, adding cooking liquid as needed to reach desired consistency. Serve warm or chilled.

Nutritional information (per serving): Calories 130, fat calories 0; total fat 0 grams, sat fat 0 grams, cholesterol 0 milligrams; sodium 0 milligrams; total carbohydrates 34 grams, fiber 5 grams, sugars 26 grams; protein 1 gram; vitamin A IUs 2%; vitamin C 20%; calcium 2%; iron 2%.

Cook's Note: If desired, substitute another variety of apple, adding sugar or agave syrup to taste, if necessary.

Waldorf Salad with Blueberries and Toasted Pecans

YIELD: 10 SERVINGS

Often we think of Waldorf Salad as a treat for a special occasion or as part of a holiday tradition. But that's a shame, because it is so easy to prepare and it's absolutely delicious. This version tops off the salad with fresh blueberries; it's an addition that not only looks pretty but also adds a welcome spark of sweet-tart flavor.

½ cup raisins

⅔ cup mayonnaise

⅓ cup sour cream

2 tablespoons sugar

2 teaspoons fresh lemon juice

6 crisp apples, such as Fuji or Gala, unpeeled, cored, cut into ½-inch cubes or ¼-inch-wide wedges

4 stalks celery, trimmed, diced

½ cup chopped toasted pecans (see Cook's Note)

Butter lettuce leaves or mixed baby greens

½ teaspoon salt

¾ cup blueberries

1 Place raisins in small bowl. Cover with warm water. Set aside for 20 minutes.

2 Meanwhile, in separate small bowl, place mayonnaise, sour cream, sugar, and juice; stir to combine.

3 In large, nonreactive bowl, combine apples, celery, and pecans. Drain raisins, discarding liquid. Add drained raisins and mayonnaise mixture to apple mixture; toss to combine. Cover and chill at least 1 hour or up to 24 hours.

4 Line salad plates with lettuce or mixed baby greens. Spoon salad on top. Season with salt. Top with blueberries.

Nutritional information (per serving): Calories 200, fat calories 100; total fat 11 grams, sat fat 2 grams, cholesterol 5 milligrams; sodium 260 milligrams; total carbohydrates 27 grams, fiber 4 grams, sugars 14 grams; protein 2 grams; vitamin A IUs 4%; vitamin C 15%; calcium 4%; iron 4%.

Cook's Note: To toast pecans, place in single layer on rimmed baking sheet. Toast in middle of 350°F oven until nicely toasted, about 4 or 5 minutes. Watch carefully because nuts burn easily. Cool.

Waldorf Salad with Blueberries and Toasted Pecans

Apple and Blue Cheese Salad

YIELD: 8 SERVINGS

Apples, nuts, and blue cheese form an irresistible flavor marriage in this tossed green salad. The dressing can be made several days in advance and refrigerated well-sealed. The nuts can be toasted or candied two days in advance, cooled, and stored in an airtight container.

½ cup safflower oil or extra-virgin olive oil

½ cup crumbled blue cheese

3 tablespoons balsamic vinegar

1 teaspoon salt

1 large shallot, minced

2 bunches watercress, tough stems removed

1 head butter lettuce or romaine, torn into bite-size pieces

3 crisp apples, such as Ambrosia, Granny Smith, Fuji, or Gala, unpeeled, cored, cut into thin wedges

¾ cup toasted or candied pecans or walnuts (see Cook's Notes)

1   In small bowl or glass measuring cup with handle, combine safflower oil or extra-virgin olive oil and cheese. Use fork to mash about half of cheese into oil, pressing it against side of container. Stir in vinegar, salt, and shallot.

2   Place watercress, lettuce, and apples in large bowl. Toss with enough dressing to lightly coat leaves. Divide among 8 salad plates and top with nuts. Serve.

Nutritional information (per serving with toasted nuts): Calories 270, fat calories 220; total fat 24 grams, sat fat 4 grams, cholesterol 5 milligrams; sodium 430 milligrams; total carbohydrates 12 grams, fiber 3 grams, sugars 7 grams; protein 4 grams; vitamin A IUs 60%; vitamin C 35%; calcium 10%; iron 6%.

Cook's Notes: To toast nuts, place in single layer on rimmed baking sheet. Toast in middle of 350°F oven until nicely toasted, about 4 or 5 minutes. Watch carefully because nuts burn easily.

To candy nuts, combine ¼ cup sugar and 1 teaspoon coarse salt, such as kosher, in small bowl; set next to stove along with ¾ cup untoasted pecan or walnut halves in a separate container. Next to ingredients place a rimmed baking sheet. Heat large, deep skillet or wok on medium-high heat; add nuts and toss about 1 minute to heat nuts. Add half of sugar-salt mixture; stir nuts constantly until sugar dissolves. Add remaining sugar-salt mixture and stir until sugar dissolves and coats nuts. *Immediately* turn nuts out on baking sheet to cool. When cool enough to handle, break nuts apart.

Rustic Apple Galette

YIELD: 8 SERVINGS

Here is an easy version of apple pie. The almond-enriched crust is simply rolled out and the apple mixture placed on top. A clean, apple-free border is left around the dough's edge and it is folded higgledy-piggledy over the apples to partially enclose them.

Filling

4 tablespoons unsalted butter

1 tablespoon apple juice or sherry

½ cup light brown sugar

4 apples, such as Ambrosia, Fuji, Gala, or Golden Delicious, peeled, cored, cut into ¼-inch-wide wedges

1 cup dried cherries or dried cranberries

2 tablespoons cornstarch

Crust

½ cup whole skin-on almonds, toasted (see Cook's Notes, page 18)

1 tablespoon sugar

1¼ cups all-purpose flour, plus flour for dusting work surface and rolling pin

Pinch of salt

6 tablespoons (¾ stick) chilled unsalted butter, cut into 8 pieces

1 to 2 tablespoons ice water

1 egg white

Optional garnish: powdered sugar

Optional for serving: whipped cream or ice cream

1 Adjust oven rack to middle position. Preheat oven to 350°F.

2 Prepare filling: Melt butter in large, deep skillet. Add juice or sherry, brown sugar, apples, cherries or cranberries, and cornstarch; cook on medium heat 3 minutes (apples should still be firm), stirring frequently. Remove from heat, set aside, and let cool.

3 Prepare crust: Place almonds and sugar in food processor fitted with metal blade. Process until almonds are finely ground. Add flour and salt; pulse 4 times to combine. Add butter and pulse about 6 times or until butter is cut into very small pieces (the largest pieces of butter should be no bigger than a pea). With processor running add enough ice water (without ice) in thin stream until dough just barely starts to come together and leaves sides of bowl. Form dough into a disk, wrap in plastic wrap, and chill for 30 minutes.

4 On a lightly floured surface using a lightly floured rolling pin, roll dough into ¼-inch-thick round circle (approximately a 13-inch round). Don't worry if dough edges are ragged. Transfer to rimmed baking sheet. Place apple mixture in center, leaving 1½- to 2-inch border without fruit mixture. Fold dough border over apples; smooth and fold dough as necessary to form a 9-inch round (area in center will be open).

5 Brush exposed dough with egg white. Bake for 45 to 60 minutes, or until apples are soft. If top starts to get too brown before apples have softened, cover loosely with aluminum foil.

6 Serve warm or at room temperature. If desired, dust top of galette with powdered sugar and serve with either whipped cream or ice cream.

Nutritional information (per serving without whipped cream or ice cream): Calories 400, fat calories 170; total fat 19 grams, sat fat 9 grams, cholesterol 40 milligrams; sodium 20 milligrams; total carbohydrates 52 grams, fiber 5 grams, sugars 27 grams; protein 6 grams; vitamin A IUs 10%; vitamin C 6%; calcium 4%; iron 10%.

Apricot

At its tree-ripened best, the juicy flesh looks like deep-pile velvet. Apricot's taste, enhanced by flowery perfume, is a perfect balance of sweet and tart flavors. A rosy blush may adorn one cheek. It graces the downy orange-gold skin, promising apricot lovers that inside, the fruit is fragrant and flavorful.

Organic apricots have intensely sweet flavors; typically on a Brix refractometer they measure 4 to 5 percent higher than conventionally grown apricots. Crops mature naturally without being manipulated by growth-regulating chemicals, so the apricots ripen randomly; organic apricots are harvested four to five times during the two-month season. Organic crops yield about 30 percent less than conventional, and a greater amount is lost in the warehouse because they bruise easily during packing.

There are primarily two varieties that are grown organically: Helena and Patterson. Helena apricots are large and very sweet. Patterson apricots are slightly smaller than the Helena variety.

BUYING AND STORING: Buy plump fruit that are fragrant and a little firm but not hard (they should be just on the verge of softening but not mushy). Avoid fruit that are green-tinged or bruised. If ripe, wash and eat as soon as possible. Ripe fruit can be stored, unwashed, in refrigerator crisper drawer in plastic bag up to 3 days. If unripe, ripen by placing in loosely sealed paper bag at room temperature away from heat or direct sunlight for 2 to 3 days; check daily to monitor ripeness.

PREP AND USE: Rinse with cold running water. Skin is thin, so it is seldom removed. But in some baked goods, peeling is recommended. Remove peel by submerging in boiling water for 15 to 20 seconds; drain and refresh with cold water. Slip paring knife under skin and pull off skin; it should slip right off. To halve, cut along the lengthwise seam (called the suture) and twist each side in opposite directions; discard pit. To prevent browning if the cut fruit is going to sit a long time, dip cut sides in acidulated water (water with small amount of lemon juice in it).

AVAILABLE: April to June

NUTRITIONAL INFORMATION (per 1 cup halved, raw): Calories 74, fat calories 5; total fat 1 gram, sat fat 0 grams, cholesterol 0 milligrams; sodium 2 milligrams; total carbohydrates 17 grams, fiber 3 grams, sugars 14 grams; protein 2 grams; vitamin A IUs 60%; vitamin C 26%; calcium 2%; iron 3%.

SERVING SUGGESTIONS

Apricot-Pineapple Salsa

Delectable spooned on grilled tofu, poultry, or pork, this tangy mixture can be made several hours in advance of serving and refrigerated. Combine 4 apricots (pitted, chopped), 1 cup diced fresh pineapple, 3 tablespoons fresh cilantro, ¼ cup chopped red onion, ½ jalapeño chile (seeded, minced), 2 tablespoons fresh lime juice, and 1 tablespoon olive oil; toss to combine. Use caution when working with fresh chiles; wash hands and work surface thoroughly upon completion and do *not* touch eyes or face.

Cheese-Stuffed Delicacies

In food processor, process until smooth 4 ounces crumbled blue cheese with 3 ounces room-temperature cream cheese. Fill hollow portion of pitted, halved fresh apricots with about 1 teaspoon of cheese mixture. Either serve as is for dessert (each garnished with a fresh mint leaf), or use as a topper for servings of mixed green salad dressed with a simple vinaigrette and garnished with chopped toasted walnuts or pistachios.

Apricot Grilling Glaze

Brush on grilled poultry or pork during the last 5 minutes of cooking to bring sunny apricot taste to poultry or pork. Puree enough pitted, chopped apricots in food processor or blender to make about ½ cup. Add 3 tablespoons red wine vinegar and 2 tablespoons light brown sugar, plus salt and freshly ground black pepper to taste; process to combine.

Think-Twice Rice

Prepare pilaf by heating 2 to 3 tablespoons unsalted butter (or a combination of butter and canola oil) in large saucepan on medium-high heat; add 1 cup raw long-grain rice and ¼ cup diced red onion. Lightly brown, stirring frequently. Add 2 cups chicken broth or vegetable broth; bring to boil. Cover and reduce heat to low; cook 17 minutes. Remove lid and fluff with fork (if there is liquid still present, continue to cook another few minutes). Add ½ cup diced apricots, 1 tablespoon minced fresh basil leaves, and ¼ cup toasted pine nuts; toss. Taste; add salt and freshly ground black pepper as needed.

Chicken Breasts with Apricots

YIELD: 4 SERVINGS

Unadorned skinned and boned chicken breasts can taste rather humdrum. Add some quickly sautéed apricots and things can get interesting, especially if you include an easy wine reduction sauce with lime zest, chile, and ginger.

2 teaspoons unsalted butter

5 ripe apricots, pitted, quartered

1 tablespoon extra-virgin olive oil

4 (4-ounce) skinless, boneless chicken breasts (see Meatless Tip)

Salt and freshly ground black pepper

1 teaspoon minced fresh ginger

4 green onions, thinly sliced, white parts only, reserving dark green stalks for garnish

1 teaspoon finely minced lime zest (colored portion of peel)

1 medium jalapeño chile, seeded, minced (see Cook's Notes)

½ cup dry white wine

1 tablespoon maple syrup or sugar-free maple syrup or agave pancake syrup

Garnish: ⅓ cup toasted slivered almonds (see Cook's Notes)

Optional garnish: Finely sliced reserved green onion stalks

1   In large, nonstick skillet, melt butter on medium-high heat. Add apricots, cut-side down. Cook until heated through and starting to lightly brown, about 2 to 3 minutes. Remove from heat; set aside.

2   In a separate large, nonstick skillet, heat oil on medium-high heat. Season chicken with salt and pepper to taste; add to skillet in single layer. Cook until nicely browned, about 5 minutes. Turn with tongs. Reduce heat to medium-low and cook until chicken is cooked throughout and no pink color remains, about 11 minutes. Transfer chicken to plate.

3   To skillet used for chicken, add ginger, green onions, zest, and chile; cook on medium heat about 30 seconds. Add wine and bring to boil, scraping up brown bits at bottom of pan. When wine has reduced to about 3 tablespoons, add maple syrup or agave pancake syrup and stir. Taste and adjust seasoning, adding more salt and pepper as needed. Add chicken to reheat about 1 minute; add apricots and reheat just long enough to barely get them hot.

4   Place chicken on serving plate. Spoon sauce on top. Garnish with toasted nuts, and green onion stalks, if desired.

Nutritional information (per serving): Calories 290, fat calories 110; total fat 13 grams, sat fat 3 grams, cholesterol 70 milligrams; sodium 60 milligrams; total carbohydrates 12 grams, fiber 2 grams, sugars 8 grams; protein 28 grams; vitamin A IUs 20%; vitamin C 15%; calcium 6%; iron 8%.

Cook's Notes: Use caution when working with fresh chiles. Wash hands and work surface thoroughly upon completion and do *not* touch face or eyes.

To toast almonds, place on rimmed baking sheet in single layer. Toast in middle of 350°F oven about 3 or 4 minutes until lightly toasted. Watch nuts carefully because they can burn easily. Cool.

Meatless Tip: Prepare sauce, omitting chicken (step 2). Serve sauce over Grilled Tofu with Mediterranean-Style Marinade (page 321).

Pork Chops with Curry-Apricot Sauce

YIELD: 2 SERVINGS

This quick-to-prepare dish is designed to serve two, but it can stretch to serve four with some adaptations. Instead of skinny rib chops, use a thicker cut of boneless pork loin; use medium-high heat and a little more oil, then cook about 4 minutes per side, or until thoroughly cooked through. Divide the sauce four ways, and garnish with additional diced apricots and cilantro.

¼ cup water

3 tablespoons apricot preserves or low-sugar apricot preserves

⅛ teaspoon dried red chile flakes

2 tablespoons canola oil or vegetable oil, divided use

1 large red onion, halved top to bottom, thinly sliced

1½ teaspoons mild curry powder

4 (4-ounce) bone-in rib pork chops, ⅜- to ½-inch thick (see Meatless Tip)

Salt and freshly ground black pepper

Garnish: 2 ripe apricots, pitted, cut into thin wedges, divided use

Garnish: about 3 tablespoons finely chopped fresh cilantro

1   In medium bowl, combine water, preserves, and chile flakes; stir together with fork and set aside.

2   Heat 1½ tablespoons canola oil or vegetable oil in large, deep skillet heat on medium heat. Add onion and curry powder; cook, stirring frequently, until onion softens, about 7 minutes. Add preserves mixture and stir to combine; simmer 1 minute on medium-low heat. Remove from heat.

3   Season pork chops with salt and pepper. In large, deep nonstick skillet, coat bottom of pan with remaining oil, either by tilting or using a paper towel to spread oil on surface. Heat pan on medium-high heat. Add pork chops in single layer and cook about 3 minutes on each side, browning nicely and thoroughly cooking. Add pork chops to onion-preserves mixture. Add wedges of 1 apricot. Turn to medium-high; heat until bubbling. Spoon mixture over chops.

4   Divide between 2 plates and top with remaining apricot wedges and cilantro.

Nutritional information (per serving): Calories 440, fat calories 200; total fat 22 grams, sat fat 3.5 grams, cholesterol 70 milligrams; sodium 660 milligrams; total carbohydrates 31 grams, fiber 2 grams, sugars 17 grams; protein 30 grams; vitamin A IUs 20%; vitamin C 20%; calcium 6%; iron 10%.

Meatless Tip: Omit pork. Prepare sauce as directed and spoon over Sautéed Breaded Tofu (page 320).

Apricot–White Chocolate Upside-Down Cake

YIELD: 12 SERVINGS

Using a cake mix can really speed up preparation time without sacrificing flavor or texture. This apricot cake is delectable served warm accompanied with ice cream.

6 ripe apricots

1 (16.2-ounce) box organic white or vanilla cake mix

Ingredients listed on cake mix package (substitute orange juice for amount of milk designated on package)

¾ cup white chocolate chips

4 tablespoons (½ stick) unsalted butter, melted

½ cup light brown sugar

Optional for serving: ice cream

1   Adjust oven rack to middle position. Preheat oven according to cake mix instructions.

2   Bring 2 cups water to a boil in medium saucepan on high heat. Add apricots and cook for 15 to 20 seconds. Drain in colander and refresh with cold water. When cool enough to handle, peel apricots. Cut each in half along seam and remove pit.

3   Prepare batter according to cake mix instructions, substituting orange juice for milk.

4   Using a rubber spatula, fold chocolate chips into batter.

5   Pour butter into 9 × 13-inch baking pan; tilt to coat bottom. Sprinkle evenly with sugar. Place apricots cut-side down in single layer on top of brown sugar. Carefully and slowly pour batter in pan, covering apricots.

6   Bake about 30 to 35 minutes, or until toothpick inserted in middle comes out clean. Cool on wire rack until just slightly warm. Cut into squares and serve, inverted to show off apricots, either warm or at room temperature, with ice cream if desired.

Nutritional information (per serving without ice cream): Calories 410, fat calories 210; total fat 23 grams, sat fat 7 grams, cholesterol 65 milligrams; sodium 330 milligrams; total carbohydrates 49 grams, fiber 1 gram, sugars 37 grams; protein 5 grams; vitamin A IUs 10%; vitamin C 15%; calcium 10%; iron 6%.

Cook's Note: Recipe was tested using Dr. Oetker Organics Vanilla Cake Mix.

Apricot, Cherry, and Blueberry Cobbler

Apricot, Cherry, and Blueberry Cobbler

YIELD: 8 SERVINGS

It's hard to decide which is more appealing, the sugared biscuits that top a cobbler, or the bright flavors of the fruit filling bubbling below. This distinctively American concoction comes from the phrase "to cobble," meaning to roughly patch something together. This tasty version is best served warm accompanied with ice cream.

Unsalted butter for greasing pan

Filling

2 pounds ripe apricots, unpeeled, pitted, quartered

1 cup blueberries

1 cup pitted cherries, halved

½ cup plus 2 tablespoons sugar

3 tablespoons plus 2 teaspoons cornstarch

2 teaspoons fresh lemon juice

½ teaspoon minced lemon zest (colored portion of peel)

Topping

2 cups all-purpose flour

4½ tablespoons sugar, divided use

½ teaspoon salt

2 teaspoons baking powder

5 tablespoons cold unsalted butter, cut into small pieces

½ cup whole milk

½ cup heavy whipping cream

1 teaspoon vanilla

Optional for serving: ice cream

1   Adjust oven rack to middle position. Preheat oven to 400°F. Lightly grease 2-quart shallow baking dish or 12-inch oval gratin dish (that is at least 2⅛ inches deep) with butter; set aside.

2   Prepare filling: Place apricots, blueberries, and cherries in large bowl; gently toss with rubber spatula. Add sugar, cornstarch, juice, and zest; gently toss to distribute dry ingredients. Place in prepared dish.

3   Prepare topping: In separate large bowl, stir flour, 3 tablespoons sugar, salt, and baking powder with a whisk. Add butter and use pastry cutter (gadget with 4 to 6 stiff wire loops attached to a handle) or 2 knives to cut in the butter (until the largest lumps of butter are about the size of peas). Or combine dry ingredients in food processor and pulse once or twice, then add butter and pulse until largest lumps are pea-size and transfer to bowl. Combine milk, cream, and vanilla in small bowl; pour over flour mixture. Give a few strokes with large wooden spoon. Use clean hands to gently blend. Dough will be wet.

4   Pinch off golf ball–size lumps of sticky dough and drop onto fruit, leaving small spaces between dough. Sprinkle with remaining 1½ tablespoons sugar. Bake for 50 to 60 minutes or until dough is nicely browned and fruit mixture is bubbling.

5   Cool on wire rack for 15 to 20 minutes before serving. Serve warm or at room temperature, alone or with scoop of vanilla ice cream.

Nutritional information (per serving without ice cream): Calories 410, fat calories 130; total fat 14 grams, sat fat 8 grams, cholesterol 40 milligrams; sodium 300 milligrams; total carbohydrates 69 grams, fiber 4 grams, sugars 38 grams; protein 6 grams; vitamin A IUs 50%; vitamin C 20%; calcium 10%; iron 10%.

Artichoke

Imagine the scene as mankind first tried to tame an artichoke for consumption. They had to look past the forbidding thorns posted atop the leaves and ignore the tickly hair-like choke at its core. An unopened flower bud of a thistle-like plant, the artichoke required ingenuity to make it edible. Cooking softens its heart and the base of its leaves, offering an alluring nutty, buttery-sweet taste.

In general, artichokes grown in summer or fall are more conical than those grown in springtime. Those grown in summer or fall tend to have a more purplish tinge to their outer petals.

Artichokes are a hardy organic crop in comparison to many other organic crops. Ladybugs are used to fight predatory pests and organic fish emulsion fertilizers are widely utilized. Organic yields are typically 25 percent less when compared to conventional crops. Damage caused by frost (most often in late fall and winter) is called winter kissed. Light bronze to brown coloring forms on the outer leaves, a superficial discoloration that doesn't affect taste, but often reduces price.

BUYING AND STORING: Look for artichokes that are tightly-closed, compact, and feel heavy for their size. To test for freshness, press leaves against each other; a squeaking sound is a sign of freshness. Avoid overmature, open artichokes, or those with firm tips and dry-looking leaves. Refrigerate in crisper drawer (unwashed, untrimmed) in tightly closed plastic bag up to 1 week.

PREP AND USE: To prepare for cooking, wash thoroughly in cold water; invert and tap on counter to shake out water and any debris if the leaves are in an open formation. If present, pull off small ragtag lower leaves on artichoke. Cut the stem to 1-inch length or trim at base of bulb. Using a sharp knife (not carbon steel), cut off top 1 inch of artichoke. Using kitchen scissors, snip off points of remaining leaf tips. In small bowl, combine 1 cup water and 2 tablespoons fresh lemon juice; dip all cut edges in mixture. Artichokes are now ready to cook.

To "boil," stand upright in deep, nonreactive saucepan or Dutch oven. Add enough water to come halfway up side of artichoke(s) and a pinch of salt. If desired add flavoring elements such as a bay leaf, peeled garlic cloves, or fennel seeds. Bring to boil on high heat. Partially cover and reduce heat to gentle boil; cook until fork-tender at base, 35 to 45 minutes. Drain upside down on rack, towel, or plate.

Artichokes can also be microwaved, braised, grilled, or steamed. Trimmed into wedges, they can be deep-fried.

To eat a leaf, grasp leaf by tip and tug between almost-closed teeth to scrape away the luscious meat. Using the tip of a teaspoon, pluck hair-like choke from heart and discard. The choke-free heart will be bowl-shaped and can be enjoyed in its entirety.

To prepare for stuffing, cook until tender, then spread leaves apart at the center and pull out the small leaves; use teaspoon to remove and discard fuzzy choke. Or to use as "boat" for filling, cut cooked artichoke in half lengthwise and remove choke.

AVAILABLE: Year-round, peaks March to July, harder to find December to February

NUTRITIONAL INFORMATION (per 1 medium artichoke): Calories 60, fat calories 2; total fat 0 grams, sat fat 0 grams, cholesterol 0 milligrams; sodium 120 milligrams; total carbohydrates 14 grams, fiber 7 grams, sugars 1 gram; protein 4 grams; vitamin A IUs 0%; vitamin C 25%; calcium 6%; iron 9%.

SERVING SUGGESTIONS

Mediterranean Omelets

Dice cooked artichoke hearts and toss with crumbled soft goat cheese and chopped fresh thyme leaves. Use mixture to fill omelets.

Tarragon Aïoli Dip

Combine ¾ cup mayonnaise, 2 tablespoons extra-virgin olive oil, 1 teaspoon white wine vinegar, 2 teaspoons minced fresh tarragon leaves, 1 large clove garlic (minced), pinch of salt, and a small squeeze of fresh lemon juice. Stir to combine and use as dip for cooked artichoke leaves.

Greened Gratin

Add 3 or 4 cooked artichoke hearts to a potato gratin. Cut hearts from top to bottom into ¼-inch slices and layer them along with potatoes in the casserole dish.

Cheese-Topped Leaves

Spread leaves of two cooked artichokes on a platter. They can be hot, cold, or room temperature. In small bowl, combine ½ cup extra-virgin olive oil, ½ cup grated pecorino cheese and salt and freshly ground black pepper to taste. If desired, add 1 tablespoon minced prosciutto instead of salt. Mix with fork and spoon over leaves. Sprinkle with chopped fresh Italian parsley. Serve as appetizers and provide napkins.

Quinoa-Stuffed Artichokes

YIELD: 4 SERVINGS

Quinoa, pronounced KEEN-wah, is hailed to be the grain of the future, although it was a staple of the ancient Inca civilization. It is labeled a "complete protein" because it contains all eight essential amino acids. In step 3 it says to cook the quinoa until a germ ring appears and most of the liquid has disappeared. A "germ ring" is a curlicue within the grain; it looks like a tiny curled wire.

1 lemon

4 artichokes, cleaned, trimmed

Salt

1½ tablespoons extra-virgin olive oil

1 cup minced onion

½ cup minced red bell pepper

½ cup minced celery

1 tablespoon minced garlic

2¾ cups chicken broth or vegetable broth

1⅓ cups quinoa

¼ teaspoon salt

¼ teaspoon freshly ground black pepper

½ cup grated Parmesan cheese

½ to ¾ cup Vinaigrette (see Cook's Note)

Garnish: 4 tablespoons finely chopped fresh Italian parsley

1 Remove zest (colored portion of peel) from lemon; mince zest and set aside. Juice lemon. Prepare artichokes for cooking (see Prep and Use).

2 To "boil," stand upright in deep, nonreactive Dutch oven. Add enough water to come halfway up side of artichokes, lemon juice, and pinch of salt. Bring to boil on high heat. Partially cover and reduce heat to gentle boil; cook until fork-tender at base, 35 to 45 minutes. Remove from water and drain upside down on plate or rack.

3 Heat oil in large saucepan or Dutch oven on medium-high heat. Add onion, bell pepper, and celery. Cook until onion begins to soften, about 3 minutes, stirring frequently. Add garlic; stir and cook about 30 seconds. Add chicken broth or vegetable broth, quinoa, ¼ teaspoon salt, and black pepper. Bring to a boil over high heat; reduce heat to medium and simmer, uncovered, stirring occasionally, for 10–15 minutes or until germ ring on quinoa is present and almost all liquid has evaporated. Add zest and remove from heat. While you preheat broiler and arrange artichokes in step 4, stir quinoa mixture periodically to allow steam to release.

4 Adjust oven rack 8 inches below broiler element. Preheat broiler. Place drained and cooled artichokes stem side down on a rimmed baking sheet. Use fingers to partially open each artichoke to make an open bloom. Fill between leaves with quinoa mixture. Top with cheese and broil until lightly browned. Place each artichoke in a shallow bowl. Drizzle with vinaigrette, sprinkle with parsley, and serve.

Nutritional information (per serving with vinaigrette): Calories 470, fat calories 200; total fat 22 grams, sat fat 3 grams, cholesterol 0 milligrams; sodium 340 milligrams; total carbohydrates 61 grams, fiber 11 grams, sugars 4 grams; protein 13 grams; vitamin A IUs 6%; vitamin C 50%; calcium 10%; iron 40% (note ⅓ of vinaigrette used in analysis).

Cook's Note: To make Vinaigrette, place 3 tablespoons red wine vinegar in small bowl or glass measuring cup with handle. Add ½ teaspoon coarse salt, such as kosher, and 1 teaspoon Dijon-style mustard; whisk to combine. Whisk in ¾ cup extra-virgin olive oil. Whisk again before using.

Cheese Salad Crowned Artichoke Dippers

YIELD: 8 SERVINGS

A cheese salad made of Parmesan cheese, mayonnaise, toasted nuts, garlic, and lemon juice provides a flavorful topping for artichoke leaves. If you like, add a little finely chopped roasted red bell pepper.

2 medium artichokes, washed, trimmed

2 tablespoons fresh lemon juice

Salt

4 cloves garlic, peeled

Filling

1 large clove garlic, minced

2 tablespoons mayonnaise

2 tablespoons fresh lemon juice

2 tablespoons extra-virgin olive oil

5 ounces Parmesan cheese, cut into ⅛-inch cubes or coarsely chopped into pieces about ⅛ inch wide

½ cup finely chopped celery

½ cup finely chopped toasted walnuts (see Cook's Note)

Salt and freshly ground black pepper

1 tablespoon chopped fresh Italian parsley

1 Prepare artichokes for cooking (see Prep and Use). To "boil," stand upright in deep, nonreactive saucepan or Dutch oven. Add enough water to come halfway up side of artichokes; add pinch of salt and garlic cloves. Bring to boil on high heat. Partially cover and reduce heat to gentle boil; cook until fork tender at base, 35 to 45 minutes. Remove from water and drain upside down on a plate or rack. Cool.

2 Prepare filling: In medium bowl, combine garlic, mayonnaise, juice, oil, cheese, celery, and walnuts. Stir to combine. Taste and adjust seasoning as needed, adding salt and pepper to taste.

3 Remove artichoke leaves and place in concentric circles in a single layer on large round platter, leaving a space in center empty. Remove choke from each artichoke. Dice artichoke hearts and place in center of platter; season with salt and pepper.

4 Using 2 teaspoons (one to scoop filling and the other to push filling off), place a small portion of cheese salad at base of each leaf. When each leaf has topping, sprinkle with parsley and place any remaining cheese mixture atop diced hearts in center.

Nutritional information (per serving): Calories 190, fat calories 130; total fat 14 grams, sat fat 4 grams, cholesterol 15 milligrams; sodium 480 milligrams; total carbohydrates 7 grams, fiber 2 grams, sugars 1 gram; protein 10 grams; vitamin A IUs 4%; vitamin C 10%; calcium 20%; iron 6%.

Cook's Note: To toast walnuts, place in single layer on rimmed baking sheet. Toast in middle of 350°F oven until lightly browned, about 1 minute. Watch carefully because nuts burn easily. Cool.

Artichoke Boat Filled with Chicken-Potato Salad

YIELD: 6 SERVINGS

Cooked until tender and drained, halved artichokes make stylish containers for everything from rice salad to artichoke dip. When cool enough to handle, scoop out the choke and smaller leaves to make a hollow area for the filling. The flower-like shape of the bisected artichoke looks beautiful, especially if a portion of stem is left intact. In this recipe the tasty filling is a chicken salad that showcases potatoes and fresh tarragon.

3 large artichokes, cleaned, trimmed,
  with stems preferred

Juice of 1 small lemon, divided use

Salt

Salad

1 pound small Yukon Gold potatoes or small
  red potatoes, unpeeled, scrubbed

1 cup chopped celery

¾ cup store-bought mayonnaise

¼ cup sour cream

3 tablespoons Dijon-style mustard

2 tablespoons white wine vinegar

Freshly ground black pepper

2 tablespoons minced fresh tarragon leaves

1 large sweet onion, finely chopped

3 cups chopped cooked skinless, boneless chicken
  (see Meatless Tip)

For serving: mixed baby greens

Garnish: sprigs of fresh tarragon

Artichoke Boat Filled with Chicken-Potato Salad

1   Prepare artichokes for cooking (see Prep and Use) using 2 tablespoons juice. To "boil," place in deep, nonreactive saucepan or Dutch oven. Add enough water to come halfway up side of artichokes, remaining juice, and pinch of salt. Bring to boil on high heat. Partially cover and reduce heat to gentle boil; cook until fork-tender at base, 35 to 45 minutes. Remove from water and drain upside down on a plate or rack.

2   When cool enough to handle, cut in half lengthwise with a sharp knife. Use spoon to remove choke and small, pale leaves. Place in airtight plastic bag or container; refrigerate.

3   Meanwhile, place potatoes in large saucepan and cover with water. Add pinch of salt to water and bring to boil on high heat. Reduce heat to medium and simmer until potatoes are fork-tender. Drain. When cool enough to handle, cut potatoes in half or quarters to produce small, bite-size pieces.

4   Meanwhile, in large bowl, combine celery, mayonnaise, sour cream, mustard, vinegar, pepper, tarragon, and onion. Stir to combine. Add potatoes; toss, cover, and refrigerate until chilled.

5   Add chicken to potato mixture; toss. Taste and adjust seasoning as needed. Line 6 dinner plates with small portion of mixed baby greens. Place artichoke halves in middle, cut-side up. Filled artichokes with salad. Garnish each with tarragon sprig and serve.

Nutritional information (per serving): Calories 370, fat calories 130; total fat 15 grams, sat fat 3.5 grams, cholesterol 65 milligrams; sodium 460 milligrams; total carbohydrates 36 grams, fiber 6 grams, sugars 5 grams; protein 25 grams; vitamin A IUs 6%; vitamin C 50%; calcium 8%; iron 15%.

Meatless Tip: Substitute small cubes of smoked tofu or "chicken" tofu for chicken.

Antipasti Platter with Marinated Artichoke Hearts

YIELD: 8 SERVINGS

A colorful platter brimming with antipasti is a great party starter. It can be as simple as marinated artichokes teamed with olives or diced cheese. For a more elaborate presentation, include some cold cuts, roasted carrots, radishes, and marinated shallots. Provide guests with small plates, forks, and an assortment of sliced rustic bread.

4 medium artichokes, washed, trimmed

Juice of 1 lemon, divided use

¾ cup white wine vinegar

½ cup extra-virgin olive oil

¼ teaspoon dried red chile flakes

3 medium cloves garlic, peeled, smashed

⅛ teaspoon coarse salt, such as kosher

4 sprigs fresh thyme

2 sprigs fresh rosemary

Optional additions: sliced salami, mixed olives, diced Parmesan cheese, radishes, Pickled Shallots (page 287), room-temperature Roasted Carrots (page 92).

1   Prepare artichokes for cooking (see Prep and Use) using 2 tablespoons juice. To "boil," place in deep, nonreactive saucepan or Dutch oven. Add enough water to come halfway up side of artichokes, remaining juice, and pinch of salt. Bring to boil on high heat. Partially cover and reduce heat to gentle boil; cook until fork-tender at base, 35 to 45 minutes. Remove from water and drain upside down on a plate or rack.

2   When cool enough to handle, cut in half lengthwise with a sharp knife. Use spoon to remove choke and small, pale leaves.

3   In large nonreactive saucepan or Dutch oven, place vinegar, oil, chile flakes, garlic, salt, thyme, and rosemary. Bring to a gentle simmer on medium heat; simmer until garlic is softened but not browned, about 3 minutes.

4   Add artichokes to mixture and toss to coat; cook on high heat until heated through. Remove from heat and gently toss. Taste and adjust seasoning. Set aside to marinate 2 hours or place in airtight plastic container or plastic bag; refrigerate at least 2 hours or overnight.

Nutritional information (per serving): Calories 160, fat calories 120; total fat 14 grams, sat fat 2 grams, cholesterol 0 milligrams; sodium 100 milligrams; total carbohydrates 9 grams, fiber 4 grams, sugars 1 gram; protein 2 grams; vitamin A IUs 4%; vitamin C 15%; calcium 4%; iron 6%.

Asian Pear
also called Apple Pear

The texture produces a noisy racket in the mouth, like a water chestnut or firm apple. Thinly sliced, raw Asian pear's signature juicy crispness makes it a welcome instead-of-cracker base for appetizers; or it can be a boisterous salad ingredient. When braised or poached, it keeps a little of its spunky consistency. The taste is subtly sweet with a hint of pear and a gentle melon note.

Organic Asian pears are primarily grown in Oregon and Washington State. Three varieties are most common: the early maturing Kosui, the larger Hosui, and the Twentieth Century (Nijisseiki), the latter being the most popular Asian pear in Japan. As with apples and European pears (such as Bartlett), organic Asian pears can be held in a controlled atmosphere in a warehouse setting to extend their availability.

BUYING AND STORING: They ripen on the tree, so look for fruit that is fragrant, but still a little firm. Store at room temperature up to 4 days, or refrigerate up to 2½ months in the crisper drawer.

PREP AND USE: If serving as an accompaniment to cheese or chocolate, wash, dry, and cut (unpeeled, uncored) into thin horizontal slices. For other raw uses (shredded, diced, or cut into wedges), they require peeling and coring. For coring, use a sturdy apple corer or cut in half from top to bottom and use a paring knife to remove seeds and the surrounding seed bed.

Eat raw or cooked. They require longer cooking times than European pears; braise, stir-fry, poach, or cook in slow cooker.

AVAILABLE: October to January

NUTRITIONAL INFORMATION (per 1 medium Asian pear, raw): Calories 51, fat calories 2; total fat 0 grams, sat fat 0 grams, cholesterol 0 milligrams; sodium 0 milligrams; total carbohydrates 13 grams, fiber 4 grams, sugars 9 grams; protein 1 gram; vitamin A IUs 0%; vitamin C 8%; calcium 0%; iron 0%.

SERVING SUGGESTIONS

Dessert "Salad" with Noise

To make dressing, combine 4 tablespoons fresh lime juice and 2 tablespoons honey or agave syrup; stir to blend. Peel and core 3 large or 4 small Asian pears. Cut into 1-inch-long matchsticks and toss with dressing. Spoon into martini glasses and top with generous amount of crumbled blue cheese. Serve as dessert.

Cheese Plate

Cut unpeeled Asian pears into thin crosswise slices; use on cheese platter instead of (or in addition to) bread slices or crackers.

Arugula Teammate

In a small bowl, mix 2 tablespoons fresh lemon juice and 3 tablespoons extra-virgin olive oil, plus salt and freshly ground black pepper to taste. Toss with 6 cups of small arugula leaves and 3 Asian pears (peeled, cored, cut into thin wedges). Garnish servings with small cubes of Parmesan cheese.

Asian Pear "Applesauce"

Place 6 Asian pears (peeled, cored, diced), 1 cup water, and 1 tablespoon fresh lemon juice in medium saucepan. Bring to boil on high heat; reduce heat to low and simmer until almost soft. Remove with slotted spoon and puree in food processor fitted with metal blade, adding enough cooking liquid to reach desired consistency. Sweeten with sugar or agave syrup to taste and garnish servings with ground cinnamon.

Asian Pear Slaw

YIELD: 6 SERVINGS

Think of this recipe as a coleslaw blueprint, an outline that you can augment with other ingredients to suit your taste. Chopped peanuts, pineapple cubes, grated carrots, and toasted sesame seeds are just a few of the potential add-ons.

4 Asian pears, peeled, cored, cut into matchsticks

4 cups shredded Napa cabbage

½ medium sweet onion, finely diced

2 green onions, trimmed, cut into thin crosswise slices, including ½ dark green stalks

⅓ cup sugar

1½ tablespoons seasoned rice vinegar

1 tablespoon distilled white vinegar

⅛ teaspoon salt

⅛ teaspoon freshly ground black pepper

¼ cup whole milk

½ cup mayonnaise

¼ cup buttermilk

2½ tablespoons fresh lemon juice

1   In large bowl, combine Asian pears, cabbage, and onions; set aside.

2   In medium bowl, combine sugar and vinegars; stir well to combine and dissolve sugar. Add remaining ingredients and still well to combine.

3   Add dressing to pear mixture; toss to coat. Cover and refrigerate 2 hours. Taste and adjust seasonings as needed and serve.

Nutritional information (per serving): Calories 230, fat calories 70; total fat 8 grams, sat fat 1.5 grams, cholesterol 5 milligrams; sodium 300 milligrams; total carbohydrates 41 grams, fiber 7 grams, sugars 28 grams; protein 3 grams; vitamin A IUs 45%; vitamin C 50%; calcium 8%; iron 4%.

Asian Pear and Cantaloupe Salad

YIELD: 8 SERVINGS

The crunchy texture of Asian pear contrasts nicely with the melting-soft mouthfeel of ripe cantaloupe. Here they team with goat cheese and low-acid vinaigrette boosted with mustard and mustard seeds to make an unforgettable salad.

1 tablespoon mustard seeds

⅓ cup extra-virgin olive oil

2 tablespoons white wine vinegar

1 teaspoon Dijon-style mustard

1 teaspoon ground mustard

Salt and freshly ground black pepper

1½ tablespoons hot water

8 cups mixed baby greens

2 Asian pears

1 ripe cantaloupe, halved, seeded, peeled, cut into ½-inch wedges

⅓ cup chopped fresh basil leaves

5 ounces cold soft goat cheese

Optional garnish: 4 slices prosciutto, cut in half lengthwise (see Meatless Tip)

1   Place mustard seeds in small skillet on medium-high heat. Cook until lightly browned, shaking handle occasionally to redistribute seeds as they heat. If seeds start to "jump" out of skillet, they are ready. Immediately place seeds on plate to cool.

2   In small bowl or glass measuring cup with a handle, combine oil, vinegar, Dijon-style mustard, ground mustard, and salt and pepper to taste. Whisk to combine. Whisk in water. Add toasted mustard seeds and stir. Taste and adjust seasoning, adding more salt or pepper as needed.

3   Divide greens between 8 plates. Peel and core Asian pears. Cut into ½-inch-wide wedges and place on greens. Top with cantaloupe wedges. Sprinkle with basil. Stir dressing and drizzle over salads. Crumble cheese and sprinkle on salads. If desired, drape a piece of prosciutto across top of each salad.

Nutritional information (per serving without prosciutto garnish): Calories 200, fat calories 140; total fat 15 grams, sat fat 5 grams, cholesterol 15 milligrams; sodium 270 milligrams; total carbohydrates 12 grams, fiber 3 grams, sugars 3 grams; protein 6 grams; vitamin A IUs 80%; vitamin C 60%; calcium 10%; iron 8%.

Meatless Tip: Omit prosciutto.

Asian Pear Bites

Asian Pear Bites

YIELD: ABOUT 20 TO 30 APPETIZERS

The focus of these scrumptious appetizers is the cubes of Asian pear that have been slowly braised in butter and brown sugar. The sweet, buttery fruit sits atop a crunchy cracker and is balanced with the salty tang of feta cheese and prosciutto. If you prefer, eliminate the meat and top each with a small leaf of fresh tarragon that will bring a subtle taste of anise to each bite.

4 tablespoons unsalted butter

2 small Asian pears, peeled, cored, cut into ¼-inch dice

¼ cup light brown sugar

1 (8-ounce) box crackers

6 to 8 ounces sliced prosciutto, cut into cracker-size pieces (see Meatless Tip)

4-ounces crumbled feta cheese, about 1 cup

Optional garnish: small fresh Italian parsley leaves

1   Melt butter in medium saucepan on low heat. Add pears and stir to coat with butter; add sugar and stir to coat. Cook on low, stirring occasionally, until tender. Remove from heat and set aside to cool.

2   Assemble pear bites: Place prosciutto on cracker, then add small spoonful of pear and top with small amount of feta cheese. Repeat with remaining crackers. If desired, garnish each with small parsley leaf.

Nutritional information (per appetizer): Calories 90, fat calories 40; total fat 4.5 grams, sat fat 2.5 grams, cholesterol 15 milligrams; sodium 320 milligrams; total carbohydrates 10 grams, fiber 1 gram, sugars 2 grams; protein 4 grams; vitamin A IUs 2%; vitamin C 0%; calcium 2%; iron 0%.

Meatless Tip: Omit prosciutto and if desired, garnish each with small fresh tarragon leaf instead of parsley.

Tea-Poached Asian Pears

YIELD: 8 SERVINGS

Desserts that can be prepared in advance are great for entertaining at home. Poach these Asian pears up to 2 days in advance and refrigerate them in their poaching liquid. Top each serving with a generous spoonful of crème fraîche, plain yogurt, or sour cream. Pass crisp vanilla cookies as an optional accompaniment.

3½ cups sugar

3½ cups water

1 medium orange or tangerine

2½ cups dry white wine

3 cinnamon sticks

2 tablespoons loose Earl Grey or English Breakfast tea or 4 tea bags

2 crosswise slices fresh ginger, ¼-inch thick

4 Asian pears, peeled, cored, quartered

For serving: crème fraîche or plain yogurt or sour cream

Optional garnish: sprigs of fresh mint

Optional for serving: crisp vanilla cookies

1   Adjust oven rack to middle position. Preheat oven to 300°F. Combine sugar and water in large nonreactive Dutch oven; place on medium-high heat and bring to simmer. Stir and simmer until sugar dissolves. Use swivel-bladed vegetable peeler to remove wide strips of zest from orange or tangerine, colored portion only, without white pith. Add strips of zest to sugar mixture and simmer 1 minute.

2   Add wine, cinnamon, tea, and ginger; bring to boil on high heat. Add pears. Liquid should cover pears; if necessary add enough water to cover. Cover and place in middle of preheated oven. Poach until crisp-tender, about 1 hour. Cool 30 minutes. Strain, reserving liquid, discarding solids. Combine strained liquid and pears in nonreactive container (such as glass or ceramic). Cover and refrigerate up to 2 days.

3   Serve either warm or chilled in small bowls or martini glasses along with half the poaching liquid. If desired top with a generous dollop of crème fraîche or sour cream or plain sweetened yogurt. If desired, garnish each with sprig of fresh mint and provide cookies.

Nutritional information (per serving without topping or cookies): Calories 270, fat calories 0; total fat 0 grams, sat fat 0 grams, cholesterol 0 milligrams; sodium 0 milligrams; total carbohydrates 62 grams, fiber 5 grams, sugars 55 grams; protein 1 gram; vitamin A IUs 0%; vitamin C 20%; calcium 2%; iron 0%.

Asparagus

Connoisseurs argue about whether fat or thin stalks are preferable. Those preferring pencil-thin asparagus spears contend that they have better flavor and cook faster. As for plumper stalks with cigar-size waistlines, fans argue that the additional flesh adds tenderness that is missing in the thinner spears. Whether lean or fat, spears should be fairly uniform in size for best results when cooking. And they should have firm closed tips.

Growers report that asparagus is one of the most difficult crops to grow organically because the delicate tips are extremely vulnerable. Those pointed crowns can mold or burn; often organic farmers grow asparagus in shade houses to protect it from cold or heat.

BUYING AND STORING: Look for deep green color with tips that are closed and compact; partially opened or mushy tips are a sign of aging or mishandling. Choose stalks that are about the same size for even cooking. Asparagus needs to be kept cold; refrigerate, unwashed, in plastic bag up to 4 days in crisper drawer. Or store standing upright in about 1 inch of water, covering container with plastic bag.

PREP AND USE: Wash thoroughly in cold running water. If tips are sandy, dunk in and out of bowl of cold water. Trim tough, woody ends or grasp both ends and snap at the breaking point. If stem "skin" is tough, peel with swivel-bladed vegetable peeler from base about halfway to the tip.

To cook in boiling water (blanch): Cook only until just barely tender but not limp; the color should be bright green. Refresh with plenty of cold water to stop cooking and freshen the color.

To roast: Adjust oven rack to upper third position and preheat oven to 400°F. Toss with enough extra-virgin olive oil to coat stalks. Place on rimmed baking sheet, season with coarse salt, such as kosher; roast about

7 to 12 minutes, until tender-crisp and tips are lightly caramelized, giving the pan a shake to redistribute stalks after 5 minutes. Turn oven light on and take a peek from time to time after 6 minutes. Do not overcook.

To grill: Toss asparagus in mixture of 2 tablespoons extra-virgin olive oil and 1 tablespoon soy sauce. On medium-high heat, grill on oiled and heated vegetable screen (or place at 90-degree angle to grate so spears don't fall through), turning with tongs as needed. Grill about 2 to 4 minutes per side depending on fire and size.

To steam: Place in steamer basket over boiling water on high heat (water should not touch bottom of basket). Cover, reduce heat to medium; steam until tender-crisp, 7 to 12 minutes.

AVAILABLE: Year-round

NUTRITIONAL INFORMATION (per 1 cup chopped, raw): Calories 27, fat calories 1; total fat 0 grams, sat fat 0 grams, cholesterol 0 milligrams; sodium 3 milligrams; total carbohydrates 5 grams, fiber 3 grams, sugars 3 grams; protein 3 grams; vitamin A IUs 20%; vitamin C 13%; calcium 3%; iron 16%.

SERVING SUGGESTIONS

Quick Asparagus Couscous

Preheat oven to 400°F. Prepare a 10-ounce box couscous according to package directions. Meanwhile, toss ½ pound trimmed asparagus and 2 medium zucchini (cut in half lengthwise) with enough olive oil to lightly coat. Place in single layer on rimmed baking sheet. Sprinkle with coarse salt. Roast in upper third of oven until tender-crisp and lightly caramelized, about 8 to 12 minutes. Cut into bite-size pieces and toss with couscous. Add salt and freshly ground black pepper to taste. Garnish with finely diced red bell pepper and chopped fresh basil leaves.

Grilled and Gingered

For sauce, combine ⅓ cup soy sauce, 3½ tablespoons rice vinegar, 2 tablespoons water, 1 tablespoon sugar, and 1½ tablespoons minced fresh ginger. For asparagus, toss 1 pound trimmed asparagus with 1 tablespoon vegetable oil. Grill on medium-high heat until tender-crisp, about 2 to 4 minutes on each side, turning halfway through with long tongs. Grilling times vary depending on heat and asparagus diameter. Place on rimmed platter and top with sauce.

Prosciutto Wrap

Roast trimmed asparagus until tender-crisp. Wrap each stalk with 1 thin slice prosciutto (prosciutto should be long enough to go around stalk 2 times). Serve as finger food garnished with a smidgen of Lemon-Infused Olive Oil (see page 191) or extra-virgin olive oil, and a little grated Parmesan cheese. Or cool and place ungarnished atop mixed green salad.

No-Fuss Soup

Cut 2 pounds trimmed asparagus into 1-inch pieces. Slice 5 large shallots. In large saucepan or Dutch oven, heat 2 tablespoons extra-virgin olive oil and 2 tablespoons unsalted butter on medium-high heat. Add shallots and cook until starting to soften, about 3 to 4 minutes. Add asparagus and 2 (14-ounce) cans vegetable or chicken broth. Bring to boil on high heat; reduce heat to medium-low and simmer 5 minutes or until asparagus is tender. Cool 5 minutes and puree in batches in blender (use caution and hold top down with potholder) or food processor. Season with salt and freshly ground black pepper. Top each serving with dollop of sour cream, minced fresh basil, and minced lemon zest (colored portion of peel).

Rosemary Spaghetti with Roasted Asparagus

YIELD: 8 APPETIZER SERVINGS

Lightly clothed in a garlic-rosemary butter sauce, this delectable pasta dish showcases fresh asparagus. The beautiful spears are roasted to lightly caramelize the tips and give the stalks a just-right crunch. Roasting times will vary according to asparagus width. Turn on oven light and keep an eye on the stalks after 6 or 7 minutes of roasting.

- 1 pound asparagus, trimmed
- 2 tablespoons extra-virgin olive oil
- ½ teaspoon coarse salt, such as kosher
- 5 tablespoons unsalted butter, divided use (see Cook's Note, page 40)
- 1 large yellow onion, coarsely chopped
- 5 medium cloves garlic, sliced
- 1½ cups chicken broth or vegetable broth
- 1½ tablespoons chopped fresh rosemary leaves
- 1 pound spaghetti, thick spaghetti preferred
- ¼ cup freshly grated Parmesan cheese, plus cheese for optional topping
- Salt and freshly ground black pepper
- Garnish: 8 sprigs fresh rosemary

Rosemary Spaghetti with Roasted Asparagus

1 Adjust oven rack to upper third of oven. Preheat oven to 400°F. Spread asparagus on rimmed baking sheet in a single layer; brush with oil and sprinkle with salt. Roast until fork-tender, about 7 to 12 minutes, shaking pan halfway through cooking to redistribute stalks (roasting time varies depending on thickness of asparagus). Cut stalks into 1½-inch pieces. Set aside.

2 In large, deep skillet melt 4 tablespoons butter on medium-low heat. Add onion and cook until nicely browned, about 15 minutes. Add garlic and cook 1 minute. Add chicken broth or vegetable broth and chopped rosemary; increase heat to high and reduce by half.

3 Meanwhile, bring large pot of salted water to boil on high heat. Add spaghetti and cook according to package directions until al dente (tender with a little bite); drain, reserving 2 tablespoons pasta water.

4 Add pasta and reserved cooking water to butter mixture. Add cheese, 1 tablespoon butter and asparagus. Gently toss. Season with salt and plenty of pepper. Garnish each serving with rosemary sprig.

Nutritional information (per serving): Calories 330, fat calories 100; total fat 11 grams, sat fat 5 grams, cholesterol 15 milligrams; sodium 280 milligrams; total carbohydrates 47 grams, fiber 4 grams, sugars 3 grams; protein 11 grams; vitamin A IUs 15%; vitamin C 8%; calcium 6%; iron 20%.

Cook's Note: If you prefer, substitute half of butter added in step 2 with extra-virgin olive oil.

Asparagus, Garbanzo, and Bell Pepper Salad

YIELD: 4 SERVINGS

To save preparation time, instead of roasting bell peppers use drained store-bought roasted red bell pepper strips. If cooking the asparagus in advance, refresh with cold water after cooking. Drain and cool until lukewarm. Wrap in kitchen towel; enclose towel in plastic bag and refrigerate up to 24 hours. If desired, strips of leftover cold steak or chicken are a delectable addition to this salad, as well as thick slices of hothouse cucumber or tomato wedges.

2 large bell peppers, red or yellow, or a combination

8 ounces asparagus, trimmed, cut on diagonal into 1-inch pieces

2 medium cloves garlic, minced

3 tablespoons fresh lemon juice

2 teaspoons minced fresh oregano leaves

1 tablespoon minced fresh basil leaves

Salt and freshly ground black pepper

½ cup extra-virgin olive oil

1 (14 ounce) can garbanzo beans, drained, rinsed

12 kalamata olives, pitted

6 cups mixed baby greens

4 ounces crumbled feta cheese

1 Preheat broiler. To roast bell peppers, line a baking sheet with aluminum foil, leaving some extra foil on the ends. Place whole peppers in a single layer on foil. Place 6 to 8 inches below broiler element. Broil until lightly charred. Rotate peppers with tongs and char on all sides. Remove from oven and draw up ends of foil to enclose peppers for 5 minutes. Open foil; when cool enough to handle, peel peppers and discard seeds. Resist temptation to wash skin off with water; use hands, the pepper will be more flavorful. Tear or cut into ½-inch-wide strips.

2 Blanch or steam asparagus until tender-crisp (see Prep and Use). Drain and refresh with cold water. Drain again and set aside.

3 In large bowl, place garlic, juice, oregano, basil, and salt and pepper to taste. Stir with fork. Add olive oil and stir to combine. Taste and adjust seasoning as needed. Add garbanzo beans, red pepper strips, and olives; toss.

4 Add asparagus and gently toss. Divide greens between plates. Spoon asparagus mixture on top of greens. Top with feta cheese and serve.

Nutritional information (per serving): Calories 480, fat calories 350; total fat 36 grams, sat fat 8 grams, cholesterol 25 milligrams; sodium 610 milligrams; total carbohydrates 29 grams, fiber 10 grams, sugars 8 grams; protein 13 grams; vitamin A IUs 60%; vitamin C 150%; calcium 25%; iron 30%.

Crostini with Asparagus and Tarragon Sauce

YIELD: 25 SERVINGS

Tarragon tastes completely different when it is fresh rather than dried. When fresh it has a sweet, subtle licorice scent and flavor that pairs beautifully with fresh green vegetables, especially asparagus. These appetizers showcase an easy-to-prepare fresh tarragon sauce teamed with both asparagus and, for added richness, thinly sliced ripe avocado.

25 medium crackers or ½ of 1-pound baguette, cut into 25 thin crosswise slices (plus 1½ tablespoons olive oil)

5 ounces asparagus, trimmed, cut on the diagonal into 1½-inch lengths

1 cup mayonnaise

1 tablespoon minced fresh tarragon leaves

2 teaspoons white wine vinegar

1 medium clove garlic, minced

1 teaspoon fresh lemon juice

1½ tablespoons extra-virgin olive oil

1 ripe avocado, halved, pitted, peeled, cut into thin crosswise slices

Seasoned salt and freshly ground black pepper

1   If using baguette, adjust oven rack to about 6 inches below broiler element. Preheat broiler. Lightly brush both sides of baguette slices with 1½ tablespoons oil. Place in single layer on rimmed baking sheet and broil until golden, turning once. It is helpful to turn on oven light to watch them carefully to make sure they don't "over-brown."

2   Blanch or steam asparagus until tender-crisp (see Prep and Use). Drain and refresh with cold water. Drain again and pat dry with clean kitchen towel or paper towels. Set aside.

3   Prepare tarragon sauce: In medium bowl, combine mayonnaise, tarragon, vinegar, garlic, juice, and 1½ tablespoons oil. Whisk to combine.

4   Place avocado slice atop each cracker or toasted bread slice and season with seasoned salt and freshly ground pepper to taste. Top each with small dollop of tarragon sauce and top with either one or two pieces of asparagus (depending on asparagus diameter). Serve.

Nutritional information (per crostini): Calories 100, fat calories 60; total fat 7 grams, sat fat 1 gram, cholesterol 0 milligrams; sodium 170 milligrams; total carbohydrates 10 grams, fiber 1 gram, sugars 1 gram; protein 1 gram; vitamin A IUs 2%; vitamin C 2%; calcium 0%; iron 2%.

Asparagus Salad with Raspberry Vinaigrette

YIELD: 6 SERVINGS

Raspberry-based vinaigrette is a fabulous combination of sweet and tart flavors. In this lovely salad it marries with the earthy-vegetal taste of asparagus and spinach, further balanced with the subtly bitter, crunchy walnuts.

1 cup fresh or frozen (thawed) raspberries

6 tablespoons extra-virgin olive oil

¼ cup heavy whipping cream

2 tablespoons white wine vinegar

1 tablespoon honey or agave syrup

Salt and freshly ground black pepper

2½ cups small fresh spinach leaves or mixed baby greens

Asparagus, cooked tender-crisp (roasted, boiled, or grilled; see Prep and Use; see Cook's Notes)

Garnish: about 18 fresh raspberries

Garnish: ⅓ cup toasted walnut halves (see Cook's Notes)

1 Using food processor fitted with metal blade, process raspberries until pureed. Strain through a sieve to remove seeds; discard seeds. Add to strained raspberries oil, cream, vinegar, honey, and salt and pepper to taste; process until blended, about 1 minute. Taste and adjust seasoning if needed.

2 Divide spinach between 6 plates. Top with asparagus, dividing it equally. Drizzle dressing on top, adding enough to nicely coat asparagus. Garnish each salad with about 3 raspberries and walnut halves.

Nutritional information (per serving without garnishes): Calories 180, fat calories 160; total fat 17 grams, sat fat 4 grams, cholesterol 15 milligrams; sodium 105 milligrams; total carbohydrates 6 grams, fiber 1 gram, sugars 4 grams; protein 0 grams; vitamin A IUs 4%; vitamin C 10%; calcium 2%; iron 2%.

Cook's Notes: Use 5 large spears per person for a first-course dish. If you are using thin spears, increase the number to 7 or 8 per person.

To toast walnuts, place on rimmed baking sheet in 350°F oven until lightly browned, 3 to 5 minutes Watch them because they can burn easily.

If you like, add some crumbled blue cheese as a final garnish.

Year-Round

Best Buy

Avocado

Yes, the avocado is a fruit. The confusion seems to center around the luxurious nut-buttery taste. Most fruits have sweet-tart flavor combinations. But because ripe avocados aren't the least bit sweet or tart, they are often thought of as a vegetable.

The Hass variety makes up 95 percent of the organic avocados available in the marketplace. Their thick, bumpy skin darkens as they ripen, signaling that the flesh inside will have velvety texture and rich taste. Other varieties include Lamb-Hass, a medium-size avocado with smooth skin that is growing in popularity, as well as the Fuerte and Reed. Both Fuerte and Reed have thin skin that stays green when ripe. Reed avocados are large, papaya-size fruit with a milder flavor profile.

BUYING AND STORING: They ripen after they are picked. Push the skin to determine ripeness. If it is hard, it will require 2 to 6 days for ripening (see page 323). If it yields slightly with gentle pressure, it's ripe and good for slicing or dicing. If it leaves a small dent when pressed, it's very ripe and good for mashing. If it leaves a large dent when pressed, it is overripe and will probably be discolored. Refrigerate ripe avocados loose in crisper drawer up to 5 days.

PREP AND USE: Wash and dry. To remove pit, cut in half lengthwise; twist halves in opposite directions to separate. Use teaspoon to pry out pit. If mashing, scoop flesh out with small spoon. If dicing, place avocado in one hand, cut-side up (as a safety precaution, place a potholder or thick kitchen towel underneath avocado). Using a small knife, make parallel cuts about ½ inch apart going side to side (do not cut through rind). Make parallel cuts about ½ inch apart going top to bottom (do not cut through rind). Scoop out with bowl of small spoon, getting as close to rind as possible.

If slicing, remove skin. Some varieties have skin that peels easily; others are stubborn. Remove pit, then quarter lengthwise. Use a paring knife to grasp skin at small end and pull to opposite end.

To prevent discoloration, squeeze lemon or lime juice on cut avocado. Cover mashed avocado with plastic wrap pressed snugly on surface (to press out air). Some contend that placing the pit in the mixture also helps.

Eat raw or use as garnish on warm dishes. Add to salsa, vinaigrette, salad, sandwiches, sushi, and hamburgers.

AVAILABLE: Hass variety year-round, all four varieties February to May

NUTRITION INFORMATION (per 1 cup cubes, raw): Calories 240, fat calories 184; total fat 22 grams, sat fat 3 grams, cholesterol 0 milligrams; sodium 11 milligrams; total carbohydrates 13 grams, fiber 10 grams, sugars 1 gram; protein 3 grams; vitamin A IUs 4%; vitamin C 25%; calcium 2%; iron 5%.

SERVING SUGGESTIONS

Bumpy Green Bowls

Use avocado halves as a container for your favorite chicken salad. Halve avocado(s) and remove pit. Season with freshly ground black pepper and place cut-side up on plates lined with baby greens or watercress. Fill with chilled chicken salad or tofu salad (see Artichoke, page 30).

Salsa-fied Avocado Rice

Top individual servings of cooked rice with a tangy avocado-based salsa. To make the salsa, gently toss 1 large ripe avocado (seeded, peeled, diced) with ½ cup prepared salsa or salsa verde and ½ cup diced mango. Spoon over rice.

Sick Day Soup

Here is a delectable cold cure. Place 6 cubes ripe avocado in bottom of soup bowl and top with a squeeze of fresh lemon juice and a few grinds of black pepper. Top with hot chicken broth and serve.

'Cado Mayo

This flavored mayonnaise is delicious on sandwiches, grilled chicken, or asparagus. In the blender, combine 1 peeled, pitted ripe avocado, 3 tablespoons mayonnaise, 2 teaspoons fresh lime juice, and dash of hot sauce. Puree, stopping to scrape down sides as needed.

'Cado Fruit Salad

YIELD: 8 FIRST-COURSE OR SIDE-DISH SERVINGS

This tasty fruit salad is a great side dish with spicy main courses such as enchiladas, chile, or curry. If desired, serve salad in a pineapple boat (a fresh pineapple that has been cut in half lengthwise with flesh removed).

4 tablespoons fresh lime juice

2 tablespoons honey

½ teaspoon ground cinnamon

1 ripe avocado, pitted, peeled, cut into ¾-inch chunks

1 ripe papaya, peeled, seeded, cut into ¾-inch chunks

½ ripe pineapple, peeled, cored, cut into ⅓-inch chunks

Coarse salt, such as kosher

Optional garnish: sprigs of fresh mint

1   In large bowl, place lime juice, honey, and cinnamon; vigorously stir to combine. Add avocado and gently toss.

2   Add papaya and pineapple; gently toss. Spoon salad onto small salad plates or bowls. Sprinkle with small amount of salt. If desired, garnish with mint.

Nutritional information (per serving): Calories 70, fat calories 50; total fat 6 grams, sat fat 1 gram, cholesterol 0 milligrams; sodium 310 milligrams; total carbohydrates 5 grams, fiber 2 grams, sugars 2 grams; protein 1 gram; vitamin A IUs 4%; vitamin C 10%; calcium 2%; iron 2%.

Bacon Guacamole

YIELD: ABOUT 3½ CUPS

Use turkey bacon if you prefer, or leave it out to make a classic guacamole mixture. Not only is it delicious served as a dip with tortilla chips, it is great spooned over grilled chicken breast or pork chop, or atop the patty in a hamburger. Or for a whole new presentation, serve it bruschetta style: spoon small mounds of guacamole on toasted slices of rustic bread and top with a thin wedge of tomato or mango. If preparing guacamole in advance, toss all ingredients except bacon, cover, and refrigerate. Gently toss in bacon just before serving.

6 strips thick-cut bacon (see Meatless Tip)

4 ripe avocados, halved, pitted, diced

2 to 3 tablespoons fresh lime juice

1 ripe plum tomato, seeded, diced

½ medium red onion, finely chopped

1 serrano chile, seeded, finely minced (see Cook's Notes)

2 tablespoons finely chopped fresh cilantro

Salt

For serving: tortilla chips

Optional for serving: hot sauce

1 Cook bacon in single layer in large skillet on medium-high heat until crisp, turning to cook both sides, about a total of 8 to 10 minutes. Drain on paper towels. Roughly chop into small pieces and set aside.

2 In medium bowl, combine avocado and juice; gently toss.

3 Add bacon, tomato, onion, chile, and cilantro; gently toss. Taste and adjust seasoning as needed, adding salt if necessary. Serve with tortilla chips and provide a bottle of hot sauce for those who might prefer a spicier bite.

Nutritional information (per tablespoon with bacon): Calories 30, fat calories 25; total fat 2.5 grams, sat fat 0.5 gram, cholesterol 0 milligrams; sodium 50 milligrams; total carbohydrates 1 gram, fiber 1 gram, sugars 0 grams; protein 1 gram; vitamin A IUs 0%; vitamin C 4%; calcium 0%; iron 0%.

Cook's Notes: 1 minced serrano chile (without seeds or veins) is about 1 tablespoon. If you generally prefer concoctions without much spicy heat, use half as much chile. Then taste and add more to suit your palate.

Use caution when working with fresh chiles. Upon completion wash hands and work surface thoroughly and do *not* touch face or eyes.

Meatless Tip: Omit bacon.

Chilled Avocado Soup

YIELD: 6 (1-CUP) SERVINGS OR 12 (½-CUP) SERVINGS

What better way to start a hot summer meal than with a little cup of chilled soup? The ingredients for this tasty avocado-based soup are simply pureed in either a food processor or blender; there's no cooking required. To ensure the best consistency, make sure the avocados used are ripe. If desired, serve small portions as an appetizer in espresso cups or demitasse cups.

2 ripe avocados

¼ cup chopped green onions, including ½ dark green stalks

2 tablespoons fresh orange juice

1 teaspoon salt

½ teaspoon freshly ground black pepper

¼ teaspoon ground cumin

8 ounces unsweetened, plain yogurt

3 cups vegetable broth

Optional garnish: small amount of finely diced red onion or crumbled bacon or thin lime slices

1   Working in two batches, place all ingredients (except garnishes) in food processor fitted with metal blade or in blender. Cover and process until smooth. Taste and adjust seasoning as needed. Chill at least 1 hour or up to 4 hours.

2   Ladle into bowls or small cups. Garnish as desired and serve.

Nutritional information (per ½ cup serving, without garnishes): Calories 90, fat calories 35; total fat 4 grams, sat fat 0.5 gram, cholesterol 0 milligrams; sodium 0 milligrams; total carbohydrates 15 grams, fiber 3 grams, sugars 10 grams; protein 1 gram; vitamin A IUs 10%; vitamin C 70%; calcium 2%; iron 2%.

Chilled Avocado Soup

Mediterranean Chopped Salad

YIELD: 6 SERVINGS

This versatile salad goes together quickly. If desired, give it even more pizzazz by adding garnishes such as pitted kalamata olives or chopped fresh basil or Italian parsley. The salad is very lightly coated with vinaigrette. If you like, you can double the amount of oil and vinegar and add to suit your taste.

- 4 Roma tomatoes, seeded, coarsely chopped
- ¼ cup finely chopped red onion
- 1 medium cucumber, peeled, halved lengthwise, seeded, coarsely chopped
- 2 medium cloves garlic, minced
- 4 ounces crumbled feta cheese
- 3 tablespoons red wine vinegar
- 1 tablespoon extra-virgin olive oil
- ½ teaspoon salt
- ¼ teaspoon ground black pepper
- 2 to 3 ripe avocados, pitted, peeled, diced (about 2¾ cups)

1   In medium bowl, combine tomato, onion, cucumber, garlic, feta, vinegar, oil, salt, and pepper. Toss.

2   Add avocado and gently toss. Taste and adjust seasoning as needed. Serve.

Nutritional information (per serving): Calories 220, fat calories 170; total fat 19 grams, sat fat 5 grams, cholesterol 15 milligrams; sodium 420 milligrams; total carbohydrates 11 grams, fiber 6 grams, sugars 3 grams; protein 5 grams; vitamin A IUs 10%; vitamin C 25%; calcium 10%; iron 4%.

Banana

The disease-resistant Cavendish banana is the most commonly grown organic variety. It is grown in subtropical regions where frequent rains provide natural pest control. There are no fertilizers used, and no need for weed control.

After harvest, bananas bunches are cut into "hands" (clusters of 4 to 8 bananas). Conventionally grown bananas are then dipped in fungicide to prevent mold, a process that is forbidden with organics. With organic bananas, the area at the top (where the bananas were cut into hands) is dipped in wax.

BUYING AND STORING: Bananas are picked green (unripened). They develop better flavor when ripened off the plant. Avoid any with broken skin or moldy stems. Ripen at room temperature, uncovered. Ripe bananas can be stored in refrigerator for 3 to 4 days, but peel will discolor. To freeze, peel and cut into 1-inch slices; freeze in single layer on baking sheet. When frozen, store airtight in plastic bag or container up to 3 months.

PREP AND USE: Peel and eat, raw or cooked. When exposed to air, flesh discolors. To avoid discoloration, brush with lemon (or lime) juice or dip in acidulated water (cold water with small amount of vinegar, or lime or lemon juice). Use in shakes, smoothies, and ice creams, or dip in chocolate. Puree and use in baked goods. Also delectable in savory dishes: broil, bake, grill, or sauté.

AVAILABLE: Year-round

NUTRITIONAL INFORMATION (per 1 cup mashed, raw): Calories 200, fat calories 6; total fat 1 gram, sat fat 0 grams, cholesterol 0 milligrams; sodium 2 milligrams; total carbohydrates 51 grams, fiber 6 grams, sugars 28 grams; protein 3 grams; vitamin A IUs 3%; vitamin C 33%; calcium 1%; iron 3%.

SERVING SUGGESTIONS

Banana Blender Breakfast

Combine ¾ cup plain nonfat yogurt, ½ banana (sliced, fresh or frozen), 2 ice cubes, and 2 hulled strawberries in blender (if you prefer a sweeter drink, add a little agave syrup or honey). Whirl until smooth.

West Indies Banana Pilaf

In a large saucepan, melt 2 tablespoons unsalted butter or heat 2 tablespoons vegetable oil. Add 1 small onion (chopped), 1 medium clove garlic (minced), and 2 medium carrots (finely chopped). Cook on medium-high heat until onion softens, about 3 minutes. Add 1 cup long-grain rice; cook, stirring frequently, until rice is lightly browned. Remove from heat and add 2 cups chicken or vegetable broth. Bring to boil on high heat. Reduce heat to low; cover and cook 18 minutes. Remove lid and fluff with a fork. Melt 2 tablespoons unsalted butter in large skillet; add 2 bananas (cut in quarters lengthwise and sliced), and cook on medium-high heat, tossing occasionally to lightly brown. Sprinkle bananas with ¼ teaspoon ground cinnamon and add to rice; gently toss. Sprinkle with a smidgen of minced fresh cilantro.

Quick Microwave Bananas Foster

In 4-cup microwave-safe glass bowl (or measuring container), place ½ cup (1 stick) unsalted butter and 1 cup packed dark brown sugar; cover with waxed paper, and microwave on high for 2 minutes. Stir in ¼ teaspoon ground cinnamon, 1 teaspoon vanilla, ¼ cup dark rum, and 4 large bananas (coarsely chopped). Cover and microwave on high power for 1 minute. Spoon mixture over scoops of vanilla or chocolate ice cream.

Parmesan Bananas

Serve these as a side dish with grilled chicken or spicy pork chops. Cut 6 peeled firm but ripe bananas in half lengthwise, then cut in half crosswise. In large, deep nonstick skillet, heat 3 tablespoons unsalted butter on medium-high heat until melted. Swirl to coat bottom of pan. When butter is hot, add bananas. Cook until heated through, but not soft. Place on serving dish and sprinkle on ½ cup grated Parmesan cheese, ⅛ teaspoon coarse salt, such as kosher, and ⅛ teaspoon freshly ground black pepper.

Cranberry-Banana Breakfast Coffeecake

YIELD: 12 SERVINGS

Rustic and not very sweet, this breakfast treat heralds the tart taste of cranberries. It is best either topped with the glaze or sliced and topped with butter and honey. For best results, use frozen cranberries. Coarsely chop the frozen berries in the food processor, pulsing 2 or 3 times, enough so that some berries are whole, some chopped.

Nonstick vegetable oil spray

1¾ cups all-purpose flour

½ cup wheat germ, toasted

2 teaspoons baking powder

⅓ cup honey

¼ cup (½ stick) unsalted butter, softened

1 cup mashed ripe bananas, about 2 medium bananas

2 egg whites, lightly beaten

1 cup coarsely chopped frozen cranberries

Glaze

½ cup powdered sugar

4 teaspoons milk

1   Adjust oven rack to middle position. Preheat oven to 350°F. Lightly spray an 8-inch square baking dish with nonstick spray; set aside.

2   In medium bowl, combine flour, wheat germ, and baking powder; stir with whisk to combine. Set aside.

3   In large bowl of electric mixer, beat honey and butter on medium speed until creamy. Add bananas and egg whites; mix until blended, scrapping down sides of bowl as needed. Add flour mixture; mix until blended, scraping down sides of bowl with rubber spatula as needed. Fold in cranberries using a rubber spatula; place in prepared baking dish. Press to even the surface. Bake 40 to 50 minutes or until toothpick inserted in center comes out clean. Cool in dish on wire rack.

4   If desired, glaze cake. To make glaze, combine powdered sugar and milk in small bowl; stir until combined. Drizzle glaze over cooled cake.

Nutritional information (per serving without glaze): Calories 200, fat calories 40; total fat 4.5 grams, sat fat 2.5 grams, cholesterol 10 milligrams; sodium 90 milligrams; total carbohydrates 38 grams, fiber 2 grams, sugars 20 grams; protein 4 grams; vitamin A IUs 2%; vitamin C 2%; calcium 6%; iron 8%.

Blueberry Banana Bread

YIELD: 1 (9 × 5-INCH) LOAF, 10 SLICES

Banana bread enriched with plump, juicy fresh blueberries is a worthy treat. To doll it up, cut into thick slices and lightly toast it (place on baking sheet under broiler—watch carefully—don't burn it). Top the toasted slice with a scoop of ice cream and more fresh blueberries. Or cut the toasted slice into fingers and serve with pudding or custard.

Vegetable oil or canola oil for greasing pan

1½ cups all-purpose flour plus additional ¼ cup flour if using agave syrup instead of sugar

½ cup quick-cooking rolled oats

¼ teaspoon salt

1 teaspoon baking soda

1 cup sugar or ¾ cup agave syrup

½ cup vegetable shortening

2 large eggs

½ cup chopped pecans

½ cup blueberries

1 cup mashed ripe bananas, about 2 medium bananas

1   Adjust oven rack to middle position. Preheat oven to 325°F. Lightly oil a 9 × 5-inch loaf pan; line bottom with parchment paper.

2   In medium bowl, combine flour (add additional ¼ cup if using agave syrup), oats, salt, and baking soda. Use a whisk to thoroughly combine; set aside.

3   Place sugar or agave syrup and shortening in large bowl of electric mixer. Beat on medium-high speed until smooth and fluffy. Add eggs 1 at a time, beating between additions to thoroughly combine. Scrape down sides of bowl with rubber spatula as needed. Add dry ingredients and mix just until blended. Add bananas and fold until well combined. Gently fold in berries.

4 Pour batter into prepared pan and bake for about 65 to 75 minutes or until a toothpick inserted in center comes out clean and top is golden brown. Cool on wire rack for 15 minutes. Invert pan and remove bread. Cool completely on wire rack. If desired, dust with powdered sugar before slicing. Cooled bread without powdered sugar can be frozen for future use for up to 3 months; first wrap in parchment paper or plastic wrap, then tightly wrap in aluminum foil.

Nutritional information (per slice without powdered sugar): Calories 330, fat calories 140; total fat 15 grams, sat fat 4.5 grams, cholesterol 200 milligrams; sodium 200 milligrams; total carbohydrates 45 grams, fiber 3 grams, sugars 25 grams; protein 5 grams; vitamin A IUs 2%; vitamin C 4%; calcium 2%; iron 8%.

Blueberry Banana Bread

Nuthouse Chicken with Roasted Bananas

YIELD: 6

Coated with a tasty pecan mixture, these baked chicken breasts team nicely with the slightly sweet flavor profile of baked bananas. If desired, accompany the dish with basmati rice, or Tangerine Coconut Rice (page 306).

2 tablespoons unsalted butter

3 tablespoons extra-virgin olive oil

1 egg, lightly beaten

½ cup buttermilk

½ cup all-purpose flour

1 cup coarsely ground pecans

1 teaspoon paprika

1 teaspoon salt

1 tablespoon sesame seeds

6 (4-ounce) skinless, boneless chicken breasts

Roasted Bananas

Nonstick vegetable oil spray or canola oil spray

3 ripe bananas, peeled, cut in half lengthwise

2 tablespoons fresh lime juice

1 tablespoon dark rum

½ teaspoon ground cinnamon

1 tablespoon dark brown sugar

1 tablespoon unsalted butter, cut into tiny pieces

Optional garnish: toasted pecan halves (see Cook's Note)

1   Adjust oven rack to middle position. Preheat oven to 375°F. Place butter and oil in 9 × 13-inch baking dish and place in oven long enough for butter to melt; stir to combine and set aside.

2   Place egg and buttermilk in shallow bowl or pie pan; stir to combine.

3   Place flour, pecans, paprika, salt, and sesame seeds in separate shallow bowl or pie pan; stir to combine.

4   Roll a chicken breast in egg mixture, then in flour mixture; gently roll in butter mixture in baking dish and place rounded side up in dish. Repeat with remaining chicken breasts. Bake for 45 minutes or until cooked through. If topping needs to be browned, place under broiler until topping is crisp and nicely browned; watch closely because it can easily burn.

5   Meanwhile, roast bananas. Spray a 9-inch baking dish with nonstick spray; add bananas in single layer, cut side up. Sprinkle with juice and rum. Sprinkle with cinnamon and sugar; dot with butter. Bake in 375°F oven for 15 minutes or until tender and lightly glazed.

6   Accompany chicken with baked bananas. If desired, garnish bananas with toasted pecan halves.

Nutritional information (per serving): Calories 510, fat calories 31; total fat 31 grams, sat fat 7 grams, cholesterol 115 milligrams; sodium 480 milligrams; total carbohydrates 29 grams, fiber 5 grams, sugars 15 grams; protein 28 grams; vitamin A IUs 8%; vitamin C 8%; calcium 6%; iron 15%.

Cook's Note: To toast optional pecan halves, place on rimmed baking sheet in single layer. Toast in middle of a 350°F oven for about 5 minutes, or until lightly toasted. Watch carefully because they burn easily. Cool.

Frozen Bananas on a Stick

YIELD: 4 SERVINGS

Coated with chocolate and nuts, frozen bananas are real crowd-pleasers. Children may prefer to use granola, mini chocolate chips, or brightly colored sprinkles instead of toasted nuts to coat their bananas. Either way, these treats are delectable.

- ¾ cup coarsely chopped pistachios or pecans or walnuts, or a combination (see Cook's Note, this page)
- 2 bananas, ripe but not mushy
- 4 Popsicle sticks or short sturdy bamboo skewers without pointed ends
- 6 ounces semisweet chocolate chips
- 1 tablespoon vegetable oil or canola oil

1   Toast nuts and cool. Peel bananas and cut in half crosswise. Insert stick into cut end to make a handle. Line rimmed baking sheet with waxed paper and add banana halves. Freeze 15 minutes.

2   Place chocolate and oil in 4-cup glass measuring cup with a handle. Place measuring cup in saucepan filled with 2 inches of simmering water on medium heat. Or, melt chocolate in top of double boiler over barely simmering water, stirring frequently. Remove from heat as soon as it melts; chocolate should just get hot enough to melt.

3   Roll each partially frozen banana in chocolate to coat; sprinkle each with toasted nuts. Return to waxed paper and freeze at least 30 minutes. Enjoy, or place in airtight plastic container and freeze up to 10 days.

Nutritional information (per serving): Calories 370, fat calories 220; total fat 24 grams, sat fat 7 grams, cholesterol 0 milligrams; sodium 5 milligrams; total carbohydrates 37 grams, fiber 6 grams, sugars 28 grams; protein 7 grams; vitamin A IUs 2%; vitamin C 8%; calcium 4%; iron 10%.

Bean

Fava Bean

Green Bean

Soybean

Fresh beans have one thing in common: The beans lined up inside their pods are immature and tender. Left to mature, those soft inner seeds can harden. Some fresh beans, such as green beans, have pods that are edible. Others are classified as shell beans, such as fava beans and soybeans (also called edamame), because their pods aren't particularly pleasant to eat.

Organic soy bean growers use crop rotation to reenergize the soil, augmenting with rich natural compost. Fava growers use drip irrigation to hold down weed growth on organic crops and say that hot weather can be their biggest challenge. Organic green bean growers say that cold, wet weather can prevent their crop from developing good color. Production levels decrease using organic methods over conventional, about 20 percent less for fava and green beans, and about 15 percent for soybeans.

Green

Fava

Soybean

BUYING AND STORING: Green beans should snap crisply when broken and should be flexible but not limp. If seeds can be detected through the pod, the beans are probably too mature and will be tough. Fava and soy bean pods should be plump and green, not yellowed. If sold shelled, beans should look plump, shiny, and moist. Refrigerate in pods in plastic bag up to 1 week in crisper drawer. Store shelled fava beans in refrigerator—in single layer, because they are delicate—up to 3 days covered loosely with plastic wrap. Refrigerate shelled or unshelled soybeans in unopened vacuum pack up to 5 days. Once opened, refrigerate in airtight container up to 3 days. Shelled, cooked soybeans and shelled fava beans can be frozen in airtight containers up to 6 months.

PREP AND USE FOR FAVA BEANS: Fava beans are most often eaten cooked. Only very immature beans can be eaten raw. When mature, beans should be shelled, cooked, and skinned. Wash in cold water and remove beans from pods: Snap off stem end and pull string toward opposite end; use thumbnail to open along seam and push out beans. Blanch 1 minute; drain and place in ice water. Drain and use thumbnail to break skin; squeeze to pop bean from skin. Most recipes call for further cooking, often simmering them in water with herbs, garlic, and a little olive oil for about 5 minutes. Note that people who have inherited a particular enzyme deficiency can experience a serious reaction from eating fava beans. Use as appetizer or snack, or include in soups, salads, or stir-fries. Include in rice or pasta dishes.

PREP AND USE FOR GREEN BEANS: Wash with cold water. Although they are sometimes referred to as string beans, few green beans have strings. If present, to remove them partially snap off stem end so string stays attached; pull toward opposite end to remove string. Snap off ends by hand or cut off with paring knife. Leave whole or cut crosswise on diagonal into 2-inch lengths. Cook in boiling water until tender-crisp, 2 to 8 minutes, depending on size and your texture preference. Drain and refresh with cold water (purists suggest ice water). Or simmer beans slowly or steam. Include in stir-fries, salads, stews, or casseroles. To serve with creamy dips, blanch just enough to take away the raw taste, 30 to 60 seconds, drain, and refresh with cold water.

PREP AND USE FOR SOYBEANS (EDAMAME): Most often sold cooked, either frozen or fresh-cooked in vacuum packs, both in pods and shelled. If in pod, remove beans from pod. Pull string and pop beans out with thumbnail; discard pod. To serve in the pod, boil in large amount of boiling salted water for 3 minutes; drain, refresh with cold water, and pat dry. Cool and toss with coarse salt, such as kosher. Use as appetizer or snack. To eat beans from pod, hold on to one end and pull the slightly fuzzy green pods through your teeth to pop the beans into your mouth. Provide bowls for the empty pods. Use shelled beans in soups or salads, or pasta- or grain-based dishes.

AVAILABLE:

Fava Beans (broad beans): March to June

Green Beans (string beans): Year-round

Soybeans (edamame): Year-round

NUTRITIONAL INFORMATION (per 1 cup raw fava beans): Calories 111, fat calories 8; total fat 1 grams, sat fat 0 grams, cholesterol 0 milligrams; sodium 31 milligrams; total carbohydrates 22 grams, fiber 9 grams, sugars 3 grams; protein 10 grams; vitamin A IUs 8%; vitamin C 8%; calcium 5%; iron 11%.

NUTRITIONAL INFORMATION (per 1 cup raw green beans): Calories 34, fat calories 1; total fat 0 grams, sat fat 0 grams, cholesterol 0 milligrams; sodium 7 milligrams; total carbohydrates 8 grams, fiber 4 grams, sugars 2 grams; protein 2 grams; vitamin A IUs 15%; vitamin C 30%; calcium 4%; iron 6%.

NUTRITIONAL INFORMATION (per 1 cup raw soybeans): Calories 376, fat calories 146, total fat 17 gram, sat fat 2 grams, cholesterol 0 milligrams; sodium 38 milligrams; total carbohydrates 28 grams, fiber 11 grams, sugars 1 gram; protein 33 grams; vitamin A IUs 9%; vitamin C 124%; calcium 50%; iron 50%.

SERVING SUGGESTIONS

Green Beans Caprese

In a medium saucepan on medium-low heat, place ¼ cup extra-virgin olive oil, 1 medium shallot (sliced), pinch dried red chile flakes, 1 tablespoon drained capers, and 1 teaspoon fresh thyme leaves. Gently heat for 8 to 10 minutes on medium-low. Spoon sauce over cooked green beans. Season to taste with coarse salt, such as kosher. Beans can be served hot, warm, cold, or room temperature. If not serving hot, beans can be spooned over tomato slices that are topped with slices of fresh mozzarella cheese.

Fava or Soybeans Go Wild

Toss cooked fava beans or soybeans with sautéed wild mushrooms. On medium-high heat in large, deep skillet, heat 1 tablespoon olive oil and 2 tablespoons unsalted butter. Add ¾ pound sliced fresh wild mushrooms (such as shiitake or cremini) and cook, tossing occasionally, until golden brown and any liquid exuded by the mushrooms has evaporated. Season with salt and freshly ground black pepper and remove from skillet. To skillet, add 1 tablespoon extra-virgin olive oil and 2 cloves garlic (minced); cook until fragrant, about 40 seconds. Return mushrooms and add 2 cups shelled and cooked (peeled) fava beans or cooked soybeans, as well as 2 tablespoons minced fresh tarragon leaves. Taste and add salt and freshly ground black pepper if needed.

Green Olive Tapenade and Green Beans

Tapenade, that delicious Provençal-style olive spread, is delicious tossed with warm, cooked green beans. For tapenade, place 1 cup pitted green olives in food processor fitted with metal blade; add 1 teaspoon drained capers, 1 large clove garlic (chopped), and 2 tablespoons chopped fresh Italian parsley. Pulse on and off until roughly chopped (not pureed); stir in 1 teaspoon extra-virgin olive oil and add salt and freshly ground black pepper to taste. Use enough tapenade to lightly coat the green beans.

Vegetable Soup

Augment vegetable soups with shelled cooked soybeans or peeled cooked fava beans during the last few minutes of cooking. Or add ½-inch pieces of trimmed green beans, allowing enough time for them to cook in the soup's broth, about 4 minutes.

Baked Risotto-Style Rice with Chicken and Edamame

YIELD: 8 SERVINGS

Risotto is made by stirring hot broth into an Arborio rice mixture, half cup by half cup, cooking and stirring between additions. The delectable dish requires time and patience. Here's an easy-to-make casserole that hits some of the flavor and texture notes of the classic dish without very much work and very little stirring.

2 tablespoons extra-virgin olive oil

6 (4-ounce) skinless, boneless chicken thighs, cut in half crosswise (see Meatless Tip)

Salt and freshly ground black pepper

3 large shallots, finely diced

1 tablespoon minced lemon zest (colored portion of peel)

2 cups Arborio rice

5 cups fat-free, low-sodium chicken broth or vegetable broth

1 cup shelled, cooked soybeans (edamame; see Cook's Note)

2 tablespoons fresh lemon juice

½ cup grated Parmesan cheese

1 tablespoon minced fresh mint

Optional for serving: extra Parmesan cheese for passing

1   Adjust oven rack to middle position. Preheat oven to 400°F.

2   Heat oil in large, deep skillet on medium-high heat. Add chicken in single layer and season with salt and pepper to taste. Brown chicken on both sides, about 4 to 5 minutes per side; don't crowd pan, if necessary, brown chicken in 2 batches.

3   Remove chicken from pan. Add shallots and zest; cook, stirring occasionally, until shallots soften and start to brown, about 3 minutes.

4   Place shallot mixture, rice, and broth in 9 × 13-inch baking dish. Stir to combine. Cover tightly with aluminum foil. Bake in preheated oven for 25 minutes. Remove from oven and cautiously remove foil, opening it on side of pan facing away from you. Add chicken and any accumulated juices, distributing chicken in single layer on rice mixture; push chicken down into rice. Cover tightly and bake 20 minutes.

5   Cautiously remove foil. Add edamame, juice, cheese, and mint, plus salt and pepper to taste. Gently toss. Pass bowl of cheese for optional topping.

Nutritional information (per serving): Calories 380, fat calories 110; total fat 12 grams, sat fat 3 grams, cholesterol 60 milligrams; sodium 400 milligrams; total carbohydrates 43 grams, fiber 3 grams, sugars 1 gram; protein 25 grams; vitamin A IUs 6%; vitamin C 8%; calcium 8%; iron 8%.

Cook's Note: 12 ounces of cooked soybean (edamame) pods yields about 1 cup shelled beans.

Meatless Tip: Omit chicken. Instead, sauté 10 ounces diced fresh shiitake mushrooms (stems removed and saved for another purpose) or sliced white mushrooms in 2 tablespoons extra-virgin olive oil on medium-high heat until softened and nicely browned. Add mushrooms in step 4, after the initial 25 minutes of baking. If desired, add tiny pinch of dried red chile flakes to shallot mixture in step 3.

Light-Style Green Bean Casserole

YIELD: 6 SERVINGS

The traditional green bean casserole is a holiday classic. Here's a fresher, more healthful rendition. Note that it employs a technique that uses ice to refresh the cooked beans immediately after blanching. This keeps the beans a beautiful, bright green color. If you prefer to simplify the process, drain beans in a colander in the sink and run plenty of cold water over them.

1 pound green beans, trimmed, cut into 1-inch lengths on the diagonal

Nonstick spray

½ cup sliced sweet yellow onion

⅓ cup sliced common white (button) mushrooms

2 tablespoons unsalted butter, divided use

2 tablespoons all-purpose flour

1¼ cups whole milk, warm

⅛ teaspoon ground nutmeg

Salt and freshly ground black pepper

¾ cup herb stuffing, ground or crushed

1 tablespoon unsalted butter, melted

1   Fill medium bowl with ice cubes and enough water to make ice float; place in sink.

2   In large saucepan, bring 2 quarts salted water to boil on high heat. Add beans to boiling water. Return to boil and cook until tender but still a little crisp. Cooking times will vary depending on thickness of beans, 2 to 8 minutes. Drain beans and place in ice water. Drain and pat dry.

3   Adjust oven rack to middle position. Preheat oven to 350°F. Spray ovenproof 2-quart casserole dish with nonstick spray; set aside.

4   In large, deep skillet on medium-high heat, melt 1 tablespoon butter. Add onion and mushrooms. Cook until limp and very little liquid remains. Transfer to a dish and set aside.

5   In same pan, melt remaining 1 tablespoon butter. Lower heat to medium and add flour. Cook, stirring, 1 minute (do not brown). Gradually whisk in milk in small amounts, keeping sauce a smooth consistency. Bring to a simmer, stirring constantly. When sauce thickens, add nutmeg, and salt and pepper to taste. Remove from heat. Add onion-mushroom mixture and drained beans; stir to combine. Place mixture in prepared cassserole.

6   In a small bowl, combine crushed herb stuffing and melted butter; stir to combine. Top bean mixture evenly with herb stuffing. Cover with aluminum foil and bake for 40 minutes, or until heated through.

7   Adjust oven rack to 6 to 8 inches below broiler element. Turn oven to broil. Remove foil and place casserole under broiler to brown topping, about 1 to 2 minutes. Watch carefully because it can burn easily. Serve hot.

Nutritional information (per serving): Calories 140, fat calories 70; total fat 8 grams, sat fat 4.5 grams, cholesterol 20 milligrams; sodium 120 milligrams; total carbohydrates 15 grams, fiber 3 grams, sugars 5 grams; protein 4 grams; vitamin A IUs 8%; vitamin C 10%; calcium 10%; iron 4%.

Tabbouleh with Edamame and Kumquats

YIELD: 6 (½-CUP) SERVINGS

Traditional tabbouleh, a bulgur wheat–based Middle Eastern salad, most often contains fresh green herbs, tomatoes, onions, olive oil, and lemon juice. This colorful rendition substitutes sweet-tart kumquats for the tomatoes and pumps up the green with shelled soybeans as well as diced cucumber. Place individual servings in butter lettuce cups.

1 cup bulgur wheat

¾ cup finely chopped fresh Italian parsley

¾ cup vegetable broth

1 large clove garlic, minced

¼ cup finely minced red onion

1 tablespoon extra-virgin olive oil

1 ½ teaspoons agave syrup or honey

2 teaspoons minced lemon zest (colored portion of peel)

1 tablespoon fresh lemon juice

½ cup diced hothouse (English) cucumber

½ cup cooked shelled soybeans (edamame)

½ cup finely chopped seeded kumquats

⅛ teaspoon salt

⅛ teaspoon freshly ground black pepper

Optional: additional fresh lemon juice, salt or freshly ground black pepper

Optional for serving: butter lettuce cups

1   Place bulgur wheat in sieve and rinse with cold water.

2   In medium bowl, place bulgur wheat and 1 cup room-temperature water for 2 hours. Drain and gently shake sieve to remove excess water.

Tabbouleh with Edamame and Kumquats

3   Place drained bulgur wheat, parsley, broth, garlic, onion, olive oil, and agave syrup in large bowl; toss.

4   Add zest, juice, cucumber, edamame, kumquats, salt and pepper; gently toss. Cover and set aside for 2 hours for flavors to build. Taste and adjust seasoning, adding a little more juice or salt or pepper as needed. If desired, spoon each serving into a butter lettuce cup.

Nutritional information (per serving): Calories 150, fat calories 30; total fat 3.5 grams, sat fat 0 grams, cholesterol 0 milligrams; sodium 115 milligrams; total carbohydrates 26 grams, fiber 7 grams, sugars 4 grams; protein 5 grams; vitamin A IUs 15%; vitamin C 35%; calcium 4%; iron 8%.

Spicy Pickled Green Beans

YIELD: 2 QUARTS

Make a Bloody Mary irresistible by garnishing it with a couple of these spicy beans. They are also delicious on an antipasto platter. Or for a spicy finger food, wrap beans with thinly sliced prosciutto and serve with a creamy dip.

½ teaspoon salt

1½ pounds green beans, trimmed

1½ cups distilled white vinegar

1½ cups water

4 tablespoons sugar

1 tablespoon salt

1 medium yellow onion, halved, sliced

2 large cloves garlic, minced

1½ teaspoons dried red chile flakes

1½ teaspoons dill seed

1   Fill a medium bowl with ice cubes and enough water to make ice float; place in sink.

2   In large saucepan, bring 2 quarts salted water to boil on high heat. Add beans to boiling water. Return to boil and cook until tender-crisp. Cooking times will vary depending on thickness of beans, 2 to 8 minutes. Drain beans and place in ice water. Drain and pat dry.

3   To make brine: In medium nonreactive saucepan, bring vinegar, water, sugar, and salt to boil on medium-high heat. Add onion, garlic, chile flakes, and dill seed. Remove from heat and periodically stir until steam no longer appears but liquid is still warm.

4   Meanwhile, in 2 tall 1-quart canning jars, place drained beans on end. Carefully pour warm liquid and seasonings to completely cover beans, transferring all onions, garlic, and chile flakes into containers. Discard any leftover brine.

5   Seal and refrigerate up to 3 months. The flavor improves as the beans marinate.

Nutritional information (per ¼ cup drained beans): Calories 45, fat calories 0; total fat 0 grams, sat fat 0 grams, cholesterol 0 milligrams; sodium 300 milligrams; total carbohydrates 11 grams, fiber 3 grams, sugars 6 grams; protein 1 gram; vitamin A IUs 6%; vitamin C 15%; calcium 6%; iron 2%.

Beet

Red (Common)

Gold

These bulb-shaped wonders are a feast for the eyes; some are a glorious gold, and others are a snappy magenta. Available both in grown-up sizes and diminutive "babies," the taste is somewhere between sweet carrots and earthy mushrooms. Because they "bleed," these delectable roots can be a challenge, unless you know the tidy trick: Bake them first in foil, and then tackle the peeling and cutting. It's easy and a lot less messy.

Organic beets are generally available year-round, but there can be gaps when production decreases, often between December and February with heavy rain and snow, or in severe heat in July, August, and September.

BUYING AND STORING: Look for beets with crisp, fresh-looking greens. Bulbs should be firm with fairly smooth skin. Small and medium bulbs are generally more tender. Remove all but 1 inch of stem. Refrigerate in plastic in crisper drawer up to 3 weeks. Store greens in plastic in crisper up to 2 days. Wash just before cooking. Tiny baby beets can be the exception. Because they can be steamed whole with stems attached, store untrimmed and refrigerate; use within 1 day.

PREP AND USE: Eat raw, peeled, and finely grated in salad, or cook. Can be roasted, steamed, baked, or boiled. To bake, wash beets with 1-inch stems attached and wrap (still wet, three to a packet) in heavy-duty aluminum foil. Bake in 400°F oven until fork-tender, 30 to 60 minutes, depending on size. When cool enough to handle, slip off peel. Cooked beets can be served hot or cold. Stain remover: If your cutting board or hands get red beet juice stains, use coarse salt to scrub them clean.

The green leaves and stems that top the bulb can be delicious, too. They are best matured to about 4 to 6 inches in length. Before using, rinse them twice in tubs of cold water, and then blanch until tender; drain, squeeze out excess water, and briefly cook in olive oil along with some minced garlic.

AVAILABLE: Year-round

NUTRITIONAL INFORMATION (per 1 cup raw chopped): Calories 59, fat calories 2; total fat 0 grams, sat fat 0 grams, cholesterol 0 milligrams; sodium 106 milligrams; total carbohydrates 13 grams, fiber 4 grams, sugars 9 grams; protein 2 grams; vitamin A IUs 1%; vitamin C 11%; calcium 2%; iron 6%.

SERVING SUGGESTIONS

Pickled Salad

Cut 1 small red onion in half from top to bottom; thinly slice. In glass or ceramic bowl, combine sliced onion with 3 tablespoons red wine vinegar. Toss and set aside for 2 to 3 hours. Dice 5 large cooked, peeled beets. Add to onion mixture and toss. Serve over mixed greens and top with crumbled goat cheese with herbs.

Golden Hummus

Puree cooked golden beets along with cooked garbanzo beans to make a tasty dip. In food processor, combine 1 large golden beet (baked, peeled, sliced) and 1 (15-ounce) can drained, rinsed garbanzo beans; process until smooth, and then add 2 tablespoons unsweetened plain nonfat yogurt, 2 tablespoons fresh lemon juice, 1 tablespoon tahini, and 1 teaspoon ground cumin. Process until smooth and serve with toasted pita triangles.

Raw Grated Beet Salad

Peel 3 medium beets with swivel-bladed vegetable peeler. Cut beets so they will fit in food processor's feed tube; using the processor's shredding disk, grate beets. In medium bowl, whisk 1 tablespoon seasoned rice vinegar, 1 tablespoon fresh lemon juice, 2 teaspoons Dijon-style mustard, 1 teaspoon honey, 3 tablespoons extra-virgin olive oil, and salt and freshly ground black pepper to taste. Add grated beets and 1 tablespoon minced fresh basil leaves. Toss and serve.

Sandwich Surprise

Add baked, peeled, and sliced beets atop filling in chicken salad, turkey salad, or egg salad sandwiches.

Hearts of Romaine Salad with Beets, Apples, and Creamy Blue Cheese Dressing

YIELD: 6 SERVINGS

The flavor combinations in this salad are irresistible. Beets and creamy blue cheese dressing are a perfect pairing. The salad is further complemented by the addition of crisp apple wedges and the crunchy, subtle bitter edge of toasted walnuts.

Dressing

2 tablespoons fresh lemon juice

½ cup unsweetened, plain yogurt

2 tablespoons extra-virgin olive oil

Salt and freshly ground black pepper

6 ounces crumbled blue cheese

Salad

3 hearts of romaine, each quartered lengthwise

4 medium beets, 2 gold and 2 red preferred, baked, peeled, cut into ¼-inch cubes

1 crisp apple, unpeeled, cored, cut into ¼-inch wedges

1 cup coarsely chopped toasted walnuts (see Cook's Note)

Optional for thinning dressing: 1 to 2 tablespoons milk

2 to 3 tablespoons finely chopped fresh Italian parsley

1   Place juice, yogurt, oil, and salt and pepper to taste in blender. Whirl until smooth, about 1 minute, stopping to scrape down sides with rubber spatula if needed. Taste and adjust seasoning as needed. Stir in cheese.

2   On each plate, place 2 romaine quarters. Dice the beets after cooking, cooling, and peeling. Arrange beet cubes and apple wedges next to romaine. Spoon dressing across plate from side to side, spilling dressing across middle of romaine and a portion of the beets and apples. (If dressing is too thick, stir in 1 to 2 tablespoons milk.) Scatter toasted walnuts on top. Sprinkle with parsley and serve.

Nutritional information (per serving): Calories 320, fat calories 230; total fat 25 grams, sat fat 7 grams, cholesterol 20 milligrams; sodium 460 milligrams; total carbohydrates 14 grams, fiber 4 grams, sugars 9 grams; protein 14 grams; vitamin A IUs 30%; vitamin C 30%; calcium 25%; iron 10%.

Cook's Note: Place walnuts on rimmed baking sheet in single layer. Toast until lightly browned in a 350°F oven, about 5 minutes. Watch carefully because nuts burn easily. Set aside to cool.

Hearts of Romaine Salad with Beets, Apples, and Creamy Blue Cheese Dressing

Green Bean and Beet Salad

YIELD: 4 SERVINGS

The colors in this salad are so beautiful, especially if both red and gold baby beets are used. To make this salad ahead, place cooked and cooled green beans in a clean kitchen towel and refrigerate up to 8 hours ahead. Steam beets, peel, and place in airtight container; refrigerate up to 8 hours. Dressing can be prepared days in advance and refrigerated in small, sealed jar. To prevent discoloration, toss green beans with dressing no more that 15 minutes before serving.

- 8 ounces green beans, trimmed, broken into 3-inch lengths
- 8 ounces baby beets, greens trimmed ½ inch above bulb
- ¼ cup balsamic vinegar
- 1½ teaspoon Dijon-style mustard
- ¼ cup extra-virgin olive oil
- ½ teaspoon freshly ground black pepper
- 2 cups mixed baby greens
- ¼ cup sliced toasted almonds (see Cook's Note)

1 Bring a large saucepan of salted water to boil on high heat. Add beans and boil until tender-crisp, 2 to 7 minutes depending on width of beans. Drain and refresh with cold water to stop cooking and maintain a bright green color.

2 Meanwhile, steam beets, covered, over simmering water until tender. When cool enough to handle, peel and cut into quarters. Or bake (see Prep and Use), peel, and quarter. Place beets and beans in medium bowl.

3 Prepare dressing: In a separate bowl, whisk vinegar, mustard, oil, and pepper. Pour over beets and beans and toss. Taste and adjust seasoning as needed.

4 Divide mixed baby greens between 4 salad plates. Top with beet salad and garnish with toasted almonds.

Nutritional information (per serving): Calories 220, fat calories 150; total fat 17 grams, sat fat 2 grams, cholesterol 0 milligrams; sodium 80 milligrams; total carbohydrates 17 grams, fiber 5 grams, sugars 10 grams; protein 3 grams; vitamin A IUs 20%; vitamin C 20%; calcium 6%; iron 8%.

Cook's Note: To toast nuts, spread out on rimmed baking sheet and toast in middle of 350°F oven until lightly browned, about 2 to 3 minutes. Watch carefully because nuts burn easily. Cool.

Beet Sauce

YIELD: ABOUT 2 CUPS, 4 SERVINGS

A tangy, slightly spicy sauce pairs well with roast game, chicken, or pork. Spoon small portions next to the meat on rimmed plates. Try it with Green Onion–Horseradish-Crusted Chicken Breasts (see page 231).

- 1½ cups coarsely chopped baked and peeled red or gold beets
- ½ cup reserved beet juice (see Cook's Note)
- 2 teaspoons freshly squeezed lemon juice
- 1 tablespoon rice vinegar
- 1 teaspoon freshly grated horseradish
- 1½ teaspoons sugar
- ½ teaspoon salt
- ⅛ teaspoon freshly ground black pepper

In a blender, add all ingredients. Process until smooth and pourable. Taste and adjust seasoning as needed. Best served at room temperature.

Nutritional information (per ½ cup): Calories 40, fat calories 0; total fat 0 grams, sat fat 0 grams, cholesterol 0 milligrams; sodium 500 milligrams; total carbohydrates 10 grams, fiber 1 gram, sugars 6 grams; protein 1 gram; vitamin A IUs 0%; vitamin C 8%; calcium 2%; iron 8%.

Cook's Note: If there isn't enough juice from the cooked beets, add water or vegetable broth to measure ½ cup.

Rustic Mashed Potatoes with Beet Greens and Roasted Garlic

YIELD: 8 SERVINGS

Smashed in their jackets along with tender beet greens and roasted garlic, these luscious spuds are delicious paired with just about any roasted or grilled meat. If you can't find small Yukon Gold potatoes, substitute an equal amount of small red potatoes. Chard can be substituted for the beet greens.

1 small head garlic, roasted (see page 139)

2 pounds small Yukon Gold potatoes, scrubbed

1 teaspoon salt

1 pound beet greens, washed, roughly chopped into 2-inch-long pieces

3 tablespoons extra-virgin olive oil

Salt and freshly ground black pepper

1   When roasted garlic is cool enough to handle, squeeze cloves out of parchment-like covering into small bowl; mash with fork and set aside.

2   Place potatoes in Dutch oven or large saucepan. Add enough water to cover by 1 inch and add 1 teaspoon salt. Bring to boil on high heat; boil for 10 minutes. Add greens and boil until potatoes are fork-tender, about 10 minutes more. Drain; reserve 1 cup cooking water. Return potato-greens mixture to pot. Add mashed roasted garlic, oil, and about ½ cup of reserved cooking water. Roughly mash with potato masher, adding more reserved cooking water if needed to reach desired consistency. Season with salt and pepper to taste.

Nutritional information (per serving): Calories 160, fat calories 45; total fat 5 grams, sat fat 0.5 grams, cholesterol 0 milligrams; sodium 410 milligrams; total carbohydrates 24 grams, fiber 3 grams, sugars 0 grams; protein 4 grams; vitamin A IUs 70%; vitamin C 60%; calcium 6%; iron 10%.

Bell Pepper

also Sweet Pepper

Green

Red

Yellow

The skin is glossy, so slick that water beads into tiny droplets on the smooth surface. No waxes or polishes are used; that shiny coating is *au naturel*. Inside, the thick flesh is crisp and pleasantly herbal without a hint of capsaicin, the heat-producing compound found in other pepper family members.

Green bells have the strongest flavor profile; a grassy herbal quality teams with a gentle spicy finish. Red bells are sweeter than green, with only a small amount of herbal notes, while yellow bells are even milder than reds.

Organic bell peppers are grown in either hothouses or fields. Organic crops yield about 30 percent fewer bell peppers than conventional farming. Bell peppers are harvested by hand.

BUYING AND STORING: Select those with glossy, smooth skin without soft spots or wrinkles. Choose those that feel heavy for their size. Store them, unwashed, in plastic bag in refrigerator crisper drawer up to 2 weeks. Green peppers often last longer than red or yellow. Hothouse-grown bell peppers will keep longer than field-grown.

PREP AND USE: Wash with cold water and pat dry. Cut off top and bottom, then cut down one side. You now have a ribbon of pepper; remove ribs and seeds with either a knife or a finger. Cut into strips, chop, or dice, always starting the cut on the soft inner flesh rather than the slippery skin.

Use raw or cooked. To roast bell peppers, line a baking sheet with aluminum foil, leaving some extra foil on the ends. Place peppers in a single layer on foil. Place 6 to 8 inches below broiler element. Broil until lightly charred. Rotate peppers with tongs and char on all sides. Remove from oven and draw up ends of foil to enclose peppers for 5 minutes. Open foil; when cool enough to handle, peel peppers and discard seeds. Resist temptation to wash skin off with water. Use hands; the peppers will be more flavorful.

To grill peppers, place whole on hot, oiled barbecue grid. Turn with tongs after side next to heat starts to char. Continue to rotate until all sides are charred. Seal in paper bag for 5 minutes. Open bag; when cool enough to handle, peel and discard seeds.

AVAILABLE: Year-round

NUTRITIONAL INFORMATION (per 1 cup chopped raw green, red, or yellow bell pepper): Calories 40, fat calories 0; total fat 0 grams, sat fat 0 grams, cholesterol 0 milligrams; sodium 0 milligrams; total carbohydrates 9 grams, fiber 3 grams, sugars 4 grams; protein 1 gram; vitamin A IUs 15%; vitamin C 180%; calcium 2%; iron 4%.

SERVING SUGGESTIONS

Full-Color Omelet

Cut roasted (cored, seeded) red and yellow bell peppers into small pieces. Combine with favorite cheese, such as grated white cheddar or crumbled goat cheese. Use as omelet filling. Garnish with sliced chives if desired.

Sweet Pepper Sauté

Core and seed 2 red bell peppers and 1 yellow bell pepper. Cut into ⅜-inch-wide lengthwise strips. Heat 2 tablespoons vegetable oil in large, deep skillet on medium-high heat. Add peppers and cook, stirring occasionally, until soft but not limp, about 4 to 5 minutes. Season with salt and freshly ground black pepper. Spoon over rice, grilled meat, or cooked vegetables.

Burger Topper

Toss wide strips of roasted bell peppers with a little extra-virgin olive oil and minced garlic. Place a couple of strips atop veggie patties or turkey patties or beef patties to add both color and flavor to burgers.

Pepper Puree

Here's a simple sauce to serve with grilled chicken or pork, or atop cooked ravioli. It can also be added to béchamel sauce, marinara sauce, or vegetable soup. Add 4 roasted red bell peppers to food processor or blender. Pulse to finely chop. Add 3 tablespoons vegetable or chicken broth or extra-virgin olive oil; process until pureed. Season to taste with salt.

Bells with Beans and Rice

YIELD: 8 SERVINGS

Here is a blueprint for an easy weeknight meatless meal. If you want to add meat, add a cup of either chopped cooked chicken or pork in step 2. If desired, top each serving with a smidgen of crumbled goat cheese.

    2 tablespoons extra-virgin olive oil

    1 medium red bell pepper, cored, seeded, chopped

    1 medium yellow bell pepper, cored, seeded, chopped

    ½ large red onion, finely chopped

    2 large cloves garlic, minced

    6 cups cooked brown rice

    1¼ cup salsa

    1 (15-ounce) can black beans, drained, rinsed

    Salt

    2 tablespoons chopped fresh Italian parsley

1   In large, deep skillet, heat oil on medium-high heat. Add peppers, onion, and garlic; cook, stirring occasionally, until softened, about 7 minutes

2   Add rice, salsa, and beans. Bring to boil; reduce heat to medium-low and simmer about 4 minutes or until heated through. Add salt to taste and stir to combine. Spoon into bowls and top with parsley.

Nutritional information (per serving): Calories 260, fat calories 45; total fat 5 grams, sat fat 1 gram, cholesterol 0 milligrams; sodium 10 milligrams; total carbohydrates 46 grams, fiber 7 grams, sugars 2 grams; protein 7 grams; vitamin A IUs 6%; vitamin C 60%; calcium 4%; iron 10%.

Roast Pepper and Feta Jumble

YIELD: 20 TO 30 SERVINGS

Roasted red bell pepper gives these appetizers a spark of both flavor and visual appeal. The colorful jumble is made up primarily of crumbled feta cheese, peppers, and green onions. It seems a perfect topping for Belgian endive leaves, but if you prefer, it is delicious atop crackers as well.

    4 roasted medium red bell peppers, cored, seeded, chopped or 1 (7-ounce) jar roasted red bell peppers, drained, chopped

    1 large clove garlic, minced

    1 tablespoon extra-virgin olive oil

    1 teaspoon fresh lemon juice

    ¼ cup minced green onions (using half of dark green stalks)

    4 ounces crumbled feta cheese

    3 to 4 Belgian endives

1   In medium bowl, combine peppers, garlic, oil, juice, green onions, and cheese.

2   Place a spoonful of mixture on each endive leaf (amount will vary depending on the size of leaves). Arrange on platter and serve.

Nutritional information (per serving): Calories 25, fat calories 15; total fat 15 grams, sat fat 1 grams, cholesterol 5 milligrams; sodium 50 milligrams; total carbohydrates 2 grams, fiber 1 gram, sugars 1 gram; protein 1 gram; vitamin A IUs 2%; vitamin C 30%; calcium 2%; iron 0%.

Sweet-Sour Vegetarian Stuffed Bell Peppers

YIELD: 5 WHOLE STUFFED PEPPERS, 10 HALVES

There is something very alluring about edible containers, especially if they are bright red, green, or yellow-skinned bell peppers. This delectable vegetarian version of stuffed bell peppers offers a hearty blend of sweet and tart flavors, supplementing the rice filling with ingredients such as raisins, lemon zest, and pine nuts.

¾ cup raisins

5 large bell peppers, red, or green, or yellow, or combination

3 tablespoons extra-virgin olive oil

1 large yellow onion, finely diced

1 tablespoon pine nuts

1 cup raw long-grain rice

⅛ teaspoon salt

⅛ teaspoon freshly ground black pepper

1 teaspoon sugar

1¾ cups water

Juice of 1 lemon, Meyer lemon preferred, divided use

⅓ cup chopped fresh Italian parsley

2 teaspoons chopped fresh dill

2 teaspoons chopped fresh mint

1 teaspoon ground cinnamon

1 medium-large tomato, finely diced

1   Adjust oven rack to middle position. Preheat oven to 350°F. Place raisins in small bowl and cover with hot water; set aside.

2   Cut about ¼ inch from top of each bell pepper. Scoop out core and seeds and discard; set peppers aside.

3   Prepare stuffing: Heat oil in large, deep skillet on medium heat. Add onion and cook, stirring occasionally, until onion turns golden brown, about 7 to 10 minutes on medium-low heat. Add pine nuts; cook until pine nuts turn golden. Add rice and stir to combine to coat rice. Drain raisins and add to mixture. Add salt, black pepper, sugar, and water. Bring to gentle boil on high heat. Cover and reduce heat to medium-low. Simmer until rice is tender and liquid is absorbed, about 25 minutes.

4   Remove from heat and uncover. Set aside to cool slightly, about 15 minutes. Stir in half of lemon juice, parsley, dill, mint, and cinnamon. Taste and add more salt and black pepper as needed.

Sweet-Sour Vegetarian Stuffed Bell Peppers

5 To assemble: Fill each bell pepper with stuffing mixture until slightly mounded at top. Sprinkle diced tomatoes over top of stuffing. Cover with tops. Place peppers standing up in Dutch oven; pan should be just big enough to accommodate them easily, yet snug enough to retain their shapes while cooking. Peppers should be at least 1 inch apart. Pour a little water into the pan to a level where it just starts to come up the side of the peppers. Cook, uncovered, until stuffing begins to brown in exposed area and peppers are tender, 35 to 45 minutes. Sprinkle with remaining lemon juice and serve.

Nutritional information (per whole stuffed pepper): Calories 350, fat calories 90; total fat 10 grams, sat fat 1.5 grams, cholesterol 0 milligrams; sodium 75 milligrams; total carbohydrates 62 grams, fiber 5 grams, sugars 7 grams; protein 6 grams; vitamin A IUs 20%; vitamin C 30%; calcium 6%; iron 15%.

Grilled Sausage and Vegetable Sandwiches

YIELD: 4 LARGE SANDWICHES

Use hot Italian sausage to give these versatile **sandwiches a spicy edge. Or for a meatless rendition, omit the meat and increase the amount of squash and bell peppers, using some hot sauce–spiked mayonnaise to offer an inviting spicy edge.**

¼ cup mayonnaise

2 medium cloves garlic, minced

Juice of ½ lemon

4 (4-ounce) hot Italian sausages (see Meatless Tip)

2 tablespoons extra-virgin olive oil or enough to thinly coat vegetables

3 red bell peppers, cored, seeded, cut into 1-inch-wide strips

1 zucchini, cut into lengthwise strips ¼-inch thick

1 yellow crookneck squash, trimmed, cut into lengthwise strips ¼-inch thick

1 sweet onion, such as Maui, cut into ¼-inch slices

⅛ teaspoon salt

⅛ teaspoon freshly ground black pepper

4 French bread rolls, cut in half lengthwise

4 slices Muenster cheese

1 Prepare sauce: In small bowl, combine mayonnaise, garlic, and lemon juice; cover and refrigerate.

2 Heat grill to high heat. Clean grates. Grill sausages until completely cooked, turning frequently.

3 Meanwhile, toss vegetables with olive oil, salt, and black pepper. Grill on both sides until heated through and tender with some grill marks.

4 Spread sauce on both pieces of bread. Split sausages in half lengthwise and place on bread. Evenly divide the vegetables; top with cheese, and serve.

Nutritional information (per ½ sandwich): Calories 330, fat calories 180; total fat 20 grams, sat fat 7 grams, cholesterol 35 milligrams; sodium 820 milligrams; total carbohydrates 22 grams, fiber 2 grams, sugars 4 grams; protein 14 grams; vitamin A IUs 6%; vitamin C 15%; calcium 15%; iron 10%.

Cook's Note: To prevent vegetables from slipping through the barbecue grate during grilling, there are special screens that can be placed directly on the barbecue grate. They are designed for grilling small vegetables such as sliced onions and are sold at stores that stock barbecue equipment.

Meatless Tip: Omit sausage and increase amounts of squash and bell pepper. And for a hint of spiciness, add a small amount of hot sauce to mayonnaise-based sauce.

Berry

Blackberry

Blueberry

Cranberry

Raspberry

Strawberry

Packed into thin colorful skin, berries provide a delightful balance of sweet-tart flavors. Cranberries differ in that their super-tart flavor profile completely edges out sweetness, their assertiveness delightfully tamed with added sweetener. Some berries, such as blackberries and raspberries, are made up of clusters of tiny sacs. Strawberries are speckled with dry, diminutive yellow seeds. Blueberries and cranberries have slick, smooth skin.

Organic cranberries grow in bogs fed with clean springwater. Beneficial insects include wasps and bees; spiders are also used. Most berries require a good chill during the dormant season. Organic blueberries grow best when soil is mulched with bark, sawdust, or leaf mold. During the growing season, organic fertilizers such as organic chicken manure (pressed into compact dry pellets) or organic seaweed fertilizer is used to nourish the plants, helping them to grow rapidly and avoid attacks from pests. Strawberries are most commonly fertilized with fish emulsion when grown organically. Ladybugs are used to help control pests. Organic strawberries often have a lower water content, which results in more flavorful, deep-red flesh.

BUYING AND STORING: Choose brightly colored, plump berries without mold, soft spots, or discoloration. If boxed, check to see if berries move freely when container is tilted; if they stick together, they are probably moldy. Refrigerate (unwashed, untrimmed) in single layer on paper towel, discarding any that are moldy. Blackberries, raspberries, and strawberries can be stored up to 5 days; store blueberries up to 7 days; store cranberries up to 14 days. To freeze, spread unwashed berries on rimmed baking sheet in single layer; freeze, then store in airtight container. Except for cranberries, freezing changes texture of berries, making them a little mushy, but perfectly fine for cooked dishes (most often not requiring defrosting before use).

PREP AND USE: Rinse very briefly in cold water; many berries tend to absorb water. Strawberries require hulling; remove leaves and stem with point of paring knife, pointed end of swivel-bladed vegetable peeler, or strawberry huller.

Use berries raw or cooked. Use uncooked berries (except cranberries) in fruit salads, smoothies, pureed dessert sauces, and compotes. Or use atop pancakes, cereal, ice cream, mousse, or shortcake. All berries are delicious in baked goods, jams, jellies, and sauces for game such as duck or goose.

AVAILABLE:

Blackberry: June to April (peak is June and July)

Blueberry: Year-round (peak is June and July)

Cranberry: October to December

Raspberry: April to December

Strawberry: February to August

NUTRITIONAL INFORMATION (per 1 cup raw blackberries): Calories 62, fat calories 6; total fat 1 gram, sat fat 0 grams, cholesterol 0 milligrams; sodium 1 milligram; total carbohydrates 15 grams, fiber 8 grams, sugars 7 grams; protein 2 grams; vitamin A IUs 6%; vitamin C 50%; calcium 4%; iron 5%.

NUTRITIONAL INFORMATION (per 1 cup raw blueberries): Calories 84, fat calories 4; total fat 0 grams, sat fat 0 grams, cholesterol 0 milligrams; sodium 1 milligram; total carbohydrates 21 grams, fiber 4 grams, sugars 15 grams; protein 1 gram; vitamin A IUs 2%; vitamin C 24%; calcium 1%; iron 2%.

NUTRITIONAL INFORMATION (per 1 cup raw cranberries): Calories 15, fat calories 1; total fat 0 grams, sat fat 0 grams, cholesterol 0 milligrams, sodium 0 milligrams; total carbohydrates 3 grams, fiber 0 grams, sugars 0 grams; protein 0 grams; vitamin A IUs 1%; vitamin C 10%; calcium 1%; iron 1%.

NUTRITIONAL INFORMATION (per 1 cup raw raspberries): Calories 64, fat calories 7; total fat 1 gram, sat fat 0 grams, cholesterol 0 milligrams; sodium 1 milligram; total carbohydrates 15 grams, fiber 8 grams, sugars 5 grams; protein 1 gram; vitamin A IUs 1%; vitamin C 54%; calcium 3%; iron 5%.

NUTRITIONAL INFORMATION (per 1 cup raw halved strawberries): Calories 49, fat calories 4; total fat 0 grams, sat fat 0 grams, cholesterol 0 milligrams; sodium 2 milligrams; total carbohydrates 12 grams, fiber 3 grams, sugars 7 grams; protein 1 gram; vitamin A IUs 0%; vitamin C 149%; calcium 2%; iron 3%.

SERVING SUGGESTIONS

Blueberry–Blue Cheese Vinaigrette

In blender, combine 1 cup fresh or frozen blueberries, ½ teaspoon Dijon-style mustard, 1 large shallot (chopped), 2 tablespoons cider vinegar, and 2 tablespoons balsamic vinegar; cover and whirl until blended. Add ½ cup extra-virgin olive oil and garlic salt to taste; whirl to combine. Stir in ¼ cup crumbled blue cheese.

Smoothie Dessert

In blender, combine 1 cup frozen yogurt (vanilla, chocolate, or strawberry), ⅓ cup cold milk, ⅓ cup raspberries, ½ cup hulled strawberries, and ½ cup blueberries. Cover and whirl until smooth. Pour into 2 glasses and garnish each with a sprig of fresh mint.

Cranny Chutney

This sauce is delicious on turkey or ham sandwiches, or roasted butternut squash. In a medium, heavy-bottomed saucepan combine 4 cups cranberries (fresh or frozen), 2½ tablespoons minced crystallized ginger, ¾ cup light brown sugar, ⅛ teaspoon dried red chile flakes, and ⅛ teaspoon salt. Bring to boil on high heat; reduce heat to medium and simmer 10 minutes, stirring frequently. Refrigerate well sealed in nonreactive container up to 10 days.

Angelic Blueberries

In medium bowl, combine 3 cups blueberries, 3 tablespoons sugar, and 3 tablespoons orange liqueur; toss to combine and set aside for 45 minutes. Cut 6 slices angel food cake and place in 6 shallow bowls. Top each with 2 tablespoons store-bought lemon curd. Toss blueberries and spoon on curd. If desired, dust with powdered sugar.

Wild Rice Salad with Raspberry-Orange Vinaigrette

YIELD: 16 SERVINGS

This salad is delicious served with baked ham, pork roast, or roast goose. Assemble salad and refrigerate 2 hours before serving. Colorful and delicious, it is a welcome addition to the holiday table as well as a casual outdoor gathering. If you can't find organic wild rice, use all long-grain white rice (omit step 2 and double the ingredients in step 3).

Wild Rice Salad

3 cups diced mixed dried fruit, such as a mixture of dried cranberries, dried apricots, dried peaches, and dried pears

¾ cup orange-flavored liqueur

1½ cups raw wild rice, well-rinsed

6¾ cups vegetable broth or chicken broth, divided use

Salt

2 cups long-grain white rice

⅓ cup chopped fresh Italian parsley

Vinaigrette

¾ cup fresh raspberries

⅓ cup raspberry vinegar or ⅓ cup red wine vinegar

½ teaspoon salt

½ cup canola oil or vegetable oil

1 generous tablespoon Dijon-style mustard

Freshly ground black pepper

Garnish: about ½ cup additional fresh raspberries

1   Prepare salad: In medium bowl, combine dried fruit and liqueur; stir to coat fruit with liqueur. Cover with plastic wrap and set aside at least 2 hours, stirring mixture from time to time. Or for a speedier approach, combine in microwave-safe bowl; cover and microwave 90 seconds on high and set aside to cool.

2   In large saucepan, combine wild rice, 3¾ cups vegetable broth or chicken broth and generous pinch of salt. Bring to boil on medium-high heat; cover and reduce to simmer on low heat. Cook 45 to 55 minutes (cooking time varies) or until liquid is absorbed and most grains have started to crack open to reveal white interior. Remove cover and set pan aside to cool.

3   Meanwhile, in large saucepan, combine long-grain rice, remaining broth and generous pinch salt. Bring to boil on high heat. Cover and reduce temperature to low. Cook about 17 minutes or until liquid is absorbed. Set aside to cool.

4   Drain fruits in fine strainer set over mixing bowl, pressing fruits with back of wooden spoon to extract liqueur; reserve liquid for vinaigrette. In large glass or ceramic salad bowl, combine the two varieties of rice, fruit, and parsley; set aside.

5   Prepare vinaigrette: In food processor, puree raspberries. Add reserved liqueur, vinegar, and salt; pulse to combine. Add oil, mustard, and pepper to taste; pulse to combine.

6   Pour vinaigrette over rice salad and toss to combine. Taste and add more salt and pepper if needed. Cover lightly with plastic wrap and refrigerate at least 2 hours or up to 4 hours; toss again before serving. Serve chilled, garnished with fresh raspberries.

Nutritional information (per serving): Calories 340, fat calories 70; total fat 8 grams, sat fat 0.5 gram, cholesterol 0 milligrams; sodium 260 milligrams; total carbohydrates 60 grams, fiber 4 grams, sugars 22 grams; protein 5 grams; vitamin A IUs 8%; vitamin C 2%; calcium 2%; iron 10%.

Summertime Sangria

YIELD: 10 SERVINGS

A glass of sangria on a hot day is such a refreshing treat. It's a classic combination of red wine and sparkling water augmented with plenty of tasty fresh berries and stone fruit. Salted almonds are an appealing accompaniment to this classic Spanish cooler.

6 tablespoons water

5 tablespoons sugar

1 cup blackberries

1 cup blueberries

1 cup pitted cherries

1 cup diced peaches

1 orange, unpeeled, cut in half lengthwise and cut into ¼-inch slices

10 medium strawberries, hulled, quartered lengthwise

5 cups dry red wine

1½ cups fresh orange juice

½ cup orange liqueur

1½ cups sparkling water

Ice

1   Prepare sugar syrup: Place water and sugar in small saucepan and bring to boil on high heat. Lower heat to medium and simmer until sugar dissolves. Remove from heat and cool.

2   In large pitcher, combine all fruit, wine, juice, liqueur, and cooled sugar syrup. Gently stir. Serve or cover and refrigerate up to 5 hours.

3   To serve, place several ice cubes in each of 10 glasses. Use slotted spoon to remove most of fruit from pitcher and add about ⅓ cup of fruit mixture to each glass. Add sparkling water to wine mixture in pitcher and gently stir; pour over fruit and ice in glasses. Serve.

Nutritional information (per serving): Calories 220, fat calories 0; total fat 0 grams, sat fat 0 grams, cholesterol 0 milligrams; sodium 0 milligrams; total carbohydrates 29 grams, fiber 3 grams, sugars 21 grams; protein 1 gram; vitamin A IUs 4%; vitamin C 70%; calcium 2%; iron 2%.

Summertime Sangria

Blueberry Gingerbread

YIELD: 9 SERVINGS

Blueberries and gingerbread are great partners. The berries give the quick bread a sweet-tart spark of flavor. Don't worry if the berries sink to the bottom of the bread. That is exactly where they are supposed to be. Top each serving with either crème fraîche or sour cream that is sweetened to taste with powdered sugar.

- 7 tablespoons unsalted butter plus butter for greasing pan
- 1¾ cups all-purpose flour, divided use, plus flour for dusting pan
- 1 cup blueberries
- 1 teaspoon baking soda
- ⅛ teaspoon salt
- 2 teaspoons ground cinnamon
- 1 tablespoon ground ginger
- ½ cup packed light brown sugar
- 2 tablespoons granulated sugar
- ⅓ cup molasses
- ⅓ cup light corn syrup
- 2 eggs
- 1¼ cups buttermilk
- Garnish: crème fraîche or sour cream sweetened to taste with powdered sugar

1   Adjust oven rack to middle position. Preheat oven to 350°F. Grease an 8-inch square baking dish with butter. Dust with flour; invert and shake out excess flour. Set aside.

2   In a small bowl, toss blueberries with 1 tablespoon of flour; set aside.

3   Place remaining flour, baking soda, salt, cinnamon, ginger, and sugars in large bowl. Use whisk to mix together.

4   In small saucepan, combine butter, molasses, and corn syrup; heat over medium heat until butter melts, stirring occasionally. Remove from heat.

5   In medium bowl, combine eggs and buttermilk; beat with fork or whisk to blend.

6   Add butter-molasses mixture and egg mixture to flour mixture; mix with wooden spoon until thoroughly combined. Transfer to prepared pan. Sprinkle flour-dusted blueberries on top of batter, leaving any excess flour behind in bowl.

7   Bake 45 to 50 minutes, until springy to the touch and toothpick inserted in middle comes out clean. Cool on wire rack. Cut into squares and serve with sweetened crème fraîche or sweetened sour cream.

Nutritional information (without topping): Calories 320, fat calories 90; total fat 11 grams, sat fat 6 grams, cholesterol 75 milligrams; sodium 240 milligrams; total carbohydrates 53 grams, fiber 1 gram, sugars 24 grams; protein 5 grams; vitamin A IUs 8%; vitamin C 4%; calcium 10%; iron 15%.

Crumble-Topped Cranberry Jumbles

YIELD: 4 LARGE SERVINGS

Sweet, yet still alluringly tart, this cranberry-focused dessert is a great choice for a holiday meal. It can be served either warm or at room temperature. Be sure to serve it with either sweetened whipped cream or ice cream.

Unsalted butter for greasing ramekins

5 cups fresh or frozen (thawed) cranberries

1 cup granulated sugar

Minced zest of 1 orange (colored portion of peel)

Pinch of salt

Topping

⅓ cup all-purpose flour

¼ cup light brown sugar, packed

½ teaspoon ground cinnamon

½ teaspoon ground nutmeg

¼ teaspoon ground cardamom

⅓ cup quick-cooking rolled oats

¼ cup (½ stick) cold unsalted butter, cut into 8 pieces

For serving: sweetened whipped cream or vanilla ice cream

1   Adjust oven rack to lower third of oven. Preheat oven to 375°F. Generously butter 4 (10-ounce) ramekins or soufflé cups. Line rimmed baking sheet with parchment paper. Set aside.

2   In large bowl, combine cranberries, granulated sugar, zest, and salt. Toss to combine. Fill each ramekin with cranberry mixture. Don't worry about overfilling because berries will break down during baking. Place on prepared rimmed baking sheet.

3   Prepare topping: In food processor fitted with metal blade, add flour, brown sugar, spices, and oats; pulse until well blended. Add butter; pulse until crumbly and pieces in mixture are about pea size. Do *not* overprocess, because mixture will form a dough. Distribute mixture over cranberries and pat topping down gently.

4   Bake 50 to 55 minutes or until cranberries are bubbly and topping is nicely browned. Serve warm topped with sweetened whipped cream or ice cream.

Nutritional information (per serving without whipped cream or ice cream): Calories 530, fat calories 190; total fat 21 grams, sat fat 13 grams, cholesterol 55 milligrams; sodium 85 milligrams; total carbohydrates 87 grams, fiber 7 grams, sugars 64 grams; protein 3 grams; vitamin A IUs 15%; vitamin C 35%; calcium 4%; iron 8%.

Broccoli

Sturdy stalks support umbrella clusters of tightly closed buds. Children say that it looks like a tree, while many adults see broccoli as a verdant vitamin powerhouse. The flavor of bud and stalk is a strong vegetal taste with hints of sweetness edged with a whisper of pepper. The stalks are somewhat fibrous and tougher than the tickly, tender buds. Peeling the stalk tames its toughness.

To ready the soil, organic growers compost the fields 45 days before planting broccoli. Alyssum flowers are often planted around the crop to keep aphids away. Ladybugs and lacewings are also used to control pests. Organic yields are about 5 to 10 percent less than conventional broccoli crops.

BUYING AND STORING: Buds should be tightly closed and uniformly green. If leaves are present, they should be green without any yellowing. Stalk bottom should be green. Avoid broccoli with soft spots or discoloration; it should have a fresh smell. Refrigerate, unwashed, in plastic bag in crisper drawer up to 7 days.

PREP AND USE: Rinse well with cold water. Some markets sell fresh broccoli without thick stalks attached (called crowns). If buying stalk-on broccoli, cut the stalk off, making sure you cut high enough so that large individual florets fall away as you cut. Cut florets in half or quarters lengthwise if large (for even cooking, you want them all about the same size). If stalks are large, peel off skin with swivel-bladed vegetable peeler or paring knife. Trim off bottom end of stalk; cut stalk into ¼-inch crosswise slices.

Eat raw or cooked. To cook, blanch, steam, stir-fry, or roast. To blanch, bring enough water to generously cover broccoli to a boil on high heat. Add stalk slices; boil 2 or 3 minutes. Add florets and cook about 5 to 7 minutes, or until tender-crisp (do *not* overcook). Drain in colander in sink and refresh with cold water. Another alternative is to cook florets in steamer basket while cooking the stalk in the simmering water below the steamer. If stir-frying, fry in hot oil first with a little ginger, then add about ¾ cup broth augmented with soy sauce and roasted sesame oil; cover. Cook on medium until tender-crisp, about 2 minutes.

AVAILABLE: Year-round

NUTRITIONAL INFORMATION (per 1 cup, chopped, raw): Calories 31, fat calories 3; total fat 0 grams, sat fat 0 grams, cholesterol 0 milligrams; sodium 30 milligrams; total carbohydrates 6 grams, fiber 2 grams, sugars 2 grams; protein 3 grams; vitamin A IUs 11%; vitamin C 135%; calcium 4%; iron 4%.

SERVING SUGGESTIONS

Quick Broccoli Stalk Soup

Peel 2 broccoli stalks and cut into ¾-inch chunks; place in large, deep skillet with 1 tablespoon vegetable oil. Heat on medium-high and add 1 large onion (roughly chopped) and 1 stalk celery (sliced). Cook, stirring frequently, until onion starts to soften. Add 1 large garlic clove (minced), small pinch of dried red chile flakes, and 1 tablespoon minced fresh ginger; cook 30 seconds, stirring frequently. Add 6 cups chicken broth or vegetable broth and 2 tablespoons soy sauce. Bring to boil on high heat; reduce heat and simmer until broccoli is tender.

Citrus Topping

In medium nonreactive bowl, combine juice of 2 limes, juice of 1 lemon, juice of 1 orange, 2 tablespoons agave syrup, 2 tablespoons rice vinegar, and 2 tablespoons soy sauce. Stir to combine; cover and refrigerate at least 1 hour or up to 24 hours. Bring sauce to room temperature. Blanch or steam broccoli florets until tender-crisp (see Prep and Use). Spoon a little sauce over each serving of broccoli.

Broccoli and Eggs

Add chopped, cooked broccoli to omelet fillings, or use in frittata or quiche.

Stem Slaw

Grate peeled broccoli stalks and peeled carrots; add to shredded cabbage and toss with coleslaw dressing. If desired, garnish with raisins.

Broccoli, Potato, and Cheese Soup

YIELD: 8 SERVINGS

The delectable flavors of the vegetables shine through in this simple pureed soup. If you prefer, instead of pureeing it in batches, either in a blender or food processor, use a handheld immersion blender to puree it to the desired consistency.

6 tablespoons unsalted butter

½ cup finely chopped celery

1 cup finely chopped sweet onion

1 cup broccoli florets

2 large Yukon Gold potatoes, peeled, cubed, about 2 cups

¼ cup all-purpose flour

2 cups whole milk

2½ cups fat-free, low-sodium chicken broth

8 ounces cheddar cheese, grated

Salt and freshly ground black pepper

Garnish: Roasted Garlic Crostini (see page 139)

1   Melt butter in heavy-bottomed Dutch oven or large saucepan on medium heat. Add celery, onion, broccoli, and potatoes; cook 10 minutes, stirring occasionally. Stir in flour; cook, stirring, 60 seconds (do *not* brown). Slowly add milk and broth, stirring constantly. Add the cheese and bring to a boil on medium-high heat, stirring constantly. Reduce heat to low heat; gently simmer 25 minutes.

2   Remove from the heat and let cool for a few minutes. In a food processor fitted with metal blade, puree soup in batches until smooth. Return to pan and gently reheat. Garnish with crostini. Serve immediately.

Nutritional information (per serving without crostini): Calories 290, fat calories 180; total fat 20 grams, sat fat 13 grams, cholesterol 60 milligrams; sodium 350 milligrams; total carbohydrates 17 grams, fiber 1 gram, sugars 4 grams; protein 11 grams; vitamin A IUs 30%; vitamin C 30%; calcium 30%; iron 6%.

Broccoli, Beef, and Brown Rice Combo

YIELD: 6 SERVINGS

Bejeweled with colorful vegetables and slices of perfectly grilled steak, this classic broccoli-beef combination gets an irresistible makeover in this one-bowl meal. The fragrant brown rice–vegetable mixture is lightly napped with a tangy peanut dressing before a topping of thinly sliced steak is added.

Marinade

2 large cloves garlic, minced

2 tablespoon soy sauce

1 tablespoon agave syrup or honey

1 teaspoon toasted sesame oil

1 tablespoon rice vinegar

1 pound boneless sirloin steak (see Meatless Tip, page 78)

Rice Mixture

1 cup long-grain brown rice

2¼ cups water

½ teaspoon salt

1 teaspoon vegetable oil or canola oil

2 medium carrots, peeled, sliced on diagonal ¼-inch thick

1¾ cups broccoli florets

Sauce

3 tablespoons smooth peanut butter

3 tablespoons hot water

2 tablespoons seasoned rice vinegar

1 tablespoon soy sauce

⅛ teaspoon dried red chile flakes

2 teaspoons toasted sesame oil

Garnish: 1 ½ tablespoons toasted sesame seeds (see Cook's Note, page 78)

Optional garnish: chopped fresh cilantro

1 Prepare marinade: Set large zipper-style plastic bag in bowl to hold it upright. Add garlic, soy sauce, agave syrup or honey, oil, and vinegar. Poke steak at 1-inch intervals with tines of fork. Add steak to bag with marinade and seal. Refrigerate at least 2 hours or up to 8 hours, turning bag occasionally to redistribute marinade.

2 Prepare rice: In large saucepan place rice, water, salt, and oil. Bring to boil on high heat; stir once. Cover with tight-fitting lid; reduce heat to low and simmer 45 minutes. Remove from heat and let stand, covered, 5 to 10 minutes. Remove lid and fluff rice with fork.

3 Meanwhile, bring about 5 cups water to boil on high heat in separate large saucepan. Add carrots and cook until tender-crisp, about 4 minutes. Remove with slotted spoon and set aside. Add broccoli and cook in boiling water until tender-crisp, about 6 to 7 minutes. Drain and set aside. Heat grill.

4 Prepare sauce: In medium bowl, stir peanut butter and 3 tablespoons hot water to combine. Add vinegar, soy sauce, chile flakes, and sesame oil; stir vigorously to combine. Place rice in large bowl; add sauce and vegetables. Toss. Taste and add salt if needed. Set aside at room temperature.

5 Remove steak from marinade; discard marinade. Grill over medium-high heat about 3 minutes on each side; cooking times vary depending on degree of doneness preferred, heat of fire, and thickness of steak. Set steak aside on cutting board and allow to rest 5 to 10 minutes.

6 Slice steak into ¼-inch-thick slices. Spoon rice salad into 6 bowls. Top with steak slices and sprinkle with sesame seeds. If desired, garnish with cilantro.

Nutritional information (per serving): Calories 310, fat calories 100; total fat 11 grams, sat fat 2.5 grams, cholesterol 30 milligrams; sodium 790 milligrams; total carbohydrates 34 grams, fiber 4 grams, sugars 4 grams; protein 21 grams; vitamin A IUs 80%; vitamin C 35%; calcium 4%; iron 10%.

Broccoli, Beef, and Brown Rice Combo

Cook's Note: To toast sesame seeds, place in small skillet on medium-high heat. Shake handle to redistribute seeds, toasting until lightly browned. Watch carefully because they burn easily. Cool.

Meatless Tip: This dish is lovely without meat, so simply leave it out. If you like, top with Quick Stir-Fried Tofu (page 322) or Grilled Tofu with Asian-Style Marinade (page 321).

Broccoli Mac 'n' Cheese

YIELD: 8 SERVINGS

Cheddar cheese brings out the best in broccoli. Even those convinced that they don't like broccoli might change their minds after a bite or two of this lovely macaroni and cheese dish that is bound with creamy cheddar cheese sauce.

- 1 pound broccoli crowns
- 1 tablespoon plus 1 teaspoon salt, divided use
- 1 cup rotini or fusilli
- 3 tablespoons unsalted butter plus butter for greasing casserole
- 3 tablespoons all-purpose flour
- 2 cups whole milk
- ½ cup sour cream
- ¼ teaspoon freshly ground white pepper
- ¼ teaspoon dried red chile flakes
- ⅛ teaspoon ground nutmeg
- 2 ounces sharp cheddar cheese, grated
- ⅓ cup fresh breadcrumbs
- 1 tablespoon unsalted butter, melted

1   Cut broccoli into bite-size florets and pieces. In 6-quart pan or Dutch oven, bring enough water to generously cover broccoli to boil on high heat. Add florets. Return to boil; immediately remove broccoli with slotted spoon and drain well in colander.

2   Return water in pan to a boil on high heat. Add 1 tablespoon salt and rotini or fusilli. Cook until al dente—tender but with a little bite, about 10 minutes. Drain well, but do not rinse.

3   Adjust oven rack to middle position. Preheat oven to 350°F. Lightly butter a 2-quart casserole; add florets and rotini.

4   Melt butter over medium heat in medium heavy-bottomed saucepan. Add flour and stir to combine. Slowly add milk, whisking to prevent lumps. Simmer until flour taste disappears, about 3 to 5 minutes, stirring frequently. Stir in sour cream, remaining 1 teaspoon salt, pepper, chile flakes, and nutmeg. Off heat, stir in grated cheddar; stir until smooth and cheese thoroughly melts. Carefully pour cheese sauce over broccoli and rotini; gently toss to coat. In separate small bowl, combine breadcrumbs and melted butter. Sprinkle buttered crumbs over top of casserole. Place casserole on rimmed baking sheet.

5   Bake until heated through, crumbs are golden, and sauce is bubbly, about 1 hour. Cool 5 to 10 minutes; serve.

Nutritional information (per serving): Calories 210, fat calories 100; total fat 11 grams, sat fat 7 grams, cholesterol 25 milligrams; sodium 380 milligrams; total carbohydrates 23 grams, fiber 2 grams, sugars 4 grams; protein 7 grams; vitamin A IUs 40%; vitamin C 90%; calcium 15%; iron 8%.

Broccoli and Mushroom Pasta Alfredo

YIELD: 8 APPETIZER SERVINGS

I f you like, augment this rich dish with a cup of cooked, shredded chicken or cubes of ham. Or if you prefer, instead of ladling it over pasta, spoon it over grilled tofu in individual shallow bowls.

2 cups broccoli florets

1 teaspoon salt plus salt for seasoning

6 tablespoons unsalted butter, divided use

½ cup sliced common white (button) mushrooms

½ cup sliced cremini mushrooms

2 large cloves garlic, minced

2 cups heavy whipping cream

1 cup freshly grated Parmesan cheese

Freshly ground black pepper

1 pound egg noodles, cooked, drained

Optional garnish: minced fresh basil leaves

1   In large saucepan, bring enough water to boil to cover broccoli. Add broccoli and 1 teaspoon salt and cook until tender-crisp, about 5 to 7 minutes. Drain and refresh with cold water; drain and set aside.

2   In large, deep nonstick skillet, melt 2 tablespoons butter on medium-high heat; add mushrooms, cook, stirring occasionally, until moisture is gone and mushrooms are starting to brown. Add garlic; cook, stirring frequently, for 30 seconds.

3   Add remaining butter and stir in the cream. Gradually stir in cheese; continue to cook until thickened (do *not* boil). Add broccoli, season with salt and pepper to taste, and pour over noodles. If desired, garnish with fresh basil. Serve immediately.

Nutritional information (per serving): Calories 520, fat calories 330; total fat 36 grams, sat fat 21 grams, cholesterol 155 milligrams; sodium 710 milligrams; total carbohydrates 39 grams, fiber 2 grams, sugars 1 gram; protein 12 grams; vitamin A IUs 35%; vitamin C 30%; calcium 20%; iron 15%.

Brussels Sprout

How glorious these tiny cabbage-like vegetables look in garden or farm. Attached to a long, thick stalk, the verdant green heads grow close together in a circular pattern. Often the larger orbs are positioned at the bottom, graduating in size to smaller ones at the top. Most often in the marketplace they are trimmed from the stem, sometimes stocked loose in bins, other times tidily piled in small bucket-like containers.

Brussels sprouts like cool coastal climates and cold nights. Organic growers often use organic soap products for pest control, as well as beneficial insects such as ladybugs. When it comes to the harvest, everything is done by hand, from picking to washing.

BUYING AND STORING: Look for bright green orbs that are firm and tightly packed. Avoid those with yellow leaves, soft spots, or black discoloration. If buying them loose from a bin, look for those that are the same size for even cooking. If loose, refrigerate unwashed in perforated plastic bag in crisper drawer up to 10 days. If on the stalk, it will be awkward to fit into a crisper drawer. Refrigerate stalk (anywhere you can fit it) up to 14 days.

PREP AND USE: Rinse with cold water. If on stalk, cut off each sprout at the base. Gently wash sprouts in cold water. Trim off any wilted or discolored leaves. Trim off small portion at base end. If sprouts are large, cut them in half lengthwise. If they are really big, say the size of a golf ball, quarter them. If small, leave whole. If you want to leave them whole and want to speed up cooking, cut a shallow X at the base. Blanch, braise, roast, sauté, microwave, or steam. To bring out their nutty, sweet flavor and appealing texture, do not over- or undercook. They should be fork-tender, not crisp; on the other hand, they shouldn't be mushy.

AVAILABLE: November to May (peak is November to February)

NUTRITIONAL INFORMATION (per 1 cup Brussels sprouts, raw): Calories 38, fat calories 2; total fat 0 grams, sat fat 0 grams, cholesterol 0 milligrams; sodium 22 milligrams; total carbohydrates 8 grams, fiber 3 grams, sugars 2 grams; protein 3 grams; vitamin A IUs 13%; vitamin C 125%; calcium 4%; iron 7%.

SERVING SUGGESTIONS

Balsamic Butter

A mixture of butter and balsamic vinegar enhances the natural sweetness in Brussels sprouts. Blanch 1 pound Brussels sprouts until fork-tender. Drain. Toss with 1 tablespoon unsalted butter and 1 tablespoon balsamic vinegar. Season with salt and freshly ground black pepper. Toss.

Braised, but Crunchy, with Gremolata

In large skillet, cook ½ medium onion (chopped) until softened in 2 tablespoons extra-virgin olive oil on medium-high heat. Add 1 pound Brussels sprouts and cook 4 minutes, stirring frequently. Add ¼ cup water, toss, and cover. Reduce heat to medium and cook until fork-tender (adding more water if necessary), about 7 minutes. To make topping, toss ½ cup large fresh breadcrumbs (from sourdough or French bread) with 2 teaspoons extra-virgin olive oil in skillet. Toast on medium-high heat, tossing frequently until brown and crunchy. Off heat, toss crumbs with 2 teaspoons finely minced orange or tangerine zest (colored portion of peel), 3 tablespoons chopped fresh Italian parsley, and 3 tablespoons freshly grated Parmesan cheese. Sprinkle topping over sprouts.

Pancetta and Sprouts

Line bottom of broiler pan with foil and top with broiler rack. Position oven rack about 5 inches below broiler element and preheat broiler. Arrange 5 thin pancetta slices (usually slices are circular in shape) on broiler rack. Broil until crisp, about 1 minute. Cool. Blanch or braise 1 pound Brussels sprouts; drain and crumble pancetta on top.

Crudités Platter

Select small Brussels sprouts. Blanch until just fork-tender. Drain; refresh with cold water, or submerge in ice water. Drain, pat dry, and serve with assorted raw vegetables and your favorite dip.

Brussels Sprouts and Cherry Tomato Salad

YIELD: 6 TO 8 SERVINGS

I f you like, cut down on preparation time by using your favorite store-bought bottled vinaigrette dressing. If desired, toss cooked and cooled Brussels sprouts with vinaigrette and spoon over sliced tomatoes.

4 medium cloves garlic, peeled, divided use

1½ pounds Brussels sprouts, trimmed

1 pound cherry tomatoes

Vinaigrette

⅓ cup balsamic vinegar

2 tablespoons red wine vinegar

2 shallots, minced

1 teaspoon dried red chile flakes

Salt and freshly ground black pepper

1 cup extra-virgin olive oil

1   In large saucepan or Dutch oven, bring about 6 cups salted water to boil on high heat. Cut two cloves of garlic into thin slices and add to water. Add Brussels sprouts and cook until just barely tender, about 5 minutes (cooking times vary depending on size). Drain and refresh with cold water. Set aside to cool.

2   Mince remaining garlic and place in large bowl. Cut tomatoes in half and add to bowl.

3   In separate medium bowl, prepare vinaigrette: combine vinegars, shallots, chile flakes, and salt and pepper to taste; whisk in oil in thin steam. Taste and adjust seasoning as needed.

4   When Brussels sprouts are cool, add to tomatoes. Stir vinaigrette; add just enough vinaigrette to lightly coat vegetables; toss very gently. Serve. Leftover vinaigrette can be stored in airtight container in refrigerator up to 2 weeks.

Nutritional information (per serving): Calories 190, fat calories 130; total fat 14 grams, sat fat 2 grams, cholesterol 0 milligrams; sodium 30 milligrams; total carbohydrates 15 grams, fiber 4 grams, sugars 7 grams; protein 4 grams; vitamin A IUs 25%; vitamin C 130%; calcium 4%; iron 10%.

Roasted Brussels Sprouts with Candied Pecans

YIELD: 6 SERVINGS

Candied pecans make an irresistible sweet foil to the vegetal taste of Brussels sprouts. The nuts offer a hint of spice along with sweetness. They are candied in a mixture of brown sugar, corn syrup, and cayenne pepper.

Olive oil nonstick spray

1 cup pecan halves

2 tablespoons light corn syrup

1 tablespoon dark brown sugar

Pinch ground cayenne pepper

1½ pounds Brussels sprouts, trimmed, cut in half lengthwise

3 tablespoons extra-virgin olive oil

1 medium clove garlic, minced

¼ cup balsamic vinegar

Minced zest of 1 lemon (colored portion only)

⅛ teaspoon salt

⅛ teaspoon freshly ground black pepper

¼ cup (½ stick) unsalted butter

1   Adjust oven rack to middle position. Preheat oven to 325°F. Spray rimmed baking sheet with nonstick spray. Set aside.

2   In large bowl, combine pecans, corn syrup, sugar, and cayenne pepper; toss. Spread nuts into single layer on prepared sheet. Bake 15 minutes, stirring nuts every 5 minutes to keep them from sticking together. Remove them from the oven and set aside to cool.

3   Set oven to 425°F and line rimmed baking sheet with aluminum foil. In bowl, toss Brussels sprouts with oil, garlic, vinegar, zest, salt, and pepper. Place mixture on a foil-lined baking sheet and roast in the oven until Brussels sprouts are tender, about 15 minutes. Remove them from the oven and place them in a bowl. Toss them with butter and pecans; serve.

Nutritional information (per serving): Calories 330, fat calories 250; total fat 28 grams, sat fat 7 grams, cholesterol 20 milligrams; sodium 85 milligrams; total carbohydrates 19 grams, fiber 6 grams, sugars 7 grams; protein 6 grams; vitamin A IUs 20%; vitamin C 160%; calcium 6%; iron 10%.

Roasted Brussels Sprouts with Candied Pecans

Chard and Brussels Sprouts Mélange

YIELD: 6 SERVINGS

Green vegetables show off in this tasty concoction. The chard adds creaminess to the dish, as well as a mild, spinach-like flavor.

- 2 tablespoons extra-virgin olive oil
- 3 tablespoons unsalted butter, divided use
- 2 medium cloves garlic, minced
- 1½ pounds Brussels sprouts, trimmed, cut in half lengthwise
- Salt and freshly ground black pepper
- ¾ cup water, divided use
- 2 bunches chard, ribs removed, leaves chopped (see Cook's Note)
- Pinch ground cayenne pepper
- Optional for serving: cooked brown or wild rice

1   Heat oil and 2 tablespoons of butter in large, deep skillet over medium-high heat. Add garlic and cook 30 seconds. Add Brussels sprouts, toss, and season with salt and pepper to taste. Increase heat to high and cook 5 minutes, tossing frequently.

2   Add ½ cup water and cover. Reduce heat to low and cook until almost tender, about 5 minutes. Add remaining ¼ cup water and chard; cook until just wilted, about 3 minutes. Stir in remaining 1 tablespoon butter and cayenne pepper. If desired, serve over cooked rice.

Nutritional information (per serving without rice): Calories 150, fat calories 100; total fat 11 grams, sat fat 4.5 grams, cholesterol 15 milligrams; sodium 105 milligrams; total carbohydrates 12 grams, fiber 5 grams, sugars 3 grams; protein 5 grams; vitamin A IUs 60%; vitamin C 180%; calcium 6%; iron 15%.

Cook's Note: Only the chard leaves are used here. Reserve and chop ribs for use in soups and stir-fries.

Brussels Sprouts with Bacon and Fresh Basil

YIELD: 6 SERVINGS

The sweet, smoky, salty taste of bacon gives Brussels sprouts a new personality. Add a pinch of chile and some fresh basil, and the dish reaches for the stars. If you don't eat bacon, serve this dish over cooked brown rice and sprinkle on some vegetarian bacon.

- 1½ pounds Brussels sprouts, trimmed
- 3 slices thick bacon (see Meatless Tip)
- ⅛ teaspoon salt
- ⅛ teaspoon freshly ground black pepper
- 1 large pinch dried red chile flakes
- 6 large basil leaves, cut into narrow crosswise strips

1   In large saucepan or Dutch oven, bring about 6 cups salted water to boil on high heat. Add Brussels sprouts and cook until just fork-tender, about 5 minutes (but cooking times vary depending on size). Drain and refresh with cold water. Cut each in half lengthwise.

2   Cook bacon in large, deep skillet over medium-high heat until crisp. Place bacon on paper towels to drain. Remove all but 2 tablespoons of bacon grease from skillet.

3   Add Brussels sprouts to skillet; add salt, pepper, and chile flakes. Cook on medium-high heat until heated through. Crumble bacon and add to mixture. Toss. Remove from heat; add basil and toss. Taste and adjust seasoning as needed.

Nutritional information (per serving): Calories 140, fat calories 80; total fat 9 grams, sat fat 3 grams, cholesterol 15 milligrams; sodium 240 milligrams; total carbohydrates 10 grams, fiber 4 grams, sugars 3 grams; protein 6 grams; vitamin A IUs 20%; vitamin C 160%; calcium 4%; iron 10%.

Meatless Tip: Omit bacon. In step 2, add 2 tablespoons vegetable oil to skillet. If desired, spoon completed mixture over cooked brown rice and top with vegetarian bacon.

Cabbage

Green (Common)

Red (Purple)

It's a shame that cabbage can have a stodgy reputation. Raw or properly cooked, it has an appealing texture and delicious spicy-sweet taste. Overcooked or cooked with too much water, it gets soggy, loses nutrients, and takes on an unpleasant sulfur smell.

Organic growers say that cabbage is much heartier than other leafy greens, and report that pests are often controlled by planting sweet alyssum around the crops. Beneficial insects such as ladybugs and lacewings are also used. Mildew can be a problem and occurs when the weather changes in spring and fall. Organic crops generally yield about 20 percent less than conventionally grown cabbage crops.

BUYING AND STORING: Look for firm heads that feel heavy for their size and have crisp leaves. Avoid those with discoloration or limp areas. Store in plastic bag placed in refrigerator crisper drawer up to two weeks.

PREP AND USE: Remove any wilted or discolored leaves. To shred, cut into quarters; remove and discard core (hard central white area). Place cut-side down on cutting board and cut crosswise into narrow shreds. A food processor fitted with the slicing blade can also be used for shredding. Use a stainless-steel knife when cutting red cabbage to prevent discoloration. Red cabbage turns a funky blue when cooked; add acid to cooking liquid (such as lemon juice, dry white wine, or vinegar) to maintain the bright color, and be sure to use a nonreactive pan (not aluminum or cast iron).

Eat raw or cooked. Braise, simmer, steam, or stir-fry.

AVAILABLE: Year-round

NUTRITIONAL INFORMATION (1 cup chopped raw green cabbage): Calories 22, fat calories 1; total fat 0 grams, sat fat 0 grams, cholesterol 0 milligrams; sodium 16 milligrams; total carbohydrates 5 grams, fiber 2 grams, sugars 3 grams; protein 1 gram; vitamin A IUs 2%; vitamin C 54%; calcium 4%; iron 2%.

NUTRITIONAL INFORMATION (1 cup chopped raw red cabbage): Calories 28, fat calories 1; total fat 0 grams, sat fat 0 grams, cholesterol 0 milligrams; sodium 24 milligrams; total carbohydrates 7 grams, fiber 2 grams, sugars 3 grams; protein 1 gram; vitamin A IUs 20%; vitamin C 85%; calcium 4%; iron 4%.

SERVING SUGGESTIONS

Stir-Fried Green

Shred ½ of large cored green cabbage. Mince 1 large clove of garlic and thinly slice 3 trimmed green onions (including dark green stalks). Heat 2 tablespoons vegetable oil in wok or large, deep skillet on high heat; swirl to coat pan. Add garlic and cook, stirring, about 20 seconds. Add cabbage and toss. Cook, without stirring, about 1 minute. Add 2 tablespoons water or vegetable broth. Stir and cook until tender-crisp, about 2 minutes. Add green onions and salt to taste; toss to combine. Remove from heat and serve. Provide hot sauce for optional topping. Serve with cooked brown rice.

Suds and Sausage

Cut ½ pound kielbasa sausage into ½-inch crosswise slices. Heat 2 tablespoons vegetable oil in large, deep skillet on medium-high heat. Add sausage and brown lightly on both sides. Add ½ cup beer and 1 teaspoon Dijon-style mustard; stir to combine and bring to simmer. Add ½ large green cabbage (cored, shredded) and 1 medium bulb fresh fennel (trimmed, thinly sliced crosswise); toss and cover. Reduce heat to medium and cook until cabbage is wilted, about 7 to 8 minutes. Season with freshly ground black pepper to taste. Garnish with 1 tablespoon minced fresh Italian parsley.

Easy Pineapple Slaw

In small bowl, combine 6 tablespoons red wine vinegar, 2 teaspoons sugar or agave syrup, 5 tablespoons vegetable oil, and salt and freshly ground black pepper to taste. In large bowl, toss ½ large green cabbage (cored, shredded), ½ ripe pineapple (peeled, cored, diced), and 2 carrots (peeled, shredded). Add vinaigrette; toss. Add ½ cup chopped salted peanuts; toss.

Taco Crunch

Use cored and finely shredded green cabbage or red cabbage in tacos instead of lettuce.

Tortilla Wraps with Cabbage and Asian Dressing

YIELD: 4 LARGE WRAPS

This is a delicious way to use leftover cooked chicken. If roasting skinless and boneless chicken breasts, place them in a small baking dish in a single layer, then drizzle with a smidgen of extra-virgin olive oil. Rub surface to thinly coat with oil and roast in preheated 350°F oven for about 25 to 30 minutes or until cooked through. Leftover dressing can be covered and refrigerated; use as a dip for raw vegetables or dress finely shredded cabbage to make an appealing coleslaw.

Dressing

1 cup mayonnaise

1 tablespoon soy sauce

Zest of 1 orange (colored portion of peel)

2 tablespoons fresh orange juice

2 teaspoons toasted sesame oil

⅛ teaspoon dried red chile flakes

Wraps

4 10-inch flour tortillas

1 cup shredded green cabbage

1 cup shredded red cabbage

½ pound cooked skinless, boneless chicken breasts, cut into thin strips (see Meatless Tip)

1 cup sno peas, strings removed, cut into 3 lengthwise strips

¼ cup shredded peeled daikon

1 medium avocado, pitted, peeled, cut into ¼-inch-wide lengthwise slices

4 green onions, roots trimmed, halved lengthwise (use half of dark green stalks)

4 to 8 sprigs fresh cilantro

Coarse salt, such as kosher, and freshly ground black pepper

1   Place dressing ingredients in small bowl; stir to combine.

2   Spread enough dressing on one tortilla to thinly coat entire surface. Place ¼ of cabbage on lower half of tortilla; place ¼ of each remaining ingredient on top of cabbage, adding salt and pepper to taste. Roll up as tight as possible, starting at lower edge, folding over ends (to tuck in contents) halfway through rolling up tortilla. Give it a gentle push to seal. Cut in half crosswise and place on plate.

3   Repeat with remaining ingredients.

Nutritional information (per ½ wrap with chicken): Calories 320, fat calories 170; total fat 18 grams, sat fat 3 grams, cholesterol 25 milligrams; sodium 540 milligrams; total carbohydrates 27 grams, fiber 5 grams, sugars 4 grams; protein 11 grams; vitamin A IUs 6%; vitamin C 40%; calcium 4%; iron 6%.

Meatless Tip: These wraps are delectable without meat, so omit the chicken. If desired, add cubes of firm Asian-flavored tofu.

Tortilla Wraps with Cabbage and Asian Dressing

Spinach, Carrot, and Red Cabbage Salad

YIELD: 8 SERVINGS

The brilliant colors—purplish red, plus bright green and orange—combine with refreshing flavors to make this salad a welcome counterpoint to rich entrées such as duck, pork, or lamb. To prevent any discoloration when using raw red cabbage, toss with dressing after cutting it into shreds. To add a sweet nuance to the salad, dice 3 pitted dates and top each salad with a few pieces.

Vinaigrette

3 tablespoons balsamic vinegar

1 teaspoon Dijon-style mustard

1 teaspoon honey or agave syrup or raspberry jam

1 teaspoon garlic salt

1/3 cup extra-virgin olive oil

1 tablespoon chopped fresh Italian parsley

Salad

1/2 large red cabbage, cored, shredded

2 medium carrots, peeled, shredded

4 cups baby spinach

1/3 cup toasted pine nuts (see Cook's Notes)

3 ounces soft goat cheese, crumbled

1 In small bowl or glass measuring cup with handle, whisk vinegar, mustard, honey or agave syrup or raspberry jam, and garlic salt with a fork. Add oil in thin stream, whisking constantly. Add parsley and stir.

2 In large bowl, toss cabbage, carrots, spinach, and pine nuts. Add vinaigrette and toss. Taste and add more garlic salt if needed.

3 Divide salad between 8 plates. Top with goat cheese and serve.

Nutritional information (per serving): Calories 160, fat calories 110; total fat 12 grams, sat fat 3.5 grams, cholesterol 10 milligrams; sodium 210 milligrams; total carbohydrates 10 grams, fiber 2 grams, sugars 6 grams; protein 4 grams; vitamin A IUs 80%; vitamin C 70%; calcium 8%; iron 6%.

Cook's Notes: To toast pine nuts, place pine nuts in small skillet on medium-high heat. Shake handle to redistribute pine nuts as they lightly brown. Watch carefully because they burn easily. Cool.

Cabbage Soup with Potatoes and Apples

YIELD: 8 SERVINGS

A squeeze of fresh lemon juice added at the table intensifies the flavors of this tasty soup. Pass small lemon wedges, as well as warm, crusty bread.

2 tablespoons extra-virgin olive oil

1 large yellow onion, chopped

2 large red potatoes, unpeeled, scrubbed, cut into 1/2-inch dice

7 cups thinly shredded green cabbage

1/2 cup dry white wine

8 large sprigs fresh thyme

10 cups low-fat, low-sodium chicken broth or vegetable broth

Salt and freshly ground black pepper

2 tablespoons unsalted butter

3 Fuji or Gala apples, peeled, cored, cut into 1/2-inch dice

Garnish: 2 teaspoons chopped fresh thyme leaves

Optional: 8 small lemon wedges

1   Heat oil in large saucepan or Dutch oven on medium-high heat. Add onion and potatoes; stir to coat with oil. Cook, stirring occasionally, until onions start to brown, about 10 minutes, reducing heat to medium after 5 minutes. Add cabbage; cook, stirring occasionally, until cabbage starts to wilt, about 5 minutes. Add wine and thyme sprigs; bring to boil; reduce heat to medium and simmer until wine reduces by half, about 3 minutes, stirring occasionally.

2   Add broth and bring to boil on high heat. Reduce heat to medium and simmer 5 minutes. Season with salt and pepper to taste.

3   Meanwhile, in large, deep skillet, heat 2 tablespoons butter on medium-high heat. Add apples and cook until tender and starting to brown, about 12 to 14 minutes. Season with salt and pepper to taste.

4   Remove and discard woody thyme stems, pulling off any leaves and adding to soup.

5   Taste soup and adjust seasoning as needed. Ladle into warm soup bowls and top each serving with apples and a pinch of chopped thyme leaves. Pass lemon wedges.

Nutritional information (per serving): Calories 190, fat calories 60; total fat 7 grams, sat fat 2.5 grams, cholesterol 10 milligrams; sodium 580 milligrams; total carbohydrates 27 grams, fiber 4 grams, sugars 9 grams; protein 4 grams; vitamin A IUs 4%; vitamin C 50%; calcium 4%; iron 6%.

Twice-Baked Potatoes with Cabbage and Pancetta

YIELD: 8 SERVINGS

Pancetta is Italian bacon that is cured with salt and spices but is not smoked. If you can't find it, substitute 4 slices bacon.

4 large baking potatoes, such as russets

Optional: vegetable oil or canola oil

4 ounces pancetta, finely diced (see Meatless Tip)

2½ cups chopped green cabbage

1 cup water

2 tablespoons unsalted butter

½ teaspoon caraway seeds

Salt and freshly ground white pepper

1   Adjust oven rack to middle position. Heat oven to 425°F. Scrub and dry potatoes. Rub with vegetable oil or canola oil, if desired. Prick in several places with fork. Bake 1 hour or until fork-tender. Remove potatoes from oven. Reduce oven temperature to 350°F.

2   Cook pancetta in small skillet over medium heat until crisp; drain on paper towel.

3   Combine cabbage, water, butter, and caraway seeds in large saucepan. On high heat, bring to boil; cover and reduce heat to medium-low. Simmer until cabbage is tender, about 10 minutes. Remove cabbage mixture with slotted spoon; drain in colander. On high heat, bring cooking liquid to boil and reduce to about ½ cup.

4   Cut potatoes in half lengthwise; cool 5 minutes. Hold potato half with thick potholder or oven mitt; scoop out flesh, being careful to leave shells intact (about ¼-inch thick). Mash potato flesh with potato masher or beat with electric mixer. Add drained cabbage mixture, half of pancetta, and enough reduced cabbage water to reach desired smooth, mashed potato consistency. Season with salt and pepper to taste.

5   Fill potato shells with mixture. Bake 15 minutes. Sprinkle with remaining pancetta; bake 5 minutes.

Nutritional information (per serving): Calories 200, fat calories 5; total fat 5 grams, sat fat 2.5 grams, cholesterol 15 milligrams; sodium 280 milligrams; total carbohydrates 33 grams, fiber 4 grams, sugars 3 grams; protein 6 grams; vitamin A IUs 2%; vitamin C 35%; calcium 4%; iron 10%.

Meatless Tip: Omit pancetta. If desired, in step 3, substitute ¼ cup shredded white cheddar cheese for pancetta.

Carrot

The feathery leaves atop the long, tapered root offer hints about the carrot's lineage. It's a relative of parsley, dill, and fennel, as well as the oh-so-delicately blossomed wildflower known as Queen Anne's lace. Occasionally boutique carrots with unexpected flesh tones surface in the marketplace, but most organic carrots are tried-and-true orange. They are naturally sweet with rich crunchiness.

Bagged baby carrots are handy, but they aren't really immature carrots. They are mature carrots that are whittled down to resemble small carrots.

Organic carrots grow in sandy loam and are fertilized with composted manure or fish emulsion. Pests generally aren't a problem, but mildew can nag carrot crops. A propane burner is sometimes used to burn weeds when carrots are in the germination stage.

BUYING AND STORING: Look for firm, crisp carrots with unblemished skin that are well shaped; avoid those that look withered, gnarled, or have discoloration or cracks. Feathery tops should look green, without any yellowing or black areas. The top of the root next to the stem, often called the shoulder, can have green tinges, but shouldn't be blackened. Remove green tops before storing; give them a vigorous twist to remove them. Refrigerate, unwashed, in plastic bag in crisper drawer up to 2 weeks.

PREP AND USE: Scrub well under cold running water, or peel with swivel-bladed vegetable peeler and rinse with cold water. Proper cooking brings out the sweetness in carrots; they are best when cooked tender-crisp. Boil, stir-fry, braise, or roast. Great for snacking, and delectable in soups, salads, marinades, and sauces.

AVAILABLE: Year-round

NUTRITIONAL INFORMATION (1 cup chopped raw): Calories 52, fat calories 3; total fat 0 grams, sat fat 0 grams, cholesterol 0 milligrams; sodium 88 milligrams; total carbohydrates 12 grams, fiber 4 grams, sugars 6 grams; protein 1 gram; vitamin A IUs 428%; vitamin C 13%; calcium 4%; iron 2%.

SERVING SUGGESTIONS

Carrot Vinaigrette

This simple dressing is delicious on a chopped vegetable salad or mixed baby greens or cold cooked pork. Whisk ¼ cup red wine vinegar with ½ teaspoon salt, 1 tablespoon minced fresh basil leaves or tarragon leaves, and ½ cup extra-virgin olive oil. Stir in 3 tablespoons minced peeled carrot and 1 teaspoon minced fresh ginger.

Quick Bean Soup

In large saucepan, heat 1 tablespoon extra-virgin olive oil on medium heat. Add 1 medium onion (chopped); cook until softened, about 4 minutes. Add 1 medium clove garlic (minced) and cook 30 seconds. Add 4 cups vegetable or chicken broth, 1 bay leaf, and 1 rosemary sprig. Bring to boil on high heat; lower heat to medium-low and simmer 10 minutes. Add 3 medium carrots (peeled, sliced ¼-inch thick) and pinch of dried red pepper flakes. Simmer until carrots are tender-crisp, about 10 minutes. Add 2 (15-ounce) cans cannellini beans (drained, rinsed) and simmer until heated through. Remove rosemary sprig and bay leaf. Season with freshly ground black pepper to taste.

Added Sweetness

Add finely chopped carrot to marinara sauce or meatloaf mixture to add just-right sweetness.

Sautéed and Marinated

Peel 2 pounds carrots and cut into ⅜-inch diagonal slices. In large, deep skillet, heat 3 tablespoons extra-virgin olive oil on medium-high heat. Add 1 medium onion (halved, cut into ¼-inch slices); cook, stirring occasionally, until starting to brown. Remove with slotted spoon and set aside. Add 2 more tablespoons oil to skillet and heat; add half of carrots and cook, stirring occasionally, until golden, about 5 minutes. Remove and add remaining carrots; cook in same manner. Place carrots and onion in large, glass or ceramic bowl, and season well with salt and freshly ground black pepper. Add ¼ cup red wine vinegar, ¼ cup chopped fresh Italian parsley, and ¼ cup chopped fresh basil leaves; toss. Taste and adjust seasoning. Cool; cover and refrigerate up to 12 hours. Serve cold or at room temperature.

Tunisian-Style Carrots

YIELD: 6 SERVINGS

Sweet-sour vinaigrette augmented with ground cumin and a few dried red chile flakes give these carrots a wake-up taste. Serve it over cooked rice or couscous. And if you like, garnish with diced pitted dates or raisins.

- 3 tablespoons extra-virgin olive oil, divided use
- 1 medium yellow onion, coarsely chopped
- 2 pounds carrots, peeled, cut into ⅜-inch-wide diagonal slices
- 1 teaspoon salt
- 2 tablespoons fresh lemon juice
- 1 to 2 teaspoons honey or agave syrup
- 2 teaspoons ground cumin
- ½ teaspoon dried red chile flakes
- 1 large clove garlic, minced
- 1 tablespoon parsley, minced
- 1 tablespoon cilantro, minced

1 Heat 1 tablespoon oil in medium skillet on medium-high heat. Add onion and cook, stirring occasionally, until starting to brown, about 7 minutes. Set aside.

2 Place carrots in large saucepan; cover by 1 inch with water and add salt. Place on high heat and bring to boil. Cook until tender-crisp, about 6 minutes. Drain.

3 Prepare vinaigrette: In small bowl or measuring cup with handle, combine lemon juice, honey, cumin, chile flakes, and garlic; stir with fork to combine. Add remaining 2 tablespoons oil and stir to combine.

4 In medium bowl, combine carrots, onion and vinaigrette; gently toss. Add parsley and cilantro. Toss. Taste and add salt if needed. Serve over cooked rice or couscous, if desired.

Nutritional information (per serving): Calories 120, fat calories 80; total fat 9 grams, sat fat 1.5 grams, cholesterol 0 milligrams; sodium 460 milligrams; total carbohydrates 9 grams, fiber 2 grams, sugars 5 grams; protein 1 gram; vitamin A IUs 210%; vitamin C 80%; calcium 4%; iron 6%.

Carrot and Farro Soup

YIELD: 10 TO 12 SERVINGS

Farro lends a pleasing chewy texture and nutty flavor to this carrot soup. Often mislabeled spelt (which is a different grain), farro is an ancient grain that cooks in about 20 minutes when purchased semi-pearled, meaning semi-peeled. Serve this rustic soup in mugs at informal gatherings. Accompany it with crusty bread or garlic toast. If making ahead, prepare through step 3, cool, and refrigerate. At serving time, reheat and finish with final steps 4 and 5.

1 cup semi-pearled or semi-peeled farro

2½ tablespoons extra-virgin olive oil

1 medium fennel bulb, trimmed, thinly sliced

1 cup sliced celery, including leaves

1 cup diced yellow onion

2 cups roughly chopped peeled carrots

Bouquet garni (2 sprigs fresh thyme, 2 bay leaves, 2 peeled garlic cloves)

1 (14.5-ounce) can diced tomatoes with juice

3 quarts fat-free, low-sodium chicken broth or vegetable broth

1 (19-ounce) can garbanzo beans, drained, rinsed

2 cups coarsely chopped chard leaves or kale leaves

½ cup chopped fresh Italian parsley

¼ cup chopped fresh basil leaves

Salt and freshly ground black pepper

Optional garnish: 1 cup grated Parmesan cheese

1 Place farro in medium bowl and add enough cold water to cover by about 1 inch; set aside.

2 Heat oil in large saucepan or Dutch oven on medium-high heat. Add fennel, celery, onion, and carrots. Cook, stirring occasionally, until softened but not browned, about 6 to 10 minutes.

3 Drain farro and add to mixture. Tie bouquet garni ingredients in double layer of cheesecloth and secure with cotton string; add to mixture. Add tomatoes with juice and chicken broth or vegetable broth. Bring to boil on high heat; reduce heat to medium-low and simmer 30 minutes, or until farro is tender.

4 Add garbanzos, chard or kale, parsley, and basil; simmer about 4 minutes or until chard or kale is wilted. Remove and discard bouquet garni. Add salt and pepper to taste.

5 Ladle into bowls or mugs. Pass cheese for optional topping.

Nutritional information (per serving): Calories 110, fat calories 35; total fat 4 grams, sat fat 0 grams, cholesterol 0 milligrams; sodium 810 milligrams; total carbohydrates 15 grams, fiber 2 grams, sugars 3 grams; protein 4 grams; vitamin A IUs 45%; vitamin C 25%; calcium 4%; iron 8%.

Cook's Note: Farro is sold at Italian markets and some health food stores.

Roasted Carrots

YIELD: 8 SERVINGS

Parsnips add a delicious earthy tone to this dish, so if you like, add 3 or 4 peeled parsnips along with the carrots. Roasted carrots can be served hot, warm, or cold.

- 3 pounds medium carrots, peeled, trimmed, leaving 1 inch of stem attached
- ⅓ cup extra-virgin olive oil
- 2 teaspoons coarse salt, such as kosher
- 2 teaspoons freshly ground black pepper
- 2 teaspoons chopped fresh rosemary leaves
- 2 teaspoons chopped fresh sage leaves
- 3 tablespoons water

1 Adjust oven rack to lower third of oven. Preheat oven to 350°F.

2 In large, shallow baking pan, toss carrots with oil, salt, pepper, rosemary, and sage. At a corner, pour water into pan.

3 Roast vegetables until tender, 45 to 55 minutes (depending on size of carrots). Serve hot, warm, or cold.

Nutritional information (per serving): Calories 140, fat calories 80; total fat 9 grams, sat fat 1.5 grams, cholesterol 0 milligrams; sodium 720 milligrams; total carbohydrates 14 grams, fiber 3 grams, sugars 8 grams; protein 1 gram; vitamin A IUs 470%; vitamin C 25%; calcium 6%; iron 10%.

Orange-Zested Chocolate Carrot Cake

YIELD: 18 VERY GENEROUS SLICES TO 32 THIN SLICES

Unlike traditional carrot cakes, this one isn't augmented with spices and fruit. It tastes like an incredible chocolate layer cake, but with an appealing subtle-sweet earthiness. During baking, the carrots melt into the chocolate. Use carrots shreds that aren't any longer than ⅜ inch. Use a box grater or the food processor's shredding disk, feeding the carrots into the feed tube so they are standing up. If using store-bought shredded carrots that are often several inches long, roughly chop them. Use a serrated knife for best results when cutting this cake, especially if cutting into thin slices.

- Vegetable or canola oil nonstick cooking spray
- 2 (17.1-ounce) packages organic chocolate cake mix (see Cook's Note)
- Ingredients listed on cake mix package, such as eggs, milk, and oil
- 3 tablespoons orange zest (colored portion of peel), minced, and 1½ cups juice from 4 Valencia oranges, divided use
- 6 cups shredded peeled carrots

Frosting

- 5 cups semisweet chocolate chips (about 30 ounces)
- 2 cups (4 sticks) unsalted butter, softened, cut into chunks
- ⅔ cup sifted powdered sugar
- 2 teaspoons vanilla
- Optional: about 3 to 4 tablespoons milk or heavy whipping cream

1 Adjust oven rack to middle position. Preheat oven according to cake mix instructions. Coat three 9-inch round cake pans with nonstick spray and set aside.

2 Prepare batter as according to cake mix instructions. Mix in half of zest and half of juice; add carrots and stir to combine.

3 Place an equal amount of batter in each cake pan. Bake according to cake mix instructions, or until tops are springy. Place pans on cooling racks for 10 minutes. Run a knife around edge of each cake to loosen it from sides. Invert each on a wire rack; invert again on second wire rack so that the smooth tops face up. Cool completely.

4 For frosting, stir chocolate chips in double boiler or heavy-bottomed, medium saucepan over very low heat until melted and smooth. Remove from heat and cool to lukewarm.

5 In large bowl of electric mixer, place butter and sugar; beat on medium speed until lightly and fluffy about 4 to 5 minutes, scraping down sides of bowl as needed. Add melted chocolate, vanilla, and remaining juice and zest. Mix on medium-high speed until thoroughly mixed and fluffy, about 5 minutes. If frosting is too stiff to be spreadable, add milk or cream 1 tablespoon at a time, beating between additions, until desired consistency is reached.

6 Place 1 cake layer on a cake plate. Spread ¼ of frosting on top. Add another cake layer and frost it with about the same amount used atop the first layer. Add final layer and frost sides and top with remaining frosting. Serve or place in covered container designed for storing layer cake and refrigerate up to 2 days.

Nutritional information (per slice, using 32 slices): Calories 410, fat calories 260; total fat 29 grams, sat fat 13 grams, cholesterol 63 milligrams; sodium 260 milligrams; total carbohydrates 40 grams, fiber 2.5 grams, sugars 27 grams; protein 4.5 grams; vitamin A IUs 10%; vitamin C 10%; calcium 8%; iron 13%.

Cook's Note: This recipe was developed using Dr. Oetker Organics Chocolate Cake Mix.

Orange-Zested Chocolate Carrot Cake

Cauliflower

Unlike its cousins—broccoli, cabbage, Brussels sprouts, and kale—cauliflower has a mild, almost sweet flavor profile. The compact head of undeveloped white flower buds forms beneath sturdy, thick leaves that protect it from sunlight.

Organic growers use crop rotation to nourish the soil and utilize ladybugs to control aphids that can cause severe damage, especially in the warmer days of August and September. The crops are hand-planted and hand-picked. Most often organic yields are reduced by 25 to 30 percent compared to cauliflower crops grown using conventional methods.

BUYING AND STORING: Select heads that are firm and tightly packed, white or creamy white. Avoid any with discoloration or soft spots. Look for leaves that are bright green, not wilted. Refrigerate, unwashed, in plastic bag in crisper drawer up to 1 week.

PREP AND USE: Trim off any discolored area. Pull off outer leaves. Cut in half from top to bottom. Cut out core and separate into florets. Rinse with cold water. Florets that are large can be cut in half and quarters lengthwise. For even cooking it is best to have them all about the same size. Eat raw or cooked. Boil, bake, steam, roast, or stir-fry. Do not use aluminum or cast-iron pans that can discolor cauliflower.

AVAILABLE: Year-round

NUTRITIONAL INFORMATION
(per 1 cup chopped, raw): Calories 25, fat calories 1; total fat 0 grams, sat fat 0 grams, cholesterol 0 milligrams; sodium 30 milligrams; total carbohydrates 5 grams, fiber 3 grams, sugars 2 grams; protein 2 grams; vitamin A IUs 0%; vitamin C 77%; calcium 2%; iron 2%.

SERVING SUGGESTIONS

Kicked-Up Pickled Cauliflower

Place ¾ cup distilled white vinegar, ¼ cup water, and ¼ cup sugar in large saucepan or Dutch oven; bring to boil on high heat. Add about 1 pound cauliflower florets, 1 medium carrot (peeled, cut into ½-inch-wide slices) and 3 or 4 fresh serrano chiles (stemmed, halved lengthwise); return mixture to boil, stirring occasionally. Remove from heat and cool slightly before transferring to a 2-quart glass or nonreactive container. Store well-sealed in refrigerator up to 10 days.

Roast Chicken with Cauliflower

Roast a whole chicken surrounded with quartered shallots, thickly sliced carrots and medium head cauliflower (in large florets). Before cooking drizzle the vegetables (not chicken) with about ½ cup water (see Roast Chicken, page 167).

Cauliflower Puree

In large heavy-bottomed saucepan or Dutch oven, place medium florets from 1 large cauliflower, ½ cup heavy whipping cream, and ½ cup milk. Bring to simmer on medium heat; simmer uncovered until cauliflower is tender, about 13 to 15 minutes, stirring frequently. Puree in 3 batches in food processor. Stir in 2 teaspoons unsalted butter, plus salt and freshly ground black pepper to taste. Stir. Taste and adjust seasoning.

Roasted and Coated with Basil-Parsley Pesto

Preheat oven to 425°F. Place 1 head of cauliflower (torn or cut into small florets) on rimmed baking sheet. Brush with extra-virgin olive oil and season with coarse salt, such as kosher, to taste. Roast about 15 minutes, or until tender and lightly browned. Toss with enough Basil-Parsley Pesto (page 167) to lightly coat.

Cauliflower Fritters with Prosciutto Dust

YIELD: 6 SERVINGS

Serve these lovely appetizers with small plates and forks, or use them as a side dish. Much of the work can be done in advance. The mashed cauliflower (through step 3) and crunchy topping can be prepared a day in advance and refrigerated well-sealed (bring to room temperature before use). The topping is made by frying thin layers of prosciutto, and then hand-crumbling or processing them in a food processor, until ground into "dust." The dust is also delectable sprinkled on fruit salads and green salads.

Canola oil for frying

6 thin slices prosciutto, torn into 3-inch-long pieces (see Meatless Tip)

1 teaspoon salt, plus salt for seasoning

1 small head cauliflower, trimmed, cut into short ½-inch-wide florets

2 large eggs

1 medium clove garlic, minced

2 tablespoons all-purpose flour

2 tablespoons chopped fresh Italian parsley

1 tablespoon chopped fresh dill

1 tablespoon chopped fresh chives

Freshly ground black pepper

¼ cup sour cream or crème fraîche

Garnish: chopped fresh chives

1 Layer 2 or 3 sheets of paper towels next to stove. Heat about 1 inch of oil in a medium skillet using medium-high heat. Fry 4 to 6 pieces prosciutto at a time, turning when one side is dark red and crisp, about 30 to 60 seconds. Cook until both sides are crisp and dark red. Drain on paper towels. Repeat until all of prosciutto is cooked. Cool. Crumble by hand or place in food processor and pulse until almost finely ground.

2   In Dutch oven or large saucepan, place about 7 cups water (enough to generously cover cauliflower). Bring to boil on high heat; add 1 teaspoon salt and cauliflower. Cook until fork-tender, about 9 minutes. Drain in colander and refresh with cold running water. Drain and give colander a good shake to remove water.

3   Place half of cauliflower in large bowl; mash with fork or potato masher.

4   In separate medium bowl, whisk eggs. Whisk in garlic, flour, parsley, dill, chives, and salt and pepper to taste. Add egg mixture to mashed cauliflower; stir to combine. Add reserved cauliflower florets and stir to combine.

5   In large, deep nonstick skillet, add about ⅛ inch oil; heat on medium-high until hot, but not smoking. Working in batches, drop spoonfuls of cauliflower mixture into skillet, about 1 heaping tablespoon per fritter. Flatten with back of spoon to form a patty about 3 inches across. Fry, turning once to brown on both sides and thoroughly cook. Repeat procedure, adding more oil to skillet with each batch. If desired, keep fritters warm in single layer on rimmed baking sheet in 275°F oven.

6   Top each fritter with a small dollop of sour cream or crème fraîche; sprinkle each generously with prosciutto dust. Garnish with chives and serve.

Nutritional information (per serving): Calories 160, fat calories 100; total fat 11 grams, sat fat 3 grams, cholesterol 85 milligrams; sodium 430 milligrams; total carbohydrates 8 grams, fiber 3 grams, sugars 2 grams; protein 9 grams; vitamin A IUs 6%; vitamin C 80%; calcium 4%; iron 6%.

Meatless Tip: Omit prosciutto dust. Instead, top each fritter with a smidgen of sweet paprika or Spanish smoked paprika.

Cauliflower Au Gratin

YIELD: 6 SERVINGS

This classic French technique for enriching blanched cauliflower elevates it to regal richness. Serve it in place of potatoes along with roast lamb, chicken, beef, or game. Or use it as the centerpiece of a vegetable feast, surrounded with steamed carrots, blanched Brussels sprouts, and sautéed mushrooms.

1 large cauliflower, trimmed, cut into medium florets

2 cups whole milk, warm

3 tablespoons unsalted butter, divided use

2 tablespoons all-purpose flour

½ cup grated Swiss cheese plus 2 tablespoons, divided use

Salt and freshly ground white pepper

Pinch of ground nutmeg

3 tablespoons medium-fine fresh white breadcrumbs

Optional garnish: 2 teaspoons minced fresh marjoram leaves or fresh Italian parsley

1   Adjust oven rack to middle position. Preheat oven to 375°F. In large saucepan or Dutch oven, bring about 3 quarts water to boil. Add cauliflower; cook until just barely tender, about 8 minutes. Drain; refresh with cold water. Drain again and set aside.

2   Prepare béchamel sauce: Melt 2 tablespoons butter in large, heavy-bottomed saucepan on medium heat. Add flour and stir about 2 minutes (do not brown). Remove from heat. Add warm milk in thin stream, whisking constantly. Increase heat to medium-high. Bring to simmer, stirring constantly. Simmer gently 1 minute, stirring constantly. Remove from heat and stir in ½ cup cheese. Add salt and pepper to taste. Add nutmeg and stir.

3 Pour ⅓ of sauce into a 12-inch oval gratin pan or 11 × 7-inch baking dish. Add drained cauliflower in single layer. Season cauliflower with salt and pepper to taste. Pour remaining sauce over top. Toss breadcrumbs and remaining 2 tablespoons cheese in small bowl; sprinkle mixture on top. Melt remaining butter and drizzle on top. If desired, gratin can be covered and refrigerated at this point for several hours.

4 Bake 30 minutes. If you want a browner, crisper top, place under broiler until lightly browned, watching carefully to prevent burning. Serve immediately.

Nutritional information (per serving): Calories 170, fat calories 100; total fat 11 grams, sat fat 7 grams, cholesterol 30 milligrams; sodium 75 milligrams; total carbohydrates 12 grams, fiber 3 grams, sugars 4 grams; protein 8 grams; vitamin A IUs 8%; vitamin C 90%; calcium 20%; iron 47%.

Cauliflower Au Gratin

Cauliflower Soup

YIELD: 8 SERVINGS

Apple, carrot, and potato offer a distinctive taste to the soup that is delectably starchy-sweet.

2 tablespoons extra-virgin olive oil

1 medium head cauliflower, cut into florets

1 large yellow onion, sliced

1 carrot, peeled, chopped

1 Gala or Fuji or Ambrosia apple, peeled, cored, chopped

1 large russet potato, peeled, cut into chunks

7 cups vegetable broth, divided use

Salt and freshly ground black pepper

Garnish: 6 to 8 teaspoons sour cream or crème fraîche

Garnish: about 10 fresh chives

1 Heat oil in large pot or Dutch oven on medium-high heat. Add cauliflower, onion, carrot, and apple; cook, stirring frequently, until onion softens and cauliflower starts to brown, 10 to 12 minutes.

2 Add potato and 6 cups broth and bring to a boil on high heat. Reduce heat to medium-low and simmer until all vegetables are softened, about 20 minutes.

3 Let cool 5 minutes. Puree in small batches in blender or food processor (if using blender, hold down lid with potholder). Return to pot; add enough remaining broth to reach a creamy consistency. Season with salt and a generous amount of pepper. Reheat.

4 Garnish each serving with dollop of sour cream or crème fraîche. Top with thinly sliced chives.

Nutritional information (per serving without garnish): Calories 130, fat calories 35; total fat 4 grams, sat fat 0 grams, cholesterol 0 milligrams; sodium 430 milligrams; total carbohydrates 21 grams, fiber 4 grams, sugars 7 grams; protein 4 grams; vitamin A IUs 45%; vitamin C 90%; calcium 4%; iron 6%.

Cauliflower and Ham Quiche

YIELD: 8 SERVINGS

The saltiness of ham is a welcome foil to the sweet, tender cauliflower in this mouthwatering quiche. For a vegetarian version, omit the ham and add some sautéed fresh spinach along with a small amount of crumbled feta cheese.

Dough

- 1 ½ cups all-purpose flour, plus flour for dusting work surface
- ⅛ teaspoon salt
- ½ cup (1 stick) cold unsalted butter, cut into ¼-inch cubes
- ¼ cup cold buttermilk

Filling

- 2 cups small cauliflower florets, blanched until tender, drained, cooled
- ¼ cup cored, seeded, finely diced red bell pepper
- ½ cup diagonally sliced green onions (use half of dark green stalks)
- ½ cup finely diced ham (see Meatless Tip)
- 3 eggs, lightly beaten
- ¾ cup heavy whipping cream
- ⅛ teaspoon salt
- ¼ teaspoon freshly ground black pepper
- 2 tablespoons grated Swiss cheese

1   Prepare dough: In food processor fitted with metal blade, combine flour and salt. Add butter cubes. Pulse until butter is in pea-size pieces. With motor running, add buttermilk in thin stream. Process just until dough comes together. The dough should not be wet or loose. Remove from processor and shape into a ball. Flatten into a disk, wrap tightly in plastic or zipper bag, and refrigerate at least 1 hour.

2   Lightly flour work surface; place well-chilled dough disk in center. Rolling from the center of disk out, and turning one-quarter turn after each roll, shape into a 10- or 11-inch disk, about ⅛-inch thick. Dust bottom of a 9-inch tart or pie pan with flour. Transfer dough to pan and gently fit into pan. Trim or flute edges. Chill while preparing filling.

3   Adjust oven rack to middle position. Preheat oven to 400°F.

4   In medium bowl, combine cauliflower, bell pepper, green onions, and ham. Place prepared crust on baking sheet. Place vegetables evenly being careful not to tear dough.

5   In medium mixing bowl, whisk eggs with cream, salt, and black pepper until well blended but not bubbly. Carefully pour into prepared tart or pie pan. Sprinkle with cheese.

6   Bake for 45 minutes or until a knife inserted in center comes out with little or no egg adhering to blade. Eggs will continue to set even though the custard has been removed from the oven. Remove from oven and allow to cool 15 minutes before cutting into wedges and serving.

Nutritional information (per serving): Calories 330, fat calories 210; total fat 24 grams, sat fat 14 grams, cholesterol 145 milligrams; sodium 240 milligrams; total carbohydrates 21 grams, fiber 2 grams, sugars 2 grams; protein 9 grams; vitamin A IUs 20%; vitamin C 30%; calcium 6%; iron 10%.

Meatless Tip: Omit ham. Instead add 1½ cups chopped fresh spinach; sauté spinach in 1 tablespoon olive oil until limp. Place spinach in strainer and gently press out excess liquid with back of spoon; stir into egg mixture along with 2 tablespoons crumbled feta cheese just before adding to crust.

Celery

Although the crunchy character might be the first attribute that comes to mind, celery also adds a refreshing, slightly sweet note to dishes. The root end holds the alluring bunch together, the outer thick ribs sport feathery leaves. The tender heart rests at its compact core where the stalks are more delicate, the taste more intense.

California is the largest provider of organic celery. Organic growers often use marigolds and/or bean crops as borders around their celery to repel pests. They say that crop rotation is essential and report that their fields are most often weeded by hand.

BUYING AND STORING: Look for bunches with the leaves still attached because fresh-looking green leaves are a good indication of quality. Stalks should be crisp. Avoid those with brown spots or yellow leaves. To store, trim base and remove any damaged stalks. Rinse in cold water and place in plastic bag. Place in refrigerator vegetable drawer up to 2 weeks. If needed, refresh by chilling in ice water.

PREP AND USE: Wash separated stalks (sometimes referred to as ribs) under cold running water and trim root end. Tough strings on large outer stalks can be removed; use paring knife to barely cut into celery (at large end on stringy side). Pull knife away, catching strings between thumb and blade, and pull toward leaves. Discard strings. A swivel-bladed vegetable peeler can also be used to remove strings. Cut into sticks, slice, or dice, as

needed. For a quick way to dice outer stalks: Cut in half or thirds lengthwise, cutting from base toward leaf end, leaving leaf end intact, then cut crosswise.

Use raw or cooked. Raw and chopped, add to salads, such as chicken or potato salad or use plentiful amount in poultry stuffing or tomato-based salsa. Add to marinara sauce, stir-fries, and soups, or braise as a vegetable side dish.

AVAILABLE: Year-round

NUTRITIONAL INFORMATION (per 1 cup chopped, raw): Calories 16, fat calories 2; total fat 0 grams, sat fat 0 grams, cholesterol 0 milligrams; sodium 81 milligrams; total carbohydrates 3 grams, fiber 2 grams, sugars 2 grams; protein 1 gram; vitamin A IUs 9%; vitamin C 5%; calcium 4%; iron 1%.

SERVING SUGGESTIONS

Celery Pilaf

Heat 2 tablespoons canola or vegetable oil and 1 tablespoon unsalted butter in large saucepan on medium-high heat. Add 1 medium yellow onion (chopped) and 1 cup diced celery. Cook, stirring frequently, until onion starts to soften. Add 1 cup long-grain rice and stir to coat; cook, stirring occasionally until rice starts to brown. Add 2 cups chicken or vegetable broth and bring to boil. Cover and turn heat to low. Simmer about 17 minutes or until all broth is absorbed. Fluff with a fork and top with 1 thinly sliced green onion (including dark green stalks).

Picnic Fans

Wash 8 large leaf-on celery stalks. Cut into fans, making 4 lengthwise cuts from base halfway up the stalk. Place in large bowl of ice water, cover, and refrigerate 1 to 3 hours. In small bowl, mix 2 tablespoons fresh lemon juice, 2 tablespoons extra-virgin olive oil, and 2 teaspoons chopped fresh cilantro. Drain celery and pat dry with paper towels or clean kitchen cloth; place on platter and drizzle with dressing. Season with seasoned salt and sprinkle with 2 tablespoons shredded Parmesan cheese.

Blue Cheese Dip

In a food processor fitted with metal blade place 4 ounces room-temperature cream cheese, ½ cup crumbled blue cheese, ½ cup mayonnaise, ½ cup sour cream, ¼ cup finely chopped onion, ½ teaspoon seasoned salt, and ½ teaspoon celery seeds. Pulse until smooth. Use celery sticks and apple slices as dippers.

Apple and Celery Salad

Toss diced apple and diced celery with enough vinaigrette to lightly coat (see Cook's Note, page 28). Toss with toasted pecan halves and garnish with crumbled feta cheese.

Gazpacho

YIELD: ABOUT 35 (2-OUNCE) APPETIZER SERVINGS OR ABOUT 8 (8-OUNCE) SERVINGS

Small servings of cold, celery-spiked gazpacho make a classy appetizer. Use 2-ounce shot glasses and garnish each with a celery leaf and narrow, oven-crisped tortilla strips. If desired, rim each glass with a mixture of coarse salt and seasoned salt.

1 medium hothouse (English) cucumber, peeled, finely diced (see Cook's Notes)

2 stalks celery, trimmed, finely diced, leaves reserved for garnish

½ medium sweet onion or red onion, finely diced

½ yellow bell pepper, cored, seeded, finely diced

½ green bell pepper, cored, seeded, finely diced

½ red bell pepper, cored, seeded, finely diced

4 ripe Roma tomatoes, seeded, finely diced

1 medium clove garlic, minced

1 small jalapeño chile, seeded, minced (see Cook's Notes)

1 tablespoon minced fresh cilantro

1 tablespoon minced fresh Italian parsley

32 ounces tomato juice

2 tablespoons extra-virgin olive oil

1 cup chicken broth or vegetable broth

Freshly ground black pepper

Optional: hot sauce

Optional: seasoned salt

For garnish: celery leaves, lime slices, toasted tortilla strips (see Cook's Notes)

For serving in glasses: 2 tablespoons seasoned salt mixed with 2 tablespoons coarse salt, and fresh lime juice for moistening glass rims

1   In nonreactive container such as glass or ceramic, combine all ingredients except optional seasoning and garnishes. Taste and adjust seasoning as needed. Cover and refrigerate overnight or about 8 hours.

2   Stir and taste. Adjust seasoning as needed.

3   If serving in small glasses, place salt mixture in one saucer and lime juice in another. Dip lip of each glass in lime juice, then into salt mixture. Ladle gazpacho into each glass. Garnish glasses with celery leaf, lime slices, and 2 tortilla strips. If serving large servings, ladle into soup bowls and garnish each with a couple of tortilla strips, celery leaf, and fresh lime slice.

Nutritional information (per 2-ounce serving, about 35 appetizer servings): Calories 20, fat calories 10; total fat 1 gram, sat fat 0 grams, cholesterol 0 milligrams; sodium 90 milligrams; total carbohydrates 3 grams, fiber 1 gram, sugars 2 grams; protein 1 gram; vitamin A IUs 4%; vitamin C 20%; calcium 0%; iron 2%.

Cook's Notes: Hothouse cucumbers generally have very small seeds that do not require removal. If using another cucumber variety, remove seeds by cutting in half lengthwise; run bowl of spoon down center of cut edge to scoop out seeds.

Use caution when working with fresh chiles. Wash work surface and hands thoroughly upon completion and do *not* touch face or eyes.

To make toasted tortilla strips, preheat oven to 375°F. Cut 3 corn tortillas into ¼-inch-wide strips. Place on rimmed baking sheet in single layer. Bake in middle of preheated oven until crisp and lightly browned, about 10 to 11 minutes

Gazpacho

Breaded Chicken Breasts with Celery Salad

YIELD: 4 SERVINGS

Rather than frying these breaded chicken cutlets, they are baked on a rack. A topping of celery salad gives the chicken a welcome crunchiness along with the tangy spark of blue-veined cheese.

Chicken

1 cup fresh breadcrumbs

3 tablespoons extra-virgin olive oil

¼ cup all-purpose flour

2 eggs, lightly beaten

Salt and freshly ground black pepper

4 (4-ounce) skinless, boneless chicken breasts (see Meatless Tip)

Salad

1½ cups sliced celery, cut ¼-inch thick

½ small red onion, thinly sliced

2 ounces crumbled blue cheese

2 tablespoons balsamic vinegar

1 teaspoon cider vinegar

¼ cup extra-virgin olive oil

1 tablespoon minced fresh basil leaves or minced fresh Italian parsley or minced fresh tarragon leaves

Salt and freshly ground black pepper

1½ cups baby spinach

1   Prepare chicken: In large skillet, toss breadcrumbs and oil until combined. Toast on medium-high heat until golden brown, about 2 to 3 minutes, stirring frequently. Remove from heat.

2   Place flour and eggs in separate shallow bowls or pie pans. Season eggs with salt and pepper to taste.

3   Adjust oven rack to middle position. Preheat oven to 400°F. Place wire rack (the kind used to cool baked goods) on rimmed baking sheet; set aside. Place each chicken breast between sheets of plastic wrap. Pound with mallet or bottom of heavy saucepan or skillet until ½-inch thick, and remove wrap. Working one at a time, coat chicken breast lightly with flour, then dip in eggs, then in crumbs, coating both sides and pressing crumbs down to make them stick. Place each on rack in single layer.

4   Bake 10 to 15 minutes, or until thoroughly cooked. Check with instant-read thermometer; temperature should be 160°F.

5   Prepare celery salad: Place celery and onion in small bowl. In separate small bowl, combine blue cheese, vinegars, oil, and basil or parsley or tarragon. Add salt and pepper to taste. Stir to combine. Taste and adjust seasoning if needed. Add dressing to celery mixture and toss.

6   Top each chicken breast with a small handful of spinach and about ¼ cup of celery salad. Pass remaining celery salad for optional servings.

Nutritional information (per serving): Calories 490, fat calories 240; total fat 26 grams, sat fat 6 grams, cholesterol 180 milligrams; sodium 410 milligrams; total carbohydrates 29 grams, fiber 2 grams, sugars 3 grams; protein 34 grams; vitamin A IUs 20%; vitamin C 6%; calcium 15%; iron 20%.

Meatless Tip: Instead of chicken, use Sautéed Breaded Tofu (page 320).

Celery Soup with Dill and Croutons

YIELD: 6 SERVINGS

f celery is not on your favorite vegetable list, this creamy soup may change your mind. Cooking sweetens celery while giving it a hint of a more herbaceous character. Its subtle flavor profile makes this soup a perfect first course for menus that showcase a hearty main dish.

- 2 tablespoons unsalted butter
- 1 tablespoon extra-virgin olive oil
- 1 small yellow onion, chopped
- 1 medium leek, white and pale green parts only, chopped
- 2 large shallots, chopped
- 2 medium Yukon Gold potatoes, peeled, chopped
- 8 stalks celery, strings removed, cut into 2-inch pieces, including leaves
- ½ cup dry white wine
- 4 cups low-fat sodium-reduced chicken broth or vegetable broth, plus additional broth if needed
- ½ cup heavy whipping cream
- ½ teaspoon salt
- ¼ teaspoon freshly ground black pepper
- 2 tablespoons fresh dill, coarsely chopped
- Garnish: seasoned crostini (see Cook's Note)

1   In Dutch oven or large pot, heat butter and oil on medium-high heat. Add onion, leek, and shallots. Cook, stirring frequently, until onion softens, about 5 minutes.

2   Add potatoes and celery; cook 2 minutes, stirring occasionally. Add wine and boil 1 minute. Add chicken broth or vegetable broth and bring to boil; cover and lower heat to medium-low. Simmer about 40 minutes, or until celery is tender.

3   Puree soup in batches in a blender or food processor fitted with metal blade until very smooth (use caution when blending hot liquids—hold top down with potholder).

4   Return soup to pot and stir in cream, salt, and pepper. If soup is too thick, add a little additional broth and stir until heated.

5   Ladle soup into bowls and garnish with dill. Top with crostini.

Nutritional information (per serving): Calories 340, fat calories 150; total fat 16 grams, sat fat 8 grams, cholesterol 55 milligrams; sodium 550 milligrams; total carbohydrates 38 grams, fiber 3 grams, sugars 3 grams; protein 10 grams; vitamin A IUs 15%; vitamin C 35%; calcium 8%; iron 15%.

Cook's Note: To make crostini, cut 6 thin baguette slices and brush both sides with extra-virgin olive oil. Place in single layer on rimmed baking sheet. Bake in middle of preheated 350°F oven until golden, about 12 minutes. Season with seasoned salt.

Potato and Celery Salad

YIELD: 4 SERVINGS

Crisp celery gives potato salad a crunchy edge. This version uses mustardy vinaigrette to dress the salad and offers the option of including a garnish of smoky bacon. The salad is best served warm, but can be served chilled or at room temperature.

- Optional: 2 thick slices bacon, cut crosswise into ¼-inch-wide pieces
- 1½ pounds Yukon Gold potatoes, unpeeled, scrubbed, cut into ¾-inch chunks
- 1½ tablespoons white wine vinegar
- ½ teaspoon salt
- 2 teaspoons Dijon-style mustard
- 3 tablespoons extra-virgin olive oil
- 2 teaspoon chopped fresh chives or 2 thinly sliced green onions, including ½ dark green stalks
- Freshly ground black pepper
- 4 stalks celery, trimmed, diced
- For serving: 3 cups mixed baby greens

1 If using, cook bacon slices in medium skillet on medium-high heat until crisp; place on paper towels to drain.

2 Place potato chunks in steamer basket over boiling water (water should come just below bottom of steamer basket) on high heat. Cover and reduce heat to medium; simmer water and steam until tender, about 16 to 18 minutes.

3 Meanwhile make vinaigrette: In small bowl or glass measuring cup with handle, place vinegar, salt, and mustard. Stir with fork to combine and dissolve salt. Stir in oil. Add chives or green onions; stir to combine.

4 In large bowl, toss vinaigrette with hot potatoes. Taste and adjust seasoning, adding more salt if needed, and a generous amount of pepper. Add celery and toss. Serve each portion of warm salad over small handfuls of baby greens. If desired, top each with crisp bacon pieces.

Nutritional information (per serving with bacon): Calories 310, fat calories 170; total fat 19 grams, sat fat 4.5 grams, cholesterol 15 milligrams; sodium 550 milligrams; total carbohydrates 27 grams, fiber 5 grams, sugars 2 grams; protein 7 grams; vitamin A IUs 25%; vitamin C 90%; calcium 6%; iron 10%.

Meatless Tip: Omit bacon.

Cherry

There's a crisp crunch as teeth break through fresh cherry skin, spreading vibrant sweet-tart juices throughout the mouth. A plump, ripe cherry is a culinary treasure, providing a uniquely vibrant flavor profile and toothsome texture. The most common organically grown red varieties (bright red to mahogany red) include Bing, Sweetheart, Skeena, Lambert, Van, and Lapin. Rainiers (a cross of Van and Bing varieties) are the most common organically grown yellow variety; their skin is yellow with a red blush.

Organic cherry growers use beneficial insects to control pests and make use of natural fertilizers such as composted manure, bone meal, and rock minerals. Organic crops yield about 25 percent fewer cherries than those grown with conventional farming methods.

BUYING AND STORING: Look for cherries that are bright, plump, and firm. Avoid any with bruises, soft spots, or cracks. Stems should be pliable and a lively green color. Refrigerate, unwashed, in plastic bag in crisper drawer up to 7 days. Pitted cherries can be frozen (without stems) in single layer on a rimmed baking sheet. Place frozen cherries in sealed airtight containers; freeze up to 6 months.

PREP AND USE: Wash cherries in cold, running water. The easiest way to remove pits is to use a cherry pitter. It's a gizmo that works something like a paper punch, pushing a shaft through the fruit to push out the seed. Trying to squeeze out the seed by hand is a messy proposition. Eat raw or cooked, in either sweet or savory dishes. They can be poached, brined, roasted, or baked; pureed, frozen, or dehydrated.

AVAILABLE: May to August

NUTRITIONAL INFORMATION (per 1 cup sweet, unpitted, raw): Calories 87, fat calories 2; total fat 0 grams, sat fat 0 grams, cholesterol 0 milligrams; sodium 0 milligrams; total carbohydrates 22 grams, fiber 3 grams, sugars 18 grams; protein 1 gram; vitamin A IUs 2%; vitamin C 16%; calcium 2%; iron 3%.

SERVING SUGGESTIONS

Heat Wave Red Wine Slush

Freeze 1 cup pitted cherries. In blender, combine 2 cups ice cubes, ⅔ cup orange juice or tangerine juice, 1 cup fruity red wine, and 2 tablespoons fresh lime juice. Add frozen cherries, cover, and whirl until slushy. Pour into 4 chilled martini glasses.

Cherrific Pancakes

Augment thick buttermilk pancakes with pitted fresh cherry halves. Before turning pancake, push 2 or 3 halves into each pancake (rounded side down).

Chocolate-Dipped Cherries

Line baking sheet with waxed paper. Gently heat about 6 ounces semisweet chocolate chips in top of double boiler over barely simmering water, stirring constantly until just melted. Remove from heat. Chocolate should be melted, but not hot. If it is too thick, stir in a little vegetable oil to make it a dipping consistency. Holding by the stem, dip 1 unpitted fresh cherry in chocolate, coating just bottom half; place stem up on waxed paper. Repeat with more cherries. Refrigerate to harden chocolate, about 10 minutes. Can be refrigerated up to 2 days. Caution guests to eat around pits.

Cherry Picks

Pit 2 cherries and skewer on cocktail pick through "waistline" of each cherry. Place in single layer in plastic container. Seal and freeze up to 3 months. Use frozen to garnish glasses of lemonade or herb tea. Or use as garnish for tropical cocktails.

Grilled Pork Tenderloin with Fresh Cherry Relish

YIELD: 6 SERVINGS

With its appealing sweet-sour flavor profile, sweet cherry relish can accompany myriad entrées. It is delicious served with grilled pork tenderloins, but it also teamed with ham, game, chicken, or sautéed tofu. Or serve it cold spooned over Brie cheese. This version has very little heat. For added spiciness, add a little more cayenne.

Pork Tenderloin

¼ cup vegetable oil or canola oil, plus extra oil for brushing grate

4 large cloves garlic, thinly sliced crosswise

½ teaspoon ground cumin

¼ cup fresh lime juice

¼ cup fresh orange juice

1 teaspoon coarse salt, such as kosher

½ teaspoon freshly ground black pepper

¼ cup water

2 (10-ounce) pork tenderloins, sinew trimmed if present (see Meatless Tip)

Relish

1 tablespoon vegetable oil or canola oil

1 medium yellow onion, coarsely chopped

2 teaspoons minced orange zest (colored portion of peel)

2 cups cherries, pitted

¼ teaspoon ground cayenne pepper

1 teaspoon minced fresh rosemary leaves

½ cup cherry preserves

2 tablespoons balsamic vinegar

¼ teaspoon ground cloves

Salt

1   Prepare tenderloin: On medium heat, heat vegetable oil or canola oil in deep, medium saucepan. Add garlic and cumin; cook until garlic is very pale golden color, 1 to 2 minutes. Remove from heat and cautiously add juices, salt, pepper, and water. Bring to boil on high heat. Remove from heat and cool to room temperature. Set large zipper-style plastic bag in bowl to hold it upright. Add cooled marinade and pork tenderloins; seal. Marinate in refrigerator at least 2 hours or up to 8 hours, turning occasionally to redistribute marinade.

2   Prepare relish: Heat vegetable oil or canola oil in large, heavy-bottomed saucepan over medium-high heat. Add onion; cook until softened, about 3 minutes, stirring occasionally. Add cherries, zest, cayenne pepper, rosemary, preserves, vinegar, and cloves. Boil on medium-high heat until thickened, stirring occasionally, about 10 to 12 minutes. Season with salt to taste.

3   Preheat grill. Remove pork from marinade; discard marinade. Clean grate and brush with vegetable oil. Grill tenderloins about 4 minutes on each of their 4 sides. Check for doneness with instant-read thermometer.

Grilled Pork Tenderloin with Fresh Cherry Relish

Interior temperature should be between 155°F and 160°F. Remove from heat and set on cutting board. Allow to rest 5 minutes.

4   Cut meat crosswise into ¾-inch slices. Serve pork slices accompanied with cherry relish.

Nutritional information (per serving): Calories 410, fat calories 140; total fat 16 grams, sat fat 3 grams, cholesterol 65 milligrams; sodium 650 milligrams; total carbohydrates 46 grams, fiber 1 gram, sugars 37 grams; protein 21 grams; vitamin A IUs 2%; vitamin C 25%; calcium 2%; iron 20%.

Meatless Tip: Instead of pork, serve cherry Relish atop Grilled Tofu with Mediterranean-Style Marinade (page 321).

Cherry, Chocolate, and Toasted Almond Ice Cream

YIELD: 1½ QUARTS, 12 (½-CUP) SERVINGS

Cherries and chocolate are very compatible players in this creamy cold confection. Almond slivers add a toasty component, but if you prefer a creamier concoction, chop them into tiny pieces or leave them out. Accompany the ice cream with a crisp cookie, or use it as the base for a delectable hot fudge sundae.

    1 cup apple juice

    2 cups pitted fresh cherries, about 2½ pounds whole cherries

    1 teaspoon vanilla

    4 egg yolks

    ⅓ cup sugar

    1 vanilla bean

    1 cup whole milk

    1 cup heavy whipping cream

    ½ cup toasted slivered almonds (see Cook's Note)

    ½ cup chopped bittersweet chocolate

1　Pour juice into medium saucepan and bring to boil on high heat; reduce heat to medium-low and simmer to reduce juice to ¾ cup, about 10 minutes. Add cherries and cook, uncovered, on medium high heat until cherries are softened but not mushy and very little liquid remains. Remove from heat and stir in vanilla. Cool, stirring occasionally.

2　Meanwhile, place yolks and sugar in medium bowl. Whisk until blended. Split vanilla bean lengthwise. Using the tip of a knife, open bean and scrape out seeds. Place seeds in medium saucepan; add milk, cream, and vanilla pod. Scald over medium high heat until steaming, but not boiling. Discard vanilla pod.

3　Cautiously remove about ¾ cup hot milk from saucepan and add in thin stream to egg yolk mixture, whisking constantly. Gradually add egg yolk mixture to milk mixture, whisking constantly. Place on medium heat and cook, stirring constantly, just until mixture thickens enough to coat the back of the spoon (if you drag a finger down the back of the spoon, it should leave a clean trail). Do *not* boil, or mixture will curdle.

4　Pour thickened mixture through medium sieve and into a medium glass or metal bowl. Stir until steam is no longer present. Cover with plastic wrap that is touching surface of mixture to prevent a skin from forming. Refrigerate until cold, about 2 hours.

5　Process mixture in ice cream machine according to manufacturer's instructions. Fold in cherry mixture, almonds, and chocolate. Place in plastic container with lid; freeze completely before serving.

Nutritional information (per serving): Calories 190, fat calories 120; total fat 14 grams, sat fat 7 grams, cholesterol 95 milligrams; sodium 20 milligrams; total carbohydrates 16 grams, fiber 1 gram, sugars 10 grams; protein 3 grams; vitamin A IUs 8%; vitamin C 2%; calcium 6%; iron 4%.

Cook's Note: To toast almonds, place in single layer on rimmed baking sheet. Place in middle of 350°F oven until nicely browned, about 3 minutes. Watch carefully because nuts burn easily. Cool.

Warm Cherry-Mango Compote

YIELD: 4 SERVINGS

This tasty mixture can certainly stand delectably on its own, but it can also top scoops of vanilla ice cream, frozen yogurt, or pudding.

1 tablespoon unsalted butter

1 tablespoon sugar

2 teaspoons fresh lime juice

1 teaspoon honey

1 cup pitted cherries

¾ cup diced mango

Optional: coarse sea salt

1 tablespoon minced fresh mint

1　In medium saucepan, combine butter, sugar, juice, and honey. Place on medium heat and cook until bubbly, stirring frequently, about 2 minutes. Add cherries and cook until heated through, about 2 minutes. Stir in mango and remove from heat.

2　Spoon into 4 small bowls. If desired, sprinkle each serving with a smidgen of coarse sea salt. Sprinkle each serving with mint. Serve warm.

Nutritional information (per serving without salt): Calories 130, fat calories 25; total fat 3 grams, sat fat 2 grams, cholesterol 10 milligrams; sodium 10 milligrams; total carbohydrates 27 grams, fiber 1 gram, sugars 22 grams; protein 1 gram; vitamin A IUs 6%; vitamin C 20%; calcium 0%; iron 10%.

Cherry Almond Buckle

YIELD: 9 SERVINGS

A fruit buckle is a simple streusel-topped dessert that is often served as a coffeecake. Cherries bring their bright flavor profile to the dish, along with beautiful color and aroma.

Unsalted butter for greasing dish

Topping

½ cup sugar

⅓ cup all-purpose flour

½ teaspoon ground cinnamon

½ teaspoon ground cardamom

2 ounces (½ stick) cold unsalted butter, cut into small cubes,

Cherry Mixture

1⅓ cups all-purpose flour

¼ teaspoon baking powder

½ teaspoon salt

6 ounces (1½ sticks) unsalted butter, softened

¾ cup sugar

1 teaspoon almond extract

3 eggs

1 teaspoon minced lemon zest (colored portion of peel)

1½ pounds fresh cherries, pitted

½ cup sliced almonds

Garnish

2 cups chilled heavy whipping cream

⅓ cup sifted powdered sugar

1   Adjust oven rack to middle position. Preheat oven to 350°F. Lightly butter an 8-inch square baking dish or 2-quart casserole.

2   Prepare topping: In medium bowl, stir sugar, flour, cinnamon, and cardamom to combine. Add butter; using pastry blender or two knives, cut butter into dry ingredients until mixture is the consistency of coarse meal, or pulse in food processor fitted with a metal blade until crumbly and the consistency of coarse meal. Place in refrigerator.

3   Prepare cherry mixture: In medium bowl, whisk in flour, baking powder, and salt; set aside.

4   In large bowl of electric mixer, combine butter and sugar; mix on medium-high speed until creamy. Add almond extract and mix to combine. Add eggs, 1 at a time, beating well after each addition. Add flour mixture and zest; mix on medium speed until blended.

5   Add cherries and almonds; stir to combine. Place batter in prepared dish; evenly sprinkle on topping. Bake for 60 minutes, or until toothpick inserted in center comes out clean, cherries are bubbling, and topping is golden.

6   Meanwhile, in large bowl of electric mixer, beat cream until it starts to thicken. Add powdered sugar and beat on high speed until stiff. Store whipped cream in refrigerator until ready to garnish. Serve buckle warm or at room temperature; top servings with whipped cream.

Nutritional information (per serving without whipped cream): Calories 470, fat calories 220; total fat 25 grams, sat fat 14 grams, cholesterol 125 milligrams; sodium 170 milligrams; total carbohydrates 58 grams, fiber 3 grams, sugars 37 grams; protein 6 grams; vitamin A IUs 15%; vitamin C 8%; calcium 4%; iron 10%.

Corn

Corn lovers used to follow the pick-it-eat-it rule. They knew that the sugar inside the corn kernels converts to starch very quickly after harvest, and to enjoy the sweetest taste they needed to eat it very soon after it was cut from the stalk. New supersweet hybrids are very sweet and maintain bold sweetness for up to a week after picking.

Yellow corn, sometimes called common corn, has plump, tightly packed bright yellow kernels. White corn kernels are often smaller than yellow ones, and are delectably moist and creamy. Bicolor ears are a mixture of white and yellow kernels.

Organic growers report that corn crops love heat and sun, adding that their corn is exceptionally sweet. They utilize crop rotation and compost the soil to maximize production. Beneficial insects, including ladybugs and lacewings, are used to control pests. But worms can be problematic to the tender top portion of the ears, so often that part is removed before they get to market.

BUYING AND STORING: For the freshest taste, buy in-the-husk corn. Look for plump and milky kernels that are tightly packed, and green husks. In the marketplace, pull back a portion of the husk to check out the kernels. Avoid any that look dry or discolored.

Refrigerate with husks intact in plastic bags in crisper drawer; refrigerate up to 7 days, but use as soon as possible. Or to freeze, cook corn on the cob in boiling water for 2 minutes, then refresh with cold water, pat dry, and cut kernels off cob. Freeze kernels in single layer on rimmed baking sheet, then place in airtight container and freeze up to 3 months.

PREP AND USE: Pull off and discard husks. Pull off silks, running a cupped hand over top of corn, or use dry, soft vegetable brush to remove silk between kernels. If you want to use kernels off the cob, stand husked cob upright on rimmed baking sheet. Using sharp knife, start at top and cut down slowly, between base of kernels and cob (leave about ¼ of kernel base attached to cob). Rotate cob and repeat until all kernels are removed.

Most often corn is eaten cooked; either boiled, grilled, toasted, or roasted. Add cooked kernels to soups, salads, stir-fries, baked goods such as muffins, or pancakes. Raw kernels can be used in salads and salsas.

AVAILABLE: June to August

NUTRITIONAL INFORMATION (per 1 cup kernels, raw): Calories 132, fat calories 15; total fat 2 grams, sat fat 0 grams; cholesterol 0 milligrams; sodium 23 milligrams; total carbohydrates 29 grams, fiber 4 grams, sugars 5 grams; protein 5 grams; vitamin A IUs 0%; vitamin C 17%; calcium 0%; iron 4%.

SERVING SUGGESTIONS

Pan-Toasted Kernels

Heat a dry, 9- or 10-inch cast-iron skillet on medium heat. Add kernels from 2 ears of corn; heat, stirring frequently, until browned in spots, 3 to 5 minutes. Place on rimmed baking sheet and season with coarse salt, such as kosher. Use kernels as garnish atop soup, or include in tamale or taco fillings. Or cool and use atop mixed green salad.

Mac 'n' Cheese

Include some cooked corn kernels in macaroni and cheese.

Corncake Appetizers

In blender, puree 2 cups cooked corn kernels and ⅔ cup half-and-half. In large bowl, combine corn mixture with ⅓ cup yellow cornmeal, ⅔ cup all-purpose flour, 1 teaspoon baking powder, and ⅛ teaspoon salt. Stir to combine and add 3 lightly beaten eggs and ⅓ cup melted unsalted butter. Stir to combine. Heat 1 tablespoon canola oil in large, deep nonstick skillet on medium-high heat. Add batter in heaping tablespoons, leaving space between each mound. Cook about 1½ minutes on each side and drain on paper towels. Serve topped with a dollop of sour cream. Sprinkle with seasoned salt and serve. If desired, also top with a pinch of crumbled fried prosciutto (see Cauliflower Fritters with Prosciutto Dust, page 95).

Brown Rice with Corn and Cheese

In large, deep skillet heat 2 tablespoons unsalted butter and 2 tablespoons extra-virgin olive oil on medium-high heat. Add 1 onion (chopped), 1 red bell pepper (cored, seeded, chopped), 2 cups raw corn kernels, and 1 Roma tomato (chopped); cook until tender, about 8 minutes. Stir in 3 cups cooked brown rice, 1 tablespoon chopped fresh thyme leaves, 1 cup grated Swiss cheese and 3 tablespoons half-and-half. Toss and cook until cheese melts, and mixture is piping hot. Add salt and freshly ground black pepper to taste.

Garden Enchiladas

YIELD: 12 ENCHILADAS

Tomatillo sauce brings a bright, tart edge and mild spicy heat to these cheese and vegetable filled enchiladas. The fresh corn lends a nice sweetness along with chewy texture. If you have an abundance of corn, double the amount of kernels used in this recipe and omit the squash.

Tomatillo Sauce

- 30 tomatillos
- 5-6 jalapeño chiles, stemmed
- 9 medium cloves garlic, peeled
- 1½ medium yellow onion, sliced ½ inch thick
- 1 tablespoon salt
- 3 tablespoons vegetable oil
- 1 tablespoon fresh lime juice

Filling

- 2 tablespoons extra-virgin olive oil or vegetable oil
- 1 small yellow onion, chopped
- 1 red bell pepper, cored, seeded, diced
- 1 cup diced zucchini
- 1 cup diced yellow crookneck squash
- 2 cups corn kernels
- 8 ounces cremini mushrooms, diced
- 1 tablespoon dried oregano or 3 tablespoons finely chopped fresh oregano leaves
- 1½ teaspoons ground cumin
- Salt

Assembly

- 12 (6-inch) corn tortillas
- Nonstick vegetable oil cooking spray
- 2 cups shredded Monterey Jack cheese

1   Adjust oven rack to middle position. Preheat oven to 400°F.

2   Prepare sauce: Peel husks off tomatillos and rinse with water; dry with paper towel, rubbing surface to remove any sticky film. Place on rimmed baking sheet(s) with chiles, garlic, and onion. Roast 10 to 15 minutes or until tomatillos are soft and begin to char. Place mixture in blender in several batches and whirl until pureed (hold down top firmly with potholder). Add salt, oil, and juice; stir to combine. Pour about ⅔ of mixture into an 8-inch square baking dish (use to dip tortillas); reserve ⅓ of sauce for topping in step 6.

3   Prepare filling: In large, deep skillet heat olive oil or vegetable oil on medium-high heat. Add onion, pepper, zucchini, crookneck squash, corn, and mushrooms; cook, stirring occasionally, until softened about 5 to 7 minutes. Add oregano and cumin, and season with salt to taste.

4   Heat a griddle or heavy skillet over medium heat. Mist both sides of each tortilla with cooking spray. Warm tortillas on griddle until heated through, about 40 to 60 seconds per side. They should be heated enough so they are crusty on exterior, but still completely flexible. Dip each tortilla into sauce just to moisten.

5   Coat a 9 × 13-inch baking dish with cooking spray. Spoon 1 cup of the leftover tomatillo sauce over bottom of dish. Place ½ cup vegetable mixture in center of 1 tortilla and top with about 1 tablespoon cheese; roll up to enclose filling. Place enchilada seam side down in baking dish. Repeat with remaining tortillas and vegetable mixture. Pour remaining sauce over enchiladas (keeping reserved sauce for serving), then sprinkle with remaining cheese. Cover with aluminum foil and bake until heated through, about 25 minutes.

6   Heat reserved sauce for optional topping. Spoon a little sauce over each serving and serve.

Nutritional information (per enchilada): Calories 250, fat calories 120; total fat 14 grams, sat fat 4.5 grams, cholesterol 15 milligrams; sodium 320 milligrams; total carbohydrates 15 grams, fiber 5 grams, sugars 7 grams; protein 9 grams; vitamin A IUs 8%; vitamin C 50%; calcium 20%; iron 10%.

Cook's Note: If sauce is too thick, stir in a little chicken broth or vegetable broth.

Garden Enchiladas

Stuffed Chicken Breasts

YIELD: 4 SERVINGS

A filling of corn kernels, grated cheese, chiles, and fresh cilantro offer an appealing herbal-yet-sweet creaminess to chicken breasts. If you like, use this recipe as a blueprint and substitute different cheeses and fresh herbs in place of those listed in the ingredients.

4 (4-ounce) skinless, boneless chicken breasts (see Meatless Tip)

Filling

¼ cup corn kernels, fresh or frozen (thawed)

3 ounces grated low-fat or whole-milk Monterey Jack cheese

1 green onion, trimmed, thinly sliced, including dark green part

1½ tablespoons minced fresh cilantro

½ small fresh jalapeño chile, seeded, minced

Optional garnish: ½ teaspoon minced fresh cilantro

Assembly

⅓ cup all-purpose flour

Garlic salt and freshly ground black pepper

1½ tablespoons olive oil or canola oil

¼ cup balsamic vinegar

⅔ cup low-fat chicken broth, plus more if needed

Optional garnish: 1 tablespoon chopped cilantro

1   Using a small sharp knife, cut a horizontal pocket in each chicken breast, starting on the long, curved side. Leave 3 sides intact and try not to pierce top or bottom (if you do, it still will work—it just won't look as glamorous).

2   Combine filling ingredients in medium bowl. Fill each breast with stuffing and close with a wooden toothpick. Dredge lightly in flour and season with salt and pepper to taste.

3   Heat olive oil or canola oil in large, deep nonstick skillet over medium-high heat. Add breasts and brown nicely on both sides. Increase to high heat; add vinegar and broth and bring to boil. Reduce heat and simmer for 3 to 4 minutes per side or until completely cooked.

4   Remove chicken and reduce sauce on high heat if needed to thicken it. Add optional garnish to sauce, if desired, and cook an additional 30 seconds. Taste and add salt and pepper, if needed. Ladle sauce over chicken and serve.

Nutritional information (per serving using low-fat cheese): Calories 310, fat calories 110; total fat 12 grams, sat fat 4 grams, cholesterol 80 milligrams; sodium 620 milligrams; total carbohydrates 16 grams, fiber 1 gram, sugars 5 grams; protein 33 grams; vitamin A IUs 10%; vitamin C 8%; calcium 35%; iron 10%.

Meatless Tip: Instead of using the filling mixture inside of poultry, use it as a topping. Prepare Sautéed Breaded Tofu (see page 320). Place in single layer on rimmed baking sheet and top with filling mixture. Heat in 350°F oven until cheese starts to melt, about 8 minutes.

Corn and Edamame Salad

YIELD: 12 SIDE-DISH SERVINGS

Grassy and sweet flavors meld together beautifully in this colorful salad mixture. It's bound with assertive vinaigrette spiked with hot sauce and ground cumin. If you like, serve it in butter lettuce cups.

Dressing

½ cup rice vinegar

¼ cup fresh lime juice

½ cup vegetable oil

½ teaspoon ground cumin

2 teaspoons hot sauce

Salt and freshly ground black pepper

Salad

2 cups shelled cooked soybeans (edamame), 24 ounces of cooked pods yield about 2 cups shelled soybeans

4 cups cooked corn kernels, cooled

1 small red bell pepper, cored, seeded, diced

1 small orange bell pepper, cored seeded, diced

1 small red onion, diced

1 small jalapeño chile, seeded, minced (see Cook's Note)

¼ cup chopped fresh cilantro

1   In medium bowl, whisk dressing ingredients until well combined.

2   Place salad ingredients in large bowl. Add dressing and gently toss. Cover and chill 3 to 4 hours before serving.

Nutritional information (per serving): Calories 160, fat calories 100; total fat 11 grams, sat fat 1 gram, cholesterol 0 milligrams; sodium 120 milligrams; total carbohydrates 15 grams, fiber 3 grams, sugars 3 grams; protein 5 grams; vitamin A IUs 6%; vitamin C 30%; calcium 2%; iron 6%.

Cook's Note: Use caution when working with fresh chiles. Wash work surface and hands thoroughly upon completion and do *not* touch eyes or face.

Spicy Grilled Corn on the Cob with Parmesan

YIELD: 4 SERVINGS

Chewy, smoky, and irresistible, hot-off-the-grill corn on the cob topped with mayonnaise and Parmesan cheese is a treat that is hard to beat. For an easy approach, put out all the fixings—a bowl of mayonnaise, a bowl of cheese, and the chile powder–based mixture—and let family and guests top their own to suit individual tastes.

1 teaspoon chile powder

⅛ teaspoon dried oregano

⅛ teaspoon onion powder

Pinch ground cayenne pepper

⅛ teaspoon garlic powder

4 ears corn, husked

4 tablespoons unsalted butter, melted

Coarse salt, such as kosher, and freshly ground black pepper

½ to ¾ cup mayonnaise

About ½ to ¾ cup grated Parmesan cheese

1 Heat grill for medium-high heat. Clean grate and brush with vegetable oil.

2 In small bowl, combine chile powder, oregano, onion powder, cayenne pepper, and garlic powder; set aside.

3 Brush corn cobs with melted butter and season with the salt and black pepper to taste. Grill, turning with tongs to lightly brown on all sides. Place ears on rimmed baking sheet or platter. Brush on all sides with mayonnaise and sprinkle with cheese and chile powder mixture to taste. Serve.

Nutritional information (per serving using 2 tablespoons cheese and 2 tablespoons mayonnaise): Calories 350, fat calories 240; total fat 27 grams, sat fat 10 grams, cholesterol 45 milligrams; sodium 380 milligrams; total carbohydrates 24 grams, fiber 2 grams, sugars 7 grams; protein 8 grams; vitamin A IUs 20%; vitamin C 10%; calcium 10%; iron 4%.

Cucumber

Common

Hothouse (English)

Cucumber's crunchy texture teams with a fragrance that is pleasingly grassy. Neutral but noisy-nice, they're ready for endless flavor variations, both simple and complex. About 12 to 15 inches long, hothouse cucumbers (often labeled English cucumbers) are most often grown in greenhouses and sealed in plastic wrap. They are eaten with their thin skin intact, and because most are essentially seedless, no seeding is necessary. Thicker-skinned common cucumbers (sometimes called plain or pole cucumbers) have plentiful seeds and are often seeded before use.

Organic common cucumbers are not coated with wax as with the conventional product, so peeling is optional. Without the wax, they have a slightly shorter shelf life. Organic cucumber growers report that composting soil prior to planting is vital to their crops. A low amount of moisture is needed at all times to keep cucumbers growing straight rather than arching into a curved shape.

BUYING AND STORING: Look for firm cucumbers without shriveling or discoloration. Check ends for desired rigid texture; ends generally are the first area to soften. Refrigerate (unwashed, uncut) in crisper drawer up to 6 days, but check sooner for softening.

PREP AND USE: Wash and, if desired, peel with swivel-bladed vegetable peeler or paring knife. To remove seeds from common cucumbers, cut in half lengthwise; run bowl of spoon from end to end to scoop out seeds. Cucumbers can be sliced, diced, or grated. Use in salads, slaws, sandwiches, or garnishes. Generally eaten raw, but can be sautéed and served warm topped with chopped fresh herbs.

AVAILABLE: Year-round

NUTRITIONAL INFORMATION (per 1 cup peeled chopped, raw): Calories 16, fat calories 2; total fat 0 grams, sat fat 0 grams, cholesterol 0 milligrams; sodium 3 milligrams; total carbohydrates 3 grams, fiber 1 gram, sugars 2 grams; protein 1 gram; vitamin A IUs 2%; vitamin C 7%; calcium 2%; iron 2%.

SERVING SUGGESTIONS

Infused Water

The subtle taste and aroma of cucumber turns water into something very special. Add several slices of hothouse cucumber and lemon to large pitcher. Fill with water; cover and chill for several hours. Strain into glasses filled with ice.

Cold Rice Salad

In large bowl, combine 3 tablespoons white wine vinegar, 2 teaspoons fresh lemon juice, ⅓ cup extra-virgin olive oil, and garlic salt to taste; whisk to blend. Add 1 large hothouse (English) cucumber (unpeeled and diced) or 2 common cucumbers (peeled, seeded, and diced) and ⅓ cup minced fresh mint; toss. Add 3 to 4 cups cold or room-temperature cooked rice. Taste and adjust seasoning as needed. Garnish with tomato wedges or sliced radishes.

Chilled Soup

In blender, combine 1 peeled, sliced hothouse (English) cucumber or 2 peeled, seeded, sliced common cucumbers, 2½ cups honeydew melon chunks, 2 tablespoons fresh lime juice, 1 tablespoon minced fresh mint, and 1 cup unsweetened, plain nonfat yogurt. Cover and whirl until smooth. Season to taste with salt and freshly ground black pepper.

Hot, Hot, Hot

Yes, cucumbers make a pleasing hot vegetable dish. Peel, seed, and cut about 1 pound of common cucumbers into 2-inch-thick slices (they will be halved lengthwise, because seeds are removed first). Heat 1 tablespoon extra-virgin olive oil in large, deep skillet on medium-high heat. Add cucumbers and cook about 3 minutes, stirring frequently. Add ¼ cup water and 1 pinch ground cumin. Boil until water evaporates. Remove from heat and stir in 2 tablespoons minced fresh basil leaves or fresh tarragon leaves or fresh dill, salt, and freshly ground black pepper to taste.

Tomato, Cucumber, and Roasted Shallot Salad

YIELD: 8 SERVINGS

The sweet taste of roasted shallots lends an irresistible edge to this vegetable salad. Serve the salad as is, or toppled over a crusty slab of bread. Cut 8 thick diagonal slices from a baguette. Brush slices with a little olive oil and grill bread on both sides until nicely toasted. Place one slice of grilled bread on each salad plate, spoon salad on top of bread and serve immediately.

12 shallots, peeled

3 teaspoons extra-virgin olive oil, divided use

Salt and freshly ground black pepper

6 medium ripe tomatoes, cut into wedges

3 common cucumbers, peeled, seeded, thinly sliced

2 tablespoons sherry vinegar

3 cloves roasted garlic, minced (see Garlic, page 139)

1 teaspoon chopped fresh thyme leaves

1 teaspoon chopped fresh oregano leaves

1 Adjust oven rack to middle position. Preheat oven to 350°F. Cover rimmed baking sheet with aluminum foil and set aside.

2 In medium bowl, toss shallots in 2 teaspoons oil; place on prepared sheet. Season with salt and pepper to taste. Roast until fork-tender, about 20 minutes. Cool. If shallots are large, cut in half lengthwise.

3 In small bowl, whisk together vinegar, garlic, remaining 1 teaspoon oil, and herbs. Season with salt and pepper to taste.

4 In medium-large bowl, combine cooled shallots, tomatoes, and cucumbers. Spoon on dressing and gently toss. Taste and adjust seasoning as needed. Serve at room temperature or chill up to 1 hour.

Nutritional information (per serving): Calories 60, fat calories 20; total fat 2 grams, sat fat 0 grams, cholesterol 0 milligrams; sodium 10 milligrams; total carbohydrates 10 grams, fiber 2 grams, sugars 5 grams; protein 2 grams; vitamin A IUs 25%; vitamin C 30%; calcium 4%; iron 4%.

Quinoa, Black Bean, and Cucumber Salad

YIELD: 8 SERVINGS

Arranged in butter lettuce cups on a large platter, this salad is a tasty addition to buffets or picnics. If you like, add a little finely chopped ham or crumbled cooked bacon.

5 cups water

½ cup quinoa

Dressing

6 tablespoons extra-virgin olive oil

2 tablespoons white wine vinegar

2 tablespoons chopped fresh Italian parsley

2 teaspoons chopped fresh basil leaves

1 tablespoon fresh lemon juice

2 large cloves garlic, chopped

¼ teaspoon dried red chile flakes

¼ teaspoon dried oregano or ½ teaspoon minced fresh oregano leaves

Salad

1 medium hothouse (English) cucumber, diced

2 Roma tomatoes, diced

2 green onions, trimmed, thinly sliced, including ½ dark green stalks

1 (15-ounce) can black beans, drained, rinsed

½ cup sliced pitted green olives

For serving: 1 head butter lettuce

1   Bring water to boil in medium saucepan. Add quinoa; boil, uncovered, 11 minutes. Strain. Fluff gently with fork and set aside uncovered to cool to room temperature.

2   In large bowl, whisk dressing ingredients together. Add cucumber, tomatoes, and green onions; gently toss. Add beans, olives, and quinoa; gently toss. Taste and adjust seasoning as needed. Serve in butter lettuce cups.

Nutritional information (per serving): Calories 210, fat calories 120; total fat 13 grams, sat fat 2 grams, cholesterol 0 milligrams; sodium 230 milligrams; total carbohydrates 19 grams, fiber 5 grams, sugars 2 grams; protein 5 grams; vitamin A IUs 20%; vitamin C 15%; calcium 4%; iron 15%.

Pita Sandwiches Stuffed with Chopped Salad and Cheese

YIELD: 8 SANDWICH HALVES

Peppery Jack cheese adds a perky edge to this chopped salad mixture. If you like, roasted bell peppers make a colorful addition to these stuffed pitas. Or augment the mixture with ½ cup cooked garbanzo beans.

¼ cup fresh lime juice

¼ cup extra-virgin olive oil

1 tablespoon honey

2 tablespoons chopped fresh mint or fresh basil leaves

1 teaspoon salt

1 teaspoon freshly ground black pepper

1 ripe avocado, pitted, peeled, diced

2 hothouse (English) cucumbers, cut in half lengthwise, sliced crosswise into ¼-inch slices

3 Roma tomatoes, diced

½ cup sliced pitted green olives

1 cup grated pepper Jack cheese

2 hearts of romaine lettuce, coarsely chopped, about 6 cups

4 (6-inch) pitas

1   In large bowl, combine juice, oil, and honey; stir to combine. Add mint, salt, and pepper; stir to combine.

2   Add avocado, cucumbers, tomatoes, and olives; gently toss. Add cheese and lettuce; toss. Taste and adjust seasoning as needed. Cut pitas in half, open pocket, and fill each half with salad. Do not overfill or pita will tear.

Nutritional information (per sandwich): Calories 270, fat calories 150; total fat 17 grams, sat fat 4 grams, cholesterol 15 milligrams; sodium 560 milligrams; total carbohydrates XX grams, fiber 3 grams, sugars 5 grams; protein 8 grams; vitamin A IUs 60%; vitamin C 30%; calcium 15%; iron 10%.

Pita Sandwiches Stuffed with Chopped Salad and Cheese

Spicy Grilled Chicken Thighs with Cucumber Raita

YIELD: 4 SERVINGS

Working like a yogurt-based fire extinguisher, cucumber raita is delicious served with spicy dishes. These zesty chicken thighs are moderately spicy, so if you want to pump up the heat, increase the hot pepper sauce in the marinade.

2 tablespoons vegetable oil

1½ tablespoons hot sauce

2 teaspoons honey

1 teaspoon paprika

4 (4-ounce) skinless, boneless, chicken thighs
   (see Meatless Tip)

Raita

1 medium common cucumber

2 cups unsweetened, plain whole-milk yogurt

1 teaspoon toasted cumin seeds (see Cook's Note)

2½ tablespoons chopped fresh mint or fresh cilantro

1 medium clove garlic, minced

1 Stir oil, hot sauce, honey, and paprika to combine in medium glass or ceramic bowl. Remove 1 tablespoon of mixture and set aside to use as garnish. Add chicken and toss to coat. Set aside to marinate 15 minutes.

2 Heat grill. Clean grates and brush with vegetable oil.

3 Meanwhile, prepare raita. Peel cucumber and cut lengthwise into ¼-inch-thick slices; cut slices crosswise into thin slices. Spread on double layer of paper towels and top with single layer. Pat to remove excess moisture. Stir yogurt and cumin seeds in medium bowl. Add cucumber, mint or cilantro, and garlic; stir to combine.

4 Discard marinade. Grill chicken until cooked through, turning occasionally, about 10 minutes. Remove chicken from grill and drizzle with reserved hot sauce mixture. Serve chicken with raita on the side.

Nutritional information (per serving): Calories 270, fat calories 150; total fat 16 grams, sat fat 4.5 grams, cholesterol 70 milligrams; sodium 240 milligrams; total carbohydrates 11 grams, fiber 1 gram, sugars 9 grams; protein 19 grams; vitamin A IUs 10%; vitamin C 10%; calcium 15%; iron 8%.

Cook's Note: To toast cumin seeds, place in small skillet on medium-high heat. Shake handle to redistribute seeds. Cook until seeds start to brown. Remove from heat. If you leave them on the heat too long, they will start to pop out of pan.

Meatless Tip: Substitute Grilled Tofu with Mediterranean-Style Marinade (page 321) for chicken, increasing the amount of dried red chile flakes to ½ teaspoon.

Eggplant

Rather than the smaller Asian varieties, it's the larger, purple-black globe eggplants that are most commonly organically grown. Either an elongated pear shape or almost cylindrical, these shiny-skinned beauties vary from mild to moderately acrid. Typically eggplants are harvested when they reach about one-third of their full growth. Once the skin turns glossy they are ready for picking. An eggplant with dull skin is past its prime and, most likely, will be heavily seeded.

Organic growers boast that eggplant is drought resistant and, in fact, say that because the crop is vulnerable to root rot, it should not be overwatered. They are a delicacy for pests; aphids, spider mites, and caterpillars are the primary predators, and organic farmers use lacewings and ladybugs to help control them.

Commonly thought of as a vegetable, this member of the nightshade family (along with tomatoes) is really a fruit.

BUYING AND STORING: Look for those that are heavy for their size with smooth glossy skin. Avoid those with cracks or discoloration. Bruises on surface indicate flesh below will be discolored. A medium-size common purple eggplant, about 4 to 6 inches in diameter, will generally be milder, and have more-tender skin and fewer seeds than a more mature, larger one. Refrigerate, unwashed, in plastic in crisper drawer up to 7 days.

PREP AND USE: Wash in cold running water and pat dry. Trim off cap and stem end using a stainless steel knife (don't use a carbon steel knife; it will discolor eggplant). Cook, skin-on or peeled, depending on the dish. When roasted whole or sliced for roasting, sautéing, broiling, or grilling, the skin is generally left intact. If peeling, use paring knife or vegetable peeler.

To eliminate excess water and to prevent eggplant from absorbing too much oil, slice and salt eggplant 30 to 40 minutes before cooking. To do this, line rimmed baking sheet with paper towels. Arrange eggplant slices on towels in single layer and lightly salt on both sides. Allow to sit for 30 to 40 minutes. Rinse with cold water and thoroughly pat dry.

Eggplant is always eaten cooked; grill, bake, boil, braise, microwave, sauté, or steam. Eggplant is often used as a meat substitute. Use mashed in dips and spreads, or add diced and sautéed. Use grilled slices as a layer below sliced tomatoes topped with basil and fresh mozzarella in Caprese salad, or top with a mixture of crumbled feta and chopped olives tossed with minced fresh tarragon.

AVAILABLE: May to August

NUTRITIONAL INFORMATION (per 1 cup, raw): Calories 20, fat calories 1; total fat 0 grams, sat fat 0 grams, cholesterol 0 milligrams; sodium 2 milligrams; total carbohydrates 5 grams, fiber 3 grams, sugars 2 grams; protein 1 gram; vitamin A IUs 0%; vitamin C 3%; calcium 1%; iron 1%.

SERVING SUGGESTIONS

Eggplant Pasta

Cube, salt, roast, and season eggplant (see step 2 of Ratatouille recipe). Toss with ¾ pound cooked penne or fusilli, 8 halved cherry tomatoes, pinch dried red chile flakes and ¼ cup chopped fresh basil. Taste and adjust seasoning as needed. Top with ⅓ cup freshly grated Parmesan cheese.

Marinated Grilled Eggplant Slices

Cut large unpeeled eggplant into ¾-inch-thick crosswise slices. Brush surfaces with olive oil and grill over medium coals until cooked through, turning as needed. Place in nonreactive container. In small bowl, combine 2 tablespoons white wine vinegar, 1 large garlic clove (minced), pinch dried red chile flakes, 1 tablespoon minced fresh basil, and salt and pepper to taste. Whisk in ⅓ cup extra-virgin olive oil. Pour over eggplant and set aside 30 minutes. Serve at room temperature as is, or arranged over mixed baby greens and topped with crumbled goat cheese.

Grilled Eggplant Topped with Chermoula Sauce

Cut 3 large eggplants into slices and grill (see Marinated Grilled Eggplant Slices, above). Arrange, slightly overlapping, on rimmed platter. To prepare sauce, heat 2 tablespoons extra-virgin olive oil in large, deep skillet on medium-high heat. Add 1 large clove garlic (minced), 1 large shallot (sliced), 1 teaspoon ground cumin, and 1 teaspoon sweet paprika; cook, stirring, until garlic softens, about 1 minute. Add 1½ pounds chopped and seeded Roma tomatoes, 3 tablespoons chopped fresh cilantro, and ¼ cup chopped fresh parsley; simmer, adjusting heat as needed, about 10 minutes. Add salt and freshly ground black pepper to taste and spoon over grilled eggplant.

Over Rice with Cannellini Beans

Cut 1 large (about 1 pound) unpeeled eggplant into ½-inch cubes. Heat 2 tablespoons extra-virgin olive oil in large, deep skillet on medium-high heat. Add eggplant and 1 large sweet onion (roughly chopped); cook until eggplant starts to brown and soften, about 10 minutes, gently tossing occasionally. Stir in 1 (15.5-ounce) can cannellini beans with juice, 1 tablespoon fresh lemon juice, 1 tablespoons chopped fresh basil leaves, and a pinch of dried red chile flakes. Bring to simmer; taste and add salt and freshly ground black pepper to taste. Serve over cooked rice.

Quick Ratatouille

YIELD: 6 SERVINGS

The famous Provençal vegetable stew–like concoction is delicious served hot or at room temperature. It is best made a day in advance, chilled in a well-sealed container, and then either reheated or brought to room temperature before serving. This rendition uses canned diced tomatoes to make it faster to put together, but if you wish, substitute ¾ pound fresh, roughly chopped Roma tomatoes (if those fresh tomatoes aren't juicy, add a little tomato juice).

- 1 large eggplant, about 1 pound, unpeeled, cut into ½-inch cubes
- 1 teaspoon salt
- 3 tablespoons extra-virgin olive oil, divided use
- 2 teaspoons chopped fresh thyme leaves
- ¼ teaspoon fennel seeds
- ¼ teaspoon dried oregano
- 1 large yellow onion, halved, cut into thin crosswise slices
- 2 red bell peppers, cored, seeded, cut into ½-inch dice
- 1 pound yellow crookneck squash, cut into ½-inch crosswise slices
- 4 large cloves garlic, minced
- 1 (15-ounce) can diced tomatoes with juice
- ⅓ cup coarsely chopped fresh basil leaves
- Salt and freshly black ground pepper

1 Spread 2 or 3 paper towels on countertop. Top with eggplant cubes and sprinkle with salt. Allow to sit 30 minutes. Pat eggplant dry, wiping off some salt in the process. Meanwhile, adjust oven rack to middle position. Preheat oven to 450°F.

2 Place eggplant on rimmed baking sheet. Drizzle with 1½ tablespoons oil and roast, tossing once or twice, until lightly browned, about 20 minutes. Gently toss with thyme, fennel, and oregano; set aside.

3 In large, deep skillet, cook onions in 1 tablespoon oil on medium-high heat until softened, about 5 minutes. Add bell peppers and squash; cook, stirring occasionally, until vegetables soften, about 8 to 10 minutes. Stir in garlic and cook until garlic starts to soften, about 2 minutes.

4 Add tomatoes along with juice and eggplant with any juices. Bring to simmer on medium-high heat; lower heat to medium and gently simmer 20 minutes. Add basil and gently toss.

5 Taste and adjust seasoning as needed, adding salt and black pepper to taste. Serve or cool and refrigerate in well-sealed container.

Nutritional information (per serving): Calories 130, fat calories 70; total fat 70 grams, sat fat 1 gram, cholesterol 0 milligrams; sodium 430 milligrams; total carbohydrates 16 grams, fiber 5 grams, sugars 6 grams; protein 4 grams; vitamin A IUs 20%; vitamin C 120%; calcium 6%; iron 8%.

Baba Ghanoush

YIELD: ABOUT 1½ CUPS (24 TABLESPOONS)

This mild-mannered but irresistible version of roast eggplant dip doesn't contain tahini, the sesame seed paste that is generally used in the classic Middle Eastern dish. The fresh taste of eggplant and lemon shines through in this simple rendition. Provide a bowl of mixed olives as a tasty accompaniment, along with toasted pita triangles for dipping.

- 1 large eggplant, about 1 pound
- 2 tablespoons extra-virgin olive oil, divided use
- 1 large clove garlic, minced
- Minced zest of 1 lemon, about 1 tablespoon (colored portion of peel)
- 2 tablespoons fresh lemon juice
- ⅛ teaspoon salt
- ⅛ teaspoon freshly ground black pepper
- Garnish: chile powder
- Garnish: 1 tablespoon chopped fresh Italian parsley
- For serving: toasted pita bread triangles (see Cook's Note)

1   Adust oven rack to middle position. Preheat oven to 400°F. Wash eggplant and pat dry. With a fork, prick eggplant well on all sides (leave calyx, the leaves at stem, intact). Use 1 tablespoon oil to rub eggplant skin; place on rimmed baking sheet. Roast for 30 minutes, turn over, and roast additional 30 minutes. The skin should look almost black, but not burned, and the flesh should be very soft. Remove from oven and cool completely.

2   Remove calyx and peel back skin. Place eggplant flesh in food processor; discard skin. Add garlic. Process until smooth and no fibers or lumps appear. Place in small serving bowl. Add remaining 1 tablespoon oil, zest, juice, salt, and pepper; stir to combine. Cover and refrigerate at least 2 hours (or up to 48 hours) before serving. Bring to room temperature before serving.

3   Taste and adjust seasonings if needed. Sprinkle with a little chile powder and parsley. Serve accompanied with toasted pita triangles.

Nutritional information (per 1 tablespoon without pita): Calories 15, fat calories 10; total fat 1 gram, sat fat 0 grams, cholesterol 0 milligrams; sodium 15 milligrams; total carbohydrates 1 gram, fiber 1 gram, sugars 0 grams; protein 0 grams; vitamin A IUs 0%; vitamin C 2%; calcium 0%; iron 0%.

Cook's Note: To make toasted pita bread triangles, preheat oven to 350°F; cut several pita bread rounds into eighths and place in single layer on rimmed baking sheet. Bake until lightly browned and crisp, about 6 minutes. Cool.

Baba Ghanoush

Curried Eggplant

YIELD: 6 SERVINGS

Coconut milk is an important ingredient in this creamy eggplant concoction. It is available in cans at many supermarkets in the Asian specialty section and shouldn't be confused with sweetened "cream of coconut," which is used mainly for cocktails and desserts. Coconut milk is made by simmering water and fresh shredded coconut (or desiccated coconut), then straining it through cheesecloth and squeezing the remnants to extract as much coconut flavor as possible.

1 medium onion, coarsely chopped

1 large eggplant, about 1 pound, unpeeled, cut into 1-inch dice

1 large sweet potato, peeled, cut into ½-inch dice

1 red bell pepper, cored, seeded, cut into ½-inch dice

3 tablespoons extra-virgin olive oil

¼ teaspoon salt

¼ teaspoon freshly black ground pepper

1 tablespoon ground coriander

2 teaspoons ground cumin

1 teaspoon ground turmeric

¼ teaspoon ground cayenne pepper

2 tablespoons unsalted butter

1 tablespoon all-purpose flour

1 cup whole milk, heated

1 cup coconut milk

½ cup fresh basil leaves, cut into thin strips

For serving: 6 cups hot cooked basmati or jasmine rice

1 Adjust oven rack to middle position. Preheat oven to 375°F. In large mixing bowl, toss onion, eggplant, sweet potato, bell pepper, oil, salt, and black pepper until lightly coated. Transfer to rimmed baking sheet. Roast in middle of preheated oven for 10 minutes. Toss. Roast until eggplant is lightly browned and sweet potato is fork-tender, about 10 to 15 additional minutes. Transfer roasted vegetables to a 2-quart casserole dish. Cover; keep warm.

2 Meanwhile, over medium-high heat, place coriander, cumin, turmeric, and cayenne pepper in medium, deep skillet and toast until just becoming fragrant and just starting to brown, shaking handle to redistribute contents. Transfer to a small dish and set aside. In same pan, melt butter on medium heat and add flour. Mash together until blended into a smooth paste, being careful not to brown the paste (roux). While stirring the roux, slowly add the heated milk, whisking to combine. Simmer until thickened and flour taste is gone, whisking constantly, about 3 to 4 minutes. Slowly whisk in coconut milk and cook until a creamy consistency.

3 Pour sauce over roasted eggplant mixture and top with basil strips. Serve over hot rice.

Nutritional information (per serving without rice): Calories 270, fat calories 180; total fat 20 grams, sat fat 11 grams, cholesterol 15 milligrams; sodium 150 milligrams; total carbohydrates 20 grams, fiber 5 grams, sugars 7 grams; protein 4 grams; vitamin A IUs 140%; vitamin C 40%; calcium 10%; iron 15%.

Eggplant Lasagna

YIELD: 8 SERVINGS

Lengthwise slices of grilled eggplant substitute for the noodles in this robust one-dish meal. If possible, use fresh herbs; they are far more aromatic than dried, lending a perfumy edge to the tomato-based sauce. If you only have dried herbs, use only one-third as much as fresh.

3 pounds eggplant

Kosher salt

2 tablespoons vegetable oil plus oil for brushing eggplant slices

½ cup diced sweet onion

1 large clove garlic, minced

½ cup dry red wine

¼ cup chopped fresh basil leaves

Leaves from 2 sprigs fresh thyme, minced

1 tablespoon chopped fresh oregano leaves

1 (26-ounce) jar marinara sauce

1 (16-ounce) container part-skim ricotta cheese

1 cup grated part-skim mozzarella cheese

1 cup grated Parmesan cheese, divided use

1 egg, lightly beaten

Salt and freshly ground black pepper

1   Peel eggplants and cut into ½-inch-thick lengthwise slices. Place in single layer on a paper towel–lined baking sheet, sprinkle with a little kosher salt and place another layer of paper towel on top of eggplant and another baking sheet or a heavy plate on top to weight down eggplant. Set aside for 20 to 30 minutes.

2   Heat grill to medium-high heat or adjust oven rack to 8 inches below broiler element and preheat broiler. Remove eggplant from paper towels and lightly brush both sides with oil. Grill or broil on rimmed baking sheet until nicely browned on both sides. Set aside.

3   In large, deep skillet, heat oil on medium-high heat. Add onion and cook, stirring frequently, until softened. Add garlic and stir; cook 30 seconds. Add wine, basil, thyme, oregano, and marinara sauce; lower heat to medium-low and simmer 20 to 25 minutes. Remove from heat to cool to room temperature.

4   Meanwhile, mix ricotta, mozzarella, and ½ cup remaining Parmesan together in medium bowl. Stir in egg, and salt and pepper to taste. Preheat oven to 400°F.

5   In a 9 × 13-inch baking dish, add enough marinara sauce mixture to just barely cover bottom of dish. Top with single layer of eggplant slices, ¼ of remaining marinara and ⅓ of ricotta mixture, added in small spoonfuls. Repeat two more times. Add a final topping of sauce. Sprinkle with ½ cup Parmesan.

6   Tightly cover baking dish with oiled aluminum foil (oiled-side down), then set dish in foil-lined rimmed baking sheet (to catch drips) and bake 30 minutes. Cautiously remove foil. Bake 15 more minutes, or until golden and bubbling. Let stand 15 to 20 minutes before serving.

Nutritional information (per serving): Calories 260, fat calories 110; total fat 12 grams, sat fat 7 grams, cholesterol 60 milligrams; sodium 380 milligrams; total carbohydrates 19 grams, fiber 6 grams, sugars 8 grams; protein 17 grams; vitamin A IUs 15%; vitamin C 15%; calcium 40%; iron 10%.

Fennel

The sweet, gentle flavor of the green-tinged, almost-white bulb is reminiscent of licorice or anise. When eaten raw, the texture is crunchy-crisp; heated until tender, it has a cooked-asparagus texture. Atop the bulb, thin feathery leaves sprout from narrowing stalks; the leaves are deep green and look like dill. Often fennel is incorrectly labeled "anise" or "sweet anise."

Organic growers report that composting the soil well before planting fennel is highly beneficial, as is crop rotation. Too much prolonged hot weather can cause fennel to bolt, forming flowers and seeds. All in all, fennel is a hardy crop.

BUYING AND STORING: Chose bulbs that are unblemished, without browning; they should be fragrant, firm, and rounded. Green feathery leaves at top should be a fresh and bright green. Refrigerate, unwashed, wrapped in plastic bag up to 5 days.

PREP AND USE: Rinse with cold water. Cut off fern-like greenery at top (reserve it for garnish or flavor enhancer).

Trim at base, removing and discarding any browned layers. To cut into crosswise strips, cut bulb in half lengthwise; place cut-side down and cut in half lengthwise again (if there is a core in center, generally it is small and doesn't need to be removed, but if it's large, cut it out and remove it with a small paring knife). Cut into crosswise slices. Or, for braising, cut fennel into lengthwise halves or quarters.

Eat raw or cooked. Can be braised, sautéed, baked, or grilled.

AVAILABLE: Year-round

NUTRITIONAL INFORMATION (per 1 cup sliced, raw): Calories 27, fat calories 1; total fat 0 grams, sat fat 0 grams, cholesterol 0 milligrams; sodium 45 milligrams; total carbohydrates 6 grams, fiber 3 grams, sugars 0; protein 1 gram; vitamin A IUs 2%; vitamin C 17%; calcium 4%; iron 4%.

SERVING SUGGESTIONS

Fried and Drizzled

Cut 2 large, trimmed fennel bulbs into lengthwise quarters, leaving base intact. Blanch in boiling water until tender, about 8 minutes. Drain and pat dry with paper towels. In one shallow bowl or pie pan, beat 1 egg with 2 teaspoons milk. In another shallow bowl or pie pan, place 1 cup fine fresh breadcrumbs seasoned with salt and freshly ground black pepper. Heat ⅛ inch canola oil or vegetable oil in large, deep skillet on medium-high heat. Dip each fennel quarter in egg mixture, then in breadcrumbs. Fry, browning all sides until crisp, lowering heat to medium as needed. Serve as is or drizzle with a little blue cheese dressing (see Hearts of Romaine Salad with Beets, Apples, and Creamy Blue Cheese Dressing, page 60).

Fennel in Foil

Preheat oven to 400°F. Cut 2 large trimmed fennel bulbs into lengthwise quarters, leaving base intact; core if needed. Place in center of large sheet of aluminum foil. Add 4 large cloves garlic, each cut in half lengthwise. Top 1 tablespoon fresh thyme leaves. Drizzle with 2 tablespoons extra-virgin olive oil and close foil, making a sealed packet. Bake until tender, about 25 minutes.

Feathery Fronds

Use stalks with leaves that are trimmed from top of fennel bulb to flavor dishes. Place some fronds inside chicken cavity before roasting, or use a bed of fennel fronds under fish when roasting.

Instead of Celery

Substitute chopped fennel for celery in soup, salad, stuffing, or rice dishes; or use raw as part of crudités accompanied with a tasty dip.

Tomato and Fennel Soup

YIELD: 4 SERVINGS

Although this soup is delectable on its own, garlic-enriched crostini (toasted baguette slices) are a very pleasing garnish.

- 2 tablespoons extra-virgin olive oil
- 1 medium, yellow onion, chopped
- 2 medium cloves garlic, minced
- 4 cups diced seeded Roma tomatoes
- 1 medium fennel bulb, trimmed, cored, diced, feathery leaves reserved for garnish
- 1½ cups diced peeled Yukon Gold potatoes
- 4½ cups vegetable broth
- 4 tablespoons chopped fresh basil leaves
- 3 tablespoons dry white wine
- 1 sprig fresh thyme
- 1 sprig fresh oregano
- Salt and freshly ground black pepper
- Optional: 8 garlic crostini, see Cook's Note

1 Heat oil in large saucepan or Dutch oven on medium-high heat. Add onion and cook, stirring occasionally, until softened. Add garlic and cook 30 seconds. Add all remaining ingredients except salt and pepper and crostini.

2 Bring to boil on high heat; reduce heat to medium-low and simmer 25 minutes or until vegetables are softened. Remove herb sprigs. Season with salt and pepper to taste. Cool 15 minutes.

3 Working in batches, puree in blender or food processor fitted with metal blade. If using blender, hold top in place with potholder.

4 Reheat and serve. Garnish each serving with a sprig of feathery fennel leaves. If desired, serve each with one or two garlic crostini (float on top of soup or serve on the side).

Nutritional information (per serving without crostini): Calories 190, fat calories 60; total fat 7 grams, sat fat 1 gram, cholesterol 0 milligrams; sodium 410 milligrams; total carbohydrates 27 grams, fiber 4 grams, sugars 4 grams; protein 3 grams; vitamin A IUs 15%; vitamin C 50%; calcium 4%; iron 8%.

Cook's Note: To make garlic crostini, start by roasting a head of garlic (see page 139); when cool enough to handle, pinch to remove 2 or 3 cloves from skin and mash with fork. Cut a portion of a baguette into 8 thin slices and lightly brush with extra-virgin olive oil. Place in single layer on rimmed baking sheet. Bake in middle of preheated 350°F oven until golden, about 8 to 10 minutes. Cool and spread with mashed garlic to taste, plus salt and pepper to taste. If desired, spread on a little soft goat cheese.

Tomato and Fennel Soup

Fennel with Pasta and Toasted Breadcrumbs

YIELD: 8 SERVINGS

Sautéed fennel and onion bring sweet, licorice-scented flavor to this simple pasta dish. A topping of coarse, crunchy breadcrumbs offers a buttery taste and appealing texture. If you like, add some Italian sausage (pick a sausage that is nicely seasoned with fennel seeds). Grill sausages until thoroughly cooked, allowing them to cool about 5 minutes before slicing; add to pasta in step 4.

Toasted Breadcrumbs

  1 cup coarse fresh breadcrumbs

  1 ½ tablespoons extra-virgin olive oil

  ¼ teaspoon salt

  ½ teaspoon freshly ground black pepper

Pasta

  2 tablespoons extra-virgin olive oil

  1 large yellow onion, halved from top to bottom, thinly sliced

  3 cups trimmed, cored, thinly sliced fennel bulb

  2 tablespoons finely chopped garlic

  2 teaspoons dried oregano

  ½ teaspoon dried red chile flakes

  1 pound penne

  Salt and freshly ground black pepper

  ½ cup grated Parmesan cheese

1   Prepare toasted breadcrumbs: Adjust oven rack to middle position. Preheat oven to 325°F. On rimmed baking sheet, toss breadcrumbs with oil, salt, and pepper. Spread out crumbs and bake for about 10 to 12 minutes or until nicely browned (tossing after 5 or 6 minutes).

2   Prepare pasta: Heat oil in large, deep skillet on medium-high heat; add onion and cook until tender, about 7 minutes, stirring occasionally. Add fennel, garlic, oregano, and chile flakes. Continue to cook over medium heat until fennel is tender.

3   Meanwhile, bring large pot of salted water to boil on high heat. Add penne and cook according to package directions until al dente. Drain, reserving ½ cup cooking water.

4   Add pasta to fennel mixture and season to taste with salt and pepper; add enough cooking water to make mixture moist.

5   Divide pasta between 6 plates. Top with toasted breadcrumbs and Parmesan cheese.

Nutritional information (per serving): Calories 330, fat calories 80; total fat 9 grams, sat fat 2 grams, cholesterol 5 milligrams; sodium 220 milligrams; total carbohydrates 52 grams, fiber 3 grams, sugars 4 grams; protein 11 grams; vitamin A IUs 2%; vitamin C 10%; calcium 10%; iron 15%.

Roasted Fennel, Carrots, and Red Onions

YIELD: 4 SERVINGS

Served hot, cold, or at room temperature, these delectable vegetables make a beautiful side dish. Or use them as a filling in hearty sandwiches along with slices of fresh mozzarella cheese on sturdy rustic buns.

1 large or 2 small fennel bulbs, trimmed, cored, cut into ½-inch-thick slices

2 large carrots, peeled, cut in half lengthwise and cut into 2-inch lengths

1 large red onion, cut into 8 wedges (see Cook's Note)

2 tablespoons extra-virgin olive oil

Salt and freshly ground black pepper

2 tablespoons balsamic vinegar

1   Adjust oven rack to middle position. Preheat oven to 425°F.

2   In large roasting pan, toss vegetables with oil and salt and pepper to taste. Roast 20 minutes. Drizzle with balsamic vinegar and roast an additional 10 to 15 minutes or until vegetables are tender.

Nutritional information (per serving): Calories 140, fat calories 60; total fat 7 grams, sat fat 1 gram, cholesterol 0 milligrams; sodium 380 milligrams; total carbohydrates 18 grams, fiber 5 grams, sugars 6 grams; protein 2 grams; vitamin A IUs 120%; vitamin C 30%; calcium 8%; iron 6%.

Cook's Note: To cut onion into wedges, peel it and place on cutting board. Cut in half from top to bottom. Cut each half in half, then in half again.

Fennel Salad with Citrus Vinaigrette

YIELD: 4 SERVINGS

To add more flavor to this salad, use a feta cheese that is augmented with herbs and/or sun-dried tomatoes. Serve this tasty salad with warm rustic bread to sop up the lovely juices.

1½ cups chilled, cooked shelled soybeans (edamame; see page 53)

1 medium fennel bulb, trimmed, cored, quartered, cut into ¼-inch slices

¼ cup trimmed sliced radishes

4 ounces crumbled feta cheese

¼ cup roughly chopped fresh mint leaves

2 tablespoons fresh lemon juice

2 tablespoons fresh orange juice

Salt and freshly ground black pepper

½ cup extra-virgin olive oil

1 In medium bowl, combine soybeans, fennel, radishes, and feta; gently toss.

2 Prepare vinaigrette: With motor running in food processor fitted with metal blade, add mint through feed tube. Process until minced. Add juices and salt and pepper to taste; pulse to blend. Add oil and pulse to blend. Taste and adjust seasoning as needed.

3 Add half of vinaigrette to vegetable mixture and toss. Divide between 4 plates and serve. Pass remaining vinaigrette to use as desired.

Nutritional information (per serving): Calories 290, fat calories 200; total fat 22 grams, sat fat 6 grams, cholesterol 25 milligrams; sodium 550 milligrams; total carbohydrates 14 grams, fiber 5 grams, sugars 2 grams; protein 11 grams; vitamin A IUs 10%; vitamin C 30%; calcium 20%; iron 10%.

Fig

Black Mission

Brown Turkey

Kadota

Fresh figs have become culinary superstars, showcased in upscale restaurants from coast to coast. Still warm from the sun, the reddish-pink or amber flesh smells like moist flower petals. Tiny seeds team with soft, honeyed flesh to provide gratifying textural pleasure.

Black Mission and Brown Turkey figs comprise about 80 percent of the organic domestic fig crop. Black Mission figs are medium-size teardrop shapes with thick, deep-purple (almost black) skin and pinkish-brown flesh. Brown Turkey figs are medium to large elongated teardrop shapes, with thick, deep-brown skin and pinkish-red flesh. A smaller amount of organic Kadota figs are grown in the United States. They are small to medium in size with greenish-yellow delicate skin and light amber or pale pink flesh.

Ninety-five percent of commercially grown organic figs are grown in California. Figs require hot, dry summers. In winter, when they are dormant, they need cold nights without snow. Birds are a problem for fig farmers. They forage primarily on the fruit at the top of the trees. Growers use fluttering, shiny Mylar tape to deter the birds; the sound and movement of the tape keep them away from the ripening figs.

Black Mission

Brown Turkey

FIG   133

BUYING AND STORING: Look for plump, ripe fruit that yields to gentle pressure. Figs are fragile; check to make sure skin is unbroken. Store unwashed in single layer at room temperature and use within 3 days. Or cover a plate or rimmed baking sheet with paper towels, place figs in single layer atop paper towels, then cover with plastic wrap and refrigerate up to 1 week.

PREP AND USE: Rinse quickly with cold running water and gently pat dry. Cut off tough stem end. Skin is edible; peel only when eating raw and skin is tough (generally only with very large figs).

Eat raw or cooked. Use raw atop green salads, or stuff with soft goat cheese and drizzle with honey. Or slice and layer in a peanut butter sandwich or dice and use as a garnish on grain-based concoctions. Cooked, use poached, roasted, or grilled. Poach in a mixture of dry red wine, spices, and sugar, or augment pork roast in the last 15 minutes of roasting. Halve and grill; use atop a salad of frisée napped with lemon vinaigrette and garnished with crisp-cooked diced pancetta and toasted walnuts.

AVAILABLE

Black Mission and Brown Turkey: June to October

Kadota: August to October

NUTRITIONAL INFORMATION (1 large fig): Calories 47, fat calories 2; total fat 0 grams, sat fat 0 grams, cholesterol 0 milligrams; sodium 1 milligram; total carbohydrates 12 grams, fiber 2 grams, sugars 10 grams; protein 0 grams; vitamin A IUs 2%; vitamin C 2%; calcium 2%; iron 1%.

SERVING SUGGESTIONS

Fig Apps

Here's an appetizer that disappears quickly—halve ripe figs lengthwise and place cut-side up on platter. Top each with generous amount of crumbled, sharp-flavored blue cheese. If desired, wrap each fig in a single layer of prosciutto. Drizzle with balsamic vinegar and serve accompanied with thinly sliced toasted baguette.

Goat Cheese with Fig Dippers

In food processor, combine 7 ounces soft goat cheese (log style, with garlic and herbs preferred), ¼ cup half-and-half, 2 teaspoons honey, 1 teaspoon finely chopped fresh rosemary leaves, and freshly ground black pepper to taste. Process until smooth. Taste and add salt if needed. Place in small bowl in center of platter. Cut ¾ pound ripe figs in lengthwise halves and place them around the bowl for dipping.

Cheese Tray

Serve quartered or halved figs along with several selections of cheese, sliced rustic bread, and toasted walnuts.

Grilled and Honeyed

Heat grill to medium-high heat. Clean grate. Cut 8 ripe, fresh figs in half lengthwise. Brush grill grate with vegetable oil and add figs, cut-side down. Grill about 3 minutes per side, or until nicely browned and heated through. Place on platter and drizzle with 1 to 2 tablespoons honey. Top with a little coarse salt, such as kosher, and 2 teaspoons finely chopped fresh basil leaves. Serve with grilled poultry or pork, or atop mixed green salad.

Figs and Port Wine Sauce-Topped Goat Cheese

YIELD: ABOUT 10 SERVINGS

This sauce is delicious warm served atop pork, chicken, or game. Or cool the mixture and serve with soft cheese, such as sliced goat cheese or Brie. If using goat cheese, slice it for easier serving (plus it looks prettier on the plate). Slicing goat cheese can be frustrating because it crumbles and/or sticks to the knife blade. A simple trick is to use dental floss instead of a knife.

3 tablespoons minced shallots

2 tablespoons unsalted butter

6 fresh figs, trimmed, halved lengthwise

½ cup port wine

½ cup dry red wine

1 cup apple juice

2 tablespoons agave syrup or honey

1 (11-ounce) log cold goat cheese, cut into ½-inch slices

Garnish: ¼ cup mixed microgreens

For serving: stone-ground whole wheat crackers, water crackers, or sliced baguette

1   In a large, deep skillet, preferably nonstick, melt butter over medium-high heat. Add shallots and cook until softened, about 2 minutes. Add figs, cut-side down. Add remaining ingredients except cheese and microgreens. Gently toss to combine.

2   Bring to a boil, then reduce heat to medium-low and simmer, jiggling pan handle occasionally to prevent sticking. Simmer until juice is thickened and coats figs, 20 to 25 minutes. Cool. Cut figs in half lengthwise (to make quarters).

3   Arrange cheese slices slightly overlapping on rimmed platter or individual cheese plates. Spoon fig mixture next to cheese slices. Top with micro greens. Accompany with crackers or sliced baguette.

Nutritional information (per serving without crackers or bread): Calories 210, fat calories 110; total fat 12 grams, sat fat 8 grams, cholesterol 30 milligrams; sodium 170 milligrams; total carbohydrates 15 grams, fiber 1 gram, sugars 12 grams; protein 7 grams; vitamin A IUs 15%; vitamin C 4%; calcium 10%; iron 4%.

Figs and Port Wine Sauce–Topped Goat Cheese

FIG   135

Whole Wheat Fig Bars

YIELD: 48 BARS

Due to the natural sweetness in figs, these bars are lower in fat and refined sugar than most cookies. Stuffing them with a fresh fig filling gives them an inviting, cozy appearance and a just-right taste.

Filling

1 pound Black Mission figs, trimmed and halved lengthwise

½ cup water

½ cup apple juice

⅓ cup agave syrup

⅛ teaspoon minced orange zest (colored portion of peel)

Dough

1 cup all-purpose flour plus flour for dusting work surface

¾ cup whole wheat flour

1 teaspoon baking powder

¼ teaspoon salt

3 ounces (¾ stick) unsalted butter, softened

¼ cup sugar

¼ cup agave syrup

1 large egg

1 teaspoon vanilla

1 teaspoon minced orange zest (colored portion of peel)

Agave water (1 tablespoon agave syrup mixed with 1 tablespoon water)

1 Prepare filling: In heavy-bottomed Dutch oven or pot, place figs, water, juice, agave syrup, and zest. Bring to full boil and reduce heat to medium-low; simmer until figs are soft and most of liquid has evaporated, about 1 hour. Transfer to food processor fitted with a metal blade; puree. Filling will thicken upon standing. Set aside or chill in refrigerator.

2 Prepare dough: In small mixing bowl, add both flours, baking powder, and salt. Whisk to combine; set aside.

3 In large bowl of electric mixer, combine butter and sugar; beat on medium speed until creamy, stopping to scrap down sides as needed. Add agave syrup and mix on medium speed until blended. Add egg, vanilla, and zest; mix on medium speed to blend well.

4 Add flour mixture in 4 batches, mixing to blend between additions. It will form a crumbly mass that will come together when pressed. Form into a cube; place in an airtight plastic bag or container and chill 2 to 3 hours. The recipe, to this point, can be done as much as three to four days in advance and stored in refrigerator.

5 Adjust oven rack to middle position. Preheat oven to 350°F. Line rimmed baking sheet with parchment paper. On a lightly floured surface, place unwrapped dough. Roll out to a 12 × 16-inch rectangle; cut into three 4 × 16-inch strips. Spread 3 generous tablespoons of fig mixture down center of each strip, being mindful to allow about 1 inch on each long side of strip, and spreading completely to the short edge of dough. Carefully fold over raw edges and pinch ends closed. Transfer bars, seam side down, to parchment-lined baking sheet. If necessary, cut bars into equal halves to accommodate cookie sheet size. Brush with agave water and place in oven.

6 Bake 12 minutes or until golden. Remove from oven and cool on pan 10 minutes. Cut into 1-inch cookies using serrated knife. Transfer to wire rack to cool completely. Store cookies in an airtight container up to 2 days.

Nutritional information (per cookie): Calories 50, fat calories 15; total fat 1.5 grams, sat fat 1 gram, cholesterol 10 milligrams; sodium 25 milligrams; total carbohydrates 9 grams, fiber 2 grams, sugars 14 grams; protein 2 grams; vitamin A IUs 2%; vitamin C 0%; calcium 2%; iron 2%.

Fig and Nectarine Salad with Lime-Honey Dressing

YIELD: 8 SERVINGS

Summertime's bounty shows off in this twist on a traditional fruit salad. The sweet-tart dressing teams well with the sweet, colorful fruit, and the salami slivers offer a salty meatiness. For a meatless version, top with chopped vegetarian bacon strips. Any ripe stone fruit can be substituted for the nectarines.

¼ cup fresh lime juice

1 teaspoon balsamic vinegar

¼ cup extra-virgin olive oil

1 tablespoon honey

Salt

2 tablespoons finely chopped fresh mint

4 ripe nectarines, pitted, cut into ½-inch-wide wedges

1 pint fresh figs, trimmed and quartered

6 thin slices cotto salami (see Meatless Tip)

1 Prepare dressing: In small bowl or glass measuring cup with handle, combine juice, vinegar, oil, and honey. Whisk to combine. Add salt to taste, keeping in mind that the salami will add a salty edge to the dish.

2 Jumble nectarines and figs on platter. Stack salami slices one on top of another. Cut them into thin strips and scatter strips over fruit. Stir dressing and spoon over fruit and salami. Serve.

Nutritional information (per serving): Calories 210, fat calories 90; total fat 10 grams, sat fat 2.5 grams, cholesterol 15 milligrams; sodium 190 milligrams; total carbohydrates 26 grams, fiber 3 grams, sugars 15 grams; protein 3 grams; vitamin A IUs 8%; vitamin C 15%; calcium 4%; iron 6%.

Meatless Tip: Omit salami and after adding dressing in step 2, top dish with cooked and chopped vegetarian bacon strips.

Pound Cake Topped with Baked Figs and Orange Liqueur

YIELD: 8 SERVINGS

Warm, juicy roasted figs are the perfect foil for cold ice cream. Although they are delectable enough to serve on their own, this dish gives figs the royal treatment, serving them over both ice cream and toasted pound cake. If you prefer, substitute untoasted angel food cake for the pound cake. And for a lighter version, use a smaller amount of ice cream, or omit ice cream and place fig mixture on the side topped with a small dollop of sour cream.

1 tablespoon unsalted butter

12 medium or 6 large fresh figs

⅓ cup water

⅓ cup sugar

¼ cup orange liqueur

2 teaspoons cornstarch

1 (16-ounce) loaf pound cake, cut into 8 (¾-inch-thick) slices

1½ tablespoons unsalted butter, melted

1 pint vanilla ice cream or coffee ice cream

1 Adjust oven rack to middle position. Preheat oven to 300°F. Grease a 9- or 10-inch ovenproof skillet with butter.

2 Using a toothpick, prick bottom of each fig in 4 or 5 places. Place figs standing up in prepared skillet. Pour water in pan and sprinkle figs with sugar.

FIG   137

3   Bake until figs are tender (but intact), about 25 minutes, basting a couple of times with pan juices. Roasting times will vary depending on fig size and degree of ripeness. Remove figs from skillet with slotted spoon. In small bowl, combine liqueur and cornstarch; beat with fork to combine. Place skillet on stove and stir in liqueur mixture. Bring to a boil on medium-high heat; reduce heat to medium and simmer until juices thicken slightly, about 3 to 4 minutes. Set aside off heat.

4   Adjust oven rack to about 8 inches below broiler element. Preheat broiler. Place pound cake slices in single layer on rimmed baking sheet. Brush tops lightly with melted butter. Broil until lightly toasted, about 2 minutes. Watch carefully because they can burn easily.

5   Place 1 slice of pound cake on each of 8 dessert plates, toasted-side up. Top each with a scoop of ice cream. Spoon warm figs and sauce over ice cream and serve.

Nutritional information (per serving): Calories 680, fat calories 140; total fat 16 grams, sat fat 9 grams, cholesterol 100 milligrams; sodium 240 milligrams; total carbohydrates 134 grams, fiber 7 grams, sugars 74 grams; protein 8 grams; vitamin A IUs 60%; vitamin C 80%; calcium 8%; iron 10%.

Garlic

Common (Purple, White)

Garlic is an aroma and taste chameleon. Raw and uncut, it has subtle aroma. Cut a garlic clove and a distinct, pungent aroma develops as elements within the garlic convert into a new compound, called alliin. It gives garlic its bite and signature scent.

The finer you cut it up, the stronger the garlic taste it will imbue. Mincing produces more alliin than chopping; smashing creates more than slicing. The alliin dissipates as cut garlic sits, so if garlic is prepped in advance, it will be less pungent. Or, if roasted whole, still tucked within its parchment-like cloak, a mellow taste and buttery mouthfeel is created.

Most organic garlic is harvested in June and July, but it is held in storage. After picking it is left to "field cure" up to two weeks; sitting atop the soil for several days decreases bruising when it is packed. Rust, a type of fungus, can be problematic for organic garlic growers. Their yield is about 30 percent less than conventional.

BUYING AND STORING: Avoid heads with shriveled or soft cloves. Purchase plump, firm bulbs with dry skins that have been stored at room temperature rather than refrigerated. Heads should feel heavy for their size. Moisture destroys garlic. Store whole heads in cool, dark location (with plenty of breathing room) up to 5 weeks. Breaking into cloves shortens the shelf life.

PREP AND USE: Garlic's papery covering is generally peeled before cooking, but there are exceptions. To peel, place clove(s) on cutting board; using a broad-bladed knife (such as a chef's knife), press down firmly with palm of hand or strike gently. Or when using several cloves, strike with bottom of skillet. Either way, skin separates easily. Or for pristine cloves, use a garlic peeler, a gizmo that looks like rubber tubing. For chopping or mincing, use a sharp knife or the "salt method." Sprinkle a little salt on cutting board. Smash clove(s) on salt using broad side of knife; then chop or mince, working salt into garlic. If using this method, reduce amount of salt in recipe.

Garlic is roasted whole and unpeeled. Also unpeeled cloves are sometimes added to dishes, such as chicken with forty cloves of garlic.

Don't burn garlic. Scorching makes it bitter. For sautéing or stir-frying, minced or chopped garlic needs only 30 to 45 seconds of cooking before adding remaining ingredients. It should be fragrant but not browned. If the recipe calls for onions and garlic cooked together, add minced or chopped garlic after the onions have been sautéed for a few minutes. Garlic takes less time to cook and onions will help protect garlic from burning.

To roast: Roasting garlic makes the natural sugars caramelize. The flesh becomes mild and creamy. Add to savory dishes or serve as an appetizer spread on rustic bread. To roast, preheat oven to 450°F. Using sharp knife, cut off one-third at pointed end of unpeeled garlic head. Enclose in aluminum foil, cut-side up; open slightly and drizzle with extra-virgin olive oil. Or to reduce fat, use 1 tablespoon water. Now, if you want creamy white roasted garlic, seal foil. Or, if you want caramelization, leave the foil open slightly at top. Roast garlic in preheated oven for about 30 minutes or until cloves are soft. When cool enough to handle, invert and squeeze cloves from papery sheath.

AVAILABLE: Year-round

NUTRITIONAL INFORMATION (per 1 cup, raw): Calories 203, fat calories 6; total fat 1 gram, sat fat 0 grams, cholesterol 0 milligrams; sodium 23 milligrams; total carbohydrates 45 grams, fiber 3 grams, sugars 1 gram; protein 9 grams; vitamin A IUs 0%; vitamin C 71%; calcium 25%; iron 13%.

SERVING SUGGESTIONS

Creamy Garlic Salad Dressing

In blender, combine pulp from 1 head roasted garlic (see Prep and Use), ¼ cup plain nonfat yogurt, 1 tablespoon fresh lime or lemon juice, 3 tablespoons grated Parmesan cheese, 1 teaspoon balsamic vinegar, 1 tablespoon chopped fresh Italian parsley, and 2 tablespoons extra-virgin olive oil. Whirl to blend and season with salt and freshly ground black pepper to taste.

Spud Topper

Instead of butter, use mashed roasted garlic on top of baked potatoes.

Garlic Whisperer

To give salads a subtle hint of garlic, cut an unpeeled, large clove in half lengthwise. Rub interior of salad bowl with cut surface.

Roasted Garlic Crostini

Adjust oven rack to middle position. Heat oven to 375°F. Cut baguette or country-style Italian bread into diagonal slices and brush with extra-virgin olive oil; arrange in single layer on rimmed baking sheet. Bake until golden, about 12 to 15 minutes; cool. Spread each with small amount of mashed roast garlic. Top each with a smear of goat cheese and strip of roasted red or yellow bell pepper or tapenade.

Rotelli with Roasted Garlic, Goat Cheese, and Baby Greens

YIELD: 4 MAIN-COURSE SERVINGS; 6 APPETIZER SERVINGS

Using a small portion of the hot water that is used to cook the pasta helps to create a lovely sauce and partially cook the baby greens. In this flavorful pasta dish, the wilted greens play an herbal role while the roasted garlic and cheese lend creaminess.

- 1 pound rotelli or fusilli
- 9 ounces mixed baby greens
- 1 tablespoon mashed roasted garlic (see Prep and Use)
- ¼ cup crumbled goat cheese
- ⅓ cup chopped oil-packed sun-dried tomatoes, drained
- ⅓ cup pitted green olives, coarsely chopped
- ⅓ cup freshly grated or shredded Parmesan cheese
- Salt and freshly ground black pepper

1 Bring large pot of salted water boil on high heat. Add rotelli or fusilli and cook according to package directions until al dente (tender but with a little bite). Drain pasta, reserving ¾ cup of cooking water; place hot pasta in large bowl.

2 Add greens, garlic, and reserved pasta water; toss to wilt greens. Add goat cheese, tomatoes, olives, and Parmesan; gently toss to combine. Season with salt and pepper to taste.

Nutritional information (per 6 appetizer serving): Calories 380, fat calories 120; total fat 13 grams, sat fat 7 grams, cholesterol 30 milligrams; sodium 910 milligrams; total carbohydrates 50 grams, fiber 4 grams, sugars 8 grams; protein 16 grams; vitamin A IUs 35%; vitamin C 15%; calcium 20%; iron 6%.

Spanish Garlic Soup

YIELD: 4 SERVINGS

Garlic and saffron give an irresistible depth of flavor to the broth that forms the base of this soup. A slice of toasted rustic wheat bread is placed in the bottom of each soup bowl. Each toast is topped with an egg that is has been quickly poached in the broth. Hot broth is ladled into each bowl, and generous amounts of freshly grated Parmesan and chopped fresh parsley add a final flourish. Serve it as a hearty first course, a light main course, or a welcoming breakfast.

- 3 tablespoons extra-virgin olive oil, divided use
- 4 thick slices rustic crusty bread, whole wheat sourdough preferred
- 5 large cloves garlic, halved lengthwise
- 1 tablespoon paprika
- ½ teaspoon ground cumin
- 5 cups fat-free low-sodium broth chicken broth or vegetable broth
- ⅛ teaspoon ground saffron
- Salt
- 4 eggs
- ¼ cup finely chopped fresh Italian parsley
- ⅓ cup grated or shredded Parmesan cheese

1 Adjust oven rack to 8 inches below broiling element. Preheat broiler. Using 1 tablespoon oil, brush bread slices on both sides. Place on rimmed baking sheet and broil until bread is lightly toasted. Turn and toast on opposite side until lightly browned. Watch carefully because bread can burn easily.

2 Heat remaining 2 tablespoons oil in heavy-bottomed, large saucepan or Dutch oven on low heat. Add garlic and cook until golden and softened, about 8 to 10 minutes. Add paprika and cumin; stir to combine and remove pan from stove.

3 Tilt pan and push ingredients to one side; mash garlic with fork tines. Return pan to stove; stir in broth and saffron. Bring to simmer on high heat; reduce heat to medium-low or medium-low and simmer 20 minutes. Taste and add salt as needed.

4 Lower heat enough so that soup is barely simmering. Break 1 egg in a small cup (such as a dry measuring cup with a handle) and, holding the cup next to the broth, tip egg into broth. Repeat with remaining eggs. Cook until egg whites set, about 5 minutes.

5 In each of 4 shallow soup bowls, place 1 toasted bread slice. Using a slotted spoon, place 1 egg atop each. Ladle soup into bowls and top with parsley and cheese. Serve.

Nutritional information (per serving): Calories 290, fat calories 160; total fat 18 grams, sat fat 4.5 grams, cholesterol 220 milligrams; sodium 910 milligrams; total carbohydrates 19 grams, fiber 2 grams, sugars 0 grams; protein 12 grams; vitamin A IUs 25%; vitamin C 10%; calcium 15%; iron 15%.

Spanish Garlic Soup

Two-Bean Salad

YIELD: 6 SERVINGS

A picnic favorite, this simple salad goes together in minutes. For variety, change the combination of beans to suit your taste. Small white beans, black beans, and kidney beans are all good choices. Or, instead of parsley, use cilantro or basil to give the dressing a different flavor profile. And if desired, just before serving, add a diced ripe avocado and gently toss.

Dressing

¼ cup cider vinegar

¼ cup extra-virgin olive oil

1 large cloves garlic, minced

2½ tablespoons agave syrup or honey

2 tablespoons minced fresh Italian parsley

Salt and freshly ground black pepper

Salad

1 (15-ounce) can pinto beans, drained, rinsed

1 (15-ounce) can black-eyed peas, drained, rinsed

1 cup corn kernels, canned, fresh, or frozen, thawed

2 stalks celery, chopped

2 green onions, thinly sliced, including ½ dark green stalks

1 red or yellow bell pepper, cored, seeded, chopped

1 In medium bowl, combine dressing ingredients. Whisk to combine and season with salt and pepper to taste.

2 Add salad ingredients and toss. Cover and refrigerate at least 2 hours or up to 2 days. Use slotted spoon for serving.

Nutritional information (per serving): Calories 230, fat calories 70; total fat 8 grams, sat fat 1 gram, cholesterol 0 milligrams; sodium 230 milligrams; total carbohydrates 33 grams, fiber 8 grams, sugars 8 grams; protein 9 grams; vitamin A IUs 4%; vitamin C 45%; calcium 4%; iron 15%.

Stir-Fried Tofu with Garlic, Mushrooms, and Green Onions

YIELD: 4 SERVINGS

The punch of minced garlic gives this stir-fry dish just-right pungency. For variety, substitute other mushroom varieties for white mushrooms, such as cremini or shiitake.

3 tablespoons rice vinegar

4 tablespoons soy sauce

1½ tablespoons agave syrup or honey

2 tablespoons dry sherry

¼ teaspoon dried red chile flakes

12 ounces extra-firm tofu, drained, cut into 1-inch cubes, patted dry with paper towels

¼ cup water

2½ teaspoons cornstarch

2½ tablespoons canola oil or vegetable oil, divided use

6 ounces common white (button) mushrooms, sliced ¼-inch thick

1 cup trimmed sugar snap peas

1 medium zucchini, trimmed cut into ½-inch slices

5 medium cloves garlic, minced

1 tablespoon minced peeled fresh ginger

4 green onions, cut into ¼-inch-long diagonal slices, including dark green stalks

Salt and freshly ground black pepper to taste

For serving: cooked rice, brown rice preferred

1 In medium bowl, combine vinegar, soy sauce, agave syrup or honey, sherry, and chile flakes; stir to combine. Add tofu and gently toss. Cover and marinate in refrigerator at least 45 minutes, or up to 4 hours.

2 Using slotted spoon, remove tofu from marinade. Whisk water and cornstarch in small bowl. Whisk into marinade.

3 Using a large, deep nonstick skillet, heat 1½ tablespoons oil on medium-high heat. Add tofu and sauté until golden, about 2 to 3 minutes. Using slotted spoon, transfer tofu to plate. Add remaining 1 tablespoon oil to skillet. Add mushrooms and stir-fry until tender, about 3 minutes. Add sugar snap peas and zucchini; stir-fry 2 minutes. Add garlic and ginger; stir-fry 30 seconds. Return tofu to skillet; add reserved marinade. Cook, stirring occasionally, until marinade thickens slightly, about 1 minute; season with salt and pepper to taste. Sprinkle with green onions. Serve over rice.

Nutritional information (per serving): Calories 240, fat calories 130; total fat 14 grams, sat fat 1 gram, cholesterol 0 milligrams; sodium 1030 milligrams; total carbohydrates 16 grams, fiber 2 grams, sugars 8 grams; protein 13 grams; vitamin A IUs 10%; vitamin C 20%; calcium 20%; iron 15%.

Ginger

Mature ginger has a pleasant peppery bite balanced with a subtle sweet finish. Cut into these knobby rhizomes and take in the spicy perfume. The deep tan skin is banded with rings; inside the flesh is fibrous yet juicy. Young ginger (spring ginger) is milder in both taste and aroma. Often cooks increase the amount when substituting it for stronger, older ginger. Its very thin skin is either ivory or a very pale yellow with sporadic pink shoots.

Organic growers plant the tubers at 10- to 12-inch intervals to give them plenty of legroom to grow. Often plastic hothouse covers are placed over the crop when the sprouts are young. The plastic protects the tender shoots from cold weather or overly hot sun. Organic yields are reduced by about 15 percent when compared to conventional crops.

BUYING AND STORING: Skin should be smooth and free of wrinkles. Ginger should feel firm and have a fresh, juicy interior. Leave at room temperature in cool location for up to 5 days, or wrap in paper towel and refrigerate in unsealed plastic bag up to 3 to 4 weeks. For longer storage, place sliced ginger in airtight jar covered with dry sherry or rice wine (then use the ginger-scented wine for cooking). Or slice and freeze in airtight container up to 3 months (freezing diminishes flavor and scent).

PREP AND USE: Skin is very thin and, whether old or young, ginger is often used unpeeled. If peeling, scrape off skin with back of small paring knife or bowl of a small spoon. Cut into matchsticks, mince, or grate across the lengthwise fiber (grain). If grating, a ginger grater or Microplane works well.

Eat raw in cold sauces, dips, salad dressings, marinades, ice cream, and beverages. Or cook in soups, casseroles, stir-fries, barbecue sauces, jams, and baked goods.

AVAILABLE: Year-round

NUTRITIONAL INFORMATION (per 1 teaspoon grated, raw): Calories 2, fat calories 0; total fat 0 grams, sat fat 0 grams, cholesterol 0 milligrams; sodium 0 milligrams; total carbohydrates 0 grams, fiber 0 grams, sugars 0 grams; protein 0 grams; vitamin A IUs 0%; vitamin C 0%; calcium 0%; iron 0%.

SERVING SUGGESTIONS

Easy-Way Flank Steak

In large zipper-style plastic bag or glass baking dish, combine ¼ cup low-sodium soy sauce, 1 tablespoon minced fresh ginger, 2 tablespoons extra-virgin olive oil, 4 large cloves garlic (minced), 1 teaspoon fresh lime or lemon juice, and 1 teaspoon cracked black pepper. Add 2-pound flank steak and seal or cover; refrigerate 3 to 5 hours. Remove from marinade and grill, brushing with marinade occasionally during the first 4 minutes of cooking (discard leftover marinade). Approximate grilling time is 4 minutes on each side.

Ginger Martini

Make ginger-infused vodka by combining 1 cup thinly sliced fresh peeled ginger and 4 cups good-quality vodka in glass container. Seal and set in cool, dark location for 2 days, shaking container 2 times a day. Strain and use, or infuse longer if you prefer a stronger ginger taste. To make martini, place ¼ cup ginger vodka in cocktail shaker filled with ice. If desired, add 2 teaspoons premium sake. Cover and shake vigorously. Strain into chilled martini glass and garnish with 2 thin slices of pickled ginger skewered on cocktail pick or a long piece of crystallized ginger draped over the lip of the glass (cut a slice halfway up the middle, then slide the cut portion onto the glass).

Pickled Young Ginger

Wash ½ pound young ginger and pat dry with paper towels. Cut unpeeled across grain to make rounds that are as thin as possible. In glass or ceramic bowl, combine slices with 2½ tablespoons kosher salt. Cover and refrigerate 24 hours. Rinse well with cold water; drain. It will be a potato-brown color; don't worry—it will turn pinkish when pickled. In medium, heavy-bottomed saucepan, combine ginger slices with ¾ cup sugar and 1 cup distilled white vinegar. Bring to boil; reduce heat and simmer 1 minute. Cool. Refrigerate airtight at least 1 day or up to 4 weeks.

Ginger Vinaigrette

This dressing is delicious spooned over cooked vegetables, such as green beans, grilled zucchini, or roasted butternut squash. In medium-small bowl or 4-cup glass measuring cup with handle, combine 2 tablespoons fresh lime juice, 2 tablespoons low-sodium soy sauce, 2 teaspoons minced fresh ginger, 1 large clove garlic (minced), and freshly ground black pepper; whisk in ⅓ cup extra-virgin olive oil. Taste and add salt if needed. Stir in 1 medium shallot (minced), and if desired, 2 teaspoons minced fresh cilantro.

Chicken Saté with Peanut Sauce and Cucumber Raita

YIELD: 24 SKEWERS

Saté (also spelled satay) is an Indonesian favorite consisting of small chunks of meat threaded on skewers and grilled, then served with a spicy peanut sauce. In this recipe the skewers are scattered party-style on a large tray. The peanut butter–based sauce is puddled below the skewered chicken. A garnish of chopped fresh cilantro is added just before serving. And a bowl of cucumber raita is offered on the side; it's a cooling East Indian cucumber-yogurt mixture.

24 bamboo skewers

Marinade

1 tablespoon minced fresh ginger

3 medium cloves garlic, minced

1 tablespoon ground coriander

1 teaspoon salt

⅓ cup vegetable oil

3 tablespoons coconut milk

1 tablespoon sugar

2 pounds skinless, boneless chicken breasts, cut into 2 x ¾ x ¼-inch strips

Sauce

1 cup smooth peanut butter

2 large cloves garlic, minced

2 tablespoons Asian sesame oil

2 tablespoons soy sauce

2 fresh jalapeño chiles, seeded, minced (see Cook's Note)

1 tablespoon sugar

3 tablespoons fresh lime juice

1 cup coconut milk, enough to thin out mixture

Optional: salt

Garnish: minced fresh cilantro

Optional garnish: mango or papaya slices

Optional for serving: Cucumber Raita (page 120)

1 To help to prevent burning, soak bamboo skewers in water for at least 30 minutes.

2 Prepare marinade: Place all marinade ingredients in glass baking dish or medium bowl. Stir to dissolve sugar. Add chicken and toss. Marinate, covered, in refrigerator for 30 minutes.

3 Meanwhile, prepare sauce: Combine all sauce ingredients except coconut milk and salt in food processor fitted with the metal blade. Pulse until mixture is smooth. Add enough coconut milk to thin out sauce to dipping consistency, about 1 cup. Taste and add salt if desired.

4 Heat grill. Remove chicken from marinade and thread onto soaked skewers (discard marinade). Clean grates and coat with vegetable oil. Grill 3 to 5 minutes per side, or until completely cooked through. Cooking times will vary depending on heat of grill. Discard marinade.

5 Make a puddle of sauce on a serving platter. Arrange skewers on top of sauce. Sprinkle on minced cilantro. If desired, garnish with papaya or mango. If desired, accompany with Cucumber Raita.

Nutritional information (per skewer without raita or fruit garnish): Calories 150, fat calories 100; total fat 11 grams, sat fat 4 grams, cholesterol 20 milligrams; sodium 250 milligrams; total carbohydrates 4 grams, fiber 1 gram, sugars 2 grams; protein 11 grams; vitamin A IUs 0%; vitamin C 2%; calcium 2%; iron 2%.

Meatless Tip: Substitute Grilled Tofu with Mediterranean-Style Marinade for chicken, increasing the amount of dried red chile to ½ teaspoon (see page 321).

Cook's Note: If you prefer a spicier dish, do not remove seeds from chiles. Use caution when working with fresh chiles. Wash work surface and hands thoroughly upon completion and do *not* touch face or eyes.

Stir-Fried Baby Bok Choy

YIELD: 6 SERVINGS

Baby bok choy has a mild flavor, more like celery than cabbage. Stir-fried, it becomes temptingly tender, yet stays a bright green color. Serve this dish spooned over your favorite rice. Or for variety, ladle it over cooked orzo tossed with warm couscous.

12 baby bok choy

2 tablespoons dry sherry

2 tablespoons low-sodium soy sauce

2 tablespoons vegetable oil or canola oil, divided use

2 medium cloves garlic, minced

1 tablespoon minced fresh ginger

1 medium-small jicama, peeled, cut into
    1 × ¼ × ¼-inch sticks

For serving: hot cooked rice

1   Wash bok choy under generous amount of cold running water; drain well. Trim small amount of root end from base of each bok choy, keeping the stalk intact. Cut into lengthwise quarters. Take a good look; if they appear to still have any grit or sand, submerge in large bowl of cold water, bobbing them up and down. Drain and pat dry with paper towels or clean towel.

2   In small bowl or cup, combine sherry and soy sauce. Set aside.

3   Place wok or large, deep skillet on high heat. Add 1 tablespoon oil. When oil is hot, cautiously add bok choy. Stir-fry, tossing bok choy quarters until they begin to wilt, about 4 to 5 minutes. If pan seems dry, add remaining oil. Add garlic and ginger; stir-fry 1 minute. Add jicama and sherry mixture; cook until heated through. Serve over hot cooked rice.

Nutritional information (per serving): Calories 100, fat calories 45; total fat 5 grams, sat fat 1 gram, cholesterol 0 milligrams; sodium 350 milligrams; total carbohydrates 11 grams, fiber 6 grams, sugars 3 grams; protein 2 grams; vitamin A IUs 60%; vitamin C 90%; calcium 8%; iron 6%.

Crystallized Ginger

YIELD: 8 OUNCES

Crystallized (often called candied) ginger is cooked in a sugar syrup. Often it is rolled in coarse sugar once it is cooked, but this version leaves it *au naturel*. Use it to flavor ice cream, crème anglaise, fruit salad, or sabayon.

Vegetable oil or canola oil for greasing pan

1 large, wide piece of ginger (about 8 ounces)

2 cups sugar

2 tablespoons water

1   Lightly oil a rimmed baking sheet and set next to stove.

2   Using the edge of a soup spoon or teaspoon, scrape off thin skin of ginger. Remove any knobs or knots with the spoon or with a knife. Slice ginger into ⅛-inch-thick rounds, cutting across the lengthwise fibers. Pierce slices several times with tines of a fork or toothpick.

3   In large, heavy-bottomed, nonreactive saucepan toss ginger and sugar. Add water and stir. Place pan on medium heat and bring just to a simmer. Lower heat and gently simmer for 60 minutes, stirring every 10 minutes to separate ginger as much as possible. Note that in the process, mixture will bubble and eventually crystallize on the edges of the pot; once syrup has thickened and crystals form in center of pan, remove ginger. Place ginger on prepared baking sheet, separating each piece. Allow ginger to cool and dry completely before transferring to an airtight container. Store in airtight container up to 3 weeks.

Nutritional information (per ½ ounce): Calories 110, fat calories 0; total fat 0 grams, sat fat 0 grams, cholesterol 0 milligrams; sodium 0 milligrams; total carbohydrates 8 grams, fiber 0 grams, sugars 25 grams; protein 0 grams; vitamin A IUs 0%; vitamin C 2%; calcium 0%; iron 0%.

Ginger Cookies

YIELD: 32 COOKIES

A double dose of ginger—both crystallized (sometimes called candied) and fresh ginger—give these cookies a gentle spicy edge. As part of an Asian menu, serve them as a finale along with fresh fruit. For a chunkier, crisper cookie, omit the baking soda.

1 cup (2 sticks) unsalted butter, softened

1 cup sugar

½ teaspoon salt

2 eggs

1½ teaspoons vanilla

2 tablespoons finely minced fresh ginger

2½ cups all-purpose flour

½ teaspoon baking soda

3 ounces crystallized ginger, chopped into ⅛-inch pieces, store-bought or homemade (page 146)

Optional garnish: powdered sugar

1   Adjust oven rack to middle position. Preheat oven to 375°F. Line 2 rimmed baking sheets with parchment paper and set aside.

2   In large bowl of electric mixer, beat butter, sugar, and salt on medium-high speed until thoroughly blended and creamy, scraping down sides of bowl as needed with rubber spatula. Add eggs; mix well until blended. Add vanilla and fresh ginger and mix well until blended.

3   In separate medium bowl, combine flour and baking soda. Add to butter mixture; mix until blended. Add crystallized ginger and mix until blended. Drop heaping tablespoons of dough 2 inches apart on baking sheets. Flatten using back of spoon to a ¼-inch thickness. Bake 12 minutes or until lightly browned. Transfer parchment to wire racks; cool completely. If desired, dust cookies lightly with powdered sugar. To get a fine powdery layer atop the cookies, place powdered sugar in sieve and shake sieve over single layer of cookies.

Nutritional information (per cookie): Calories 120, fat calories 50; total fat 6 grams, sat fat 3.5 grams, cholesterol 30 milligrams; sodium 65 milligrams; total carbohydrates 16 grams, fiber 0 grams, sugars 7 grams; protein 1 gram; vitamin A IUs 4%; vitamin C 0%; calcium 0%; iron 4%.

Ginger Cookies

Grape

Grapes are delectable unadorned. Plucked from stem, eaten one by one, they explode with juicy sweetness. But grapes make great team players, too. Tossed into salads, cooked in sauces, or teamed with cheese in appetizers, with their natural sugar and crisp texture, they add an irresistible spark to savory dishes.

Whether they're a frosty lime green or flame-colored red, grapes can turn a humdrum dish into fragrant perfection.

Organic grapes have a shorter shelf life than conventional because no sulfur dioxide fumigation is used. Conventionally grown grapes are often fumigated with sulfur dioxide while in storage.

Organic growers report that cover crops are important in spring to combat weeds and help replace nitrogen in the soil.

BUYING AND STORING: Look for firm grapes that are plump and fragrant. They should be fairly firm, but not rock hard. Grapes are picked ripe; they do not ripen removed from vine. If grapes are detached from stem, look at the area that once surrounded stem; it should be free of discoloration, mold, or soft spots. Avoid shriveled fruit. Store unwashed at room temperature up to 3 days, or in perforated plastic bag in crisper drawer up to 7 days.

PREP AND USE: Rinse well in cold running water before use. Drain or shake off excess water. To serve at table, cut into small bunches with scissors. If cooking grapes with seeds, cut in half and pluck out seeds with tip of small pointed knife. Generally eaten raw out of hand or in salads, but can be cooked. Delicious added to wild rice dressing or atop pizza, paired with an assertive cheese combination such as fontina and soft goat cheese. Or puree grapes and use in sorbet or chilled fruit soup; or use as a garnish atop a custard tart.

AVAILABLE: March to October

NUTRITIONAL INFORMATION (per 1 cup, raw): Calories 104, fat calories 2; total fat 0 grams, sat fat 0 grams, cholesterol 0 milligrams; sodium 3 milligrams; total carbohydrates 27 grams, fiber 1 gram, sugars 23 grams; protein 1 gram; vitamin A IUs 2%; vitamin C 27%; calcium 2%; iron 3%.

SERVING SUGGESTIONS

Roasted Grapes with Brie

Cut ½ pound red seedless grapes into very small clusters (or remove from stems entirely). Place on rimmed baking sheet and drizzle with about 1 tablespoon extra-virgin olive oil (or enough to nicely coat); season with coarse salt, such as kosher, and, if desired, 1 teaspoon minced fresh rosemary leaves. Roast in middle of preheated 500°F oven for about 15 minutes (or until soft inside and slightly crisp on outside). Serve with Brie cheese and thinly sliced baguette (also delicious with roast pork or poultry).

Grape Devils

Try one of these cocktails on a hot afternoon. In a blender, combine ⅓ cup spiced dark rum, 1 cup seedless grapes (use the same color, either all green or all red), 3 cups ice, 2 tablespoons agave syrup, and ¼ cup fresh lime juice. Whirl until blended and slushy. Pour into 2 tall glasses.

Grape Compote with Sweetened Mascarpone

Combine 2 pounds large seedless grapes with ½ cup sugar in large, heavy-bottomed Dutch oven. Add 4 tablespoons undiluted frozen white grape juice concentrate and ¼ teaspoon ground cinnamon; bring to boil on medium-high heat, stirring to dissolve sugar. Reduce heat to medium-low and simmer 10 minutes. Remove grapes with slotted spoon. Simmer syrup 15 more minutes. Cool syrup and grapes; combine and chill. In food processor, combine 8 ounces mascarpone, 4 tablespoons powdered sugar, and 1 teaspoon vanilla; whirl until combined. Divide mascarpone between 6 martini glasses. Top with grape compote and garnish each with a sprig of fresh mint. Accompany with crisp cookies.

Grape Salsa

In medium bowl, combine 1 cup large seedless green grapes (quartered), 1 cup large seedless red grapes (quartered), ½ cup minced sweet onion, 2 jalapeño chiles (seeded, minced), 2 tablespoons chopped fresh cilantro, 2 tablespoons rice wine vinegar, 2 cloves garlic (minced), ⅛ teaspoon salt, and ⅛ teaspoon freshly ground black pepper. Toss; cover and chill 1 to 2 hours. Spoon over grilled chicken, game, or pork or use atop fresh mozzarella cheese on crostini (toasted sliced baguette).

Quick Pork Loin Chops with Grapes

YIELD: 6 SERVINGS

Trimmed of excess exterior fat, slices of boneless pork loin are lean and quick to cook. Fresh grapes bring a sweet-tart punch to the pork, simmering the fruit in a sauce that includes a little Dijon mustard, brown sugar, and brandy.

⅓ cup all-purpose flour

Seasoned salt and freshly ground black pepper

6 (4-ounce) ½-inch-thick slices boneless pork loin, excess fat trimmed (see Meatless Tip)

1 tablespoon extra-virgin olive oil

2 large shallots, minced

1 cup seedless green grapes, halved lengthwise

¼ cup dry white wine

2 teaspoons brandy

¾ cup fat-free low-sodium chicken broth

1½ teaspoons dark brown sugar

1 tablespoon Dijon-style mustard

1   Combine flour and seasoned salt and pepper to taste on rimmed plate or pie pan; toss to combine. Dredge pork in flour mixture, shaking off excess.

2   Heat oil in a large, deep nonstick skillet (the leaner your pork is, the more oil you'll need) over high heat. Add pork in a single layer. Brown on both sides, about 4 to 5 minutes per side. Remove pork from skillet and transfer to a plate.

3   Reduce heat to medium and add shallots and grapes. Cook 4 minutes, stirring occasionally. Increase heat to high and add wine and brandy; cook until all liquid evaporates. Add broth and sugar; cook until liquid is reduced by half.

4   Return pork to skillet in a single layer. Cook on medium-high until pork is heated through and thoroughly cooked, about 3 to 5 minutes. Remove pork from pan; whisk mustard into sauce.

5   Place pork on serving plates and spoon sauce on top. Serve immediately.

Nutrition information (per serving): Calories 250, fat calories 80; total fat 9 grams, sat fat 2.5 grams, cholesterol 65 milligrams; sodium 140 milligrams; total carbohydrates 13 grams, fiber 1 gram, sugars 5 grams; protein 25 grams; vitamin A IUs 2%; vitamin C 6%; calcium 4%; iron 6%.

Meatless Tip: Prepare Grilled Tofu with Mediterranean-Style Marinade (page 321) and set aside. In this recipe, omit steps 1 and 2. Begin step 3 by heating 1 tablespoon canola oil in large, deep nonstick skillet on medium heat. Add shallots and grapes and proceed with recipe. In step 5, spoon sauce over tofu.

Grape and Muscat Wine Cake

YIELD: 10 SERVINGS

A perfect blend of red seedless grapes and muscat wine team up to give this cake a just-right sweetness. It's perfect for every occasion. Whether for dessert after dinner, a breakfast or teatime treat, or hostess gift, this cake will be an unforgettable hit.

3 tablespoons extra-virgin olive oil plus oil for greasing pan

1½ cups all-purpose flour

1 teaspoon baking powder

1 teaspoon salt

¼ teaspoon baking soda

¾ cup plus 2 tablespoons sugar, divided use

6 tablespoons (¾ stick) unsalted butter, softened

2 eggs

1 teaspoon grated lemon zest (colored portion of peel)

1 teaspoon grated orange zest (colored portion of peel)

1 teaspoon vanilla

¾ cup muscat (muscato) wine

2 cups red seedless grapes, divided use

2 tablespoons cold unsalted butter, cut into 6 pieces

For serving: ice cream or whipped cream

Garnish: powdered sugar

Optional garnish: sweetened whipped cream

1   Adjust oven rack to middle position. Preheat oven to 400°F. Brush a 10-inch springform pan with oil. Line bottom with parchment paper and brush paper with oil. Set aside.

2   In medium bowl, place flour, baking powder, salt, and baking soda. With a whisk, mix ingredients together. Set aside.

3   In large bowl of electric mixer, combine ¾ cup sugar, softened butter, and 3 tablespoons oil. Mix on medium-high speed until smooth. Add eggs, both zests, and vanilla; mix until smooth.

4   Add flour mixture alternately with wine in 3 additions each, whisking just until smooth after each addition. Pour into prepared pan; smooth top. Sprinkle 1 cup of grapes on top (place grapes so that there is a 1½-inch border around edge without fruit). Bake in preheated oven for 12 minutes. Sprinkle on remaining grapes. Bake 7 minutes.

5   Meanwhile, combine cold butter and remaining 2 tablespoons sugar in food processor. Pulse until crumbly. Sprinkle over cake, breaking up mixture with fingers. Bake 15 to 20 more minutes or until golden and a toothpick inserted in center comes out clean. Release sides of pan and cool 15 minutes. Serve warm or at room temperature.

6   Be careful not to cut through parchment paper when you cut cake. Serve with ice cream or whipped cream. Dust with powdered sugar.

Nutritional information (per serving without ice cream or whipped cream): Calories 300, fat calories 130; total fat 14 grams, sat fat 7 grams, cholesterol 65 milligrams; sodium 330 milligrams; total carbohydrates 39 grams, fiber 1 gram, sugars 23 grams; protein 3 grams; vitamin A IUs 8%; vitamin C 6%; calcium 4%; iron 6%.

Grape and Muscat Wine Cake

Green Salad with Grapes, Blue Cheese, and Macadamias

YIELD: 4 SERVINGS

The greens used in this salad have an assertive flavor edge. The arugula has a peppery flavor and the crunchy Belgium endive offers a gentle bitterness. The aromatic blue cheese, sweet grapes, and buttery macadamia nuts provide a lovely balance of flavors.

Vinaigrette

2 tablespoons sherry vinegar

1 large shallot, minced

2 teaspoons fresh lemon juice

Salt and freshly ground black pepper to taste

⅓ cup extra-virgin olive oil

Salad

3 cups small arugula leaves

2 Belgian endive, trimmed, and cut on the diagonal into ½-inch slices

⅓ cup crumbled blue cheese, divided use

1 cup seedless grapes, cut in half lengthwise

¼ cup roughly chopped macadamia nuts

1 Prepare vinaigrette: In medium bowl, whisk vinegar, shallot, juice, and salt and pepper to taste. Whisk in oil. Taste and adjust seasoning as needed.

2 Prepare salad: In large bowl, gently toss arugula, endive, about ⅔ of the cheese, and the grapes. Add enough vinaigrette to lightly coat the leaves; toss to combine.

3 Divide salad among 4 plates. Sprinkle with nuts and remaining cheese. Serve immediately.

Nutritional information (per serving): Calories 290, fat calories 230; total fat 26 grams, sat fat 5 grams, cholesterol 10 milligrams; sodium 460 milligrams; total carbohydrates 13 grams, fiber 3 grams, sugars 7 grams; protein 5 grams; vitamin A IUs 10%; vitamin C 15%; calcium 10%; iron 6%.

Grape and Gouda Quesadillas

YIELD: 6 SERVINGS

Wedges of toasted quesadillas make delectable appetizers. The foolproof technique detailed in this recipe begins with toasting tortillas in a skillet, but finishes by heating the filling in the oven atop a parchment-lined baking sheet.

Nonstick vegetable oil or olive oil spray

2 large flour tortillas

8 ounces Gouda cheese, grated

2 cups halved red seedless grapes

2 tablespoons chopped fresh tarragon leaves

1 Adjust oven rack to middle position. Preheat oven to 375°F. Line rimmed baking sheet with parchment paper and set aside.

2 Lightly spray skillet or griddle with nonstick spray. Heat 1 tortilla on medium-high until lightly toasted on both sides. Place on prepared baking sheet. Top with cheese, grapes, and tarragon. Lightly toast the second tortilla and place on top of mixture.

3 Bake in oven until cheese melts, about 3 to 4 minutes. Remove from oven. Cut into 6 wedges (it's best to use a long-bladed knife and cut across the entire tortilla to prevent filling from sliding). Serve warm.

Nutritional information (per wedge): Calories 220, fat calories 100; total fat 11 grams, sat fat 7 grams, cholesterol 45 milligrams; sodium 390 milligrams; total carbohydrates 19 grams, fiber 1 gram, sugars 9 grams; protein 11 grams; vitamin A IUs 6%; vitamin C 10%; calcium 30%; iron 4%.

Grapefruit

There's nothing namby-pamby about grapefruit. The flavor profile can be assertive, with a sassy degree of tartness and a fragrance that defines citrus perfume. In some grapefruit varieties that sourpuss taste is balanced with sweetness. In others, that acidic personality is complex, offering a hint of bitterness along with an elusive pinch of sugary allure.

Organic grapefruit is grown primarily in Arizona, California, and Texas. Heat and mild temperatures are essential to bring nice color to the fruit. Grapefruit skin is softer than that of many other citrus fruits and wind and/or insects can scar it, so organic growers take precautions to protect it.

BUYING AND STORING: Often harvested before reaching maturity, they may have a green-tinged skin. Look for fruit that is fragrant and heavy for its size, a sign that it is laden with juice. It should feel springy when pressed. Store at room temperature in cool, dry location up to 7 days, or refrigerate up to 2 weeks. Juice freezes well.

PREP AND USE: Cut in half and scoop out segments with spoon; or loosen segments from rind with grapefruit knife (serrated knife that is gently curved at end of blade) or grapefruit spoon (spoon that is serrated at tip). To cut into peeled segments, cut off top and bottom ends of fruit, deep enough to expose fruit. Set cut-side down on

cutting board. Cut in strips from top to bottom, following the contour of the fruit, deep enough to remove all pith. Hold fruit over bowl and remove each segment by cutting toward center on either side of each segment membrane. Let each segment fall into bowl. When all segments have been removed, squeeze membrane to extract any remaining juice.

Eat raw or cooked. To eat raw, cut in half and scoop with spoon. Or, sprinkle cut half with raw sugar and broil until caramelized. Use in fruit salads, vinaigrettes, or sorbets. Substitute for oranges in baked goods. Or team it with avocado, pâté, or game.

AVAILABLE: November to September

NUTRITIONAL INFORMATION (per 1 cup sections, raw): Calories 97, fat calories 3; total fat 0 grams, sat fat 0 grams, cholesterol 0 milligrams; sodium 0 milligrams; total carbohydrates 25 grams, fiber 4 grams, sugars 16 grams; protein 2 grams; vitamin A IUs 53%; vitamin C 120%; calcium 5%; iron 1%.

SERVING SUGGESTIONS

Rosemary-Cinnamon–Scented Syrup

Serve this delicious compote with cookies or fingers of buttery pound cake. To make it, combine in large saucepan 1 cup sugar, ¾ cup water, 4 sprigs rosemary, and 1 cinnamon stick. Bring to boil on medium-high heat, stirring to dissolve sugar. Boil 4 minutes. Remove from heat and cool. Cut 4 grapefruit into segments (see Prep and Use), holding over bowl to catch juice. Strain sugar mixture and place in bowl with segments and juice. Chill. If desired, garnish each serving with small rosemary sprig.

Cluck with Spunk

Arrange scoops of chicken salad on a bed of baby greens. Encircle with peeled grapefruit segments and sprinkle with minced fresh basil or parsley.

Crimson Greyhound Cocktail

Divide ⅔ cup pink grapefruit juice, ⅔ cup vodka, and 2 tablespoons pomegranate juice between 2 tall glasses; stir and fill with ice. Garnish with a narrow strip of grapefruit peel.

Chocolate-Dipped Candied Grapefruit Peel

YIELD: ABOUT 20 PIECES, ¼ INCH-WIDE STRIPS ABOUT 1¼-INCHES LONG

Served with coffee or hot tea as an after-dinner treat, candied citrus peel is a refreshing treat, especially appealing if chocolate-dipped. Or use these beauties to garnish cake, cupcakes, or frosted cookies. They can be prepared in advance and stored airtight in a parchment paper–lined plastic container up to 1 week in a cool, dark location.

½ cup sugar

½ cup water

1 medium grapefruit

3 ounces chocolate, chopped (see Cook's Note)

1 Prepare sugar syrup: Place sugar and water in large, heavy-bottomed saucepan. Bring to boil on medium-high heat, stirring to dissolve sugar. When sugar dissolves, remove from heat and set aside.

2 Use a swivel-bladed vegetable peeler to remove grapefruit peel in wide, thin strips, cutting from top to bottom. You want the colored portion of peel, not the white pith. If there is white pith on the underside of strips, turn them over with white portion up. Cautiously

remove white pith with sharp paring knife. Cut strips into narrow, lengthwise strips, about ¼ to ½ inch wide.

3   In a separate large saucepan, bring about 4 cups of water to boil on high heat. Add grapefruit peel strips and boil 1 minute. Drain. Repeat process one more time, boiling strips for 1 minute in clean water and draining. Place strips in single layer on paper towels. Blot dry.

4   Line rimmed baking sheet with parchment paper and set next to stove. Place strips in sugar syrup, in single layer or overlapping slightly. Bring to simmer on medium-high heat. Simmer for 20 minutes or until peel becomes semitranslucent, turning halfway through and adjusting heat to maintain a steady gentle simmer.

5   Remove strips from syrup using slotted spoon and place in single layer on parchment-lined sheet. Allow to dry at least 1 hour.

6   Melt chocolate in top of double boiler over barely simmering water, stirring occasionally. Get the chocolate just warm enough to melt; it should not be hot. Remove from heat. Dip one end of candied peel in melted chocolate. Place on dry sheet of parchment until chocolate hardens.

Nutritional information (per dipped strip): Calories 45, fat calories 15; total fat 2 grams, sat fat 1 gram, cholesterol 0 milligrams; sodium 0 milligrams; total carbohydrates 8 grams, fiber 1 gram, sugars 7 grams; protein 0 grams; vitamin A IUs 0%; vitamin C 6%; calcium 0%; iron 0%.

Cook's Note: Use semisweet or bittersweet chocolate. After dipping, if chocolate doesn't harden after sitting at room temperature (step 6), refrigerate for several minutes.

Jeweled Grapefruit and Avocado Salad

YIELD: 6 SERVINGS

The rich, unctuous taste and texture of a ripe avocado is balanced perfectly with grapefruit's assertive tartness. Add the jewel-red color of pomegranate seeds and you have a salad that is beautiful to look at and delectable to eat.

2 tablespoons extra-virgin olive oil

6 tablespoons rice vinegar

⅛ teaspoon salt

⅛ teaspoon freshly ground black pepper

⅛ teaspoon ground cayenne pepper

2 cups peeled grapefruit segments (see Prep and Use, page 153)

2 ripe avocados, halved, pitted, peeled, cut into lengthwise wedges about ⅜-inch thick

½ cup pomegranate seeds (see Pomegranate, page 272)

1   In small bowl, prepare dressing: Whisk together oil, vinegar, salt, black pepper, and cayenne pepper.

2   On each of 6 salad plates, fan grapefruit segments and avocado slices, alternating each. Sprinkle each with pomegranate seeds. Whisk dressing and taste; adjust seasoning as needed. Drizzle over salads and serve.

Nutritional information (per serving): Calories 160, fat calories 130; total fat 15 grams, sat fat 1.5 grams, cholesterol 0 milligrams; sodium 50 milligrams; total carbohydrates 13 grams, fiber 3 grams, sugars 2 grams; protein 2 grams; vitamin A IUs 4%; vitamin C 60%; calcium 0%; iron 0%.

Texas Ruby Red Grapefruit Pound Cake

YIELD: 12 SLICES

Ruby Red grapefruit juice lends its colorful citrus flavor profile to this dense pound cake. It makes a delicious dessert served with sweetened whipped cream or ice cream, but can stand alone served with tea or as a delicious finale at outdoor gatherings.

- 1 cup plus 2 tablespoons all-purpose flour
- 1 teaspoon baking powder
- ¼ teaspoon salt
- 4 teaspoons minced Ruby Red grapefruit zest (colored portion of peel)
- ⅔ cup fresh Ruby Red grapefruit juice plus 4 teaspoons, divided use
- ½ cup (1 stick) unsalted butter, softened, plus butter for greasing pan
- 1 cup sugar
- 3 large eggs
- ½ teaspoon lemon extract
- 2 tablespoons milk
- ½ cup sifted powdered sugar

1 Adjust oven rack to middle position. Preheat oven to 350°F. Lightly butter a 9 × 5-inch loaf pan; line bottom and long sides with parchment paper. Set aside.

2 In medium bowl, whisk together flour, baking powder, salt, and zest.

3 In large bowl of electric mixer, beat butter until light and fluffy on medium-high speed. Add sugar; beat until well combined, scraping down sides of bowl as needed.

4 Add 2 eggs, one at a time, beating well after each addition. Add lemon extract and remaining egg; beat to combine.

5 By hand, beat in half of the flour mixture. Add milk and ⅔ cup grapefruit juice. The juice will curdle. Blend ingredients well. Add remaining flour mixture and mix just until combined. Do not overmix.

6 Pour batter into prepared pan; smooth top. Bake 55 to 60 minutes or until toothpick inserted in center comes out clean. The top will be glossy. Cool cake in pan on wire rack 20 minutes. Carefully loosen sides and invert. Place on wire rack to cool completely.

7 Prepare glaze: In small bowl, blend powdered sugar and remaining 4 teaspoons grapefruit juice. Drizzle over top of cooled cake, allowing glaze to drip down sides and dry. Cake may be made up to 3 days ahead, cooled, and wrapped in plastic wrap.

Nutritional information (per serving): Calories 220, fat calories 80; total fat 9 grams, sat fat 5 grams, cholesterol 75 milligrams; sodium 110 milligrams; total carbohydrates 33 grams, fiber 0 grams, sugars 22 grams; protein 3 grams; vitamin A IUs 8%; vitamin C 10%; calcium 4%; iron 4%.

Chocolate Cupcakes with Grapefruit Smooches

YIELD: ABOUT 24 STANDARD-SIZE CUPCAKES, OR 10 JUMBO CUPCAKES

Chocolate teams beautifully with the wake-up taste of grapefruit, especially if the fruit's bold flavor profile is softened by using it in an irresistible cream cheese frosting. These cupcakes are a perfect finale for casual gatherings such as picnics, but are elegant enough for dinner party fare.

Cupcakes

- 6½ ounces unsweetened chocolate, chopped
- 2 cups all-purpose flour
- 2 teaspoons baking soda
- 1 cup (2 sticks) unsalted butter, softened

1 cup granulated sugar

1 cup packed light brown sugar

4 large eggs

1 cup buttermilk

1 teaspoon vanilla

Frosting

1 (8-ounce) package cream cheese, softened

½ cup (1 stick) unsalted butter, softened

2 cups sifted powdered sugar

4 teaspoons finely minced grapefruit zest (colored portion of peel)

1 tablespoon fresh grapefruit juice

⅛ teaspoon salt

Optional garnish: Chocolate-Dipped Candied Grapefruit Peel (page 154)

1 Place chocolate in top of double boiler over barely simmering water. Melt chocolate, stirring frequently. Chocolate should only get just hot enough to melt. Remove top pan with chocolate and set aside.

2 Adjust oven rack to middle position. Preheat oven to 350°F. Line muffin tins with paper liners and set aside.

3 Prepare cupcakes: Place flour and baking soda in medium bowl; stir with whisk to combine.

4 In large bowl of electric mixer, beat butter until smooth. Add both sugars; beat until fluffy, about 3 minutes on medium speed. Add eggs 1 at a time, beating between additions to blend. Add melted chocolate and mix to blend on medium speed, stopping to scrape down sides and bottom of bowl with rubber spatula as needed.

5 Add dry ingredients in thirds, alternating with thirds of buttermilk. Scrape down sides and bottom of bowl as needed. Add vanilla and mix until blended. Scrape down sides and bottom with spatula for one last mixing. Spoon batter into muffin tins, filling each no more than ¾ full. Bake 22 to 25 minutes, or until a toothpick inserted in center comes out with only a few dry crumbs. Baking times vary and will take longer if using jumbo-size tins, about 28 to 30 minutes. Set muffin pans on wire racks. Cool 10 minutes and remove from muffin tins. Cool cupcakes on wire rack.

6 Prepare frosting: Place cream cheese and butter in large bowl of electric mixer. Beat on medium-high speed until smooth, about 1 minute.

7 Add powdered sugar 1 cup at a time, beating to blend between additions. Scrape down sides and bottom of bowl with rubber spatula. Add zest, juice, and salt; beat on high speed until blended, about 1 minute. Frost cupcakes. If desired, garnish each with a chocolate-dipped candied grapefruit peel.

Nutritional information (per cupcake without candied peel garnish): Calories 330, fat calories 180; total fat 20 grams, sat fat 12 grams, cholesterol 75 milligrams; sodium 170 milligrams; total carbohydrates 39 grams, fiber 2 grams, sugars 28 grams; protein 4 grams; vitamin A IUs 10%; vitamin C 2%; calcium 4%; iron 10%.

Chocolate Cupcakes with Grapefruit Smooches

Greens

Chard (Green, Rainbow, Red)

Collard

Dandelion

Kale (Common Green)

Mustard

Spinach (Mature, Baby)

Along with vibrant flavor profiles, greens offer unique visual beauty. Red chard looks like a vegetal road map, as the bright-red stalk sends myriad crimson veins throughout the deep green leaf. And it's not just the ruby roadways that make it so dramatic. The glossy leaves ruffle around veins creating irregular folds that look like the texture of a crumpled organdy petticoat. Other chard varieties include common green chard (white stalk and veins) and rainbow chard (several colors of stalks and veins, including orange, pink, purple, and gold).

Collard greens show off paddle-like oval leaves that feel velvety to the touch. Green kale has frilly ruffled edges. Mustard greens have a more delicate, fragile, thin-leaf look; their apple-green leaves are edged in jagged frills.

The deep green leaves of spinach have a smooth edge and are shaped like elongated paddles. And a dandelion leaf, shaped like an elongated arrowhead, has an irregular saw-toothed edge.

When it comes to greens, one of the biggest challenges to organic growers is weed control. Another is mildew, caused by heavy rains or high humidity. Aphids and worms are controlled with beneficial insects.

BUYING AND STORING: Leaves should be brightly colored with no sign of wilting or discoloration. They should smell fresh. Except with spinach, before storing, rinse in tub of cold water; repeat if necessary, until water is clear and free of grit. Shake off excess water or drain, wrap in clean cloth or paper towels, and place in plastic bag. Refrigerate up to 3 days in crisper drawer. If buying clean spinach in cellophane bag, refrigerate in sealed package. If buying loose spinach (not sealed in plastic bags) store unwashed in plastic bag up to 2 days.

PREP AND USE: All greens except spinach should be thoroughly washed before storage (see Buying and Storing). Generally stems are removed from chard, collards, kale, and mustard greens before cooking. Both stem and leaf are edible, but the majority of dishes use just the leafy part. Large chard stalks (including the central vein that runs the length of the leaf) are fleshy and are often treated as a separate vegetable, almost like asparagus; they can be blanched, gratinéed, or braised. If chard stalks are included with the greens, they are generally sliced or diced and are added to cook a few minutes before the leafy part comes to the party.

To remove stalks, cup thumb and fingers around stem below leaf and move cupped hand toward tip of leaf, while holding leaf steady with other hand. Stack several leaves together, then roughly chop or shred. Stems on more tender greens, such as spinach or dandelion, can be pinched off at base of leaves.

Spinach and dandelion greens are eaten raw or cooked. To cook, boil, simmer, sauté, or steam. Team with salty, rich meats, such as bacon, prosciutto, or smoked turkey. Add a spark of acidity as a final touch, either vinegar or lemon juice.

The general rule is that the younger the green, the milder it will taste. Many greens need to be cooked to tame their bold flavor profiles and tenderize their shoe-leather toughness. Long simmering or steaming works, but a few-minute parboil followed with a quick sauté is a great approach. Or in the case of dandelion greens and spinach, a quick toss with hot bacon dressing wilts their tender leaves, coating them rich sweetness. Baby spinach leaves, mild and sweet, are often eaten raw.

AVAILABLE: Year-round (peak is late spring to early summer)

NUTRITIONAL INFORMATION (per 1 cup chopped raw chard): Calories 7, fat calories 1; total fat 0 grams, sat fat 0 grams, cholesterol 0 milligrams; sodium 77 milligrams; total carbohydrates 1 gram, fiber 1 gram, sugars 0 grams; protein 1 gram; vitamin A IUs 44%; vitamin C 18%; calcium 2%; iron 4%.

NUTRITIONAL INFORMATION (per 1 cup chopped raw collard greens): Calories 11, fat calories 1; total fat 0 grams, sat fat 0 grams, cholesterol 0 milligrams; sodium 7 milligrams; total carbohydrates 2 grams, fiber 1 gram, sugars 0 grams; protein 1 gram; vitamin A IUs 48%; vitamin C 21%; calcium 5%; iron 0%.

Chard (Rainbow)

Collard

Kale

Chard (Red)

NUTRITIONAL INFORMATION (per 1 cup chopped raw dandelion greens): Calories 25, fat calories 3; total fat 0 grams, sat fat 0 grams, cholesterol 0 milligrams; sodium 42 milligrams; total carbohydrates 5 grams, fiber 2 grams, sugars 0 grams; protein 1 gram; vitamin A IUs 112%; vitamin C 32%; calcium 10%; iron 9%.

NUTRITIONAL INFORMATION (per 1 cup chopped raw kale): Calories 33, fat calories 4; total fat 0 grams, sat fat 0 grams, cholesterol 0 milligrams; sodium 29 milligrams; total carbohydrates 7 grams, fiber 1 gram, sugars 0 grams; protein 2 grams; vitamin A IUs 206%; vitamin C 134%; calcium 9%; iron 6%.

NUTRITIONAL INFORMATION (per 1 cup chopped raw mustard greens): Calories 15, fat calories 1; total fat 0 grams, sat fat 0 grams, cholesterol 0 milligrams; sodium 14 milligrams; total carbohydrates 3 grams, fiber 2 grams, sugars 1 gram; protein 2 grams; vitamin A IUs 118%; vitamin C 65%; calcium 6%; iron 5%.

NUTRITIONAL INFORMATION (per 1 cup raw spinach): Calories 7, fat calories 1; total fat 0 grams, sat fat 0 grams, cholesterol 0 milligrams; sodium 24 milligrams; total carbohydrates 1 gram, fiber 1 gram, sugars 0 grams; protein 1 gram; vitamin A IUs 56%; vitamin C 14%; calcium 3%; iron 5%.

SERVING SUGGESTIONS

Sautéed Chard Italian-Style

Not only is this a great side dish, room-temperature leftovers are irresistible as an appetizer atop toasted rounds of French baguette. Remove stalks from 3 pounds of clean chard; set stalks aside for another recipe. Stack leaves and cut into thin strips. Place in Dutch oven or large pot with about 3 cups water and pinch of salt; cook on high heat until leaves are tender. Drain well in colander, pressing out excess water (can be refrigerated airtight at this point if desired). Heat ⅓ cup extra-virgin olive oil in large, deep skillet on medium-high heat. Add 2 medium garlic cloves (minced) and pinch dried red pepper flakes. Stir 30 seconds (do not brown garlic). Add chard and cook until heated through, about 4 minutes. Add salt as needed.

Chard and Goat Cheese Omelet

Use chard sautéed Italian-style as an omelet filling along with some crumbled goat cheese.

Rice and Greens

In medium saucepan that has a tight-fitting lid, melt 1 tablespoon butter in 1 tablespoon extra-virgin olive oil on medium-high heat. Add 1 medium onion (chopped) and cook until softened, about 4 minutes, stirring occasionally. Add 1 large clove garlic (minced) and 1 cup long-grained rice such as basmati. Toss rice to coat and cook, stirring occasionally, until starting to turn golden. Add 1½ cups roughly chopped spinach, chard or mustard greens; toss. Add 2 cups vegetable broth or chicken broth; bring to boil. Decrease heat to low, cover and simmer 17 minutes. Remove cover; if all liquid is absorbed, fluff rice with fork. If some liquid remains, remove cover and cook until all moisture is absorbed, then fluff with fork. Add salt and pepper to taste.

Emergency Spinach

Use the microwave to create steamed spinach in about 3 minutes. Place 3 to 5 cups baby spinach in a microwave-safe bowl. Sprinkle with a smidgen of water if leaves are dry. Cover and microwave on high power for 2 to 3 minutes or until leaves are piping hot and wilted. Cautiously remove cover opening it away from you. Toss spinach with a little butter and balsamic vinegar. Season to taste with salt.

Linguine with Baby Spinach and Blue Cheese

YIELD: 8 SERVINGS

Greens are a delectable teammate for pasta. In this recipe, baby spinach pairs with linguine, prosciutto, fresh herbs, and pine nuts. If you like, substitute roughly chopped dandelion leaves for the spinach. Or instead of spinach or dandelion leaves, add Sautéed Chard Italian-Style (see Serving Suggestions).

1 pound linguine

⅓ cup extra-virgin olive oil

6 ounces prosciutto, diced (see Meatless Tip)

2 large garlic cloves, minced

3 tablespoons minced fresh basil leaves

1 (10-ounce) bag baby spinach

4 ounces crumbled blue cheese

½ cup toasted pine nuts (see Cook's Note)

Salt and freshly ground black pepper

Optional garnish: fresh basil leaves

1 Bring large pot of salted water to boil over high heat. Add linguine and cook according to package directions until al dente (tender but with a little bite). Drain.

2 Meanwhile, heat olive oil in a large, deep skillet on medium-high heat. Add prosciutto and garlic. Cook about 2 to 4 minutes or until garlic is softened and starting to lightly brown. Add basil and spinach; cook 1 minute or until spinach starts to wilt, tossing mixture occasionally. Add cooked, drained pasta, cheese, and pine nuts. Toss. Taste and add salt and pepper to taste.

Nutritional information (per serving): Calories 450, fat calories 200; total fat 22 grams, sat fat 5 grams, cholesterol 25 milligrams; sodium 800 milligrams; total carbohydrates 46 grams, fiber 3 grams, sugars 3 grams; protein 19 grams; vitamin A IUs 50%; vitamin C 15%; calcium 10%; iron 20%.

Cook's Note: To toast pine nuts, place them in a small skillet. Place over medium-high heat and toast, shaking handle to redistribute nuts, until lightly browned. Watch carefully because pine nuts burn easily.

Meatless Tip: Omit prosciutto. If desired, top each serving with a small amount of cooked and chopped vegetarian bacon.

Joe's Baked Egg Special

YIELD: 1 SERVING

Virtuous and delicious, not one drop of fat is added to this egg casserole that is named for Joe Hernandez, who created the set of ingredients to suit his palate. The dish has the pizzazz of chile rellenos but without the fat grams. Substitute other vegetables to suit the season and your taste-bud preference.

2 tablespoons finely diced zucchini

1 tablespoon finely diced rapini leaves and buds

2 tablespoons finely diced sweet onion

1 tablespoon finely diced roasted peeled fresh poblano chile (see Bell Pepper, page 64, see Cook's Note)

½ jalapeño chile, seeded, minced (see Cook's Note)

½ Roma tomato, cored, seeded, finely diced

1 tablespoon water

1 tablespoon coarsely chopped baby spinach

Optional: ½ teaspoon salt

6 egg whites

1 Adjust oven rack to middle position. Preheat oven to 400°F. Place zucchini, rapini, onion, chiles, tomato, and water in medium skillet. Cook on medium-low heat, stirring occasionally, until vegetables are tender. Toss in spinach and remove from heat. If desired, season with salt.

2 In medium bowl, whisk egg whites until just starting to get frothy. Add egg whites to vegetable mixture; stir to combine. Place in 2-cup gratin dish.

3 Bake for 30 minutes, or until nicely browned and knife inserted in center comes out clean.

Nutritional information (per serving): Calories 130, fat calories 5; total fat 0.5 grams, sat fat 0 grams, cholesterol 0 milligrams; sodium 340 milligrams; total carbohydrates 7 grams, fiber 1 gram, sugars 4 grams; protein 23 grams; vitamin A IUs 25%; vitamin C.

Cook's Note: Use caution when working with fresh chiles. Wash hands and work surface thoroughly upon completion and do *not* touch eyes or face.

Joe's Baked Egg Special

Stir-Fried Tofu with Mustard Greens

YIELD: 4 SERVINGS

As with all stir-fry dishes, make sure to have all your ingredients ready to go before you begin. If mustard greens are wet, shake them dry as much as possible, but don't worry if some water remains on the leaves. When you add them to the hot mixture, make sure you are cautious because the oil may sputter when you add the first handful. So stand back and add it cautiously. If you prefer spicy dishes, add a good pinch of dried red chile flakes when you add the garlic and ginger.

3 tablespoons canola oil or vegetable oil, divided use

1 medium yellow onion, cut in half from top to bottom, thinly sliced

1 large clove garlic, minced

1 tablespoon minced fresh ginger

2½ cups coarsely chopped stemmed mustard greens

1½ pounds extra-firm tofu patted dry with paper towels, cut into ¾-inch cubes

3 tablespoons dry sherry

½ cup vegetable broth or chicken broth

2½ tablespoons low-sodium soy sauce

2 green onions, cut into ¼-inch thick diagonal slices, including dark green stalks

Optional for serving: cooked rice

1 tablespoon toasted sesame seeds (see Cook's Note)

1 Heat 2 tablespoons canola oil or vegetable oil on high heat in wok or large, deep nonstick skillet. Add onion and cook, stirring frequently, until softened and starting to brown. Stir in garlic and ginger; cook 20 seconds (do *not* brown). Add mustard greens a handful at a time, stirring to combine. Stir until greens are heated through and wilted. Off heat, remove with slotted spoon to bowl.

2 Return wok to heat and add remaining 1 tablespoon oil; tilt pan to swirl oil to coat sides. When oil is hot, add tofu. Cook, tossing occasionally until tofu browns. Add sherry and broth; cook, stirring frequently, until approximately half of liquid evaporates. Add mustard green mixture; toss and cook until greens heated through. Add soy sauce and green onions; toss. If desired, serve over cooked rice. Garnish with sesame seeds and serve.

Nutritional information (per serving without rice): Calories 290, fat calories 190; total fat 21 grams, sat fat 1.5 grams, cholesterol 0 milligrams; sodium 330 milligrams; total carbohydrates 10 grams, fiber 3 grams, sugars 3 grams; protein 19 grams; vitamin A IUs 80%; vitamin C 50%; calcium 35%; iron 20%.

Cook's Note: To toast sesame seeds, place in small skillet over medium-high heat. Shake handle to redistribute seeds as they toast to light brown. Watch carefully because they burn easily.

Bulgar Pilaf with Baby Spinach

YIELD: 4 SIDE-DISH SERVINGS

Spinach adds a welcome herbal note to bulgur pilaf. In this version, small pieces of fideo or vermicelli pasta are added to give it an appealing starchy balance to the bulgur wheat. Bulgur wheat is ground from steamed and dried wheat kernels. It can be found in Middle Eastern markets, health food stores, and some supermarkets. It is sold in coarse, medium, and fine grinds.

2 tablespoons unsalted butter

2 tablespoons extra-virgin olive oil

1 large yellow onion, chopped

½ cup 1-inch long fideo or vermicelli

1 cup medium-grind bulgur wheat

Seasoned salt and freshly ground black pepper

2⅓ cups boiling chicken broth or vegetable broth

1¾ cups coarsely chopped baby spinach

1 Place butter and oil in large saucepan that has a tight-fitting lid. Melt butter on medium-high heat. Add onion and cook until softened, stirring occasionally, about 4 to 5 minutes. Add fideo or vermicelli and toss to coat; cook, stirring frequently, for 1 minute. Stir in bulgur and seasoned salt and pepper to taste. Add boiling broth, cover, and reduce heat to low. Simmer, covered, 10 minutes.

2 Add spinach, but don't stir it in. Cover and remove from heat. Allow to sit off heat for 15 minutes. Toss. Taste; adjust seasoning as needed and serve.

Nutritional information (per serving): Calories 240, fat calories 60; total fat 6 grams, sat fat 3.5 grams, cholesterol 15 milligrams; sodium 280 milligrams; total carbohydrates 40 grams, fiber 8 grams, sugars 2 grams; protein 7 grams; vitamin A IUs 20%; vitamin C 10%; calcium 4%; iron 10%.

Herbs

Arugula

Basil

Chives

Cilantro

Dill

Mint

Oregano

Parsley (Curly, Italian)

Rosemary

Sage

Thyme

Fresh herbs echo the taste and aroma of the garden. These fragrant, flavorful leaves add much more pizzazz than their dried counterparts. Grown in hothouse or field, fresh herbs are essential ingredients in myriad dishes.

Organic herb growers often use sectional crop rotation to control pests; small patches of herbs that deter pests are planted next to herbs that attract pests. Plants such as hedge roses and alyssums are also planted to attract beneficial insects. With field-grown herbs, weeding is done by hand, and blowtorch-like burners are often employed to eliminate unwanted growth.

Rosemary

Dill

Chives

Oregano

Rosemary

Oregano

Sage

Dill

Thyme

Arugula: Pronounced ah-ROO-guh-lah, it delivers a taste that is pleasingly tart and peppery. It is often used as a salad green teamed with fruity olive oil and cheese. The leaves are crisp yet tender. If purchased in bunches, cut off roots and any thick stems, then dunk leaves up and down in bowl of cold water. Rinse out bowl and repeat. Spin leaves dry or drain well and pat dry, and then wrap in kitchen towel, enclose in plastic bag, and chill in crisper drawer.

Basil: Highly fragrant, these soft, pointed leaves of sweet basil balance notes of both citrus and licorice. Use raw or as finishing herb in cooked dishes, adding it during the last 5 to 10 minutes of cooking.

Chives: These grass-green, lanky leaves are tubular with pointed tips. Because they grow in clumps they are referred to in the plural. They have a delicate but pronounced onion scent and flavor. Use raw as a garnish (most often thinly sliced), or use as a more mildly flavored replacement for onions in cold dishes.

Cilantro: This is a "love it" or "hate it" herb. To some it is pleasingly aromatic with a refreshing, slightly peppery finish. To some it tastes soapy. The bright green leaves look like Italian flat-leaf parsley, but with feathery edges. Use raw or as finishing herb in cooked dishes, adding it during the last 5 minutes of cooking. The seeds are known as coriander.

Dill: These feathery green fronds have a distinct flavor that is refreshing and slightly lemon-like with an aroma that is reminiscent of caraway seeds. They look much like the fronds atop fresh fennel but are much more aromatic. Use raw or as finishing herb in cooked dishes, adding it during the last 5 minutes of cooking.

Mint: The sweet summery taste and distinctive aroma of these bright green leaves make them an essential ingredient in many sweet and savory dishes. Use raw in cold dishes, such as salads or wraps, or use as a finishing herb during the last 3 minutes of cooking. Or use as a garnish on beverages, desserts, compotes, fish, and lamb.

Oregano: These slightly fuzzy leaves have a musty, earthy taste that is a distinctive part of the flavor profiles of many Mediterranean dishes. Generally the leaves are removed from their tough stems, chopped, and added at the beginning of cooking.

Parsley (Curly and Italian): Curly-leaf parsley has a straightforward vegetal taste that is milder than flat-leafed Italian parsley. Italian parsley is the choice of most cooks because its flavor profile is more intense, relegating the curly kind for garnishing. Italian parsley is generally chopped and can be added to dishes during the last 10 minutes of cooking. Sometimes it is used two times in a recipe, during cooking and as a chopped garnish as well.

Rosemary: With its distinct aroma, both pine-like and lemony, these gray-green needle-shaped leaves are used in moderation to impart a floral, somewhat sweet taste. Pulled from their woody stem, the leaves are generally chopped or minced and added during the last 30 minutes of cooking. If whole sprigs are added, they are removed and discarded before serving.

Sage: With its earthy, somewhat lemony flavor and camphor-like aroma, sage complements a wide range of dishes. Most commonly thought of as a distinctive ingredient in poultry seasoning, breakfast sausages, and Thanksgiving stuffing, it is also delicious paired with roasted apples, game, and vegetables. Raw, it can have a fuzzy texture, so it should be cooked rather than eaten raw.

Thyme: The deep, grassy taste of garden thyme with its pleasant lemony aroma adds distinctive flavor to dressings, soups, and sauces, as well as poultry, meat, and vegetables. Most often it is added to dishes early in the cooking process; generally the leaves are removed from their woody stems before their addition, but sometimes the entire sprig is added and then fished out and discarded at the end of cooking.

BUYING AND STORING: Look for herbs that look and smell fresh and clean. Avoid any that look wilted or discolored. Use as soon after purchase as possible; most will keep up to 5 days; however, herbs with thick stems, such as rosemary or thyme, will last a little longer. For everything except arugula, refrigerate unwashed in crisper drawer loosely wrapped in barely damp paper towel enclosed in plastic bag. With softer-leaved herbs, such as basil or mint, wilted leaves can sometimes be revived by submerging herbs in an ice-water bath. If arugula is purchased in bunches, cut off roots and any thick stems, then dunk leaves up and down in bowl of very cold water. Rinse out bowl and repeat. Spin leaves dry or drain well and pat dry, and then wrap in kitchen towel, enclose in plastic bag, and chill.

PREP AND USE: Wash herbs in cold running water; shake dry and blot with paper towels. Soft-leaved herbs, such as basil or mint, chop more easily if they are very dry. To slice or chop, stack about 10 leaves on top of each other; roll into a cylinder and cut crosswise into slender slices. These skinny slices can be easily chopped or minced. Leaves of herbs with thick stems, such as rosemary or thyme, should be pulled off the stem before using. Thick stems of rosemary can be used as skewers for kebobs. The delicate leaves of mint and basil can bruise and discolor; chop or shred just before adding to dishes.

Many herbs lose flavor and aroma with long cooking, so they are added toward the end of cooking. Some cooks like to add some at the beginning of cooking and add more close to the end of the cooking.

AVAILABLE: Year-round

NUTRITIONAL INFORMATION (per 1 ounce raw arugula): Calories 7, fat calories 2; total fat 0 grams, sat fat 0 grams, cholesterol 0 milligrams; sodium 8 milligrams; total carbohydrates 1 gram, fiber 0 grams, sugars 1 gram; protein 1 gram; vitamin A IUs 13%; vitamin C 7%; calcium 4%; iron 2%.

NUTRITIONAL INFORMATION (per 1 ounce raw basil leaves): Calories 6, fat calories 1; total fat 0 grams, sat fat 0 grams, cholesterol 0 milligrams; sodium 1 milligram; total carbohydrates 1 gram, fiber 0 grams, sugars 0 grams; protein 1 gram; vitamin A IUs 30%; vitamin C 8%; calcium 5%; iron 5%.

NUTRITIONAL INFORMATION (per 1 ounce raw chives): Calories 8, fat calories 2; total fat 0 grams, sat fat 0 grams, cholesterol 0 milligrams; sodium 1 milligram; total carbohydrates 1 gram, fiber 1 gram, sugars 1 gram; protein 1 gram; vitamin A IUs 24%; vitamin C 27%; calcium 3%; iron 2%.

NUTRITIONAL INFORMATION (per 1 ounce raw cilantro): Calories 6, fat calories 1; total fat 0 grams, sat fat 0 grams, cholesterol 0 milligrams; sodium 13 milligrams; total carbohydrates 1 gram, fiber 1 gram, sugars 0 grams; protein 1 gram; vitamin A IUs 38%; vitamin C 13%; calcium 2%; iron 3%.

NUTRITIONAL INFORMATION (per 1 ounce raw dill): Calories 12, fat calories 3; total fat 0 grams, sat fat 0 grams, cholesterol 0 milligrams; sodium 17 milligrams; total carbohydrates 2 grams, fiber 1 gram, sugars 0 grams; protein 1 gram; vitamin A IUs 43%; vitamin C 40%; calcium 6%; iron 10%.

NUTRITIONAL INFORMATION (per 1 ounce raw mint): Calories 12, fat calories 2; total fat 0 gram, sat fat 0 gram; cholesterol 0 milligrams; sodium 8 milligrams; total carbohydrates 2 grams, fiber 2 grams, sugars 0 grams; protein 1 gram; vitamin A IUs 23%; vitamin C 6%; calcium 6%; iron 18%.

NUTRITIONAL INFORMATION (per 1 tablespoon raw oregano leaves): Calories 5, fat calories 0; total fat 0 grams, sat fat 0 grams, cholesterol 0 milligrams; sodium 0 milligrams; total carbohydrates 1 gram, fiber 0 grams, sugars 0 grams; protein 0 grams; vitamin A IUs 2%; vitamin C 4%; calcium 2%; iron 2%.

NUTRITIONAL INFORMATION (per 1 tablespoon raw parsley): Calories: 1, fat calories 0; total fat 0 grams, sat fat 0 grams, cholesterol 0 milligrams; sodium 2 milligrams; total carbohydrates 0 grams, fiber 0 grams, sugars 0 grams; protein 0 grams; vitamin A IUs 6%; vitamin C 8%; calcium 1%; iron 1%.

NUTRITIONAL INFORMATION (per 1 tablespoon raw rosemary leaves): Calories 5, fat calories 0; total fat 0 grams, sat fat 0 grams, cholesterol 0 milligrams; sodium 0 milligrams; total carbohydrates 0 grams, fiber 0 grams, sugars 0 grams; protein 0 grams; vitamin A IUs 2%; vitamin C 0%; calcium 0%; iron 0%.

NUTRITIONAL INFORMATION (per 1 tablespoon raw sage leaves): Calories 0, fat calories 0; total fat 0 grams, sat fat 0 grams, cholesterol 0 milligrams; sodium 0 milligrams; total carbohydrates 0 grams, fiber 0 grams, sugars 0 grams; protein 0 grams; vitamin A IUs 0%; vitamin C 0%; calcium 2%; iron 2%.

NUTRITIONAL INFORMATION (per 1 teaspoon raw thyme leaves): Calories 1, fat calories 0; total fat 0 grams, sat fat 0 grams, cholesterol 0 milligrams; sodium 0 milligrams; total carbohydrates 0 grams, fiber 0 grams, sugars 0 grams; protein 0 grams; vitamin A IUs 1%; vitamin C 2%; calcium 0%; iron 1%.

SERVING SUGGESTIONS

Getting It under the Skin

Tuck a little chopped prosciutto, minced garlic, and chopped fresh rosemary leaves under the skin of a turkey. As it roasts, the turkey develops a tempting fragrance and flavor.

Cannellini Bean Dip

In food processor fitted with a metal blade with the motor running, drop 1 large peeled garlic clove and 2 teaspoons chopped rosemary leaves in feed tube; process until finely minced. Add 1 (15-ounce) can cannellini beans (drained), minced zest of 1 lemon (colored portion of peel), ¼ cup extra-virgin olive oil, and plenty of freshly ground black pepper. Serve with tortilla chips or raw vegetables such as carrots, celery, or jicama sticks.

Basil-Parsley Pesto

In food processor, finely chop 2 cups fresh basil leaves and 2 cups fresh Italian parsley. Add about 6 cloves roasted garlic (see Garlic Prep and Use, page 139), 2 tablespoons toasted pine nuts, and ¼ cup grated Parmesan cheese; process until finely chopped. Add ⅓ cup extra-virgin olive oil, plus salt and freshly ground black pepper to taste; process until smooth. Toss with cooked vegetables or pasta.

Roast Chicken with Rosemary

Preheat oven to 425°F. Place 4 dry rosemary branches in shallow pan big enough to hold chicken. Wash 3-pound fryer with cold running water, including the cavity; pat dry thoroughly with paper towels. Sprinkle salt and freshly ground black pepper in cavity. Place 2 peeled garlic cloves, 1 tablespoon chopped fresh rosemary leaves, and ½ lemon in cavity. Place chicken on top of rosemary branches in the baking pan. Drizzle 1 tablespoon extra-virgin olive oil over top of chicken. Season with salt and generous amount of freshly ground black pepper. Roast 20 minutes. Reduce temperature to 350°F. Roast 60 minutes. Stick instant-read thermometer into thickest part of thigh beneath, but not touching, bone, reaching down to joint. It should read 170°F to 175°F. Let chicken rest 5 minutes before carving.

Rosemary Shortbread

YIELD: 12 SERVINGS

Homemade shortbread is delicious served with ice cream or sorbet. Team the basic dough with chopped fresh rosemary and the crisp, buttery cookie takes on a sophisticated herbal edge.

½ cup unsalted butter, softened

⅓ cup sugar

Pinch salt

1 teaspoon vanilla

1 cup all-purpose flour

2 teaspoons finely chopped fresh rosemary leaves

1 Adjust oven rack to middle position. Preheat oven to 300°F. Line a baking sheet with parchment paper.

2 In large bowl of electric mixer, beat butter on low speed until light in color, about 1 minute. Add sugar, salt and vanilla; beat until well combined, about 1 minute on medium speed, scraping down sides of bowl with rubber spatula as needed.

3 Add flour and beat on medium speed until blended. Add rosemary and mix until well distributed throughout dough.

4 Pat dough into a 7½-inch disk on parchment paper–lined baking sheet. Score edge with tines of fork or crimp decoratively. Prick shortbread decoratively with tines of fork. Use sharp knife to make shallow indentations where shortbread will be cut into 12 wedges. Bake for 35 to 40 minutes or until golden around the edges. Slide shortbread on parchment onto wire rack. Cool.

5 Transfer to cutting board. Cut into 12 wedges following shallow indentation made before baking.

Nutritional information (per wedge): Calories 130, fat calories 70; total fat 8 grams, sat fat 5 grams, cholesterol 20 milligrams; sodium 20 milligrams; total carbohydrates 14 grams, fiber 0 grams, sugars 6 grams; protein 1 gram; vitamin A IUs 4%; vitamin C 0%; calcium 0%; iron 2%.

Asian Noodle Salad

YIELD: 6 SERVINGS

Baby spinach gives this pasta-based salad a vibrant, fresh taste. Make the dressing and cut up the vegetables while the spaghetti cooks.

1 pound spaghetti, strands broken in half

⅓ cup smooth peanut butter

¼ cup hot water

2 tablespoons honey

4 tablespoons fresh lime juice

2 large cloves garlic, minced

2 teaspoons hot sauce

3 tablespoons vegetable oil or canola oil

¾ cup shredded peeled carrots

1½ cups shredded cooked chicken (see Meatless Tip)

5 green onions, trimmed, thinly sliced, including ½ dark green stalks (reserve unused stalks for garnish)

3 tablespoons chopped fresh cilantro

3 cups baby spinach leaves

Garnish: ⅓ cup chopped, dry-roasted, unsalted peanuts

1 Bring a large pot of salted water to boil on high heat. Add spaghetti and cook according to package directions until pasta is al dente (tender but with a little bite). Drain and refresh with cold water. Drain.

2 Meanwhile, prepare dressing: In medium bowl, vigorously stir peanut butter, water, and honey together until smooth. Add lime juice, garlic, hot sauce, and oil; whisk to combine.

3 In large bowl, combine spaghetti, dressing, carrots, chicken, green onions, and cilantro: gently toss. Add spinach and gently toss. Divide between 4 bowls. Top with peanuts and reserved green onions. Serve immediately.

Nutritional information (per serving): Calories 570, fat calories 190; total fat 21 grams, sat fat 3 grams, cholesterol 25 milligrams; sodium 500 milligrams; total carbohydrates 71 grams, fiber 5 grams, sugars 10 grams; protein 26 grams; vitamin A IUs 70%; vitamin C 20%; calcium 6%; iron 25%.

Meatless Tip: Omit chicken; if desired, add Grilled Tofu with Asian-Style Marinade (see page 321). Or serve with grilled portobello mushrooms.

Cheddar-Thyme Crisps

Cheddar-Thyme Crisps

YIELD: ABOUT 50 CRISPS

These tasty cocktail crisps can be addictive. It's almost impossible to eat just one. Serve them with a glass of chilled bone-dry sherry or Sauvignon Blanc and grapes. They are at their crispy best served within hours of baking, but if storing, layer them between sheets of parchment paper in an airtight container for up to 2 days.

2 ½ ounces white cheddar cheese, grated, about 3 ¼ cups

3 ounces Parmesan cheese, grated, grated, about 1 cup plus 2 tablespoons

2 ounces shelled, roasted, salted pistachio nuts, coarsely chopped, about ½ cup

2 tablespoons finely chopped fresh thyme leaves

1   Adjust oven rack to middle position. Preheat oven to 400°F. Line 2 baking sheets with parchment paper. You will need to use new parchment paper with each batch.

2   Combine cheeses in small bowl. Drop the mixture by rounded teaspoonfuls onto lined baking sheets, leaving about 1½ inches between them. Add a small portion of pistachios to each pile. Flatten each pile slightly with back of spoon. Add a little thyme to each.

3   Bake 5 minutes or until crisps are bubbling and edges are golden. Allow to stand for several minutes, then slide off paper with a thin metal spatula. Blot crisps gently with paper towels and serve at room temperature.

Nutritional information (per serving): Calories 20, fat calories 10; total fat 1.5 grams, sat fat 0.5 gram, cholesterol 5 milligrams; sodium 40 milligrams; total carbohydrates 0 grams, fiber 0 grams, sugars 0 grams; protein 1 gram; vitamin A IUs 0%; vitamin C 0%; calcium 2%; iron 0%.

Rice and Pecan Sage Stuffing

YIELD: 8 SERVINGS

This rice-based stuffing can be augmented with diced tart apples. Use it for stuffing a turkey or duck, or place in a buttered casserole (covered with sheet of buttered foil) and bake 15 to 20 minutes in a 350°F oven.

¼ cup (½ stick) unsalted butter, divided use

1 tablespoon extra-virgin olive oil

1 large yellow onion, chopped

3 large stalks celery, chopped

3 large garlic cloves, minced

Salt and freshly ground black pepper

½ pound fresh mushrooms, such as cremini or common white (button) mushrooms, sliced

2 teaspoons minced fresh sage leaves

6 cups cooked long-grain rice, such as basmati

1½ cups toasted pecans, coarsely chopped (see Cook's Note)

½ cup minced fresh Italian parsley

¼ teaspoon ground nutmeg

1   In a large, deep skillet, melt 2 tablespoons butter in oil over medium-high heat. Add onion and celery; cook, stirring frequently, until onion softens, about 8 minutes. Season with salt and pepper to taste; place in large bowl.

2   In same skillet melt remaining 2 tablespoons butter. Add mushrooms and cook on medium heat until mushrooms are softened and starting to brown, about 5 minutes. Add sage and cook 1 minute. Add to onion mixture. Add remaining ingredients; toss. Taste and add more salt and pepper if needed.

Nutritional information (per serving): Calories 400, fat calories 220; total fat 24 grams, sat fat 5 grams, cholesterol 15 milligrams; sodium 25 milligrams; total carbohydrates 42 grams, fiber 4 grams, sugars 3 grams; protein 7 grams; vitamin A IUs 10%; vitamin C 15%; calcium 6%; iron 15%.

Cook's Note: To toast pecans, place on rimmed baking sheet in a single layer. Toast in a 350°F oven for about 5 minutes or until lightly toasted. Watch nuts carefully because they can burn easily.

Jicama

Inside the thin, tan-colored skin, jicama's juicy white flesh has the crunchy texture of a crisp apple. It is shaped like a very plump turnip that is flattened at the top and bottom. Pronounced HEE-kah-mah, this tuber has a taste that is a cross between a water chestnut and an apple.

Organic growers do not allow post-harvest chlorine baths for their jicamas, a process that is customary with conventionally grown jicama crops; due to the no-chlorine policy, organic jicamas have a shorter shelf life. Farmers using organic methods use seaweed-based fertilizers and fish emulsions to enrich the soil. And beneficial insects are used to control unwanted pests.

BUYING AND STORING: Small or medium-size jicamas are often the best (large, thick-skinned jicama can be dry, fibrous, and pulpy at the center). Avoid those with cracks or shriveling. Store whole in cool location for several days, or refrigerate up to three weeks. Once cut, cover tightly with plastic wrap and refrigerate; use within 1 week.

PREP AND USE: Remove skin: Cut off top and bottom. Place cut side down on cutting board. Working from top to bottom and following contour of vegetable, cut off skin in strips. Or using a small paring knife, catch skin at cut top and pull down toward bottom; long jagged portions of skin can be removed this way.

Cut into desired shape: cubes, slices, or sticks. Seal airtight in plastic to prevent drying and refrigerate.

Generally eaten raw, but can be cooked. Use raw in salads, as a snack or use as dippers with creamy dips such as hummus. Substitute for water chestnuts in Asian salads and stir-fries.

AVAILABLE: April to June

NUTRITIONAL INFORMATION (per 1 cup cubed, raw): Calories 49, fat calories 1; total fat 0 grams, sat fat 0 grams, cholesterol 0 milligrams; sodium 5 milligrams; total carbohydrates 11 grams, fiber 6 grams, sugars 2 grams; protein 1 gram; vitamin A IUs 1%; vitamin C 44%; calcium 2%; iron 4%.

SERVING SUGGESTIONS

Street Style

Cut peeled jicama into sticks. Arrange with wedges of unpeeled orange, sliced mango, and cucumber sticks. Squeeze fresh lime juice on top and lightly sprinkle with chile powder. For more spice, add a smidgen of ground cayenne pepper. Sprinkle with coarse salt.

Jicama and Celery Stir-Fry

Use this as a vegetable side dish. Cut 1 medium bunch trimmed celery into ¼-inch-thick crosswise slices. Cut 1 peeled medium jicama into sticks (about ¼ × ¼ × 1 inch). Heat 2 tablespoons canola oil in large, deep skillet on medium-high heat; add celery and cook 3 minutes, tossing occasionally. Add jicama; cook, stirring frequently, for 3 minutes. Add 1 large clove garlic (minced) and cook 2 more minutes, stirring frequently. Remove from heat and toss in ¼ cup chopped fresh Italian parsley, 2 teaspoons minced fresh tarragon leaves, 1 teaspoon grated lemon zest (colored portion of peel), and fresh lemon juice to taste. Season with salt and freshly ground black pepper.

Salsa-Topped Stars

These appetizers show off jicama's crunchy texture. Peel a medium jicama and cut crosswise into 1-inch-thick slices. Use a ¾-inch-wide star cutter to cut into star shapes. Cautiously cut each 1-inch-thick star horizontally into thin star-shaped slices. Arrange in a single layer and season with seasoned salt. Top each with a dollop of Grape Salsa (page 149), or your favorite fruit salsa.

Pasta, Bean, and Jicama Salad

In large bowl, combine 8 ounces penne pasta (cooked, drained, cooled), 1 (15-ounce) can pinto beans (drained, rinsed), 1 small jicama (peeled, diced), 1 cup grape tomatoes (halved), and 1 small red onion (diced). Toss with enough Snappy-Spicy Lime Vinaigrette (page 201) to coat ingredients. Add 1 ripe avocado (peeled, pitted, diced); gently toss and serve.

Jicama and Orange Salad with Honey-Citrus Vinaigrette

YIELD: 8 SERVINGS

A great choice for a spicy Mexican-themed meal, this salad has a sweet, fruity edge that is balanced with a little fiery ground cayenne pepper. The peeled oranges sections (supremes) and jicama sticks marinate for a short time in the flavorful dressing and then serve as a tasty crown atop the baby greens. Start the recipe by cutting the oranges into supremes over a bowl to collect the juice (see page 324): use the reserved juice as part of the juice needed for the vinaigrette. Add olive oil to taste as needed.

Vinaigrette

2 cups fresh orange juice

¼ cup red wine vinegar

3 tablespoons fresh lime juice

3 tablespoons honey or agave syrup

¼ teaspoon ground cayenne pepper

2 tablespoons finely chopped fresh cilantro

Salt and freshly ground black pepper

Salad

4 oranges, cut into peeled sections

1 medium jicama, peeled, cut into 1 × ¼ × ¼-inch matchsticks

10 to 12 cups mixed baby greens

¼ cup finely chopped fresh cilantro

Salt and freshly ground black pepper

Garnish: about ⅓ cup shelled, toasted, salted
   sunflower seeds

1   In medium bowl, whisk together the first 4 ingredients
for the vinaigrette until well blended. Taste and add more
honey or agave syrup if needed to make a slightly sweet
dressing. Mix in cayenne pepper, cilantro, and salt and
black pepper. Set aside.

2   Place orange sections and jicama in separate bowls.
Pour about ¼ cup vinaigrette over each, gently toss, and
marinate at room temperature for 30 minutes.

3   Place greens in large bowl; add ¼ cup cilantro
and season with salt and pepper to taste. Add enough
vinaigrette to lightly coat leaves. Place on salad plates. Top
each serving with orange segments and jicama. Sprinkle
sunflower seeds over each salad.

Nutritional information (per serving): Calories 130, fat calories 30;
total fat 3.5 grams, sat fat 0 grams, cholesterol 0 milligrams; sodium
30 milligrams; total carbohydrates 23 grams, fiber 4 grams, sugars
17 grams; protein 4 grams; vitamin A IUs 50%; vitamin C 140%;
calcium 8%; iron 10%.

Jicama and Watermelon Salad with Fresh Herb Dressing

YIELD: 8 SERVINGS

This crunchy salad is filled with complementary sweet,
sour, and herbal notes. It is a lovely accompaniment
to spicy dishes, such as grilled carne asada, barbecued ribs,
or grilled tri-tip slathered with piquant sauce. If you like,
substitute diced mango for the watermelon, or simply add
some to the mixture.

½ cup plus 1 tablespoon fresh lime juice

1 tablespoon agave syrup, honey, or sugar

1 teaspoon salt

3 tablespoons chopped fresh cilantro leaves

¼ cup chopped fresh mint leaves

¼ cup chopped fresh basil leaves

2½ cups ½-inch-diced, peeled jicama

4 cups ½-inch-diced seeded watermelon

1 hothouse (English) cucumber, cut into ½-inch dice

½ cup microgreens

1   In large bowl, combine juice, agave syrup or honey or
sugar, and salt. Stir to dissolve salt.

2   Add cilantro, mint, basil, jicama, watermelon, and
cucumber. Gently toss. Taste and adjust seasoning,
adding a little more salt and/or lime juice if needed. Place
on salad plates and sprinkle individual servings with a
small amount of microgreens.

Nutritional information (per serving): Calories 50, fat calories 0;
total fat 0 grams, sat fat 0 grams, cholesterol 0 milligrams; sodium
300 milligrams; total carbohydrates 13 grams, fiber 3 grams, sugars
8 grams; protein 1 gram; vitamin A IUs 15%; vitamin C 40%;
calcium 2%; iron 4%.

Jicama and Watermelon Salad with Fresh Herb Dressing

Chinese New Year Stir-Fry

YIELD: 6 SERVINGS

Before you start any stir-fry dish, make sure to have all the ingredients sitting next to the stove and ready to go. This bright-colored concoction makes a great addition to an Asian New Year feast. Serve it spooned over cooked rice.

2 tablespoons canola oil

½ medium sweet onion, diced

3 medium garlic cloves, minced

1 teaspoon minced fresh ginger

1 cup fresh shiitake mushrooms, stemmed, cut crosswise into ¼-inch-thick slices

2 medium carrots, peeled, cut diagonally into ⅛-inch slices

6 small broccoli florets

½ peeled, shredded medium daikon

½ cup diced red bell pepper

3 baby bok choy, quartered, washed

1 cup peeled, diced jicama

2 tablespoons soy sauce

½ teaspoon sugar or agave syrup

¼ cup vegetable broth

For serving: cooked rice

1　Heat oil in wok or large, deep skillet on high heat, tilting pan to coat sides with oil. Add onion and stir-fry until softened, about 3 minutes. Add the garlic and ginger; cook 10 seconds. Add the mushrooms, carrots, broccoli, and daikon; stir-fry until carrots are tender-crisp.

2　Add pepper, bok choy, and diced jicama; add soy sauce, sugar or agave syrup, and broth. Toss. Simmer 3 minutes or until bok choy is wilted and just barely tender. Serve over cooked rice.

Nutritional information (per serving without rice): Calories 140, fat calories 50; total fat 5 grams, sat fat 0 grams, cholesterol 0 milligrams; sodium 410 milligrams; total carbohydrates 21 grams, fiber 6 grams, sugars 8 grams; protein 5 grams; vitamin A IUs 80%; vitamin C 250%; calcium 4%; iron 10%.

Mango, Kumquat, and Jicama Salad

YIELD: 6 SERVINGS

The bright, assertive kumquats add citrusy "flavor bling" to this fruit-based salad. Serve it as a side dish with Indian curry or spicy Asian stir-fries. If the red onion is strong (with a high degree of mouth burn), soak it in ice water for 20 minutes, then pat dry before adding to salad.

½ pound kumquats, cut into crosswise slices, seeded

1 medium jicama, peeled, diced

1 mango, peeled, seeded, diced

½ medium red onion, diced

Chili powder

2 tablespoons fresh lime juice

¼ cup chopped fresh cilantro leaves

1　Place kumquats, jicama, mango, and onion in glass or nonreactive ceramic bowl. Add chile powder to taste and toss. Add juice and cilantro. Gently toss. Cover and chill 2 hours. Serve in small, individual bowls.

Nutritional information (per serving): Calories 70, fat calories 0; total fat 0 grams, sat fat 0 grams, cholesterol 0 milligrams; sodium 5 milligrams; total carbohydrates 18 grams, fiber 5 grams, sugars 10 grams; protein 1 gram; vitamin A IUs 8%; vitamin C 60%; calcium 4%; iron 4%.

Kiwi

Apple-green flesh dotted with a ring of petite black edible seeds lie beneath kiwi's fuzzy brown camouflage. The oblong fruit is an exotic blend of pineapple, strawberry, and sweet cantaloupe flavors. A ripe melon–like texture makes it easy to slice and use as a glamorous garnish for desserts and beverages. Native to China, kiwis were called Chinese gooseberries by Westerners until New Zealand developed their commercial production and renamed them after their downy national bird.

Kiwi vines are hardy, but frost during the blooming season can be very problematic. Organic kiwi growers trim the vines so the canopy doesn't touch the ground. They use ladybugs to control pests and wind-propelled streamers to deter birds. The fields are weeded by hand.

BUYING AND STORING: Look for kiwis with unbroken skin that give slightly to gentle pressure and have fragrant scent; avoid mushy-soft kiwis. If necessary, ripen at room temperature 2 to 3 days, until fruit gives to gentle pressure. Ripening time can be shortened by placing in loosely sealed paper bag with an apple, banana, or pear at room temperature (see Glossary, page 323). Refrigerate ripe kiwi (unwashed, unpeeled) in crisper drawer up to 3 to 5 days.

PREP AND USE: Wash with cold water. Kiwi skin is almost paper-thin (except in very large fruit) and can be eaten, but most find the fuzziness unappealing. To peel, cut off ends, then use paring knife or vegetable peeler to remove skin, or cut in half lengthwise and scoop out flesh with spoon.

Generally eaten raw. Use as garnish on tarts, cakes, and sundaes, or atop pudding or chicken salad. Include in fruit salsa and fruit salads, or eat as is, as a snack. Toss green salad with a simple vinaigrette and top with kiwi slices and crumbled goat cheese. Or cut off top ¼ inch from stem end and seal in airtight container (such as a zipper-style plastic bag); partially freeze and eat sorbet-style with spoon, scooping chilly flesh from skin.

Kiwi contains an enzyme that prevents gelatin from setting (so forget the idea of molded kiwi gelatin). That enzyme has beneficial effects when it comes to tenderizing meat. To increase meat tenderness, cut kiwi in half lengthwise and rub over uncooked meat; discard kiwi and let meat stand 20 to 30 minutes before cooking.

AVAILABLE: Year-round

NUTRITIONAL INFORMATION (per 1 cup diced, raw): Calories 108, fat calories 8; total fat 1 gram, sat fat 0 grams, cholesterol 0 milligrams; sodium 5 milligrams; total carbohydrates 26 grams, fiber 5 grams, sugars 16 grams; protein 2 grams; vitamin A IUs 3%; vitamin C 273%; calcium 6%; iron 3%.

SERVING SUGGESTIONS

Kiwi Sandwich Treats

Mix ½ cup ricotta cheese with 2 teaspoons powdered sugar. Turn a crisp shortbread cookie upside down and spread a little strawberry jam on it. Top jam with peeled kiwi slice and a teaspoon of sweetened ricotta cheese; top with a second cookie.

Kiwi Cheesecake

Garnish cheesecake with slightly overlapping slices of peeled kiwi.

Jade Milkshake

In blender, place 1 cup milk, 1 large scoop vanilla ice cream or frozen yogurt, and 1 peeled, sliced kiwi. Cover and whirl until blended.

Green Mornings

Top pancakes, French toast, or cinnamon toast with thin slices of peeled kiwi.

Tropical Fruit Salsa

YIELD: ABOUT 8 CUPS

Vibrant in flavor and appearance, this fruit concoction can serve as a dip accompanied with sturdy crackers, large tortilla chips, or bagel chips. Or use as a topping for grilled chicken or pork chops. Or roll a spoonful into a warm corn tortilla and top with a little crumbled feta cheese. For the prettiest appearance, cut all fruit into ¼-inch dice.

4 kiwi, peeled, diced

2 cups peeled, seeded, diced papayas

2 cups peeled, cored, diced pineapple

2 mangoes, peeled, seeded, diced

⅓ cup chopped red onion

3 tablespoons fresh lime juice

1½ teaspoons seasoned rice vinegar

2 jalapeño chiles, seeded, finely minced (see Cook's Note)

3 tablespoons chopped fresh cilantro

Coarse salt, such as kosher

For serving: sturdy tortilla chips, bagel chips, or warm tortillas

In medium bowl, combine all ingredients. Gently toss with rubber spatula. Cover and refrigerate for 1 hour. It is best served the day it is made, but will keep, covered, for up to 24 hours in the refrigerator, draining off excess juice if needed. If storing for longer than a few hours, it is best to omit the cilantro and add it just before serving.

Nutritional information (per ¼ cup serving): Calories 25, fat calories 0; total fat 0 grams, sat fat 0 grams, cholesterol 0 milligrams; sodium 0 milligrams; total carbohydrates 6 grams, fiber 1 gram, sugars 4 grams; protein 0 grams; vitamin A IUs 4%; vitamin C 35%; calcium 0%; iron 0%.

Cook's Note: Use caution when working with fresh chiles. Wash work surface and hands thoroughly upon completion and do *not* touch eyes or face.

Tropical Fruit Salsa

Kiwi, Blackberry, and Coconut Cream Tart

YIELD: 10 SERVINGS

Delicately flavored coconut pastry cream is the base of this lovely dessert. It is topped with colorful slices of kiwi, which offer a vibrant contrast to the creamy mixture below. The crust and pastry cream can be made several hours ahead, the crust stored at room temperature, and the pastry cream chilled in the refrigerator. It should be assembled just before serving because enzymes in the kiwi might break down the surface of the pastry cream.

Easy Processor Pie Dough

1 ⅓ cups all-purpose flour, plus flour for dusting work surface

½ teaspoon salt

1 teaspoon sugar

½ cup (1 stick) cold unsalted butter, cut into 8 pieces

¼ cup ice water

Egg wash: 1 egg white mixed with ½ teaspoon water

Pastry Cream

2 cups whole milk

1 cup unsweetened shredded coconut

5 large egg yolks

⅓ cup sugar

⅓ cup plus 1 tablespoon all-purpose flour

1 tablespoon unsalted butter

½ teaspoon vanilla

Topping

1 cup unsweetened shredded coconut, toasted, and chopped (see Cook's Note)

6 kiwi

1 cup blackberries

Optional garnish: ⅓ cup apricot jam

1   Adjust oven rack to middle position. Preheat to 350°F.

2   Prepare pie dough: In food processor fitted with metal blade, pulse flour, salt, and sugar 2 or 3 times. Add butter and pulse until mixture resembles coarse meal. With motor running, add ice water through feed tube, processing until mixture just barely comes together. Pat into disk shape; place in plastic bag and refrigerate 1 hour.

3   On lightly floured work surface, roll dough into a circle, roughly 11 inches in diameter, using a floured rolling pin. Place dough in 9½-inch tart pan with removable bottom. Use top of bent finger to press dough into fluted sides of pan. To create a double layer of dough on sides of crust, trim dough ¼ inch above top of pan; fold overhanging dough over so top of fold is even with top of pan to reinforce sides; press with top of bent finger to seal sides. Roll rolling pin over top of tart pan to make top of dough even all the way around. Poke dough at 1-inch intervals with tines of fork (bottom and sides). Line dough with sheet of aluminum foil. Add about 1 cup dry beans, uncooked rice, or pie weights. Bake 15 minutes. Remove from oven; remove foil and beans, rice, or weights. Using a pastry brush, brush top edge of dough with a little egg wash. Return to oven and bake until golden brown, about 5 minutes. Set aside.

4   Prepare pastry cream: Heat milk in medium saucepan on medium heat until hot to the touch. Stir in coconut and remove from heat. Cover and set aside for 10 minutes. Working in two batches, whirl mixture in blender (use caution when blending hot mixtures—hold down lid with potholder). Place strainer over bowl and strain milk mixture. Use rubber spatula to press coconut to extract as much milk as possible; discard coconut. Place milk mixture in saucepan and place on medium-high heat; cook until bubbles form around the edges. Whisk yolks and sugar in large bowl until blended and light in color, about 2 to 3 minutes; whisk in flour. Add hot milk in very thin stream, whisking constantly to prevent eggs from scrambling.

5   Transfer mixture to medium saucepan. Cook over medium heat, stirring constantly with a utensil that comes in good contract with the bottom of the pan (such as a wooden spatula), until mixture thickens (do not boil). Be careful not to scorch the bottom. Remove from heat and stir in butter and vanilla. Pour into medium bowl and cover with plastic wrap, adjusting wrap so that it covers surface of pastry cream. Refrigerate until chilled, about 1 hour.

6   Remove tart shell from rim of pan and place on large plate (still placed on removable bottom). Spread pastry cream evenly in tart crust. Sprinkle toasted coconut over cream. Peel kiwi and cut into ¼-inch crosswise slices. Arrange kiwi slices in overlapping concentric circles on pastry cream. Dot with blackberries. If desired, brush fruit with apricot glaze. To make glaze, melt apricot jam on medium heat in small saucepan. Strain and use pastry brush to brush strained glaze on fruit. Cut into wedges and serve.

Nutritional information (per serving): Calories 340, fat calories 170; total fat 19 grams, sat fat 13 grams, cholesterol 135 milligrams; sodium 150 milligrams; total carbohydrates 36 grams, fiber 4 grams, sugars 15 grams; protein 7 grams; vitamin A IUs 10%; vitamin C 80%; calcium 10%; iron 10%.

Cook's Note: To toast shredded coconut, place in single layer on rimmed baking sheet. Place in 350°F oven until nicely browned, about 3 minutes. Watch carefully because it can burn easily. Cool.

Fruit Salad Royale

This colorful salad is a luscious addition to a buffet table. Guests who have lukewarm attitudes about fruit salad may find themselves coming back for more.

1 ½ cups peeled, sliced kiwi

2 cups hulled, quartered strawberries

2 cups green or red seedless grapes

2 cups sliced plums or plumcots or peaches

1 cup peeled orange segments (see Glossary (supremes), page 324)

¼ cup orange liqueur

3 tablespoons fresh orange juice

1 tablespoon agave syrup or sugar

Place all ingredients in glass or nonreactive ceramic bowl; gently toss with rubber spatula. Cover and chill up to 4 hours.

Nutritional information (per serving): Calories 130, fat calories 5; total fat 0.5 gram, sat fat 0 grams, cholesterol 0 milligrams; sodium 0 milligrams; total carbohydrates 30 grams, fiber 4 grams, sugars 23 grams; protein 2 grams; vitamin A IUs 6%; vitamin C 150%; calcium 4%; iron 4%.

Kiwi Martini

This frosty cocktail captures the aroma and vibrant taste of fresh lime and kiwi. Kiwi is a rather unexpected cocktail ingredient, giving this concoction a welcome element of surprise.

3 ounces vodka or citrus vodka

2 teaspoons sugar syrup (see Cook's Note)

½ kiwi, peeled, sliced

2 teaspoons fresh lime juice

Garnish: kiwi slice

In a cocktail shaker, combine vodka, sugar syrup, kiwi, and lime juice; mash with a muddler or sturdy wooden spoon. Add a generous amount of ice. Cover and shake vigorously. Strain into chilled martini glass. Garnish with a slice of kiwi.

Nutritional information (per serving): Calories 300, fat calories 0; total fat 0 grams, sat fat 0 grams, cholesterol 0 milligrams; sodium 0 milligrams; total carbohydrates 12 grams, fiber 0 grams, sugars 0 grams; protein 0 grams; vitamin A IUs 0%; vitamin C 6%; calcium 0%; iron 0%.

Cook's Note: To make sugar syrup: Combine ½ cup water and ½ cup sugar in small saucepan. Bring to boil on high heat. Reduce heat and gently boil for 2 minutes. Cool. Leftover cooled sugar syrup can be refrigerated airtight and used in cocktails and desserts such as sorbet.

Kumquat

Roll a kumquat between your palms and smell the perfume-like citrus scent. Then eat the bantam-size orange orb, skin and all. Think of an inside-out orange. The skin is subtly sweet and the interior is pleasantly tart. Some seeds dot the interior, and can be easily discarded. But the smaller seeds seem perfectly acceptable as part of the kumquat's personality.

Organic kumquats are grown primarily in California, with smaller crops in Texas and Florida. Kumquats are labor-intensive to harvest because each little kumquat needs to be hand-clipped and hand-gathered. Most are Nagami, the oval-shaped variety. About 5 percent of the crop is the smaller, rounder variety called Meiwa.

BUYING AND STORING: Choose fruit that is plump and has a shiny surface. Avoid those with bruises or soft spots. Store in cool location up to 7 days, or refrigerate unwashed in plastic bag in crisper drawer up to 2 weeks.

PREP AND USE: Wash in cold water and dry just before use. Do not peel. Eat raw or cooked. To remove seeds, cut in half lengthwise and use tip of small knife to pluck out and discard seeds. If using slices, cut crosswise and pluck seeds out as needed.

Use kumquats as substitutes for oranges in pudding, rice dishes, stir-fries, and soufflés, as well as fruit salads and marmalades. They make beautiful garnishes.

AVAILABLE: December to May

NUTRITIONAL INFORMATION (per 1 average-size kumquat, raw): Calories 14, fat calories 1; total fat 0 grams, sat fat 0 grams, cholesterol 0 milligrams; sodium 2 milligrams; total carbohydrates 3 grams, fiber 1 gram, sugars 2 grams; protein 0 grams; vitamin A IUs 1%; vitamin C 14%; calcium 1%; iron 1%.

SERVING SUGGESTIONS

Stuffed Treats

Cut 12 kumquats in half lengthwise. Remove seeds. Remove pulp from skin with small spoon or tomato shark (small tool with sawtooth edge for coring tomatoes). Place pulp in small bowl or food processor. Add 3 ounces room-temperature cream cheese and 1 tablespoon milk; mash with fork or process until smooth. Stir in 2 tablespoons finely chopped pecans or finely chopped dates. Use 2 small spoons to fill kumquat shells, one to scoop and one to push mixture off spoon into kumquat "boat."

Chocolate-Dipped Kumquat Wheels

Partially dipped kumquat slices make an elegant garnish atop chocolate cake or ice cream. Cut kumquats crosswise into slices and remove any big seeds. Melt semisweet or bittersweet chocolate in top of double boiler over barely simmering water, stirring frequently (chocolate should be just warm enough to melt). Line a baking sheet with waxed paper. Holding slice vertically, dip half of each slice in chocolate and place in single layer on prepared sheet. Set aside for chocolate to harden, or chill for about 5 minutes, or until chocolate is firm.

Candied Kumquats atop Cheesecake

Make or buy your favorite cheesecake, then top it with this tasty kumquat topping. Cut 30 kumquats into thin crosswise slices; remove and discard seeds. Place 2 cups water and 2½ cups sugar in large, heavy-bottomed saucepan on medium-high heat. Stir until sugar dissolves. Add kumquats and bring to simmer; reduce heat and simmer until semitranslucent, about 25 minutes. Remove

from heat and stir in 1 teaspoon vanilla or orange liqueur. Allow to cool. Strain, reserving syrup. Mix fruit with half of reserved syrup. Spoon mixture over wedges of cheesecake (or chocolate ice cream, angel food cake, or rice pudding). Garnish with sprigs of fresh mint.

Kumquat Crannies

Here's a condiment with attitude. Try it with turkey, ham, or game. In large, heavy-bottomed saucepan combine 2 (12-ounce) bags fresh cranberries, 12 kumquats (sliced crosswise and seeded), 1⅓ cups sugar, 1 cup water, and pinch salt. Bring to simmer on medium-high heat; reduce heat to medium-low and simmer, stirring occasionally, until cranberries pop, about 12 minutes. If desired, stir in 1 teaspoon orange liqueur or orange juice. Serve warm or chilled.

Kumquat Soufflé

YIELD: 6 SERVINGS

The kumquat mixture that is the delicious base for these individual soufflés can be simmered, seeded, and pureed in advance and stored airtight in the refrigerator for several days. An hour before you want to serve them, beat the eggs whites and fold them into the kumquat mixture and bake. Voilà!

2 cups kumquats

1 cup water

Unsalted butter for greasing ramekins

8 egg whites

Pinch of salt

3 cups sugar plus sugar for dusting ramekins

1 Place kumquats in medium saucepan; add water, bring to a boil on medium-high heat. Reduce heat to low and gently simmer, covered, for 1 hour. Check occasionally and add water as needed if mixture starts to dry.

2   Adjust oven rack to middle position. Preheat oven to 400°F. Meanwhile, butter 6 (8-ounce) ramekins and sprinkle with sugar. Set aside.

3   When cool enough to handle, cut kumquats in half lengthwise and pluck out seeds with tip of small knife. Place in food processor fitted with metal blade; process until pureed and smooth.

4   In large bowl of electric mixer, beat egg whites and salt on high speed until soft peaks form. Reduce speed to medium-high and add sugar ¼ cup at a time, beating about 30 seconds between additions. Beat until stiff. Add kumquat puree and gently fold with rubber spatula. Divide mixture between prepared ramekins. Place on rimmed baking sheet. Bake 25 minutes or until set. Serve immediately.

Nutritional information (per serving): Calories 450, fat calories 10; total fat 1 gram, sat fat 0 grams, cholesterol 0 milligrams; sodium 80 milligrams; total carbohydrates 108 grams, fiber 2 grams, sugars 105 grams; protein 6 grams; vitamin A IUs 2%; vitamin C 30%; calcium 2%; iron 2%.

Turkey Breast Cutlets with Kumquats and Fresh Spinach

YIELD: 6 SERVINGS

Kumquats bring an irresistible citrus spark to this elegant turkey dish. Turkey cutlets are available in many supermarkets. They are slices of skinned and boned turkey breast, usually about ¼ inch thick. If you prefer, substitute chicken tenders or ground turkey patties.

1 egg white

Salt

1 cup dried breadcrumbs

Freshly ground black pepper

1¼ pounds turkey breast cutlets

Vegetable oil for frying

2 shallots, thinly sliced

6 kumquats, thinly sliced crosswise, seeded

4 tablespoons sugar

⅔ cup water

⅓ cup dried cranberries or dried cherries

⅓ cup white wine vinegar

¼ teaspoon dried red chile flakes

1 tablespoon extra-virgin olive oil

1 large garlic clove, minced

6 cups packed baby spinach leaves

Turkey Breast Cutlets with Kumquats and Fresh Spinach

1 Adjust oven rack to middle position. Preheat oven to 350°F.

2 In shallow bowl or pie pan, beat egg white and pinch of salt until frothy. Place breadcrumbs in second shallow pan or pie plate. Season cutlets on both sides with salt and pepper to taste. Dip a cutlet in egg white, holding it over pan to let excess drip back into pan. Dip both sides in crumbs. Set aside and repeat process with each cutlet.

3 In large, deep skillet (preferably nonstick), heat ¼ inch vegetable oil on medium-high heat. In two batches, add cutlets and brown on both sides. Place on rimmed baking sheet in single layer and place in oven. Bake until thoroughly cooked, about 8 to 10 minutes.

4 Meanwhile, return skillet to medium-high heat. Add 1 tablespoon vegetable oil along with shallots. Stir to release browned bits. Add kumquats, sugar, water, cranberries, vinegar, and chile flakes. Bring to simmer, stirring frequently until sugar dissolves and mixture thickens, about 8 to 10 minutes.

5 Meanwhile, heat 1 tablespoon olive oil in separate large, deep skillet. Add garlic and cook 30 seconds. Add spinach and cook until wilted, stirring occasionally as needed. Divide spinach between 6 plates. Check cutlets for doneness; no pink color should remain. Cut cutlets into 1-inch strips and place on top of each portion of spinach. Top with kumquat sauce and serve.

Nutritional information (per serving with turkey cutlets): Calories 350, fat calories 130; total fat 15 grams, sat fat 3 grams, cholesterol 70 milligrams; sodium 230 milligrams; total carbohydrates 33 grams, fiber 3 grams, sugars 6 grams; protein 24 grams; vitamin A IUs 40%; vitamin C 30%; calcium 8%; iron 10%.

Meatless Tip: Prepare sauce, starting with step 4. Spoon over Sautéed Breaded Tofu (page 320).

Kumquat-Spiked Custard

YIELD: 6 SERVINGS

Simple baked custard is a delectable treat when augmented with finely chopped kumquats. The milk-egg mixture balances perfectly with the small amount of tangy citrus. For dessert, top with a smidgen of whipped cream and ground cinnamon. Or serve plain as a fast breakfast indulgence.

- 6 kumquats
- 2½ cups milk
- 3 eggs
- ½ cup sugar
- ¼ teaspoon salt
- 1½ teaspoons vanilla

1 Adjust oven rack to middle position. Preheat to 350°F.

2 Cut kumquats in lengthwise quarters. Use small pointed knife to pluck out seeds. Finely chop. Set aside.

3 Place milk in large, heavy-bottomed saucepan. Scald milk on medium-high heat. (To scald means to heat to just below the boiling point.) Remove from heat.

4 In large bowl, whisk eggs, sugar, salt, and vanilla to combine. Whisking constantly, add hot milk little by little to egg mixture. If you add the hot milk too quickly, it might curdle eggs. Stir in kumquats.

5 Ladle mixture into 6 (1-cup) custard cups. Place cups in 9 × 13-inch baking pan. Add enough hot water to the pan to come 1 inch up the sides of the cups. Place in oven and bake 40 minutes or until set and knife inserted in center comes out clean. Serve warm or chilled.

Nutritional information (per serving): Calories 170, fat calories 40; total fat 4.5 grams, sat fat 1 gram, cholesterol 115 milligrams; sodium 190 milligrams; total carbohydrates 26 grams, fiber 1 gram, sugars 24 grams; protein 7 grams; vitamin A IUs 8%; vitamin C 15%; calcium 25%; iron 2%.

Fruit-and-Nut-Topped Baked Brie

YIELD: 20 SERVINGS

Brie cheese covered with kumquats, dried fruit, and assorted nuts becomes irresistible when you top it with a buttery brown sugar mixture and bake it. It makes a delicious appetizer served with crunchy crackers, bread, or apple slices, but cut into wedges it can also be used as a garnish for mixed green salads.

1 (9-inch or 10-inch) round chilled Brie cheese

½ cup mixed nuts, salted or unsalted

4 kumquats, quartered, seeded, coarsely chopped

2 tablespoons dried cherries or dried blueberries or dried cranberries

2 tablespoons unsalted butter, melted

3 tablespoons dark brown sugar

Optional garnish: 4 to 6 whole kumquats

Optional garnish: 4 to 6 sprigs fresh Italian parsley

For serving: sliced apples or sliced French bread or crackers

1   Adjust oven rack to middle position. Preheat oven to 350°F. Unwrap cheese and place in 10-inch pie pan or quiche pan.

2   In small bowl, toss nuts, kumquats, and dried fruit; spoon mixture on top of cheese.

3   In same bowl, mix butter and brown sugar. Use fingers to sprinkle mixture evenly over nut mixture.

4   Bake 12 to 15 minutes, or until heated through. Serve with apple slices, bread slices, or crackers for scooping.

Nutritional information (per serving with sliced apple): Calories 130, fat calories 80; total fat 9 grams, sat fat 5 grams, cholesterol 25 milligrams; sodium 140 milligrams; total carbohydrates 6 grams, fiber 1 gram, sugars 4 grams; protein 5 grams; vitamin A IUs 4%; vitamin C 4%; calcium 4%; iron 2%.

Leek

A leek's deep green stalks form a chevron-patterned crown atop its pearly-white bulb. A forest of dense roots tangle at its base, creating a vegetable that looks like an enormous green onion (or scallion). Related to garlic and onions, leeks have a sweeter, more subtle scent and taste than their lily-family cousins. Whether served hot or cold, when cooked they are silken.

Organic growers use cover crops to help manage soil fertility and control weeds. Too much heat can burn tips of leeks, and extreme cold can be problematic as well. Organic leek crops generally yield about 10 percent less than conventionally grown crops.

BUYING AND STORING: Look for leeks with the largest amount of edible portion, the white and light green areas. Avoid leeks with yellowed or withered tops. White portion should be unblemished and feel crisp, not slimy, and free of any splitting. Do not trim or wash before storing. Store untrimmed and wrapped loosely in a plastic bag, in the crisper drawer of the refrigerator. They'll keep for one to two weeks, sometimes even longer. If the outer leaves turn yellow, pull them off; the remaining portion should be perfectly fine.

PREP AND USE: Leeks often have dirt lodged between their layers. Trim off the root end and the dark green stalks. Cut the remaining white and light green portion in half lengthwise. With one hand hold under cold running water, cut-side up, pulling layers apart to wash

away any dirt. Hold one portion together with opposite hand. Shake off water. If slicing, place cut-side down on cutting board. Cut crosswise into thin slices.

Substitute leeks for onions in recipes, but not vice versa. Used raw, they can be very thinly sliced and used in relishes, salads, and salsas. They can be braised, baked, stir-fried, or microwaved. Use them in casseroles, gratins, pasta, rice, or soup.

AVAILABLE: Year-round (peak is spring)

NUTRITIONAL INFORMATION (per 1 cup sliced, raw): Calories 54, fat calories 2; total fat 0 grams, sat fat 0 grams, cholesterol 0 milligrams; sodium 18 milligrams; total carbohydrates 13 grams, fiber 2 grams, sugars 3 grams; protein 1 gram; vitamin A IUs 30%; vitamin C 18%; calcium 5%; iron 10%.

SERVING SUGGESTIONS

Potato-Leek Gratin

For flavorful potato gratin, prepare your favorite potato gratin recipe, but add 2 to 3 thinly sliced leeks (white and light green parts) between the layers of potatoes, cheese, and cream.

Chicken Breasts with Leeks

Chicken breasts topped with a creamy leek sauce are delicious served with couscous or orzo. Preheat oven to 375°F. Dredge 4 large, bone-in chicken breasts in ⅓ cup all-purpose flour seasoned with salt and freshly ground black pepper. Shake off excess flour and brown chicken on both sides in 2 tablespoons extra-virgin olive oil on medium-high heat in large Dutch oven or flameproof casserole. Remove chicken and add 4 thinly sliced leeks (white and light green parts); sauté until softened. Add 8 peeled small carrots, 1 clove garlic (minced), and ⅔ cup Madeira. Bring to simmer, scraping up any brown bits sticking to bottom of pan. Add chicken and 1 cup reduced-sodium chicken broth. Cover and bake for 35 minutes. Remove chicken and vegetables from pot with slotted spoon. Bring sauce to boil and reduce on high heat to about ¼ cup. Stir in ¼ cup heavy whipping cream. Season to taste with salt and freshly ground black pepper. Spoon vegetables and sauce over chicken. Garnish with chopped fresh tarragon leaves.

Chilled Leeks Niçoise

Trim dark green stalks off 4 leeks and discard. Cook trimmed leeks in simmering water until just barely tender, about 10 minutes. Drain and refresh with cold water. Slice leeks in half lengthwise; look to see if there is any sand between layers and if so, rinse with cold water. Place leeks on rimmed platter. In small bowl, whisk 3 tablespoons balsamic vinegar, 2 teaspoons Dijon-style mustard, ¼ cup chopped pitted kalamata olives, 1 teaspoon cider vinegar, and salt and freshly ground black pepper to taste. Whisk in ⅓ cup extra-virgin olive oil. Drizzle over leeks. Garnish with chopped fresh basil leaves or chopped fresh tarragon leaves and if desired, 2 hard-cooked eggs (peeled and halved lengthwise).

Leekie Egg Salad

Add chopped leek (white and light green parts) to egg salad and, if desired, add sliced, pitted green olives as well.

Leek and Tarragon Soup with Melted Brie Cheese

YIELD: 6 SERVINGS

Soup isn't just for winter. A one-dish soup dinner, eaten outdoors in the cool of the evening, can be a welcome break from traditional summer fare. The soup can be prepared ahead, reheated, and topped with cheese.

6 thick slices French bread

4 tablespoons unsalted butter, divided use

7 large leeks, trimmed, white and green parts halved, washed, cut into thin crosswise slices

¾ pound common white (button) mushrooms, thinly sliced

2 medium cloves garlic, minced

2½ tablespoons all-purpose flour

4 cups fat-free, low-sodium chicken broth or vegetable broth

⅓ cup heavy whipping cream or milk

2 tablespoons minced fresh tarragon leaves

Freshly ground black pepper

6 ounces brie cheese, cut into ½-inch slices

1 Adjust oven rack to middle position. Preheat oven to 325°F. Place bread on rimmed baking sheet in single layer. Bake until toasted, about 12 to 15 minutes. Spread with about 2 tablespoons butter and set aside. Increase oven temperature to 425°F.

2 In Dutch oven or large saucepan, melt remaining 2 tablespoons butter over medium heat. Add leeks, mushrooms, and garlic. Cook, stirring frequently, until vegetables are soft and most of liquid evaporates, about 15 minutes.

3 Stir in flour and cook, stirring constantly, for 1 minute. Remove from heat and stir in chicken broth or vegetable broth and cream or milk. Bring to a boil, stirring constantly. Remove from heat; add tarragon and pepper to taste.

4 Ladle into 6 (2-cup) ovenproof soup bowls. Place bowls on rimmed baking sheet. Top each with a piece of toasted bread and top bread with cheese. Bake uncovered until bubbly, about 8 to 10 minutes. If you want to further brown the topping, remove baking sheet from oven and move rack to 6 to 8 inches below broiler element. Turn oven to broil and broil soup on baking sheet about 1 minute. Turn on oven light and watch carefully to prevent burning. Serve hot, cautioning guests that bowls are hot.

Nutritional information (per serving): Calories 440, fat calories 160; total fat 18 grams, sat fat 10 grams, cholesterol 50 milligrams; sodium 900 milligrams; total carbohydrates 54 grams, fiber 4 grams, sugars 6 grams; protein 16 grams; vitamin A IUs 45%; vitamin C 2%; calcium 20%; iron 25%.

Leek and Tarragon Soup with Melted Brie Cheese

Mixed Green Salad with Leek and Tarragon Dressing

YIELD: 6 SERVINGS

Salad dressings containing a little whipping cream cling lightly to lettuce. To reduce fat calories derived from whipping cream, you can substitute an equal amount of unsweetened plain, nonfat yogurt. If desired, garnish each salad with a slice or two of fresh mango or few tiny champagne grapes.

- 3 tablespoons fresh lemon juice
- 2 tablespoons heavy whipping cream or plain nonfat yogurt
- 1 tablespoon trimmed, washed, finely chopped leek (white and light green parts)
- 1½ tablespoons finely minced fresh tarragon leaves
- ¼ cup canola oil or extra-virgin olive oil
- Salt and freshly ground black pepper
- 6 cups butter lettuce, torn into bite-size pieces
- 2 cups watercress, torn into bite-size pieces

1 In a medium bowl, combine lemon juice, cream or yogurt, leek, and tarragon. Whisk in oil using fork. Add salt and pepper to taste; stir to combine.

2 Place salad greens in large bowl. Toss with enough dressing to lightly coat the leaves.

Nutritional information (per serving): Calories 110, fat calories 100; total fat 11 grams, sat fat 2.5 grams, cholesterol 5 milligrams; sodium 210 milligrams; total carbohydrates 3 grams, fiber 1 gram, sugars 1 gram; protein 1 gram; vitamin A IUs 30%; vitamin C 15%; calcium 2%; iron 0%.

Leek, Zucchini, and Pasta Brothy Soup with Fresh Herbs

YIELD: 4 SERVINGS

This blueprint recipe can be changed to suit your taste and ingredients you have on hand. If desired, omit the zucchini and/or carrot and add ½-inch green bean pieces, ⅜-inch crookneck squash slices, shelled fresh peas, or cubes of butternut squash. Or add a 15-ounce can of cannellini beans (drained, rinsed) or a cup of shelled cooked soybeans (edamame).

- 2 tablespoons extra-virgin olive oil
- 2 large leeks or 3 medium leeks (white and light green parts), trimmed, washed, cut into thin crosswise slices
- 2 medium cloves garlic, minced
- 1 medium carrot, peeled, cut into ¼-inch-thick rounds
- 2 medium zucchini, cut into ⅜-inch-thick rounds
- 5 cups vegetable broth or chicken broth
- Pinch dried red chile flakes
- ¾ cup small pasta, such as fusilli or rotini
- Freshly ground black pepper
- 2 tablespoons chopped fresh chives
- 2 tablespoons chopped fresh Italian parsley
- 4 tablespoons grated Parmesan cheese

1 In large saucepan or Dutch oven, heat oil on medium heat. Add leeks and cook, stirring occasionally, until softened, about 10 minutes. Add garlic and cook 1 minute.

2 Add carrot, zucchini, vegetable broth or chicken broth, and chile flakes. Bring to boil on high heat. Add pasta and reduce heat to medium-high. Cook until pasta is al dente (tender but with a little bite).

3   Remove from heat and season with generous amount of pepper. Stir in chives and parsley. Ladle into soup bowls and top with cheese. Serve.

Nutritional information (per serving with vegetable broth): Calories 290, fat calories 80; total fat 9 grams, sat fat 2 grams, cholesterol 5 milligrams; sodium 360 milligrams; total carbohydrates 4 grams, fiber 5 grams, sugars 11 grams; protein 9 grams; vitamin A IUs 120%; vitamin C 60%; calcium 15%; iron 20%.

Baked Radicchio Stuffed with Leeks and Goat Cheese

4 SERVINGS

Radicchio is red-leafed Italian chicory that is most often used as a salad green. In Tuscany, it is often grilled and served as a side dish. In this recipe radicchio's bold flavor profile is tamed by grilling, then stuffing with a creamy leek mixture.

2 heads radicchio, cut in half lengthwise (leave the leaves attached at root end)

2½ tablespoons extra-virgin olive oil, divided use

2 medium leeks (white and light green parts), trimmed, washed, thinly sliced

8 ounces crumbled goat cheese

½ cup shelled pistachio nuts, toasted, coarsely chopped (see Cook's Note)

2 tablespoons chopped fresh basil leaves

¼ teaspoon salt

¼ teaspoon freshly ground black pepper

1   Heat grill. Clean grates and coat with vegetable oil. Brush cut side of radicchio with 1 tablespoon oil. Place on heated grill; grill until grill marks form and radicchio is starting to soften, about 4 to 5 minutes. Remove from heat. When cool enough to handle, remove small central leaves and chop them, leaving several layers of radicchio behind to form a kind of hollow cavity.

2   Adjust oven rack to middle position. Preheat oven to 350°F.

3   In a medium, deep skillet heat remaining 1½ tablespoons oil on medium-high heat. Add leeks and cook, stirring occasionally, until softened and starting to brown, about 8 minutes. Remove from heat and cool about 15 minutes.

4   Prepare filling: In medium bowl, combine cooled leeks, chopped radicchio, goat cheese, pistachios, and basil. Add salt and pepper and toss; spoon filling into radicchio halves. Place cut-side up on rimmed baking sheet and bake until hot, about 6 to 8 minutes.

Nutritional information (per serving): Calories 360, fat calories 250; total fat 28 grams, sat fat 13 grams, cholesterol 45 milligrams; sodium 600 milligrams; total carbohydrates 13 grams, fiber 3 grams, sugars 4 grams; protein 16 grams; vitamin A IUs 35%; vitamin C 10%; calcium 20%; iron 15%.

Cook's Note: To toast pistachios, place on rimmed baking sheet in single layer. Toast in middle of 350°F oven for 3 to 5 minutes, or until lightly toasted. Watch carefully because they burn easily. Cool.

Lemon

Cooks know that the outer portion of lemon peel is culinary treasure. The irresistible oils that reside in the colored portion (known as the zest) are loaded with citrusy fragrance and flavor. A big advantage of organic lemons is in the quality of their zest. Chemicals used in conventional growing can end up in the peel; these chemicals are forbidden in organic regimens. Plus the exteriors of organic lemons are not waxed, so the taste and smell is purer. But know that waxing extends shelf life, so plan on using organic lemons within two weeks of purchase.

Organic growers say that their lemon yields are about 25 percent lower than the conventionally grown citrus. Composting takes place twice a year, generally when the trees are in bloom and mid–growing season. Gophers are major pests in lemon orchards; the little stinkers eat the tree roots.

BUYING AND STORING: Look for fruit that has brightly colored skin with no tinge of green and that is heavy for its size. Avoid lemons with nicks or soft spots. Refrigerate in plastic bag for up to 2 weeks or at room temperature for up to 1 week.

PREP AND USE: Wash before use. If using zest, remove it before cutting lemon (see page 324). When juicing, for best results first bring lemons to room temperature or heat for 10 seconds in microwave. Or, roll on counter, pressing down with palm, to help break up segments.

Use minced zest and/or juice in sauces, soups, syrups, and salad dressings; desserts, beverages, and entrées. For salt-restricted diets, substitute minced lemon zest for all or part of salt in savory dishes.

AVAILABLE: September to July (peak is December to February)

NUTRITIONAL INFORMATION (per 1 medium lemon without seeds): Calories 22, fat calories 3; total fat 0 grams, sat fat 0 grams, cholesterol 0 milligrams; sodium 3 milligrams; total carbohydrates 12 grams, fiber 5 grams, sugars 0 grams; protein 1 gram; vitamin A IUs 1%; vitamin C 139%; calcium 7%; iron 4%.

SERVING SUGGESTIONS

Lemon-Infused Olive Oil

There are myriad uses for this tasty oil. All by itself it can dress mixed greens or add flavor to cooked vegetables. Drizzle little droplets around the edge of rich dishes such as risotto or cauliflower au gratin. To make it, place 1 cup extra-virgin olive oil in small nonreactive saucepan. Add 3 tablespoons finely minced lemon zest (colored portion of peel). Cook on medium heat for 2 minutes or until tiny bubbles appear. Lower heat and gently simmer about 4 minutes. Cover and cool. Transfer to covered glass container (such as a jar) and refrigerate 1 week. Strain and use, or refrigerate well-sealed up to 2 more weeks.

Guilt-Free Corn Topper

Instead of butter, squeeze fresh lemon juice on hot corn on the cob.

Lemon-Rosemary Salt

This flavored salt is terrific on roasted vegetables, roast chicken, lamb, and pork. With motor running, drop 1 medium peeled clove of garlic in feed tube of food processor fitted with metal blade; mince garlic. Stop machine and add minced zest of 2 lemons (colored portion of peel), 2½ tablespoons chopped fresh rosemary leaves, and ½ cup coarse salt, such as kosher. Pulse 3 or 4 times. Store airtight in jar in refrigerator up to 1 week.

Lemon Slush

In blender, combine 1 cup cold water, 1 teaspoon minced lemon zest (colored portion of peel), ½ cup fresh lemon juice, 1 cup ice cubes, and 3 tablespoons sugar or agave syrup. Cover and whirl until slushy. Pour into 2 chilled glasses.

Lemon-Kissed Skillet Pancake with Whole Blueberry Syrup

YIELD: 4 SMALL SERVINGS

Puffed into a beautifully browned dome, this skillet pancake teams the tartness of fresh lemon juice and zest with palate-pleasing sweet components. Once out of the oven, the surface is dusted with powdered sugar, and warm syrup with fresh blueberries is made available for an optional topping. Sometimes called a Dutch baby, this treat is much like a popover or Yorkshire pudding. It is a great emergency treat for unexpected guests.

½ cup all-purpose flour

½ cup whole milk or 2 percent milk

2 eggs, lightly beaten

½ teaspoon minced lemon zest (colored portion of peel)

4 tablespoons unsalted butter, cut into 4 pieces

1 tablespoon powdered sugar

1 tablespoon fresh lemon juice

Whole Blueberry Syrup (see Cook's Note)

1 Adjust oven rack to middle position. Preheat oven to 425°F.

2 In medium bowl, combine flour, milk, eggs, and zest; mix until well combined, but some small lumps should remain.

3 Melt butter on medium-high heat in large, ovenproof skillet. When butter is melted and very hot (but not browned), remove from heat and pour batter in center. Bake for 18 minutes or until nicely browned and very puffy.

4 Remove skillet from oven (remember handle is very hot). Sprinkle lemon juice on top of pancake. Place sugar in small sieve and lightly dust over surface. Cut into 4 servings and accompany with warm blueberry syrup.

Nutritional information (per serving without syrup): Calories 220, fat calories 130; total fat 15 grams, sat fat 9 grams, cholesterol 140 milligrams; sodium 45 milligrams; total carbohydrates 16 grams, fiber 0 grams, sugars 3 grams; protein 6 grams; vitamin A IUs 10%; vitamin C 4%; calcium 6%; iron 6%.

Cook's Note: To make Whole Blueberry Syrup, place 1 cup agave pancake syrup or maple syrup and ½ cup blueberries in small saucepan. Place on medium heat and cook until heated through, about 4 minutes.

Sparkling Pomegranate Lemonade

YIELD: 8 SERVINGS

Not only does pomegranate juice add a tantalizing flavor element to lemonade, it also turns it an eye-popping pink color. If desired, add a splash of vodka to the mixture to make a refreshing cocktail.

1½ cups water

1½ cups sugar

2½ cups fresh lemon juice

1 cup pomegranate juice

Ice

8 thin lemon slices

1 quart sparkling water

Optional garnish: 8 small sprigs of fresh mint

1 Prepare simple syrup: In medium saucepan, combine water and sugar. Dissolve sugar over medium heat. Set aside to cool.

2 In large pitcher, combine cooled syrup, lemon juice, and pomegranate juice; stir to combine. Add sparkling water and stir.

3 Fill 8 tall glasses with ice. Pour lemonade mixture into glasses. Garnish with mint sprigs and lemon slices. Serve immediately.

Nutritional information (per serving): Calories 110, fat calories 0; total fat 0 grams, sat fat 0 grams, cholesterol 0 milligrams; sodium 0 milligrams; total carbohydrates 29 grams, fiber 0 grams, sugars 26 grams; protein 0 grams; vitamin A IUs 0%; vitamin C 40%; calcium 0%; iron 0%.

Sparkling Pomegranate Lemonade

Sautéed Rapini with Garlic and Lemon

YIELD: 6 SERVINGS

Rapini's slender stalk is topped with bright green, jagged-edged leaves that surround compact little buds. At first glance, you may mistake it for broccoli, but the stalks are much thinner. The taste is much more assertive and benefits greatly by combining it with fresh lemon juice, garlic, and onion.

- 1½ pounds rapini, trimmed
- 2 tablespoons unsalted butter
- 2 tablespoons extra-virgin olive oil
- ½ large sweet onion, thinly sliced
- 4 medium cloves garlic, minced
- 2½ tablespoons fresh lemon juice
- Coarse salt, such as kosher, and freshly ground black pepper

1 Bring large pot of water to boil on high heat. Add rapini and cook until tender-crisp. Place colander in sink and add rapini. Refresh it with cold running water. Cut rapini into 1-inch pieces.

2 In a large, deep skillet on medium-high heat, melt butter in oil. Add onion; cook, stirring occasionally, until softened, about 5 minutes. Add garlic; cook 30 seconds. Add rapini and cook, stirring occasionally, until rapini is heated, 2 to 3 minutes. Add lemon juice, salt and pepper to taste; toss. Taste and adjust seasoning as needed and serve.

Nutritional information (per serving): Calories 130, fat calories 70; total fat 8 grams, sat fat 3 grams, cholesterol 10 milligrams; sodium 45 milligrams; total carbohydrates 10 grams, fiber 3 grams, sugars 2 grams; protein 6 grams; vitamin A IUs 200%; vitamin C 240%; calcium 8%; iron 8%.

Grilled Lamb Chops with Rosemary and Lemon

YIELD: 12 SERVINGS

Lemon, garlic, and rosemary make lamb absolutely irresistible. It's a marriage that is hard to beat and in fact, also works very well with pressed tofu slices.

- ¾ cup balsamic vinegar
- 6 tablespoons extra-virgin olive oil
- 3 tablespoons fresh lemon juice
- 3 tablespoons minced fresh rosemary leaves
- 6 medium cloves garlic, minced
- 1 teaspoon coarsely ground black pepper
- 12 (3-ounce) loin lamb chops, about 1 inch thick, excess fat trimmed
- Coarse salt, such as kosher, and freshly ground black pepper
- Garnish: 1 lemon cut into small wedges

1 Prepare marinade: In small bowl, combine vinegar, oil, juice, rosemary, garlic, and pepper; stir to combine.

2 Place chops in single layer in large shallow glass baking pan. Pour marinade over chops. Cover with plastic wrap and refrigerate 4 hours, turning chops 2 or 3 times.

3 Heat grill. Season chops with salt and pepper to taste. Grill about 4 minutes per side for medium-rare, basting with marinade after 3 or 4 minutes before turning chops.

Nutritional information (per serving): Calories 290, fat calories 170; total fat 19 grams, sat fat 6 grams, cholesterol 70 milligrams; sodium 60 milligrams; total carbohydrates 7 grams, fiber 0 grams, sugars 5 grams; protein 22 grams; vitamin A IUs 0%; vitamin C 4%; calcium 2%; iron 15%.

Lettuce

Butter

Green Leaf

Iceberg

Red Leaf

Romaine

Not only is lettuce the focal point of most salads, its texture and flavor are welcome additions to many other dishes, including sandwiches and lettuce wraps. Lettuce can be a tasty backdrop for cold grain-based dishes and is at home in pureed vegetable soups. Taste and texture vary; some varieties are crisp, others are velvety. Some, such as iceberg, have very mild flavor profiles and rely on crunch to give them personality. Others have deep green leaves with a strong but pleasing vegetal taste. A rule of thumb is that the darker the leaf, the higher the amount of beta carotene.

The biggest challenges that face organic lettuce growers are weed control and disagreeable weather. Heavy rains or humidity can bring mildew, and extreme heat can burn leaves. Beneficial insects are used to control aphids.

BUYING AND STORING: Look for lettuce that looks crisp and fresh without discoloration. Wash before refrigerating. For all lettuces (except iceberg), gently separate leaves and place in large bowl or tub of cold water. Some lettuce, if it is very dirty to begin with, can require two rinses, so repeat soaking in clean tub of water a second time. Drain in colander. Spin in salad spinner or blot with paper towels. If using a salad spinner, don't overdo it. If

Romaine

Green Leaf

Butter

Red Leaf

spun too fast or too long, tender leaves will get crushed against the sides of the contraption. Wrap lettuce in clean kitchen towel and enclose in plastic bag. The towel will absorb some moisture and will gently hydrate the lettuce. Refrigerate in crisper drawer up to 4 days. For iceberg lettuce, remove cone-shaped central core that starts at the root end (preferably using a plastic knife). Fill up the cavity with cold water; invert and shake out water. Let it drip dry in colander for a few minutes (or enclose in clean kitchen towel, grab all four corners of the towel, and hand-spin it back and forth to remove water—a fun outdoor activity on a hot day). Wrap in clean kitchen towel and enclose in plastic bag. Refrigerate in crisper drawer up to 5 days.

PREP AND USE: For salads, gently tear clean, chilled lettuce into bite-size pieces (see Buying and Storing for washing techniques). Use about 2 handfuls of lettuce per person for a first course, or 3 to 4 handfuls for a main course. Use raw lettuce in salads, sandwiches, and lettuce wraps. Cooked lettuce is popular in Chinese and French cuisines, either braised, simmered, or sautéed. Stir-fried chunks of iceberg lettuce or pureed lettuce soup with peas are two examples.

AVAILABLE: Year-round (peaks in late spring to early summer)

NUTRITIONAL INFORMATION (per 1 cup raw shredded butter): Calories 7, fat calories 1; total fat 0 grams, sat fat 0 grams, cholesterol 0 milligrams; sodium 3 milligrams; total carbohydrates 1 gram, fiber 1 gram, sugars 1 gram; protein 1 gram; vitamin A IUs 36%; vitamin C 3%; calcium 2%; iron 4%.

NUTRITIONAL INFORMATION (per 1 cup raw shredded green leaf): Calories 5, fat calories 0; total fat 0 grams, sat fat 0 grams, cholesterol 0 milligrams; sodium 10 milligrams; total carbohydrates 1 gram, fiber 0 grams, sugars 0 grams; protein 0 grams; vitamin A IUs 53%; vitamin C 11%; calcium 1%; iron 2%.

NUTRITIONAL INFORMATION (per 1 cup raw shredded iceberg): Calories 10, fat calories 1; total fat 0 grams, sat fat 0 grams, cholesterol 0 milligrams; sodium 7 milligrams; total carbohydrates 2 grams, fiber 1 gram, sugars 1 gram; protein 1 gram; vitamin A IUs 7%; vitamin C 3%; calcium 1%; iron 2%.

NUTRITIONAL INFORMATION (per 1 cup raw shredded red leaf): Calories 4, fat calories 1; total fat 0 grams, sat fat 0 grams; cholesterol 0 milligrams; sodium 7 milligrams; total carbohydrates 1 gram, fiber 0 grams, sugars 0 grams; protein 0 grams; vitamin A IUs 42%; vitamin C 2%; calcium 1%; iron 2%.

NUTRITIONAL INFORMATION (per 1 cup raw shredded romaine): Calories 8, fat calories 1; total fat 0 grams, sat fat 0 grams, cholesterol 0 milligrams; sodium 4 milligrams; total carbohydrates 2 grams, fiber 1 gram, sugars 1 gram; protein 1 gram; vitamin A IUs 55%; vitamin C 19%; calcium 2%; iron 3%.

SERVING SUGGESTIONS

Green Taco
Instead of a tortilla, wrap taco filling in a large butter lettuce leaf and fold to enclose contents. This technique is also delicious using egg salad as the filling.

Lettuce Nests
Form a nest of lettuce underneath a serving of pasta salad. This extends the dish and offers a tasty crunch (see Pasta Salad with Shallot Dressing, page 289).

Steak Apps
These appetizers are both delicious and pretty. Marinate and grill flank steak (see Easy-Way Flank Steak, page 144). Cut steak into thin slices and cut slices into 2-inch lengths. Top each steak slice with sliver of tart apple or peeled mango. Wrap each steak-apple bundle in butter lettuce that is cut small, but wide enough to cover edges of meat and long enough to go around steak bundle two times. Secure with toothpick. Repeat to use entire head of butter lettuce.

Buffet Romaine Wedges

Cut 3 small hearts of romaine into lengthwise quarters leaving them attached at the root end. Place a large bowl of creamy blue cheese dressing in a bowl in the center of a platter, along with a large spoon. Surround dressing with romaine quarters. Top romaine quarters with thin slices of red onion. Invite guests to make their own wedge-style salad.

Last Course Green Salad

YIELD: 4 SERVINGS

In French homes, a mixed green salad is often served after the main course. One way to have the salad ready to go is to prepare it before dinner starts, layering it in the salad bowl so the dressing is at the bottom of the bowl, with the torn greens on top. Toss just before serving.

1 large shallot, finely chopped

1 ½ teaspoons cider vinegar

1 teaspoon Dijon-style mustard

½ teaspoon salt

½ teaspoon freshly ground black pepper

¼ cup extra-virgin olive oil

1 large head red leaf lettuce, chilled, torn into bite-size pieces

1   In large salad bowl, combine shallot, vinegar, mustard, salt, and pepper; whisk to combine. Whisk in oil in thin stream. Taste and adjust seasoning as needed.

2   Take a set of salad servers (generally a large spoon and large fork) and crisscross them over the dressing. They will form a makeshift barrier. Place lettuce on top of crossed servers. Cover bowl and refrigerate up to 1 hour.

3   At serving time, pull out the salad servers and toss salad.

Nutritional information (per serving): Calories 140, fat calories 120; total fat 14 grams, sat fat 2 grams, cholesterol 0 milligrams; sodium 330 milligrams; total carbohydrates 4 grams, fiber 1 gram, sugars 1 gram; protein 1 gram; vitamin A IUs 120%; vitamin C 6%; calcium 4%; iron 6%.

Butter Lettuce Soup

YIELD: 4 SERVINGS

This pureed lettuce soup takes about 35 minutes to prepare. If a more vegetal taste is preferred, substitute 1 ½ cups baby spinach for half of the butter lettuce. A crunchy garnish is essential. It can be cooked and crumbled crisp bacon or vegetarian bacon, or thin strips of baked corn tortillas (see Cook's Note).

2 large heads butter lettuce, shredded, including ribs

4 cups chicken broth or vegetable broth, divided use

2 tablespoons unsalted butter

½ teaspoon seasoned salt

2 tablespoons minced fresh Italian parsley

Garnish: crumbled crisp bacon or vegetarian bacon or baked thin tortilla strips (see Cook's Note, page 198)

1   In Dutch oven or large saucepan, combine lettuce and 3 cups chicken broth or vegetable broth. Bring to boil on high heat; press down lettuce to submerge in broth. Cover and reduce heat to low; simmer 25 minutes.

2   Puree in food processor or blender in 4 batches. Use caution when blending hot liquids; if using blender, hold down lid with potholder. Return soup to pan. Add enough of remaining broth to reach a creamy consistency and heat until hot on medium heat. Add butter and stir until melted. Add seasoned salt. Taste and adjust seasoning if needed.

3   Ladle into 4 bowls and top with parsley. Top each serving with either bacon or vegetarian bacon or 2 or 3 baked tortilla strips.

Nutritional information (per serving without garnish): Calories 70, fat calories 50; total fat 6 grams, sat fat 3.5 grams, cholesterol 15 milligrams; sodium 750 milligrams; total carbohydrates 2 grams, fiber 1 gram, sugars 1 gram; protein 2 grams; vitamin A IUs 70%; vitamin C 10%; calcium 4%; iron 8%.

Cook's Note: To make toasted tortilla strips, preheat oven to 375°F. Cut 3 corn tortillas into ¼-inch-wide strips about 1½ inches long. Place on rimmed baking sheet in single layer. Bake in middle of preheated oven and bake until crisp and lightly browned, about 10 to 11 minutes.

No-Noodle Chinese Chicken Salad with Peanut and Ginger Dressing

YIELD: 8 SERVINGS

Traditionally, Chinese chicken salads contain deep-fried rice stick noodles or strips of fried wonton skins. This is a noodle-free version showcases raw vegetables—two kinds of cabbage, plus carrots, romaine lettuce, and cucumbers. The colors and flavors make a very appealing concoction.

2 (5-ounce) skinless, boneless chicken breasts (see Meatless Tip)

1 teaspoon extra-virgin olive oil or vegetable oil

Seasoned salt

Dressing

⅓ cup rice vinegar

1½ tablespoons minced fresh ginger

1½ tablespoons soy sauce

3 tablespoons agave syrup or sugar

¾ teaspoon Dijon-style mustard

1 teaspoon salt

¾ cup peanut oil

Salad

½ head green cabbage, cut in half lengthwise, cored, cut into ¼-inch-wide crosswise slices

¼ head red cabbage, cored, cut into ¼-inch-wide crosswise slices

1 heart of romaine lettuce, cut into ¼-inch-wide crosswise slices

1 large carrot, peeled, cut into 1-inch-long matchsticks

2 Persian (baby) cucumbers or ½ hothouse (English) cucumber, thinly sliced

⅓ cup coarsely chopped fresh cilantro

2 green onions, cut into ¼-inch-thick diagonal slices, including dark green stalks

¼ cup chopped roasted peanuts

Garnish: 3 tablespoons toasted sesame seeds (see Cook's Note)

No-Noodle Chinese Chicken Salad with Peanut and Ginger Dressing

1   Adjust oven rack to middle position.Preheat oven to 350°F. Place chicken in small roasting pan or pie pan. Drizzle with oil and season with seasoned salt. Bake 25 to 30 minutes or until thoroughly cooked. Cool and cut into bite-size pieces.

2   Prepare dressing: In small bowl or 1-quart glass measuring cup with handle, combine vinegar, ginger, soy sauce, agave syrup or sugar, mustard, and salt. Stir to combine with fork or whisk. Stir or whisk in oil.

3   Prepare salad: In large bowl, toss cabbages, romaine, carrot, cucumbers, cilantro, green onions, peanuts, and cooked chicken. Stir dressing and pour over salad; toss. Divide between plates and top with sesame seeds.

Nutritional information (per serving): Calories 340, fat calories 240; total fat 27 grams, sat fat 4.5 grams, cholesterol 15 milligrams; sodium 760 milligrams; total carbohydrates 16 grams, fiber 4 grams, sugars 9 grams; protein 11 grams; vitamin A IUs 20%; vitamin C 90%; calcium 10%; iron 10%.

Cook's Note: To toast sesame seeds, place in small skillet over medium-high heat. Shake handle to redistribute seeds as they toast to light brown. Watch carefully because they burn easily. Cool.

Meatless Tip: Omit chicken. Substitute Grilled Tofu with Asian-Style Marinade (page 321).

Vegetarian Couscous Lettuce Wraps

YIELD: 12 WRAPS

Great for a salad-like picnic treat or lunchbox entrée, these colorful wraps are loaded with flavorful ingredients. Grapes, bell pepper, parsley, red onion, and apple give the filling a nice crunch along with vibrant color.

Couscous Filling

2 cups vegetable broth or water

½ teaspoon salt

2 teaspoons extra-virgin olive oil or unsalted butter

1⅔ cups couscous

1 red bell pepper or yellow bell pepper, cored, seeded, diced

1 small red onion, diced

½ cup unpeeled, cored apple, diced

1 cup seedless grapes, halved, or whole champagne grapes

¼ cup toasted pine nuts (see Cook's Note)

3 tablespoons minced fresh Italian parsley

Vinaigrette

1½ tablespoons red wine vinegar

½ teaspoon honey or agave syrup

Salt

3 tablespoons extra-virgin olive oil

Freshly ground black pepper

12 large red leaf lettuce leaves

1   Prepare filling: Place broth or water, salt, and oil or butter in medium saucepan; bring to boil on high heat. Stir in couscous. Cover and remove from heat. Let stand 5 minutes. Remove from heat and fluff with fork. Place couscous in medium bowl and cool to room temperature.

2   Add bell pepper, onion, apple, grapes, pine nuts, and parsley to couscous. Gently toss.

3   Prepare vinaigrette: In small bowl or glass measuring cup with handle, stir vinegar, honey or agave syrup, and salt to taste with fork. Stir in oil and season to taste with black pepper. Add to couscous mixture and toss. Taste and add more salt if needed.

4   Place 1 lettuce leaf flat on cutting board, rib down with bottom of leaf facing you. Spoon a portion of couscous mixture across leaf slightly lower than center, leaving 2 inches of leaf empty on each end. Fold bottom of leaf over mixture and fold in sides of leaf. Roll leaf into packet. Package each wrap separately with plastic wrap if taking on a picnic or packing in a lunch.

Nutritional information (per wrap): Calories 170, fat calories 60; total fat 6 grams, sat fat 0.5 gram, cholesterol 0 milligrams; sodium 230 milligrams; total carbohydrates 25 grams, fiber 2 grams, sugars 4 grams; protein 4 grams; vitamin A IUs 30%; vitamin C 20%; calcium 2%; iron 4%.

Cook's Note: To toast pine nuts, place in small skillet on medium-high heat. Shake handle to redistribute pine nuts and lightly brown on all sides. Watch carefully because they burn easily. Cool.

Lime

There's nothing wishy-washy about limes. Their piercing acidity and spicy fragrance add balance and pizzazz to everything from perky cocktails to classic Southeast Asian dishes to Latin American delicacies. A good squeeze of lime juice over low-acid fruit such as avocado or papaya adds just-right tartness. A wedge rubbed against the rim of a glass of water turns something tasteless into something that is both fragrant and super-refreshing.

A big advantage of organic limes is in the superiority of their zest, the colored portion of the peel. Chemicals used in conventional growing methods can end up in the peel; these chemicals are forbidden in organic procedures. Plus the exteriors of organic limes are not waxed, so the taste and smell of the skin's exterior is untainted. But know that waxing extends shelf life, so plan on using organic limes within two weeks of purchase.

BUYING AND STORING: Look for limes that are heavy for their size, without soft spots or shriveling. Small brown areas on the rind won't affect the quality of the juice, but will reduce the amount of zest. Refrigerate in plastic bag for up to 2 weeks or at room temperature for up to 1 week.

PREP AND USE: Wash before use. If using zest, remove it before cutting lime (see page 324). When juicing, for best results first bring limes to room temperature or microwave for 10 seconds. Or roll on counter, pressing down with palm, to help break up segments. There are

hinged gadgets designed to squeeze every drop of juice out of a lime; the contraption surrounds a lime half between a perforated cup below and a solid cup above. A small reamer is also an option for extracting fresh lime juice.

Use minced zest and/or juice in sauces, soups, and salad dressings, desserts, beverages, and entrees.

AVAILABLE: Year-round (peak is May to July)

NUTRITIONAL INFORMATION (per 1 large raw lime with 2-inch diameter): Calories 20, fat calories 1; total fat 0 grams, sat fat 0 grams, cholesterol 0 milligrams; sodium 1 milligram; total carbohydrates 7 grams, fiber 2 grams, sugars 1 gram; protein 0 grams; vitamin A IUs 1%; vitamin C 32%; calcium 2%; iron 2%.

SERVING SUGGESTIONS

Limey Roast Chicken

Before roasting whole fryer, stuff cavity with two lime halves, rosemary sprigs, and 1 small onion (quartered).

Creamy Yogurt-Lime-Curry Dressing

Combine ⅓ cup unsweetened nonfat plain yogurt, 1 tablespoon fresh lime juice, ½ teaspoon minced lime zest (colored portion of peel), 2 teaspoons curry powder, and 1 teaspoon finely grated fresh ginger, plus salt and freshly ground black pepper to taste; stir well. Stir in 1 tablespoon canola oil. Toss with cooked rice, couscous, quinoa, orzo, or wheat berries, adding just enough dressing to very lightly coat. Garnish with diced mangoes, chopped peanuts, and chopped fresh mint.

Mojito

In a squat pitcher or cocktail shaker, muddle (smash) 2 to 3 sprigs of fresh mint into 2 teaspoons sugar with wooden spoon or muddler. Add 3 tablespoons fresh lime juice and stir until sugar dissolves. Stir in 3 tablespoons rum. Pour into a glass. Add ice to top. Fill with sparkling water and stir to combine.

Snappy-Spicy Lime Vinaigrette

Drizzle this over grilled poultry, vegetables, tofu, or pork. With motor running, drop 2 medium cloves garlic into food processor. Stop motor and add 1 tablespoon chopped fresh ginger, ¼ cup chopped fresh cilantro, and 1 seeded jalapeño chile; pulse until minced. Add ⅓ cup fresh lime juice, ¼ cup honey, 1 tablespoon balsamic vinegar, plus salt and freshly ground black pepper; pulse to combine. Add ½ cup extra-virgin olive oil and process to combine.

Lime Aqua Fresca

YIELD: 3 QUARTS, 12 SERVINGS

Refreshing lime aqua fresca is similar to lemonade, but it contains less sugar and the lime gives it a more assertive tartness than lemons.

1 cup fresh lime juice

¼ cup sugar

¼ teaspoon salt

2½ quarts water

Ice

1   In a large pitcher, mix juice, sugar, and salt. Stir until sugar and salt dissolve.

2   Add water and stir to combine. Cover and chill. Pour into glasses filled with ice.

Nutritional information (per 1 cup serving): Calories 20, fat calories 0; total fat 0 grams, sat fat 0 grams, cholesterol 0 milligrams; sodium 50 milligrams; total carbohydrates 6 grams, fiber 0 grams, sugars 5 grams; protein 0 grams; vitamin A IUs 0%; vitamin C 10%; calcium 0%; iron 0%.

Lime, Avocado, and Cranberry Salsa

YIELD: 5 CUPS

Enchiladas or tacos are delectable topped with this vivid salsa. Or serve it as a dip with sturdy tortilla chips or crackers. It is also delicious piled on a turkey sandwich.

2 yellow bell peppers

12 ounces fresh or frozen cranberries, thawed

3 tablespoons fresh lime juice

¼ cup fresh orange juice

6 ripe avocados, pitted, peeled, diced

3 jalapeño chiles, seeded, minced (See Cook's Note)

¼ cup chopped fresh cilantro

1 tablespoon grated orange zest (colored portion of peel)

2 tablespoons sugar or agave syrup

¼ teaspoon ground cayenne pepper

Salt and freshly ground black pepper

1   Roast bell peppers: Adjust oven rack 6 to 8 inches below broiler element. Preheat broiler. Place peppers in a single layer on aluminum foil–lined baking sheet. Broil until lightly charred, about 5 minutes. Rotate peppers with tongs and char on all sides. Remove from oven and draw up ends of foil to enclose peppers for 5 minutes. Open foil; when cool enough to handle, peel peppers and discard seeds. Resist temptation to wash skin off with water. Use your hands; the peppers will be more flavorful. Dice peppers.

2   In food processor fitted with metal blade, combine cranberries, lime juice, and orange juice; pulse to coarsely chop.

3   In large bowl, combine the cranberry mixture, avocados, chiles, cilantro, zest, and roasted bell peppers. Add sugar or agave syrup and cayenne pepper; gently toss. Add salt and black pepper to taste. Serve.

Nutritional information (per tablespoon): Calories 25, fat calories 20; total fat 2.5 grams, sat fat 0 grams, cholesterol 0 milligrams; sodium 0 milligrams; total carbohydrates 2 grams, fiber 1 gram, sugars 1 gram; protein 0 grams; vitamin A IUs 0%; vitamin C 8%; calcium 0%; iron 0%.

Cook's Note: Use caution when working with fresh chiles. Wash hands and work surface thoroughly upon completion and do not touch face or eyes.

Lime and Raspberry Cheesecake with White Chocolate

YIELD: 16 SERVINGS

White chocolate filling rippled with a swirl of raspberry puree makes a cheesecake that has a stunning appearance. The bright flavors of lime and raspberry offer a welcome tart edge to the sweet white chocolate mixture. The dessert freezes well: Wrap the cooled cheesecake in plastic wrap and aluminum foil. Label and freeze up to 1 month. Defrost in refrigerator overnight. Uncover and place at room temperature 1 hour before serving.

Crust

Unsalted butter for greasing pan

1½ cups crumbled shortbread cookies

1 cup toasted hazelnuts (see Cook's Note)

¼ cup sugar

¼ cup (½ stick) unsalted butter, melted

1½ teaspoons minced lime zest (colored portion of peel)

Raspberry Sauce

1½ cups fresh raspberries or unsweetened frozen (thawed, drained) raspberries

1 tablespoon sugar

1 teaspoon fresh lime juice

Filling

8 ounces white chocolate, chopped

2 pounds cream cheese, softened

1¼ cups sugar

2 tablespoons all-purpose flour

4 large eggs, room temperature

2 teaspoons vanilla

2 teaspoons fresh lime juice

1 teaspoon minced lime zest (colored portion of peel)

2 tablespoons heavy whipping cream

1 Adjust oven rack to middle position. Preheat oven to 350°F. Grease a 9-inch springform pan with butter. Wrap outside of pan (bottom and sides) with a sheet of heavy-duty aluminum foil.

2 Prepare crust: Place cookies, nuts, and sugar in food processor fitted with metal blade, pulse until coarsely ground. Add melted butter and zest; process until moist crumbs form. Press onto bottom and up sides of prepared pan. Bake until crust is light golden brown, about 15 to 18 minutes. Cool on wire rack.

3 Prepare raspberry sauce: Puree raspberries in food processor fitted with metal blade or in blender. Use back of spoon or rubber spatula to press raspberries through a strainer to remove seeds. Measure ½ cup strained puree into a small bowl and mix with 1 tablespoon sugar and juice. Set sauce aside and save any additional puree for another use or to use as garnish with the cheesecake

4 Prepare filling: Place chocolate in top pan of double boiler over barely simmering water; stir often and remove from stove as soon as it melts (chocolate should be just hot enough to melt).

5 Place cream cheese in large bowl of electric mixer. Mix on low speed until smooth, about 1 minute. Add sugar and mix until smooth and creamy, about 1 minute. Mix in flour. Add eggs, 2 at a time, mixing smooth after each addition. Stop mixer and scrape sides of bowl twice during mixing. Mix in vanilla, juice, and zest. Mix in cream and melted white chocolate. Pour batter into cooled crust in springform pan.

6 Use a small spoon to drizzle raspberry sauce over the batter, leaving a 1-inch plain edge. Dip spoon or small sharp knife gently into batter and swirl some of the sauce into batter, leaving some swirls of sauce on top of batter in a marbleized pattern. Do not disturb the crumb crust.

7 Place springform pan in roasting pan with sides at least 2 inches high. Pour hot water in the larger pan to reach 1 inch up the sides of springform pan. Put baking pan containing springform pan in oven. Bake about 1 hour, or until when you give the cheesecake a gentle shake, the top looks firm.

Lime and Raspberry Cheesecake with White Chocolate

8   Cool cheesecake, covered loosely with paper towels, in the water bath in the larger pan for 1 hour on a wire rack. Carefully remove cheesecake from water bath. Remove paper towels and cool 1 hour more. The cheesecake should feel cool to the touch. Cover with plastic wrap and chill thoroughly in the refrigerator, at least 6 hours or overnight.

9   Cut into wedges and garnish with fresh raspberries and mint or leftover raspberry sauce. Leftovers can be refrigerated up to 5 days.

Nutritional information (per serving): Calories 510, fat calories 320; total fat 36 grams, sat fat 19 grams, cholesterol 135 milligrams; sodium 240 milligrams; total carbohydrates 39 grams, fiber 2 grams, sugars 29 grams; protein 9 grams; vitamin A IUs 20%; vitamin C 6%; calcium 8%; iron 8%.

Cook's Note: To toast and skin raw hazelnuts, place on rimmed baking sheet for 10 to 12 minutes in middle of a 350°F oven, or until lightly browned. Wrap nuts in clean kitchen towel and set aside 2 minutes. Rub nuts in towel to remove skin; not all of the skin will come off, but that is not a problem. Cool.

Lime Walnut Cookies

YIELD: ABOUT 36 COOKIES

These mouthwatering cookies get a pleasant crunch from toasted nuts. Lime juice and zest add a just-right citrus taste that won't knock your socks off. If desired, glaze the cookies with a mixture of 2 tablespoons fresh lime juice and 2 tablespoons powdered sugar. While still warm brush the glaze on top of each cookie.

- 1 cup (2 sticks) unsalted butter, softened
- ¾ cup granulated sugar
- ¾ cup packed light brown sugar
- 2 eggs
- 1 teaspoon vanilla
- 3 tablespoons minced lime zest (colored portion of peel)
- 5 tablespoons fresh lime juice
- 2¼ cups all-purpose flour
- 1 teaspoon baking soda
- ½ teaspoon salt
- 1 cup walnut halves, toasted, chopped (see Cook's Note)

1   Adjust oven rack to middle position. Preheat oven to 350°F.

2   In large bowl of electric mixer, combine butter and granulated sugar; mix on medium-high speed until light and fluffy, about 5 minutes. Add brown sugar, eggs, and vanilla; mix until well combined. Add zest and juice; mix to combine.

3   In medium bowl, combine flour, baking soda, and salt. Gradually mix dry mixture into butter mixture, mixing until combined. Stir in toasted, chopped walnuts.

4   Line baking sheet(s) with parchment paper. Using 2 spoons (one to scoop, and one to push dough off), drop dough in tablespoonfuls onto prepared sheet, leaving 1½ to 2 inches between each mound. Bake for 10 to 12 minutes or until light golden brown. Move parchment paper onto wire rack to cool cookies. If desired, add glaze (see introduction).

Nutritional information (per cookie without glaze): Calories 130, fat calories 60; total fat 7 grams, sat fat 3.5 grams, cholesterol 25 milligrams; sodium 75 milligrams; total carbohydrates 15 grams, fiber 0 grams, sugars 9 grams; protein 2 grams; vitamin A IUs 4%; vitamin C 2%; calcium 2%; iron 4%.

Cook's Note: To toast walnuts, place on rimmed baking sheet in single layer. Toast in middle of 350°F oven for about 5 minutes, or until lightly toasted. Watch carefully because they burn easily. Cool.

Mango

Ataulfo

Haden

Kent

Tommy Atkins

No wonder mangoes are the most widely consumed fruit in the world. The soft flesh is sweet and exotic, a blend of pineapple and tree-ripened peach. The scent is an alluring blend of pine forest and tropical jungle.

Ataulfo mangoes, sometimes labeled Mexican or Champagne mangoes, are small, kidney-shaped beauties with greenish-yellow to deep golden skin. They have a very sweet flavor profile and their smooth texture isn't the least bit fibrous. Haden, Kent, and Tommy Atkins varieties are larger and have oval shapes. They have vibrant sweet-tart flavor and are more fibrous than the Ataulfo variety. The Tommy Atkins variety makes up about 70 percent of organic mangoes sold in the U.S.

Grown in subtropical areas, frequent rain prevents pest problems for organically grown mangoes. As with conventionally grown mangoes, organic mangoes are treated with hot water before they are imported into the U.S.

Ataulfo

Tommy Atkins

BUYING AND STORING: Mangoes will ripen after they are harvested. For ripe fruit, look for mangoes that yield to light pressure. Avoid those with loose or shriveled skin. If ripening at home, place at room temperature for 1 to 3 days out of direct sunlight. Or, to speed up ripening, place 2 or more mangoes in loosely sealed paper bag (see page 323). When ripe, refrigerate in plastic bag up to 3 days.

PREP AND USE: Mangoes should always be peeled (some people have an allergic reaction when skin is eaten). To seed, peel, and dice, hold mango on work surface with stem end pointing up. Notice that it is an elliptical shape when viewed from the top. Using sharp knife, make a vertical slice along one of the long sides, about ⅜ inch from stem. If you hit the seed, move knife over a little and try again. Make a second slice on other side, about ⅜ inch from stem. The elongated seed is in the center slice left behind. Place a double layer of clean kitchen towel in your hand. Place one of the seed-free "halves" cut-side up in towel-lined hand. Using small, sharp knife, make parallel diagonal slices across mango about ¾ inch apart, taking care not to slice through peel. Make second set of slices in opposite direction. Push up the center of the slice on skin side to expose small mango cubes. Run knife just above mango skin to slice away cubes. Repeat with other "half." Peel center slice that contains seed. Cut two long strips from either side of mango seed and dice. Eat raw or cooked (seed and skin should not be eaten). Eat raw out of hand or use in sorbet or cocktails, smoothies, or fruit salads. To cook, include in sweet or savory rice dishes and pork dishes. Southeast Asian cuisines use unripened, green mangoes in tangy salads.

AVAILABLE:

Ataulfo: March to July

Haden, Kent, Tommy Atkins: Year-round

NUTRITIONAL INFORMATION (per 1 cup sliced, raw): Calories 107, fat calories 4; total fat 0 gram, sat fat 0 grams, cholesterol 0 milligrams; sodium 3 milligrams; total carbohydrates 28 grams, fiber 3 grams, sugars 28 grams; protein 1 gram; vitamin A IUs 25%; vitamin C 76%; calcium 2%; iron 1%.

SERVING SUGGESTIONS

Mango Coulis

For vibrant dessert sauce, puree diced mango in blender or food processor until smooth. Spoon over angel food cake, pudding, ice cream, or fruit salad.

Chicken Salad

Add diced mango to chilled chicken salad. If desired, also add a little minced fresh cilantro.

Mango and Mint Salsa

In medium bowl, combine 1 finely diced ripe mango, ¼ medium red onion (finely diced), ½ minced jalapeño chile (seeded), 1½ tablespoons fresh lime juice, 1 tablespoon chopped fresh mint, and 1 tablespoon extra-virgin olive oil. Gently toss and season with salt and freshly ground black pepper. Use atop grilled chicken, fish, pork, game, or grilled tofu.

Mango Lassi

To make this South Asian smoothie, place 1 cup cold plain yogurt and 1½ cups diced ripe mango in blender; whirl until smooth. Add ½ cup cold milk and 1 tablespoon sugar or agave syrup; whirl until smooth.

Mango Chutney

YIELD: ABOUT 4 CUPS

Mango chutney is the addictive relish served with classic curried East Indian dishes. It isn't limited to just curries; try this mouthwatering concoction with grilled chicken, pork, or tofu. It is also delicious atop Brie cheese. It is best to use mangoes that are partially ripe; they should be just starting to ripen—not rock hard, mango should give to firm pressure.

- 3 ripe but firm mangoes, peeled, seeded, diced
- ¼ cup distilled white vinegar
- ¼ cup seasoned rice vinegar
- 1 medium yellow onion, coarsely chopped
- ⅓ cup sugar
- 2 teaspoons salt
- ⅓ cup raisins
- 1 (¾-inch slice) fresh ginger, coarsely chopped
- 1 jalapeño chile, stemmed, halved, seeded (see Cook's Note)
- 4 large cloves garlic, peeled
- ¾ teaspoon ground cumin
- 1 teaspoon ground coriander
- ½ teaspoon ground turmeric
- 2 tablespoons vegetable oil or canola oil, plus more if needed to thin paste
- 1 cinnamon stick, about 3 inches

1 In glass or ceramic bowl, combine mangoes, vinegars, onion, sugar, salt, and raisins. Toss and set aside.

2 In blender, add ginger, chile, garlic, cumin, coriander, and turmeric. Whirl until pureed into paste, scraping down sides as needed and adding a little oil if necessary.

3 Heat 2 tablespoons oil in Dutch oven or large, heavy-bottomed saucepan on medium heat; add paste and cinnamon stick. Cook and stir frequently for about 8 minutes, or until warm and fragrant.

4 Add mango mixture and simmer, covered, on low heat, stirring occasionally, 25 minutes or until mango is tender. Remove and discard cinnamon stick. Cool. Refrigerate well-sealed in plastic, ceramic, or glass container up to 3 weeks.

Nutritional information (per 1 teaspoon): Calories 5, fat calories 0; total fat 0 grams, sat fat 0 grams, cholesterol 0 milligrams; sodium 30 milligrams; total carbohydrates 1 gram, fiber 0 grams, sugars 1 gram; protein 0 grams; vitamin A IUs 0%; vitamin C 2%; calcium 0%; iron 0%.

Cook's Note: Use caution when working with fresh chiles. Wash work surface and hands thoroughly upon completion and do *not* touch eyes or face.

Mixed Green Salad with Blueberries and Mango Dressing

YIELD: 4 SERVINGS

Mangoes and blueberries are great flavor partners. They both have sweet-tart flavor profiles, but mangoes lean toward peachy-pineapple flavors and blueberries have a finish that offers a more assertive tartness while delivering an appealing crunchy texture. Here they team with fresh greens and a tangy mango dressing that is spooned around the periphery of the salad. A small amount of crumbled blue cheese adds both salt and tang.

Mango Dressing

- 1 large ripe mango, peeled, seeded, diced
- 1 tablespoon plain yogurt
- 3 tablespoons seasoned rice vinegar
- ¼ teaspoon coarse salt, such as kosher
- ¼ teaspoon freshly ground black pepper

Salad

- 8 cups mixed baby greens
- 1½ cups blueberries
- 1 large ripe mango, peeled, seeded, diced
- 2 tablespoons extra-virgin olive oil
- 1 tablespoon seasoned rice vinegar
- Garlic salt
- Freshly ground black pepper
- 3 ounces crumbled blue cheese

1 Prepare dressing: Place dressing ingredients in blender or food processor; whirl until smooth. Taste and adjust seasoning as needed. Set aside.

2 Prepare salad: Place greens, blueberries, and mango in large bowl. Drizzle oil on top and toss to lightly coat greens with oil. Add vinegar, garlic salt to taste, pepper to taste, and blue cheese; toss.

3 Arrange salad in center of 4 dinner plates, leaving an area empty around edge of greens. Puddle mango dressing in small amounts around edge of greens.

Nutritional information (per serving): Calories 270, fat calories 120; total fat 14 grams, sat fat 5 grams, cholesterol 15 milligrams; sodium 720 milligrams; total carbohydrates 34 grams, fiber 6 grams, sugars 24 grams; protein 7 grams; vitamin A IUs 80%; vitamin C 90%; calcium 20%; iron 10%.

Pavlova with Mango and Blackberries

YIELD: 8 SERVINGS

Named for Russian prima ballerina Anna Pavlova, the Pavlova is a dessert that teams a crisp-baked meringue base with whipped cream and fresh fruit. It's the national dessert of Australia and New Zealand. This version uses a mixture of diced mango and blackberries. Feel free to substitute other berries, such as blueberries, raspberries, or sliced strawberries.

- Unsalted butter and flour for preparing baking sheet
- 4 large egg whites, room temperature (see Cook's Notes)
- ½ teaspoon salt
- 1 cup superfine sugar (see Cook's Notes), divided use
- 2 teaspoons cornstarch
- 2 teaspoons distilled white vinegar
- 2 cups cold heavy whipping cream
- 2 tablespoons powdered sugar (see Cook's Notes)
- Optional: 1 teaspoon orange liqueur
- 3 ripe mangoes, peeled, seeded, diced
- 1 cup blackberries
- 1 tablespoon chopped fresh mint
- Optional garnish: mint leaves

1 Adjust oven rack to middle position. Preheat oven to 300°F. Butter and flour a baking sheet; invert and shake off excess flour. Using a 7-inch plate or bowl as a guideline, trace a circle with your finger or with the point of a knife in the flour. Set aside.

2 Place egg whites in large bowl of electric mixer. Beat on medium speed until foamy. Add salt and increase speed to medium-high. Beat until soft peaks form. Add 1 tablespoon superfine sugar and beat for 1 minute on medium-high speed. Repeat procedure, adding 1 tablespoon of superfine sugar and beating for 1 minute, until all sugar has been incorporated.

3 In a small bowl, stir cornstarch and vinegar until blended. Fold cornstarch mixture into egg white mixture. Spread to form a circle in the traced area of prepared baking sheet. Make a well (about 6 inches wide and 1 inch deep) using the bowl of a large spoon or flexible metal frosting spatula. Straighten outside edges. Place in middle of a preheated 300°F oven; immediately turn oven to 250°F. Bake until outside of meringue is firm and pale tan in color, about 1 hour 15 minutes. Place sheet on cooling rack for 15 minutes. Using a large spatula, transfer Pavlova to serving plate. Don't worry if there are cracks in the meringue. The whipped cream will cover them up. It may stand, uncovered, at room temperature for up to 8 hours.

4 In large bowl of electric mixer, whip cream until soft peaks form. Add powdered sugar and liqueur, if desired, and beat until stiff. Fill meringue with whipped cream and spread cream over top and sides.

5 In medium bowl, toss mangoes, blackberries, and chopped mint; gently toss with rubber spatula. Make a ½-inch-deep well in center of whipped cream and spoon in fruit mixture. Garnish with mint leaves, if desired. Cut into wedges and serve.

Nutritional information (per serving): Calories 380, fat calories 200; total fat 22 grams, sat fat 14 grams, cholesterol 80 milligrams; sodium 200 milligrams; total carbohydrates 44 grams, fiber 2 grams, sugars 39 grams; protein 4 grams; vitamin A IUs 30%; vitamin C 45%; calcium 6%; iron 2%.

Cook's Notes: To bring cold eggs to room temperature, place in warm water to cover for 5 minutes; remove and dry eggs.

To create superfine sugar, place about 1½ cups sugar in food processor (perfectly clean and dry) fitted with the metal blade; process for 30 seconds. Measure 1 cup.

If assembling Pavlova more than 30 minutes before serving, increase amount of powdered sugar in the whipped cream to ¼ cup. This will help to stabilize the whipped cream.

Mango-Citrus Sorbet

YIELD: 8 SERVINGS

Sorbet creates flavor excitement with a balance of sweet and tart flavors. Here, the vibrant taste of mango combines with both lemon and orange juice to make an irresistible profile of tastes. If desired, accompany the sorbet with Rosemary Shortbread (page 168) to add a subtle herbaceous tone. And if desired, drizzle a smidgen of orange liqueur over top of each serving of sorbet.

½ cup water

½ cup sugar (see Cook's Notes, page 210)

3 large or 4 medium mangoes, peeled, seeded, diced

Juice of 1 lemon, preferably Meyer

Juice of 1 orange, preferably Cara Cara

Optional for serving: Rosemary Shortbread (page 168) or other cookie of choice

Mango-Citrus Sorbet

1 In small saucepan, combine water and sugar. Bring to boil on high heat; boil 2 minutes. Cool and chill.

2 Puree mango in batches in blender or food processor fitted with metal blade; fruit should be smooth, without any lumps. Add chilled sugar syrup and juices; whirl until combined.

3 Process in ice cream machine according to manufacturer's instructions.

4 Transfer to container. Cover and freeze at least 5 hours or up to 1 week. Place in refrigerator 20 minutes before serving to soften slightly.

Nutritional information (per ½ cup serving without cookies): Calories 120, fat calories 0; total fat 0 grams, sat fat 0 grams, cholesterol 0 milligrams; sodium 0 milligrams; total carbohydrates 32 grams, fiber 2 grams, sugars 28 grams; protein 1 gram; vitamin A IUs 15%; vitamin C 60%; calcium 2%; iron 0%.

Cook's Notes: If you prefer to use agave syrup instead of sugar, combine 1 cup water and ¾ cup agave syrup. Use 1 cup of agave-water mixture for this recipe and refrigerate leftover syrup for future use.

If desired, accompany this sorbet with Rosemary Shortbread (see page 168). They add a pleasing buttery herbal edge to the sweet–tart sorbet.

Melon

 Cantaloupe

Honeydew

Watermelon, Mini Watermelon

Fragrance-filled and temptingly tender, melons come in a wide variety of colors, shapes, and sizes. They are generally classified into two categories: watermelon (with its seeds distributed throughout the flesh) and muskmelon, which includes cantaloupe and honeydew (with seeds and strings grouped together in the center).

Over the last few years, seedless watermelons have become commonplace. Shiny black seeds have disappeared in these varieties, replaced instead with "seeds" that aren't developed. They are small, empty white "pips" that usually surround the seeds in seeded varieties. Mini watermelons are only available seedless and are a convenient size for ice chests and crowded refrigerators, usually only 5 to 8 inches in diameter. They have a thicker rind and a longer shelf life.

Organic melon growers stress the importance of composting the soil before planting. They often

Watermelon

Honeydew

Watermelon

Canteloupe

use underground drip irrigation to prevent too much moisture on the surface of the soil and to help prevent weed growth. Organic melon yields are about 15 percent less than conventionally grown melons.

BUYING AND STORING: Choose melons that feel heavy for their size and are free of bruises or cracks. Muskmelons are fragrant when ripe and blossom end gives slightly to gentle pressure. Avoid those with cracks or spongy texture. If unripe, ripen at room temperature (uncut) up to about 4 days. Once cut, refrigerate in plastic bags for 2 to 3 days. For whole watermelons, again look for those that feel heavy for their size. Look at area where melon has rested on ground during growing period. A creamy yellow area indicates ripeness at harvest. Avoid those with cracks or soft spots. Some contend that a thudding sound made by tapping with palm of hand is a sign of ripeness; although this can be fun, it isn't a surefire method. Keep at room temperature up to 1 week or refrigerate whole up to 2 weeks. Or cut and cover cut surface with plastic wrap, or store pieces in airtight container up to 2 days. Remove rind and cut into wedges or balls; freeze, well sealed, up to 3 months, and use in smoothies or blended cocktails.

PREP AND USE: Wash well with cold water. For muskmelons, cut in half through the "equator." Scoop out seeds and strings with bowl of spoon. Cut out spheres with melon baller or, if cutting into cubes or wedges, cut off rind. For watermelons, cut into wedges, or cut off both ends, then in half through equator. Place wider cut edge on work surface. Using sturdy knife, cut off rind from top to bottom. If desired, reserve rind for pickling. Cut into desired shape. Or to use watermelon rind as a container, cut in half lengthwise and remove flesh (run knife around inner edge of rind; cut into wedges, then scoop out with large spoon).

Eat raw in fruit salads, compotes, beverages, salsas, cold soups, or sorbets. Cube and skewer to use as garnish for beverages. Watermelon rind can be pickled in mixture of salt, water, vinegar, sugar, and spices.

AVAILABLE:

Cantaloupe and honeydew: Year-round

Watermelon, mini watermelon: June to September

NUTRITIONAL INFORMATION (per 1 cup balls raw cantaloupe): Calories 60, fat calories 3; total fat 0 grams, sat fat 0 grams, cholesterol 0 milligrams; sodium 28 milligrams; total carbohydrates 16 grams, fiber 2 grams, sugars 14 grams; protein 1 gram; vitamin A IUs 120%; vitamin C 108%; calcium 2%; iron 2%.

NUTRITIONAL INFORMATION (per 1 cup balls raw honeydew): Calories 64, fat calories 2; total fat 0 grams, sat fat 0 grams, cholesterol 0 milligrams; sodium 32 milligrams; total carbohydrates 16 grams, fiber 1 gram, sugars 14 grams; protein 1 gram; vitamin A IUs 2%; vitamin C 53%; calcium 1%; iron 2%.

NUTRITIONAL INFORMATION (per 1 cup balls raw watermelon): Calories 46, fat calories 2; total fat 0 grams, sat fat 0 grams, cholesterol 0 milligrams; sodium 2 milligrams; total carbohydrates 12 grams, fiber 1 gram, sugars 10 grams; protein 1 gram; vitamin A IUs 18%; vitamin C 21%; calcium 1%; iron 2%.

SERVING SUGGESTIONS

Watermelon and Herb Salad

In medium bowl, toss 3 cups cubed watermelon, 2 tablespoons fresh lemon juice, 1 tablespoon chopped fresh basil leaves, and ½ tablespoon chopped fresh mint. Drizzle with 1 tablespoon agave syrup and toss.

White Sangria

In large pitcher, combine 1 chilled bottle dry white wine, ⅓ cup agave syrup or sugar, ½ cup brandy, 6 tablespoons frozen lemonade concentrate, 1 cup halved green grapes, and 1 cup diced cantaloupe. Stir to combine; cover and chill up to 3 hours. Serve in tall glasses filled with ice.

Cheese 'n' Melon

This is good for breakfast or dessert. Place wedge of chilled watermelon on plate. Next to it place a small wedge of either feta cheese or goat cheese. Make two small piles next to the cheese, one of toasted walnuts or candied walnuts, one of dried cranberries or candied ginger.

Melon in Spiced Syrup

In medium saucepan, combine ⅔ cup water and ⅔ cup sugar. Bring to simmer on medium heat, stirring until sugar dissolves. Add 1 teaspoon grated fresh ginger, 1 teaspoon grated lemon zest (colored portion of peel), and 1 cinnamon stick. Gently simmer 6 minutes. Cool and strain. Place 4 cups watermelon chunks and 4 cups cantaloupe or honeydew chunks in bowl. Pour syrup on melons and gently toss. Cover and chill. Garnish with chopped fresh mint and a few blueberries. If serving as a dessert, accompany with crisp cookies.

Cantaloupe Sorbet

YIELD: 6 SERVINGS

The earthy taste of cantaloupe lends itself well to sorbet, that softer-than-sherbet dessert that the Italians call *sorbetto*. If you like, serve tiny portions of this sorbet between savory courses as a palate cleanser as part of an elegant meal. If you like, add a smidgen of coarse salt to the top of each just before serving.

¼ cup sugar syrup (see Cook's Notes)

1 large lushly ripe cantaloupe, seeded, peeled, cut into 1-inch cubes

1½ tablespoons fresh lemon juice

For serving: thin wedges of seeded watermelon or seeded honeydew

Optional garnish: sprigs of fresh mint

Optional for serving: crisp cookies

1 Place cantaloupe in food processor fitted with metal blade. Add lemon juice and ¼ cup sugar syrup; puree until smooth. Process in ice cream machine according to manufacturer's instructions.

2 Scoop into chilled bowls or goblets atop small wedge of either watermelon or honeydew. If desired, garnish with mint and pass an assortment of cookies.

Nutritional information (per serving without cookies): Calories 110, fat calories 0; total fat 0 grams, sat fat 0 grams, cholesterol 0 milligrams; sodium 20 milligrams; total carbohydrates 28 grams, fiber 0 grams, sugars 17 grams; protein 1 gram; vitamin A IUs 90%; vitamin C 90%; calcium 2%; iron 2%.

Cook's Notes: Prepare the sugar syrup (see page 210): This recipe makes more sugar syrup than the sorbet requires. Leftover syrup can be covered and refrigerated; use to sweeten future sorbet or cocktails.

If you wish to make sorbet richer and silkier, you can add 2 tablespoons half-and-half or heavy whipping cream; add it to the mixture in the food processor in step 1.

Mango and Melon Salad

YIELD: 6 SERVINGS

The combination of melon and mango is magical, both for eye and for palate. If you like, omit the mixed baby greens and spoon the salad into chilled martini glasses; garnish each with a sprig of either fresh mint or basil. For best results, use chilled fruit for this salad.

3 tablespoons rice vinegar

1 tablespoon minced fresh ginger

2 teaspoons soy sauce

1½ teaspoons agave syrup or honey

⅛ teaspoon dried red chile flakes, or more as needed

¼ cup vegetables oil or canola oil

1 cup 1-inch cubes honeydew

1 cup 1-inch cubes watermelon

1 cup 1-inch cubes mango

½ hothouse (English) cucumber, unpeeled, halved lengthwise, thinly sliced

2 green onions, cut into ⅛-inch diagonal slices, including dark green stalks

2 cups mixed baby greens

2 tablespoons toasted sesame seeds (see Cook's Note)

1 In medium-large bowl, place vinegar, ginger, soy sauce, agave syrup or honey, and chile flakes; whisk to combine. Whisk in vegetable oil or canola oil. Taste and add more chile flakes if desired. Add melons, mango, cucumber, and green onions. Gently toss.

2 Divide greens between 6 salad plates. Top with melon salad. Sprinkle with sesame seeds.

Nutritional information (per serving): Calories 150, fat calories 100; total fat 11 grams, sat fat 1.5 grams, cholesterol 0 milligrams; sodium 250 milligrams; total carbohydrates 0 grams, fiber 2 grams, sugars 10 grams; protein 2 grams; vitamin A IUs 25%; vitamin C 35%; calcium 2%; iron 4%.

Cook's Note: To toast sesame seeds, place in small skillet on medium-high heat. Shake handle to redistribute seeds and toast to light brown color. Watch carefully because they burn easily. Cool.

Curried Turkey and Melon Salad

Curried Turkey and Melon Salad

YIELD: 8 SERVINGS

Curry powder is used to spike the dressing with the alluring aroma and taste of dried herbs and spices. Contents of commercial curry powder blends vary from brand to brand, but generally speaking, they fall into two basic styles: standard and the hotter of the two, "Madras." In this salad, use the style that most suits your taste.

½ cup mayonnaise

⅓ cup unsweetened plain yogurt

⅓ cup sour cream

1 tablespoon curry powder

2 cups (¾ pound) cubed cooked turkey or chicken (see Meatless Tip)

1 cup green or red seedless grapes, halved if large

½ medium honeydew, seeded, peeled, cut into ¼-inch cubes

½ medium cantaloupe, seeded, peeled, cut into ¼-inch cubes

Optional: 1 large, ripe peach or nectarine, peeled, pitted, cut into ¼-inch cubes, or 2 ripe apricots, pitted, cut into ¼-inch cubes

2 large stalks celery, trimmed, cut into ¼-inch pieces

4 green onions, sliced, including ½ dark green stalks

Salt and freshly ground black pepper

6 cups mixed baby greens

1 cup toasted slivered almonds (see Cook's Note)

1 To make dressing, bowl whisk mayonnaise, yogurt, sour cream, and curry powder in small bowl; set aside.

2 In large bowl, place turkey or chicken, grapes, melons, peach or nectarine or apricots if using, celery, and green onions. Add dressing and salt and pepper to taste; gently toss to lightly coat contents with dressing. Taste and adjust seasoning as needed.

3 Place baby greens on serving platter. Spoon salad on top. Top with almonds. Season to taste with salt and pepper.

Nutritional information (per serving with turkey): Calories 260, fat calories 140; total fat 15 grams, sat fat 3 grams, cholesterol 25 milligrams; sodium 180 milligrams; total carbohydrates 20 grams, fiber 4 grams, sugars 9 grams; protein 15 grams; vitamin A IUs 50%; vitamin C 50%; calcium 10%; iron 10%.

Cook's Note: To toast slivered almonds, place on rimmed baking sheet in single layer. Toast in middle of a 350°F oven about 3 to 4 minutes, or until nicely browned. Watch carefully because nuts burn easily. Cool.

Meatless Tip: Cook 2 cups of a rice medley mixture (such as brown rice, wild rice, and barley). Cool to room temperature. Omit turkey in step 2. Place mixed greens on platter and top with rice; spoon fruit mixture on top of rice. If desired, garnish with sprigs of fresh cilantro.

Grilled Portobello Mushrooms and Honeydew Salad

YIELD: 6 SERVINGS

Grilled marinated portobello mushrooms offer a meat-like element to this tasty salad. As a side dish, it is right at home served with roast chicken or pork. Or make slightly larger servings and make it the meal. If you like fresh mint, add 1 tablespoon of minced mint to the dressing. Feta cheese, with its slightly sour and salty flavor profile, flatters the earthy taste of grilled portobello mushrooms and the sweetness of honeydew melon. Use plain feta if you prefer, or one that is augmented with complementary flavors such as sun-dried tomatoes or garlic and herbs.

¼ cup balsamic vinegar

1 teaspoon cider vinegar

½ teaspoon garlic salt

2 large shallots, minced

½ cup extra-virgin olive oil

Freshly ground black pepper

6 portobello mushrooms, stemmed (see Cook's Note)

4 cups mixed baby greens

1 honeydew, seeded, peeled, cut into ½-inch-wide wedges

4 ounces crumbled feta cheese, plain or with herbs and sun-dried tomatoes or herbs and garlic

1   Heat grill. Clean grates and brush with vegetable oil.

2   Prepare vinaigrette: In small bowl, combine vinegars, garlic salt, and shallots. Using a fork, whisk in oil; season with pepper to taste.

3   Brush both sides of each mushroom liberally with vinaigrette. Place rounded-side down on grill. Grill 2 to 3 minutes, or until grill marks form. Lift with tongs and rotate ¼ turn. Grill 1 to 2 minutes (this will create crisscross grill marks). Watch carefully to prevent burning, moving mushrooms to cooler part of grill if there are any flare-ups. Turn mushrooms over and brush again with vinaigrette. Grill 2 to 4 minutes, or until thoroughly heated and softened.

4   Place mushrooms on cutting board and drizzle with a little vinaigrette; allow to rest for 10 minutes. Cut into ½-inch-wide slices. Taste and add more salt and pepper if needed.

5   Toss salad greens with enough vinaigrette to barely coat the leaves. Divide greens among 6 plates. Alternate slices of mushrooms with melon slices. Sprinkle with feta cheese and serve.

Nutritional information (per serving with plain feta cheese): Calories 280, fat calories 150; total fat 16 grams, sat fat 4.5 grams, cholesterol 15 milligrams; sodium 370 milligrams; total carbohydrates 32 grams, fiber 3 grams, sugars 25 grams; protein 7 grams; vitamin A IUs 30%; vitamin C 90%; calcium 10%; iron 10%.

Cook's Note: For portobellos, remove stems and discard; wipe mushrooms with moist paper towel. Use bowl of teaspoon to scrape off and discard gills (delicate ridges on underside of portobellos).

Mushroom

Cremini

Common White (Button)

Portobello

Shiitake

Highly prized for their versatility, mushrooms' flavor profiles range from woodsy to nutty, meaty to mild. These fleshy cultivated fungi can have caps that look like open umbrellas or sphere-like domes that fit snugly to stem.

Common white mushrooms, sometimes labeled button mushrooms, have rounded caps with closed veils (fit snug at the stem); they taste mildly woodsy. Cremini have the same size and shape but have dark brown caps; they taste mildly earthy. When they mature, they are called portobello mushrooms. Meaty rich and earthy, portobello mushrooms have deep, dark gills under their caps. Shiitakes look like broad, open umbrellas, and have tan-colored gills; they taste steak-like beefy.

Mushrooms are grown indoors in climate-controlled sheds. Summertime heat can lower organic production due to an increase in pests. Organic growers report that their yield is about 10 percent less than conventionally grown crops. Rather than chemically sterilized compost, organic mushrooms are grown in compost that has been sterilized by heat.

Portobello

Cremini

Shiitake

White

BUYING AND STORING: Look for firm mushrooms that are free of soft spots or mold. They should be stored with cool air circulating around them; do not store in plastic bag or packaging. Instead, place unwashed in pan or sheet in single layer with barely damp paper towel on top and refrigerate up to one week. Sautéed mushrooms can be frozen up to three months.

PREP AND USE: Avoid submerging in water to wash because mushrooms absorb like a sponge and become mushy. Instead, wipe surface with moist paper towels. If extremely dirty, they can be briefly dunked into cold water and wiped dry.

Discard shiitake stems or use them to create stock (then discard them); use paring knife to cut stem where it meets the cap. Cooking doesn't soften the shiitake stems' stubborn toughness.

If using dried mushrooms, reconstitute them by soaking in hot water until pliable, usually about 20 minutes. Strained soaking liquid is often used as an ingredient in recipes calling for dried mushrooms.

Mushrooms can be marinated, sautéed, simmered, broiled, roasted, or grilled. Mushrooms with hollow caps are delicious stuffed with hot or cold fillings. Portobello caps can be grilled and used as a pizza "crust." Dried mushrooms can be ground and used to flavor breadcrumbs, soups, and sauces, or used as a dry rub for meat.

AVAILABLE: Year-round

NUTRITIONAL INFORMATION (per 1 cup sliced raw common white): Calories 15, fat calories 2; total fat 0 grams, sat fat 0 grams, cholesterol 0 milligrams; sodium 4 milligrams; total carbohydrates 2 grams, fiber 1 gram, sugars 1 gram; protein 2 grams; vitamin A IUs 0%; vitamin C 2%; calcium 0%; iron 2%.

NUTRITIONAL INFORMATION (per 1 cup sliced raw cremini): Calories 19, fat calories 1; total fat 0 grams, sat fat 0 grams, cholesterol 0 milligrams; sodium 4 milligrams; total carbohydrates 3 grams, fiber 0 grams, sugars 1 gram; protein 2 grams; vitamin A IUs 0%; vitamin C 0%; calcium 1%; iron 2%.

NUTRITIONAL INFORMATION (per 1 cup diced raw portobello): Calories 22, fat calories 1; total fat 0 grams, sat fat 0 grams, cholesterol 0 milligrams; sodium 5 milligrams; total carbohydrates 4 grams, fiber 1 gram, sugars 2 grams; protein 2 grams; vitamin A IUs 0%; vitamin C 0%; calcium 1%; iron 3%.

NUTRITIONAL INFORMATION (per 1 cup sliced raw shiitake): Calories 40, fat calories 0; total fat 0 grams, sat fat 0 grams, cholesterol 0 milligrams; sodium 0 milligrams; total carbohydrates 6 grams, fiber 1 gram, sugars 2 grams; protein 1 gram; vitamin A IUs 0%; vitamin C 0%; calcium 1%; iron 0%.

SERVING SUGGESTIONS

Fontina Mushroom Crostini

Adjust oven rack to lowest position and preheat oven to 450°F. In large bowl, toss 1 pound halved cremini mushrooms, 2 tablespoons extra-virgin olive oil, and 2 teaspoons fresh thyme leaves. Arrange mushrooms in single layer on rimmed baking sheet. As mushrooms roast, they will release juices. Roast until most of liquid evaporates and mushrooms brown, 12 to 14 minutes. Toss to turn mushrooms so they can brown on opposite side; roast 5 to 8 minutes longer, until completely browned. If they seem dry, toss with a little olive oil. Top Roasted Garlic Crostini (page 139) with mushrooms and generous pinch of grated fontina cheese.

Shiitake Noodle Soup

Add sautéed sliced shiitake mushrooms to your favorite chicken noodle soup. Shiitakes give the soup new depth, spiking it with meaty flavor.

Mixed Green Salad with Mushrooms

In bottom of large bowl, mix juice of 1 lemon with salt and freshly ground black pepper to taste; whisk in ⅓ cup extra-virgin olive oil. Add 2 teaspoons minced fresh tarragon leaves, ¾ cup sliced cremini or common white mushrooms, 6 halved cherry tomatoes, ¼ cup diced fontina or Muenster cheese, 1 hard-cooked egg (peeled and sliced), and, if you like, ¼ cup diced ham; gently toss. Tear 2 medium heads of washed butter lettuce into bite-size pieces and add to bowl. Toss and taste; adjust seasoning as needed.

Stuffed Mushies

Remove stems from 12 medium common white (button) mushrooms; toss caps with 1½ tablespoons extra-virgin olive oil and place hollow side up on rimmed baking sheet. Adjust rack to 6 to 8 inches below broiler element; preheat broiler. Combine ⅓ cup fine fresh sourdough breadcrumbs, 4 tablespoons melted unsalted butter, 4 tablespoons shredded Jack cheese, 1 teaspoon soy sauce, 1 tablespoon minced fresh Italian parsley, and 1 tablespoon dry white wine; if desired, add 2 teaspoons crumbled cooked bacon. Toss to combine. Mound the bread mixture into mushroom cavities. Broil until lightly browned, about 4 minutes.

Farro "Risotto" with Roasted Mushrooms

YIELD: 4 FIRST-COURSE SERVINGS

To turn this first-course stunner into a main dish, serve it topped with sliced roasted duck breasts.

- 1 pound common white (button) or cremini mushrooms, cleaned, quartered if large, halved if small
- 5 tablespoons extra-virgin olive oil, divided use
- 1 teaspoon minced fresh rosemary leaves
- 1 small yellow onion, chopped
- 1½ cups semi-pearled or semi-peeled farro
- ⅓ cup dry white wine
- 4 cups water, divided use
- 3 tablespoons grated Parmesan cheese
- ⅓ cup heavy whipping cream
- 1 tablespoon unsalted butter
- Salt and freshly ground black pepper
- Garnish: 6 small sprigs rosemary

1 Adjust oven rack to lowest position. Preheat oven to 450°F.

2 In large bowl, toss mushrooms, 3 tablespoons oil, and rosemary. Arrange mushrooms in single layer on rimmed baking sheet. Roast until most of liquid evaporates and mushrooms brown, about 12 to 14 minutes. As mushrooms roast, they will release juices. Toss to turn mushrooms so they can brown on opposite side; roast about 5 to 8 minutes longer, until mushrooms are completely browned. Remove from oven.

3 Meanwhile, prepare farro. In large saucepan, heat 2 tablespoons oil. Add onion and cook on medium-high heat until softened, about 5 minutes, stirring occasionally. Add farro and toss to coat with oil. Add wine and cook until wine absorbs, about 3 minutes.

4   Add water, 1 cup at a time, stirring occasionally and cooking between additions until most of liquid is absorbed. This will take about 20 to 25 minutes. Farro should be softened but with a little bite. Stir in cheese, cream, and butter. Season to taste with salt and pepper. Cook until heated through and thickened, stirring, about 3 minutes. Place farro in 6 shallow bowls. Stir in mushrooms. Garnish each with small sprig of rosemary.

Nutritional information (per serving): Calories 310, fat calories 140; total fat 16 grams, sat fat 6 grams, cholesterol 25 milligrams; sodium 50 milligrams; total carbohydrates 39 grams, fiber 1 gram, sugars 2 grams; protein 8 grams; vitamin A IUs 6%; vitamin C 2%; calcium 6%; iron 15%.

Cook's Note: Farro, sometimes mislabeled spelt (which is a different grain), is a grain with a mellow nutty flavor. It is sold at health food markets, Italian markets, and some supermarkets.

Grilled Portobello Burgers

YIELD: 4 SERVINGS

Tangy marinade adds scrumptious flavor to grilled portobello mushrooms. Use them in place of meat in burgers, supplemented with white cheddar cheese, sliced tomato, and red onion plus large leaves of fresh basil. If you like, brush grilled bread with mayonnaise or Tarragon Aïoli Dip (page 27). Or if you prefer, omit the bun and wrap the grilled mushroom, cheese, onion, and tomato in butter lettuce or iceberg lettuce and enjoy a bread-free version.

4 large portobello mushrooms

1 cup extra-virgin olive oil, plus oil for brushing grate

¾ cup red wine vinegar

¼ cup balsamic vinegar

1 tablespoon soy sauce

1 tablespoon sugar or agave syrup

½ tablespoon dried thyme

1 tablespoon minced fresh Italian parsley

Salt and freshly ground black pepper

4 sandwich buns, split, lightly brushed on cut side with olive oil

Optional: mayonnaise

4 to 8 slices white cheddar cheese or sharp yellow cheddar cheese, enough to generously cover each bun

4 tomato slices

4 very thin slices red onion

4 to 8 large leaves fresh basil

1   Remove stems and wipe mushrooms with moist paper towel. Use bowl of teaspoon to scrape off and discard gills (delicate ridges on underside of mushrooms).

2   Place large zipper-style plastic bag in bowl to hold it in place. Add oil, vinegars, soy sauce, sugar or agave syrup, thyme, and parsley. Add mushrooms and seal bag. Shake to distribute contents. Marinate in refrigerator at least 2 hours or up to 8 hours.

3   Heat grill. Clean grates and brush with vegetable oil. Remove mushrooms from marinade. Grill mushrooms on oiled grate, about 3 minutes per side, until heated through and grill marks appear. Season to taste with salt and pepper. If grill is large enough, grill cut side of buns at same time; otherwise, grill bread separately, once mushrooms have completed cooking.

4   If desired, brush cut side of buns lightly with mayonnaise. Place cheese on bottom bun. Top with tomato, onion, basil, and mushroom; cover with upper portion of bun and serve.

Nutritional information (per serving without mayonnaise): Calories 390, fat calories 230; total fat 25 grams, sat fat 8 grams, cholesterol 30 milligrams; sodium 580 milligrams; total carbohydrates 31 grams, fiber 3 grams, sugars 8 grams; protein 14 grams; vitamin A IUs 10%; vitamin C 10%; calcium 25%; iron 15%.

Cook's Note: To produce lovely grill marks on mushrooms, while grilling push each portobello against the grate for about 30 seconds using a hamburger press or small, heavy skillet.

Mushroom Barley Soup

YIELD: 12 SERVINGS

With its intense earthy flavor, this hearty soup can make a one-dish cool-weather meal. Accompany it with slices of crusty bread and a simple mixed green salad.

2 ounces dried shiitake mushrooms

1 cup boiling water

¼ cup extra-virgin olive oil

1½ cups finely chopped onions

4 large cloves garlic, minced

2 pounds common white (button) mushrooms, trimmed and sliced

1 tablespoon soy sauce

½ cup medium-dry sherry

6 cups chicken broth or vegetable broth

4 cups water

1 cup pearl barley

8 medium carrots, peeled, cut diagonally into ½-inch-thick slices

½ teaspoon minced fresh thyme leaves or crumbled dried thyme

½ teaspoon minced fresh rosemary leaves or crumbled dried rosemary

Salt and ground fresh ground black pepper

⅓ cup minced fresh Italian parsley

1   Place shiitake mushrooms in small, heatproof bowl. Add boiling water to cover and set aside for 20 minutes. Using a slotted spoon, remove mushrooms from liquid; reserve liquid. Remove stems from shiitakes, discard stems; slice caps. Pour reserved liquid through a sieve lined with a dampened paper towel into another small bowl.

2   Heat oil in large saucepan or Dutch oven over medium heat. Add onions and cook, stirring occasionally, 8 to 10 minutes, until pale golden. Add garlic and cook 1 minute. Add white mushrooms and sliced shiitakes; cook over medium-high heat, stirring occasionally, about 10 minutes, until most of liquid evaporates. Add soy sauce and sherry and boil 5 minutes until evaporated.

3   Add chicken broth or vegetable broth, water, strained mushroom soaking liquid, barley, carrots, and herbs; bring to boil over high heat. Reduce heat to low; simmer, covered, 1 hour. Season to taste with salt and pepper. Stir in parsley and serve.

Nutritional information (per serving): Calories 170, fat calories 45; total fat 5 grams, sat fat 0.5 gram, cholesterol 0 milligrams; sodium 350 milligrams; total carbohydrates 26 grams, fiber 5 grams, sugars 5 grams; protein 5 grams; vitamin A IUs 140%; vitamin C 10%; calcium 4%; iron 6%.

Grilled Portobello Burgers

Shiitake Fried Rice

YIELD: 6 SERVINGS

t is important that the rice be well chilled before stir-frying. If desired, substitute long-grain brown rice for white rice. And a small sprinkle of chopped cilantro is a welcome garnish, along with toasted sesame seeds.

2 tablespoons plus 1 teaspoon vegetable oil

1 medium carrot, peeled, finely diced

2½ tablespoons minced fresh ginger

3 green onions, cut into ⅛-inch-thick diagonal slices, including dark green stalks

¾ teaspoon coarse salt, such as kosher

8 ounces shiitake mushrooms, stemmed, thinly sliced

3 cups cold cooked long-grain white rice, such as jasmine or basmati

1 egg, lightly beaten

For garnish: 2 tablespoons toasted sesame seeds (see Cook's Note)

Optional garnish: chopped cilantro

1 Heat oil in wok or large, deep skillet over high heat. Add carrot and stir-fry 2 to 3 minutes. Add ginger and green onions, reserving half of dark green slices for garnish, and salt; stir-fry 20 seconds. Add shiitakes and stir-fry until tender, 3 to 5 minutes.

2 Crumble rice into wok and stir-fry until lightly browned, 10 to 15 minutes. Allow rice to brown in one position, then toss to break up clumps. Add egg and stir-fry 1 minute to scramble egg. Remove from heat and add reserved green portion of sliced green onions; toss. Garnish individual servings with sesame seeds.

Nutritional information (per serving): Calories 210, fat calories 70; total fat 8 grams, sat fat 1.5 grams, cholesterol 35 milligrams; sodium 320 milligrams; total carbohydrates 32 grams, fiber 3 grams, sugars 3 grams; protein 4 grams; vitamin A IUs 35%; vitamin C 4%; calcium 4%; iron 15%.

Cook's Note: To toast sesame seeds, place in small skillet over medium-high heat. Shake handle to redistribute seeds as they toast to light brown. Watch carefully because they burn easily. Cool.

Nectarine

White Flesh

Yellow Flesh

Nectarines have smooth, fuzz-free skin. The deep-colored exteriors create visual drama; maroon-splashed ivory skin covers white flesh, while golden skin that is highlighted with crimson wraps around bright yellow flesh. The white-fleshed fruit is slightly sweeter than the yellow, and has a creamier texture. In general, ripe nectarines bruise less easily than ripe peaches, so shipping them is less problematic.

Organic nectarines are most often much sweeter than those grown using conventional methods. Typically, organic nectarines have Brix readings (see page 323) that are 4 to 5 percent higher. Growers say that, grown organically, newly planted nectarine trees take longer to produce, often delaying full production up to two years when compared to conventional orchards. And the size of organic nectarines is typically smaller.

BUYING AND STORING: Look for fruit that is fragrant, plump, and gives to gentle pressure at the shoulders, but without soft spots or mushiness. Deep-colored skin isn't necessarily a sign of ripeness. Take a good whiff; ripe nectarines have rich fragrance. They do not continue to ripen after harvest; brown-bag ripening (see page 323) will improve texture but not sweetness. Store at room temperature out of direct sunlight up to 2 days or refrigerate ripe fruit loose in crisper drawer up to 9 days (but note that refrigeration is not recommended because it can change taste).

PREP AND USE: Wash and dry fruit. Peeling nectarines is a matter of personal preference. Peaches need to be peeled before using in baked goods because their skin is thick and often comes loose from the fruit when heated. Nectarine skin is thin and generally stays attached to the fruit when heated. If peeling, either use a paring knife, or for a showier result, cut a very shallow X in the blossom end and drop into boiling water for about 1 to 2 minutes, then remove with slotted spoon and refresh with cold water; slip off skin. To pit, cut fruit in half from top to bottom along suture (seam). Twist halves in opposite directions and lift out pit. For clingstones, cut into quarters or eighths, cutting toward pit; lift off sections, cutting next to pit if stubborn flesh won't pull away. Use right away, or to prevent discoloration, rub with lemon or dip in acidulated water (cold water mixed with a little lemon or lime juice; see Glossary, page 323).

Eat raw or cooked. Nectarines have lower water content than peaches. Generally nectarines require more cooking time to soften. Slice and use raw atop French toast, cereal, cake, ice cream, or pancakes. Add to fruit salad, compotes, shortcake filling, salsa, or cold soups; blended drinks, cocktails, or dessert sauce. To cook, broil, bake, grill, or sauté. Use for pie, jam, jelly, cheesecake, cobbler, clafouti, crisp, or coffeecake.

AVAILABLE: May to September

NUTRITIONAL INFORMATION (per 1 cup sliced, raw): Calories 63, fat calories 4; total fat 0 grams, sat fat 0 grams, cholesterol 0 milligrams; sodium 0 milligrams; total carbohydrates 15 grams, fiber 2 grams, sugars 11 grams; protein 2 grams; vitamin A IUs 9%; vitamin C 13%; calcium 1%; iron 2%.

SERVING SUGGESTIONS

Nectarine Barbecue Sauce

Brush ribs or chicken with this tasty concoction during the last few minutes of grilling. To make sauce, combine 2 peeled and chopped nectarines, 4 tablespoons brown sugar, ½ cup cider vinegar, ⅓ cup water, 2 tablespoons ketchup, 2 tablespoons agave syrup or honey, and 2 large cloves garlic (minced) in medium, heavy-bottomed saucepan. Bring to boil on high heat; reduce heat to low and simmer 30 minutes, stirring occasionally. Puree in blender in 2 batches, cautiously holding lid in place with potholder. Store well sealed in refrigerator.

Cheesecake Topper

Cut 1½ pounds ripe pitted nectarines into wedges. Peel them first if you prefer, but you don't have to. Toss with 1½ tablespoons sugar or agave syrup; gently toss. Set aside for 15 minutes. Cut cheesecake into wedges and place on individual dessert plates. Spoon topping over cheesecake.

Roasted White Nectarine Siders

Preheat oven to 375°F. Cut 4 ripe white nectarines in half and place cut side down in single layer in glass baking dish. Roast until softened, about 18 to 20 minutes. Turn cut side up and sprinkle with a little coarse salt, such as kosher, and freshly ground black pepper. Top each with a dollop of sour cream or crème fraîche. Serve as accompaniment to pork, beef, poultry, or grilled tofu.

Layered with Pudding

Toss unpeeled, diced ripe nectarines with a smidgen of orange liqueur. Place alternate layers of fruit and vanilla pudding in stemmed glasses. Garnish each glass with sprig of fresh mint.

Nectarine Bran Muffins

YIELD: 12 MUFFINS

A great choice for breakfast treats or wholesome snacks, these flavorful nectarine-spiked muffins are moist and chewy.

1 cup bran cereal with raisins

½ cup fresh orange juice

1 cup all-purpose flour

¼ cup sugar

2½ teaspoons baking powder

½ teaspoon ground cinnamon

¼ teaspoon ground allspice

1 large egg

¼ cup vegetable oil

½ cup diced peeled nectarine

1   Adjust oven rack to middle position. Preheat oven to 400°F. Line standard-size 12-cup muffin tin with paper liners.

2   In small mixing bowl, combine cereal and juice. Stir periodically and allow bran to absorb all of juice.

3   In large bowl, place all dry ingredients and whisk to combine.

4   In medium bowl, place egg and oil; whisk to combine. Add egg mixture and bran mixture to dry ingredients along with chopped nectarines. Stir to combine.

5   Fill prepared muffin cups ¾ full with batter. Bake for 25 minutes or until toothpick inserted in center comes out clean. Cool slightly on wire rack and serve.

Nutritional information (per serving): Calories 120, fat calories 50; total fat 5 grams, sat fat 0.5 gram, cholesterol 20 milligrams; sodium 130 milligrams; total carbohydrates 17 grams, fiber 1 gram, sugars 6 grams; protein 2 grams; vitamin A IUs 2%; vitamin C 10%; calcium 6%; iron 10%.

Grilled Nectarines with Mascarpone and Berries

YIELD: 4 SERVINGS

It's the cook's call. Some people like nectarine skin; it's a beautiful color and very thin. Others prefer to remove the skin, so peel them if you prefer. For the topping, choose berries that are at their peak of flavor. If using ripe strawberries, hull them, then cut them so they are diced about the same size as the other berries in the mixture.

2 cups mixed berries, such as blueberries, blackberries, raspberries

2 tablespoons orange liqueur

⅔ cup mascarpone cheese, softened

2 tablespoons agave syrup or honey

2 large ripe nectarines, halved, pitted

Vegetable oil or canola oil for greasing grate

1   In medium bowl, combine berries and liqueur; gently toss, cover, and chill.

2   In another medium bowl, combine mascarpone cheese and agave or honey. Stir vigorously to blend; set aside.

3   Heat grill. Clean grate and brush it with vegetable oil or canola oil. Place nectarines cut-side down on grill. Grill about 5 minutes, allowing grill marks to form. Turn with metal spatula and grill rounded sides until heated through, about 3 minutes. Grilling times vary with degree of ripeness as well as heat of fire.

4   Place hot nectarine halves on 4 dessert plates cut-side up. Place a dollop of mascarpone cheese in the well of each. Top with liqueur-spiked berries. Serve.

Nutritional information (per serving): Calories 450, fat calories 320; total fat 35 grams, sat fat 19 grams, cholesterol 95 milligrams; sodium 45 milligrams; total carbohydrates 27 grams, fiber 4 grams, sugars 21 grams; protein 7 grams; vitamin A IUs 25%; vitamin C 30%; calcium 10%; iron 4%.

Slushy Nectarine Margaritas

YIELD: ABOUT 8 SERVINGS

Frozen nectarine chunks create slushy paradise when whirled in a blender with margarita ingredients. If you have a large, heavy-duty blender, you can make the entire batch at one time. If using a standard blender, divide the ingredients in half and prepare two batches. The recipe suggests rimming the lip of each glass with sugar. If you prefer, you can skip the sugared edge and proceed to step 2.

- Optional: about ⅓ cup sugar
- Optional: 1 juicy lime, quartered
- 6 medium nectarines, peeled, pitted, cut into 1-inch chunks, frozen
- ¼ cup tequila
- ¼ cup orange liqueur or sweet-and-sour mix (see Cook's Note)
- ¼ cup fresh lime juice
- 3 cups crushed ice

1   To rim glasses with sugar: Place sugar on shallow dish or saucer (larger than the diameter of margarita glasses). Moisten rims of glasses with lime quarters. Dip rims of glasses in sugar to lightly coat.

2   Place remaining ingredients in large, heavy-duty blender. Puree until slushy. Pour into prepared glasses.

Nutritional information (per serving without sugared rims): Calories 100, fat calories 0; total fat 0 grams, sat fat 0 grams, cholesterol 0 milligrams; sodium 0 milligrams; total carbohydrates 17 grams, fiber 1 gram, sugars 13 grams; protein 1 gram; vitamin A IUs 6%; vitamin C 15%; calcium 0%; iron 2%.

Cook's Note: If you prefer margaritas that have a tart edge, use sweet-and-sour mix rather than orange liqueur. To make sweet-and-sour mix: Combine and heat 1 cup sugar with 1 cup water in a small saucepan until sugar is dissolved. Cool completely. Once cooled, add 1 cup each fresh lime juice and lemon juice. Stir well to combine. Refrigerate unused portions.

Nectarine and Berry Sabayon Gratiné

YIELD: 6 SERVINGS

Prosecco is an Italian sparkling wine made from the grapes most often grown in the Veneto region in Italy. It lends a gentle touch of sweetness to the sabayon in the fruit-filled dessert. Plan on heating the dessert under the broiler just before serving.

- 3 large egg yolks
- ⅓ cup packed light brown sugar
- ⅓ cup Prosecco
- 3 large or 4 medium ripe nectarines, unpeeled, pitted, cut into ¾-inch-wide wedges
- 2 tablespoons unsalted butter
- 1½ tablespoons granulated sugar
- ½ cup chilled heavy whipping cream
- 1 teaspoon vanilla
- ⅓ cup blueberries
- ½ cup raspberries
- Optional garnish: powdered sugar
- Optional garnish: sprigs of fresh mint

1   Prepare sabayon: In top of double boiler over simmering water, whisk yolks, brown sugar, and Prosecco. Whisk constantly until mixture thickens to the consistency of lightly whipped cream (it is important not to overheat the mixture because eggs will scramble). Transfer to bowl and cover. Refrigerate until chilled.

2   Cut nectarine wedges into bite-size pieces. In a large, nonstick skillet, melt butter on medium-high heat. Add granulated sugar and stir to dissolve. Add nectarine pieces. Cook, tossing frequently, until nectarines are just barely fork-tender; cooking time will vary according to ripeness. Set aside.

3   Adjust oven rack to 5 to 6 inches below heating element. Preheat broiler.

4   In large bowl of electric mixture, beat cream and vanilla until soft peaks form. Fold half of whipped cream mixture into chilled yolks mixture using a large rubber spatula. Add remaining cream mixture and gently fold to combine.

5   Distribute nectarine pieces and berries in 6 crème brûlée dishes (shallow dishes that hold ¾ cup to 1 cup and are about 4¾ inches wide). Spoon the sabayon mixture over fruit, dividing it evenly between the dishes. Place on rimmed baking sheet. Turn on oven light. Broil until nicely browned, 3 to 6 minutes. Watch carefully because they can burn easily. Tops should be nicely browned and a little crusty. If desired, dust with powdered sugar and garnish each serving with a sprig of fresh mint. Serve immediately.

Nutritional information (per serving): Calories 270, fat calories 120; total fat 13 grams, sat fat 8 grams, cholesterol 140 milligrams; sodium 20 milligrams; total carbohydrates 32 grams, fiber 2 grams, sugars 26 grams; protein 3 grams; vitamin A IUs 15%; vitamin C 15%; calcium 4%; iron 4%.

Nectarine and Berry Sabayon Gratiné

Onion

Cipolline

Green (Scallion)

Red

Sweet

White

Yellow

Onions display an impressive array of colors, shapes, and sizes. There are hundreds of varieties, but all of them fall into three general categories. Those that can be stored for long periods of time are called storage onions. They have more pronounced heat, a characteristic that is sometimes described as mouth burn. They have a crackly covering over firm layer-upon-layer flesh.

A second category includes onions that have bright green stalks; they are classified as spring onions. Sweet onions make up the third category; they have shorter shelf life than storage onions and are aptly named for their juicy, sweet flavor profiles. Often sweet onions are named for the location where they are grown; Vidalias are grown in and near Vidalia, Georgia, and Walla Walla onions are grown in the Walla Walla Valley in Washington.

Crop rotation and composting are used by organic onion growers to enrich the soil. Weeding is done by hand, but there is little worry

Yellow

Red

Cipolline

White

Green

about pests. Onions give off gasses that act as natural insect repellents. Onions are field-cured after harvest; they are left to rest in gunnysacks close to the picking site for about two weeks. This process lessens bruising during shipping.

BUYING AND STORING: Bulb should be firm without soft spots. Storage onions and sweet onions should have tightly closed necks; avoid those with green shoulders. Green onions (scallions) should have bright green stalks. Place dry, unwashed storage or sweet onions loose (not in plastic bag) in cool, dark location; storage onions up to 6 weeks, sweet onions up to 10 days. Or refrigerate sweet onions (keeping them dry) up to 3 weeks. Unwashed green onions should be refrigerated. Kept dry in plastic bag, refrigerate up to 7 days.

PREP AND USE: For storage onions and sweet onions, trim top and bottom, leaving enough root end intact so that layers stay together. Cut in half lengthwise. Pull off and discard skin. Place cut-side down on cutting board. Cut into wedges or slices. Or, to dice or mince, cut into parallel horizontal lengthwise slices, leaving root end intact; then cut parallel lengthwise vertical slices, leaving root end intact. Cut crosswise. For green onions (scallions), wash thoroughly in cold running water. Trim root end. Some recipes call for using dark green stalks, others do not.

Use raw or cooked. Use raw in salads, sandwiches, relishes or dips. Onions can be braised, boiled, grilled, sautéed, roasted, or pickled.

AVAILABLE:

Cipolline: September to November

Green (Scallion): Year-round

Red, White: Year-round

Sweet: March to August

Yellow: Year-round

NUTRITIONAL INFORMATION (per ½ ounce raw cipolline): Calories 7, fat calories 0; total fat 0 grams, sat fat 0 grams; cholesterol 0 milligrams; sodium 1 milligram; total carbohydrates 2 grams, fiber 0 grams, sugars 0 grams; protein 0 grams; vitamin A IUs 2%; vitamin C 1%; calcium 0%; iron 1%.

NUTRITIONAL INFORMATION (per ¼ cup chopped raw green onions): Calories 10, fat calories 0; total fat 0 grams, sat fat 0 grams, cholesterol 0 milligrams; sodium 5 milligrams; total carbohydrates 2 grams, fiber 1 gram, sugars 1 gram; protein 0 grams; vitamin A IUs 2%; vitamin C 8%; calcium 0%; iron 0%.

NUTRITIONAL INFORMATION (per 1 cup chopped raw red, white, or yellow onion): Calories 64, fat calories 1; total fat 0 grams, sat fat 0 grams; cholesterol 0 milligrams; sodium 6 milligrams; total carbohydrates 15 grams, fiber 3 grams, sugars 7 gram; protein 2 grams; vitamin A IUs 0%; vitamin C 20%; calcium 4%; iron 2%.

NUTRITIONAL INFORMATION (per 1 ounce raw sweet onion): Calories 9, fat calories 0; total fat 0 grams, sat fat 0 grams; cholesterol 0 milligrams; sodium 2 milligrams; total carbohydrates 2 grams, fiber 0 grams, sugars 1 gram; protein 0 grams; vitamin A IUs 0%; vitamin C 2%; calcium 1%; iron 0%.

SERVING SUGGESTIONS

Red Onion Marmalade

Use this as a condiment with grilled sausage, roast pork, or roasted vegetables. Well-sealed in a glass jar, the marmalade can be refrigerated up to 1 week. Heat ¼ cup olive oil in a heavy-bottomed large saucepan on medium-high heat. Add 2 large, thinly sliced red onions and ½ teaspoon dried red chile flakes. Reduce heat to low and cook onions 15 minutes or until completely softened but not browned, stirring frequently. Add ½ cup cider vinegar, 3 tablespoons balsamic vinegar, ½ cup raisins, ½ cup dry sherry, and 3 tablespoons dark brown sugar. Stir and cook 20 minutes, stirring frequently. Add salt to taste.

Grilled Green Onions

Trim root ends and toss with vegetable oil seasoned with a little ground cumin and coriander, just enough to lightly coat. Grill until lightly browned and heated through. Season to taste with salt.

Caramelized Sweet Onion and Grilled Cheese

Cut large peeled sweet onion into ¼-inch slices. In large, deep skillet on medium-high heat, toss with enough extra-virgin olive oil to lightly coat; add 1 tablespoon unsalted butter and 1 teaspoon fresh thyme leaves. Cook, stirring occasionally, until onions start to brown. Reduce heat to medium-low and cook until nicely browned. Use on top of slices of sharp cheddar cheese in grilled cheese sandwiches.

Glazed Cipolline Garnish

Preheat oven to 375°F. Peel 1 pound cipolline onions (small, squat onions) and place in small roasting pan. Add ⅓ cup extra-virgin olive oil, ⅔ cup balsamic vinegar, ½ teaspoon salt, and ½ teaspoon freshly ground black pepper; toss. Roast 40 to 60 minutes, tossing every 15 minutes. If pan starts to become dry, add water. Onions should have a nice dark golden color and vinegar should be reduced to syrup. When cool enough to handle, roughly chop and stir into glaze in pan. Use as a garnish for sautéed spinach or chard, or blanched green beans.

Prairie Caviar

YIELD: 12 SERVINGS

Casual and irresistible, this hodge-podge of vegetables and beans is a welcome appetizer at outdoor gatherings. Be sure to provide large, sturdy tortilla chips so guests can load them up with plenty of "caviar." Also, put out an assortment of hot sauces, so guests can kick up their servings to meet individual tastes.

- 2 tablespoons red wine vinegar
- 1½ teaspoons hot sauce
- 2 teaspoons vegetable oil or extra-virgin olive oil
- 1 medium clove garlic, minced
- 1 small sweet onion or ½ medium sweet onion, diced
- Freshly ground black pepper
- 1 (15-ounce) can black beans, drained, rinsed
- 1 firm-ripe avocado, halved, peeled, pitted, diced
- 1 (11-ounce) can corn kernels, drained
- ⅔ cup thinly sliced green onions, including dark green stalks
- ½ cup chopped fresh cilantro
- ½ pound Roma tomatoes, coarsely chopped
- Salt
- Tortilla chips

1 In large bowl, mix vinegar, hot sauce, oil, garlic, sweet onion, and pepper to taste. Add beans and avocado; gently toss.

2 Add corn, green onions, cilantro, and tomatoes. Mix gently to coat. Add salt to taste and additional pepper if needed. Accompany with tortilla chips for dipping.

Nutritional information (per serving without chips): Calories 90, fat calories 35; total fat 35 grams, sat fat 0.5 grams, cholesterol 0 milligrams; sodium 90 milligrams; total carbohydrates 14 grams, fiber 4 grams, sugars 2 grams; protein 3 grams; vitamin A IUs 6%; vitamin C 15%; calcium 2%; iron 6%.

Green Onion–Horseradish-Crusted Chicken Breasts

YIELD: 4 SERVINGS

Horseradish offers a fiery edge to dishes. Its biting-hot flavor profile teams well with boneless chicken breasts and green onions in this delicious entrée. For added color and flavor, team it with pureed Beet Sauce (page 61).

- 2 teaspoons Dijon-style mustard
- 3 tablespoons mayonnaise
- 2 (8-ounce) skin-on, boneless chicken breasts
- Garlic salt and freshly ground black pepper
- 1 tablespoon extra-virgin olive oil
- 4 tablespoons chopped green onions, including about ⅓ of dark green stalks
- ½ cup coarse fresh breadcrumbs
- 2 tablespoons drained bottled horseradish
- 1 teaspoon minced fresh tarragon leaves
- ½ teaspoon dried oregano
- 1 teaspoon minced fresh basil leaves
- Optional for serving: Beet Sauce (page 61)

1 Adjust oven rack to middle position. Preheat oven to 400°F.

2 In small bowl, whisk mustard and mayonnaise until well combined. Place chicken on paper towel and season with garlic salt and pepper to taste.

3 Heat oil in large, deep nonstick skillet on medium-high heat. Add chicken breasts to skillet; brown on both sides, cooking about 6 minutes per side. Place chicken in 8-inch square baking dish, skin-side up.

4 Add green onions to skillet and cook until softened, stirring occasionally, about 2 minutes. Take off heat, stir in breadcrumbs, horseradish, tarragon, oregano, basil, and garlic salt and pepper to taste. Spread mustard mixture on skin side of each chicken breast and top evenly with breadcrumb mixture. Bake chicken in middle of oven 10 minutes, or until cooked through. If topping isn't browned, adjust oven rack to 8 inches below broiler element and turn oven to broil. Broil just until nicely browned; watch carefully because breadcrumbs burn easily. If desired, serve with Beet Sauce on the side.

Nutritional information (per serving without Beet Sauce): Calories 260, fat calories 120; total fat 14 grams, sat fat 3 grams, cholesterol 70 milligrams; sodium 210 milligrams; total carbohydrates 8 grams, fiber 1 gram, sugars 1 gram; protein 25 grams; vitamin A IUs 4%; vitamin C 4%; calcium 4%; iron 8%.

Party Chili

YIELD: 6 TO 8 SERVINGS

Chili is a one-pot meal that is perfect for casual entertaining. Set out an assortment of optional toppings and guests can augment their chili to suit individual taste. Provide bowls of diced ripe avocado, minced cilantro, finely diced red onion, crumbled tortilla chips, and sour cream. Also provide an assortment of bottled hot sauces for fire-loving diners.

- 2 tablespoons extra-virgin olive oil
- 2 medium-sized sweet onions, chopped
- 1 large green bell pepper, cored, seeded, chopped
- 1 large stalk celery, trimmed, chopped
- 1 large clove garlic, minced
- 1½ pounds extra-lean ground beef or ground turkey (see Meatless Tip)

Party Chili

2 (14.5- ounce) cans whole tomatoes with juice

2 (15-ounce) cans kidney beans, drained, rinsed

1 (8-ounce) can tomato sauce

2 tablespoons chili powder

1½ teaspoons ground cumin

1 teaspoon salt

¼ teaspoon freshly ground black pepper

Ground cayenne pepper

Optional toppings: diced avocado, minced fresh cilantro, finely diced red onion, crumbled tortilla chips, hot sauce, sour cream

1   Heat oil in large saucepan or Dutch oven on medium-high heat. Add onions, bell pepper, celery, and garlic; cook until onions soften, stirring frequently and lowering heat if needed to prevent onion from browning. Add beef or turkey; cook, stirring frequently, until meat browns and is cooked through.

2   Add remaining ingredients and bring to boil on high heat. Decrease heat to medium-low and simmer, stirring occasionally, for 30 minutes. Taste and adjust seasoning as needed.

3   Ladle into bowls. Provide toppings for optional garnishes.

Nutritional information (per serving without optional toppings): Calories 270, fat calories 70; total fat 8 grams, sat fat 2 grams, cholesterol 45 milligrams; sodium 570 milligrams; total carbohydrates 27 grams, fiber 9 grams, sugars 5 grams; protein 25 grams; vitamin A IUs 30%; vitamin C 70%; calcium 10%; iron 25%.

Meatless Tip: Omit meat. Instead add 1 (15-ounce) can drained and rinsed black beans along with kidney beans in step 2. Season to taste; add additional chili powder or a pinch of dried red chile flakes, if needed.

Onion and Rosemary Loaves

YIELD: 2 SMALL LOAVES, ABOUT 18 TO 24 SLICES

Caramelized onions contribute a sweet edge to these delectable loaves. Rosemary's aromatic scent and flavor offer an herbal balance, adding hints of both lemon and pine. The freshly baked loaves are brushed with garlic butter, a final flourish that makes them irresistible.

- 4 tablespoons unsalted butter
- 3 cups chopped yellow onion
- 2¼ teaspoons active dry yeast
- 2 teaspoons sugar
- 1 cup warm water, not over 95°F
- 5 cups all-purpose flour, divided use
- 1½ teaspoons salt
- 1½ tablespoons chopped fresh rosemary leaves
- Nonstick olive oil spray or extra-virgin olive oil for greasing bowl
- 2 tablespoons unsalted butter, melted, mixed with ¼ teaspoon garlic salt

1 On medium-high heat, melt butter in large, deep nonstick skillet. Add onions and stir periodically until caramelized, about 30 minutes, reducing heat if necessary to prevent burning. Set aside and cool completely.

2 In large bowl of electric mixer, add yeast, sugar, and water. Allow yeast to become bubbly, about 15 to 20 minutes. Add half of the flour, the salt and rosemary. Mix well on low speed. Add caramelized onions with juices in pan and a small amount of the remaining flour. Knead or mix using dough hook until smooth, but not sticky. You may need to add more flour in small amounts, no more than 5 cups total; knead or mix well between additions to reach this consistency. The dough is ready when it gently springs back when pressed.

3 Turn dough out into a large, lightly oiled or sprayed bowl. Gently turn dough over in bowl to lightly coat all of dough ball with oil. Loosely cover and set in a warm area to double in size, about 1 hour.

4 Adjust oven rack to middle position. Preheat oven to 400°F. Line rimmed baking sheet with parchment paper; set aside.

5 Punch down dough and cut into 2 equal portions. Flatten each portion on floured work surface and let rest 10 minutes. Shape into 2 loaves and place on prepared baking sheet about 2 inches apart. Bake in oven for 30 minutes or until nicely browned. Remove from oven and immediately brush with garlic butter mixture. Allow to cool 20 minutes before slicing. Serve warm.

Nutritional information (per slice, with 18 slices): Calories 150, fat calories 35; total fat 4 grams, sat fat 2.5 grams, cholesterol 10 milligrams; sodium 210 milligrams; total carbohydrates 25 grams, fiber 1 gram, sugars 1 gram; protein 3 grams; vitamin A IUs 2%; vitamin C 0%; calcium 0%; iron 8%.

Orange

Blood Orange
Cara Cara
Navel
Valencia

The peel is part of the pleasure, a gift wrap filled with fragrance. Use a thumbnail to break into the juicy flesh inside and take in even more wondrous perfume. Those juice-packed segments offer irresistible tang, a lovely blend of sweet-sour flavors.

Minced orange zest (the colored portion of the peel) can add flavor to everything from baked goods to vinaigrettes. With organically grown citrus, there's no worry about any residual pesticide on the peel. Most organic oranges are grown in California with smaller crops in Florida, Texas, and Arizona.

Blood Orange

BUYING AND STORING: Look for fruit that is heavy for its size and fragrant, without soft spots or nicks. Store at cool room temperature up to 10 days, or refrigerate up to 3 weeks. Juice and zest can be frozen. To freeze zest, mince and enclose 1-tablespoon batches in small containers or storage bags, pressing out as much air as possible before freezing. Use within 3 months for best flavor. Or to dry zest, spread minced zest on waxed paper in single layer. Allow to dry at room temperature until brittle, about 2 days; store airtight in cool, dark location.

PREP AND USE: Wash in cold water. If using zest (colored portion of peel without white pith), remove it with a swivel-bladed vegetable peeler, Microplane, or other "zesting" device. Use hands to peel off skin, or for varieties that are more difficult to peel, cut off skin with knife. To supreme oranges (removing the peel and pith and cutting into segments without membranes), see Glossary, page 324.

Eat raw out of hand, use for juice, or include in salads, desserts, marinades, or dressings.

VARIETIES:

Blood Orange: Orange skin with a burgundy blush and deep crimson flesh (or streaks). Often the time of harvest influences the color both of the skin and flesh; the later in the season they are picked, the more blood-red the color. Lower in acidity than many varieties, with a slight hint of raspberry flavor.

Cara Cara: Often referred to as a pink navel because it looks like a navel in shape but has flesh that is a deep salmon-pink with yellowish-orange skin. It is sometimes difficult to peel, but the juicy, sweet flavor profile makes it worth the effort.

Navel: Generally very easy to peel off the bright orange skin by hand and segment easily. This sweet, juicy orange makes up about 30 percent of the U.S. organic orange crop. Generally seedless.

Valencia: Available throughout the summer, this variety makes up 65 percent of the U.S. organic orange crop. The skin is thin and smooth, and may have green areas when it is harvested in summertime (it doesn't affect taste). Flesh is super juicy and sweet. It's most often used for juice, but it is the orange of choice served for dessert at most U.S. sushi bars.

AVAILABLE:

Blood Orange: December to February

Cara Cara: December to February

Navel: November to March

Valencia: February to November

NUTRITIONAL INFORMATION (per 1 cup peeled orange sections, raw): Calories 85, fat calories 2; total fat 0 grams, sat fat 0 grams, cholesterol 0 milligrams; sodium 0 milligrams; total carbohydrates 21 grams, fiber 4 grams, sugars 17 grams; protein 2 grams; vitamin A IUs 8%; vitamin C 160%; calcium 7%; iron 1%.

SERVING SUGGESTIONS

Quick Sicilian Salad

Peel and slice 2 or 3 oranges and place on single layer on platter. Trim 1 fennel bulb (reserving fronds) and cut into thin slices; scatter on orange slices. Drizzle with about 3 tablespoons extra-virgin olive oil. Season to taste with salt and freshly ground black pepper. Scatter fennel fronds on top.

Orange Supreme Rice Pudding

Stir 1 tablespoon orange marmalade into warm rice pudding. Cool. Serve topped with several peeled orange segments (see supremes in Glossary, page 324).

Blood Orange Sundaes

Over a bowl (to collect the juice) cut 4 blood oranges into peeled segments (see supremes in Glossary, page 324). In bowl with collected juice, stir in 4 tablespoons sugar and 3 tablespoons vodka; stir to dissolve sugar. Add orange slices. Chill; serve over vanilla or chocolate ice cream. Accompany with crisp cookies.

Sunshine Marinade for Chicken Thighs

With motor running in food processor fitted with metal blade, add 2 cloves garlic (peeled) and process until minced. Stop machine and add ⅓ cup extra-virgin olive oil, 2 tablespoons balsamic vinegar, 2 tablespoons brown sugar, 1 teaspoon minced orange zest (colored portion of peel), ¼ cup fresh orange juice, 3 teaspoons fresh lemon juice, and 1 teaspoon salt; pulse to blend. Place in nonreactive bowl with 1½ pounds skinless, boneless chicken thighs; toss, cover, and marinate in refrigerator 30 minutes. Discard marinade Grill and garnish with trimmed, thinly sliced green onions (including dark green stalks).

Pecan-Date Muffin-Cakes with Citrus Syrup

YIELD: 4 SERVINGS

Delectable on their own, these still-warm muffins are drizzled with citrus syrup, accompanied with whipped cream, and served as a dessert. A splash of orange liqueur can be added to the syrup if desired. The muffins can be made a day in advance and reheated in a 350°F oven for 5 to 8 minutes. Smaller servings are perfectly acceptable; instead of serving 1 "muffin" per person, cut each in half and make 8 servings instead of 4.

Muffin Cake

- ¾ cup chopped toasted pecans (see Cook's Note)
- ½ cup all-purpose flour
- ½ teaspoon baking powder
- Pinch of salt
- ⅔ cup diced pitted dates
- ½ cup sugar
- 2 tablespoons milk
- 6 tablespoons (¾ stick) unsalted butter, melted
- 1 egg, lightly beaten

Syrup

- ½ cup sugar
- 3 tablespoons orange zest (colored portion of peel)
- ½ cup fresh orange juice
- 1 teaspoon fresh lemon juice

- 1 cup heavy whipping cream
- 1 tablespoon powdered sugar
- ½ teaspoon vanilla

1   Adjust oven rack to middle position. Preheat oven to 350°F. Line 4 standard 1-cup muffin cups with paper liners.

2   Prepare cake: In large bowl, combine pecans, flour, baking powder, and salt; stir to combine. Add dates and sugar; stir to combine. Add milk, butter, and egg; stir to combine.

3   Spoon batter into paper liners. Bake for 25 minutes, or until toothpick inserted in center comes out clean.

4   Meanwhile, prepare syrup: Place sugar, zest, and juices in medium, heavy-bottomed saucepan. Stir over medium heat until sugar melts. Reduce heat to low and simmer about 6 to 7 minutes.

5   In large bowl of electric mixer, beat cream, sugar, and vanilla until stiff. Refrigerate.

6   When still warm but cool enough to handle, remove paper from muffin-cakes. Place each in shallow bowl or deep rimmed dessert plate. Ladle syrup over each. Place a good dollop of whipped cream on one side of each and serve immediately.

Nutritional information (per serving, using 4 servings): Calories 890, fat calories 510; total fat 57 grams, sat fat 26 grams, cholesterol 180 milligrams; sodium 110 milligrams; total carbohydrates 96 grams, fiber 5 grams, sugars 73 grams; protein 8 grams; vitamin A IUs 30%; vitamin C 35%; calcium 15%; iron 10%.

Cook's Note: To toast pecans, place on rimmed baking sheet in single layer. Bake in 350°F oven about 3 to 5 minutes, until lightly toasted. Watch nuts carefully because they can burn easily. Cool.

Red Times Three Salad

YIELD: 6 SERVINGS

Blood orange's sweet-sour flavor profile has a subtle note of raspberry. It teams delectably with the earthiness of roasted beets and crunchy-pop texture of pomegranate seeds. Crumbled goat cheese is a classic garnish in beet salads, but it is optional (but delicious) in this dish.

3 blood oranges (see Cook's Note)

½ cup sherry vinegar

½ teaspoon salt

½ cup extra-virgin olive oil

¼ small red onion, thinly sliced

1 tablespoon minced fresh basil leaves

3 to 4 medium beets, cooked, peeled, sliced

1 cup pomegranate seeds

Optional garnish: handful of microgreens

Optional garnish: crumbled goat cheese

1   Remove zest (colored portion of peel) from 1 orange and mince; set aside. Use a sharp knife to remove skin from all the oranges; to peel, slice off top and bottom of each orange to expose flesh, then place cut side down on work surface and cut off peel and pith in strips, cutting from top of bottom following the contour of the fruit. Cut oranges into slices about ⅜-inch thick.

2   Prepare vinaigrette: In small bowl or glass measuring cup with handle, combine zest, vinegar, and salt; stir to dissolve salt. Whisk in oil. Add onion and basil. Stir and taste; adjust seasoning as needed.

3   Arrange beet slices in single layer on 6 salad plates. Top with orange slices, arranging them in single layer so part of the beet slices show. Stir vinaigrette and spoon over beets and oranges. Top with pomegranate seeds. If desired, garnish with microgreens and optional cheese garnish.

Nutritional information (per serving): Calories 230, fat calories 160; total fat 18 grams, sat fat 2.5 grams, cholesterol 0 milligrams; sodium 230 milligrams; total carbohydrates 17 grams, fiber 2 grams, sugars 11 grams; protein 1 gram; vitamin A IUs 4%; vitamin C 60%; calcium 4%; iron 4%.

Cook's Note: If blood oranges aren't available, substitute navel oranges, Cara Cara oranges, or tangerines.

Rainbow Slaw

YIELD: 8 SERVINGS

This colorful concoction combines both red and green cabbage with orange segments. The dressing is flavor-boosted with plenty of orange juice and zest. It is especially delicious served with grilled chicken, chicken teriyaki, or baby back pork ribs.

1 medium green cabbage, quartered lengthwise, cored, shredded

¼ medium-red cabbage, cored, shredded

¼ medium red onion, finely diced

4 oranges, peeled, torn into segments

Minced zest of 4 additional oranges (colored portion of peel), plus juice of those oranges (about 1 cup)

½ cup mayonnaise

2 tablespoons seasoned rice vinegar

2 tablespoons sugar

2 tablespoons minced fresh ginger

¼ teaspoon salt

¼ teaspoon freshly ground black pepper

1 tablespoon sesame seeds (see Cook's Note)

1   In large bowl, gently toss cabbages, onion, and orange segments.

2   In small bowl, prepare dressing: Mix zest, juice, and mayonnaise. Add vinegar, sugar, ginger, salt, and pepper; stir to combine.

3   Add dressing to cabbage mixture; toss. Taste and adjust seasoning if needed. Divide between 8 plates and top with sesame seeds. Serve.

Nutritional information (per serving): Calories 170, fat calories 50; total fat 6 grams, sat fat 1 grams, cholesterol 5 milligrams; sodium 280 milligrams; total carbohydrates 29 grams, fiber 7 grams, sugars 16 grams; protein 3 grams; vitamin A IUs 15%; vitamin C 230%; calcium 15%; iron 6%.

Cook's Note: If available, use black sesame seeds. They add a touch of visual drama to the dish. Or use the more common pale grayish-ivory seeds, but to give them more flavor, toast and cool them before adding to slaw. To toast, place in small skillet over medium-high heat. Shake handle to redistribute seeds as they toast to light brown. Watch carefully because they burn easily. Cool.

Red Times Three Salad

Orange-Glazed Broccoli Stir-Fry

YIELD: 6 TO 8 SERVINGS

Stir-frying brings out the best in broccoli, giving it vibrant flavor and turning it an appealing bright green. Serve with brown rice, fragrant white rice (such as basmati), or wild rice.

  6 oranges: zest and juice from 2 oranges, 4 peeled and torn into segments

  1 tablespoon cornstarch

  1 tablespoon soy sauce

  2 tablespoons canola oil

  1½ pounds broccoli, cut into bite-size florets, stems peeled and cut into bite-size pieces

  ¼ cup toasted slivered almonds (see page 215)

  1 teaspoon toasted sesame oil

  ⅛ teaspoon salt

  ⅛ teaspoon freshly ground black pepper

  For serving: cooked rice

1   In small bowl, combine zest, juice, cornstarch, and soy sauce. Set aside.

2   In large, deep skillet or wok, heat canola oil on high heat. Add broccoli and cook 4 to 5 minutes, until tender-crisp, stirring frequently.

3   Stir juice mixture and add to broccoli. Lower heat to medium-low; simmer until sauce thickens, about 2 to 3 minutes. Add oranges, almonds, sesame oil, salt and pepper; gently toss and remove from heat. Taste and adjust seasoning. Serve immediately, accompanied with rice.

Nutritional information (per serving without rice): Calories 120, fat calories 50; total fat 6 grams, sat fat 0 grams, cholesterol 0 milligrams; sodium 180 milligrams; total carbohydrates 16 grams, fiber 4 grams, sugars 7 grams; protein 3 grams; vitamin A IUs 25%; vitamin C 140%; calcium 6%; iron 4%.

Peach

Saturn

White Flesh

Yellow Flesh

Peaches are classified by how easily the flesh separates from the stone. Those that separate easily are dubbed freestone. Those that stubbornly resist are called clingstone, most of which are sold to canneries.

Unlike many conventionally grown peaches, organic peaches are not mechanically brushed to remove the natural fuzz on the exterior. Organic growers say that the fuzz is beneficial, working as a natural fungicide to impede decay.

Filled with intoxicating fragrance and sweet-tart juices, three varieties of organic peaches are most common in the marketplace. White-fleshed peaches

often have tender red-colored skin and white flesh that is streaked with red next to the pit. They are very juicy and often are the sweetest peach of all. Yellow-fleshed peaches often have fuzzy, yellow skin. The flesh is succulent and sweet. Lifesaver-shaped Saturn peaches are about one-third the size of an average peach, making them perfect for on-the-go snacking. They have juicy flesh that is fairly firm and sweet.

Organic peaches are often smaller in size, but they make up for their size with vibrant flavor

profiles. They are intensely sweet, often with 4 to 5 percent higher Brix levels (see page 323) than conventionally grown peaches. Organic growers report that their crops yield about 30 percent less than conventional orchards.

Many organic peach growers use pheromone cards in their orchards designed to confuse predatory insects and prevent their reproduction. Clover is often planted between trees to attract beneficial insects.

BUYING AND STORING: Look for fruit that is fragrant, plump, and gives to gentle pressure at the shoulders, but without soft spots or mushiness. Red blush isn't necessarily a sign of ripeness. Peaches should be perfumy, with a rich peachy smell. They do not continue to ripen after harvest; brown-bag ripening (see page 323) will improve texture but not sweetness. Store at room temperature out of direct sunlight up to 2 days or refrigerate ripe fruit loose in crisper drawer up to 8 days (but note that refrigeration is not recommended because it can change taste).

PREP AND USE: Peaches can be peeled with paring knife. Or for a showier result, cut a very shallow X in the blossom end and drop into boiling water for about 1 minute, then remove with slotted spoon and refresh with cold water; slip off skin.

To pit freestones, cut fruit in half from top to bottom along suture (seam). Twist halves in opposite directions and lift out pit. For clingstones, cut into quarters or eighths, cutting toward pit; lift off sections, cutting next to pit if stubborn flesh won't pull away. Use right away, or to prevent discoloration, rub with lemon or dip in acidulated water (cold water mixed with a little lemon or lime juice).

Eat raw or cooked. Slice and use atop cereal, pudding, ice cream, or pancakes. Add to fruit salad, shortcake filling, salsa, cold soups, blended drinks, cocktails, or dessert sauces. To cook: broil, bake, grill, or sauté. Use for jam, jelly, pie, shortcake, or coffeecake.

AVAILABLE:

Saturn: June to August

White Flesh: June to September

Yellow Flesh: May to September

NUTRITIONAL INFORMATION (per 1 cup sliced, raw): Calories 60, fat calories 3; total fat 0 grams, sat fat 0 grams, cholesterol 0 milligrams; sodium 0 milligrams; total carbohydrates 15 grams, fiber 2 grams, sugars 13 grams; protein 1 gram; vitamin A IUs 10%; vitamin C 17%; calcium 1%; iron 2%.

SERVING SUGGESTIONS

Margarita Salad

In large ceramic or glass bowl, combine 4 tablespoons powdered sugar, 3 tablespoons orange liqueur, 3 tablespoons tequila, and 2 tablespoons freshly squeezed lime juice; whisk to combine. Add 3 ripe peaches (peeled, pitted, cut into wedges), 1½ cups seedless grapes, 1½ cups hulled and halved strawberries, 1 cup blueberries. Gently toss with rubber spatula. Cover and chill 1 hour. Garnish with minced fresh mint, if desired.

Ricotta-Stuffed

Serve these as a dessert. Combine ¾ cup ricotta cheese, 3 tablespoons toasted and chopped walnuts, and 1 tablespoon sugar; stir until combined. Cut 4 ripe peaches in half from top to bottom; remove pits. Using 2 small spoons (one to scoop, another to push mixture off spoon) fill the cavity of each peach half. Garnish each with small fresh mint or basil leaf.

Peachy Smoothie

Cut peeled banana in 1-inch slices and freeze airtight. In blender, combine frozen banana slices, 2 ice cubes, ½ cup buttermilk, 1 peeled ripe peach (cut into 1-inch chunks) and 1½ teaspoons agave syrup or honey. Cover and whirl until slushy.

Stone-Fruit Shortcake

Beat 2 cups of heavy whipping cream into soft peaks. Place 2 tablespoons peach jam in small bowl and mash with fork to break it up. Fold jam into whipped cream; mound mixture on sliced pound cake and top with sliced fresh peaches.

Sweet Peach Iced Tea

YIELD: 8 SERVINGS

The sweet taste and fragrance of ripe peaches make this iced tea irresistibly refreshing. It isn't a clear, see-through drink because the fruit puree makes it cloudy. Adjust the amount of sugar or agave syrup to suit your taste. If you are using very ripe, sweet peaches, less sweetening may be required.

2 English breakfast tea bags

8 cups boiling water

4 ripe peaches, peeled, pitted, cut into wedges

¼ cup sugar or agave syrup

Ice

1   Place tea bags in large teapot or heatproof bowl; add boiling water. Cover and steep 5 minutes. Remove tea bags.

2   In blender, puree peaches and sugar or agave syrup. Add 2 cups tea and whirl until pureed. Pour into pitcher. Add remaining tea; stir to combine. Cover and chill.

3   Stir and pour into glasses filled with ice.

Nutritional information (per serving): Calories 45, fat calories 0; total fat 0 grams, sat fat 0 grams, cholesterol 0 milligrams; sodium 0 milligrams; total carbohydrates 11 grams, fiber 1 gram, sugars 10 grams; protein 0 grams; vitamin A IUs 4%; vitamin C 6%; calcium 0%; iron 0%.

Peachy French Toast

YIELD: 4 SERVINGS

French toast is glamorized in this delightful breakfast treat. Sautéed fresh peach cubes are sandwiched between slices of French bread or brioche, then the bread's exterior is dipped in an egg mixture and fried until crisp and golden brown. Serve as is, or top with syrup and sour cream.

4 tablespoons unsalted butter, divided use

2 tablespoons light brown sugar

½ teaspoon ground cinnamon, divided use

Pinch ground nutmeg

2 large ripe peaches, peeled, pitted, sliced

2 tablespoons sour cream

8 slices French bread or brioche bread, ⅜ inch thick

4 eggs

¼ teaspoon salt

Agave pancake syrup or maple syrup

Optional for serving: 2 tablespoons sour cream

1   Melt 2 tablespoons butter in medium skillet on medium-high heat. Add sugar, ¼ teaspoon cinnamon, and nutmeg; stir until sugar dissolves.

2   Add peaches and cook, stirring occasionally, until peaches are soft. Remove from heat and add 2 tablespoons sour cream. Divide peach mixture evenly on 4 pieces of bread, leaving ½-inch border all around. Top each with a second piece of bread; press down gently to seal edges.

3   Place eggs, remaining ¼ teaspoon cinnamon, and salt in pie pan; using a fork, beat well.

4   Melt 1 tablespoon butter in large, deep skillet on medium-high heat. Working in batches, dip both sides of 2 "sandwiches" in egg mixture and pan-fry in melted butter until lightly browned on both sides. Repeat with remaining butter and sandwiches. Cut each "sandwich" in half on the diagonal. If desired, top with remaining sour cream and syrup.

Nutritional information (per serving without syrup and optional sour cream): Calories 590, fat calories 210; total fat 23 grams, sat fat 11 grams, cholesterol 250 milligrams; sodium 700 milligrams; total carbohydrates 79 grams, fiber 5 grams, sugars 10 grams; protein 18 grams; vitamin A IUs 20%; vitamin C 8%; calcium 15%; iron 25%.

Peachy French Toast

Fresh Peach Ice Cream with Crystallized Ginger

YIELD: 6 SERVINGS

For many Americans, the mention of peach ice cream conjures up visions of idyllic outdoor summer gatherings. Peaches offer a fresh, sweet-yet-tart edge to the cold confection, a treat that for many is downright irresistible. This version is augmented with a small amount of finely chopped crystallized ginger and spices, giving it a subtle hint of pepper with a sweet finish.

4 egg yolks

⅓ cup sugar

1 vanilla bean

1 cup whole milk

1 cup heavy whipping cream

1 cup chopped peeled ripe peaches

¼ cup simple syrup (see Cook's Note)

¼ teaspoon ground cinnamon

⅛ teaspoon ground nutmeg

⅛ teaspoon ground allspice

3 tablespoons finely chopped crystallized ginger, store-bought or homemade (page 146)

1   Place yolks and sugar in medium bowl. Beat until blended and sugar dissolves.

2   Split vanilla bean lengthwise with sharp knife. Using the tip of knife, open bean and scrape out seeds. Place seeds in medium saucepan; add milk, cream, and vanilla pod. Scald over medium-high heat until steaming; do not boil. Remove from heat.

3   Stirring constantly, cautiously add 1 cup of hot milk mixture in thin stream to yolk mixture. Then, gradually pour all of the yolk mixture into the milk mixture, whisking constantly. Return saucepan to medium heat; stir with wooden spoon until well blended and thickened

enough for mixture to coat back of spoon (if you drag a finger down back of spoon it should leave a clean trail). Do not boil. Strain thickened mixture through sieve into medium glass or ceramic bowl. Cool, stirring, until no longer steaming. Cover with plastic wrap touching the surface to prevent skin from forming. Refrigerate until cold, about 2 hours.

4   Meanwhile, in medium, deep skillet combine all remaining ingredients except ginger. Bring to boil; reduce heat to low and simmer, stirring occasionally, until mixture thickens, about 15 minutes. Add ginger and stir to combine. Cool to room temperature.

5   Process chilled yolk mixture in ice cream machine according to manufacturer's instructions. Once it is frozen, fold in peach mixture. Place in plastic container and cover surface of ice cream with plastic wrap. Cover container and freeze.

Nutritional information (per serving): Calories 290, fat calories 170; total fat 19 grams, sat fat 11 grams, cholesterol 195 milligrams; sodium 35 milligrams; total carbohydrates 27 grams, fiber 1 gram, sugars 25 grams; protein 4 grams; vitamin A IUs 20%; vitamin C 4%; calcium 8%; iron 4%.

Cook's Note: To make simple syrup, combine ½ cup water and ½ cup sugar in small saucepan. Bring to boil on high heat; boil 2 minutes. Cool and chill. Measure ¼ cup to use in this recipe.

Peachy-Orange Parfaits

YIELD: 8 SERVINGS

These easy-to-make parfaits layer peach-spiked whipped cream and peaches in decorative glasses. Mango, nectarine, or strawberries can be substituted for the peaches. Or use a combination of berries, such as raspberries, strawberries, blackberries, and blueberries. If you like, accompany the parfaits with cookies. The parfaits can be assembled and refrigerated up to 2 hours before serving.

8 medium ripe peaches, peeled, pitted, divided use

4 tablespoons sugar, divided use

2 tablespoons fresh orange juice

1 teaspoon minced orange zest (colored portion of peel)

1 teaspoon fresh lemon juice

¾ cup heavy whipping cream

¼ cup sliced almonds, toasted (see Cook's Note)

Garnish: 8 small sprigs fresh mint

Optional for serving: biscotti or shortbread cookies

1   Cut 2 peaches into wedges and puree with 2 tablespoons of sugar in a food processor fitted with metal blade until smooth. Add orange juice and zest; pulse to combine.

2   Cut remaining peaches into ¼- to ½-inch pieces. Combine about 1 cup chopped peaches with puree. Toss remaining peach pieces with lemon juice. Cover and refrigerate each mixture in separate airtight containers. Chill 1 hour.

3   Using electric mixer, beat cream with remaining 2 tablespoons of sugar in large bowl until soft peaks form. Gently fold peach puree mixture into whipped cream.

4   Using 8 stemmed wineglasses, large martini glasses, or parfait glasses, spoon a small portion of peach pieces in bottom of each. Top with small portions of whipped cream mixture and reserved peach pieces. Continue layering until both mixtures are used up. Sprinkle tops with almonds. Garnish with the mint sprigs and serve with biscotti or cookies, if using.

Nutritional information (per serving without cookies): Calories 160, fat calories 90; total fat 10 grams, sat fat 5 grams, cholesterol 30 milligrams; sodium 10 milligrams; total carbohydrates 17 grams, fiber 2 grams, sugars 15 grams; protein 2 grams; vitamin A IUs 15%; vitamin C15%; calcium 2%; iron 2%.

Cooks' Note: To toast sliced almonds, place on rimmed baking sheet in single layer. Toast in middle of 350°F oven for about 4 minutes or until lightly toasted. Watch carefully because they burn easily. Cool.

Pear

Bartlett

Bosc

D'Anjou

Red Bartlett

Starkrimson

A lush, juicy pear offers melt-in-the-mouth texture combined with charismatic aroma. But purchasing pears needs to be premeditated. In the market, they are often baseball-hard and almost scent-free. That is because when left on the tree to ripen, pears become mushy. Let them ripen at home and that patience will be generously rewarded.

Bartletts and Red Bartletts are smooth textured and juicy. Their skin is thin, and due to its colorful eye appeal, they should be left unpeeled in salads and garnishes. Starkrimson pears (often the first organic pear of the season) supply their share of red-skinned glory; it is difficult to resist simply eating one of these beauties right out of hand due to their oh-so-sweet flavor profile.

Bosc pears, with their long tapered neck and sandy texture, maintain their attractive shape when cooked, so they are perfect for poaching or baking whole. The fine-textured D'Anjou (sometimes labeled Anjou) is best cooked before it becomes overly soft and yielding.

Bartlett

Bosc

Starkrimson

D'Anjou

Organic growers compost the soil in fall and spring. The trees are pruned, thinning the yield to produce larger-size fruit. Many farmers report that their organic orchards produce about 25 percent fewer pears than conventionally grown crops. Organic pears are not waxed or dipped.

BUYING AND STORING: Buy several days in advance of serving to allow time to ripen them. Once ripened, refrigerate 3 to 5 days. Or for slower ripening, store firm pears at room temperature out of direct sunlight. They are ripe when they give to gentle pressure at the neck. Look for unblemished fruit without bruises. Handle gently; even hard, unripe fruit can bruise.

PREP AND USE: Once cut and cored, pears discolor quickly. To prevent browning, dip cut fruit in acidulated water (cold water with a little lemon or lime juice). Can be eaten with or without skin, raw or cooked. Generally, peel before cooking. If poaching or baking whole fruit, choose pears that are naturally firm, such as Bosc. If cut for baking, use ripe Bartlett, D'Anjou, or Starkrimson.

Pears can be baked, braised, grilled, poached, roasted, or sautéed. They are delicious in baked goods, chutneys, and sauces, or served raw with cheese. In savory dishes, they pair well with meats and game. Pears are delightful when paired with fresh berries, dried fruit (cherries, raisins), butterscotch, honey, chocolate, mint, or ginger. Generally, they can be substituted for apples in recipes.

AVAILABLE:

Bartlett: August to April

Bosc: September to June

D'Anjou: October to July

Red Bartlett: August to April

Starkrimson: August to January

NUTRITIONAL INFORMATION (per 1 cup cubed, raw): Calories 93, fat calories 2; total fat 0 grams, sat fat 0 grams, cholesterol 0 milligrams; sodium 2 milligrams; total carbohydrates 25 grams, fiber 5 grams, sugars 16 grams; protein 1 gram; vitamin A IUs 1%; vitamin C 11%; calcium 1%; iron 2%.

SERVING SUGGESTIONS

Potato-Pear Salad

Add cubes of cored, ripe pear to potato salad dressed with simple vinaigrette.

Spud Mash with Pears

Using a potato masher, roughly mash 3 (peeled, cored, roasted or poached) pears with the flesh of 3 large baked russet potatoes. There should be small chunks of pear and potato left in the mixture. Stir in 2 tablespoons unsalted butter, plus salt and freshly ground black pepper to taste.

Crostini Appetizers with Pears and Cheese

Slice a baguette into thin slices. Brush lightly with extra-virgin olive oil and place in single layer on rimmed baking sheet. Bake in 350°F oven until tops are nicely browned. Cool. Spread with Gorgonzola and top with slivers of cored, fresh ripe pear.

Cosmo Garni

Use a slice of ripe red-skinned pear to garnish a Cosmopolitan cocktail.

Individual Puff Pancakes with Pears

YIELD: 8 SERVINGS

Richly browned and puffed, the interiors of these glorious breakfast treats are custardy. Right from the oven, the warm pear mixture is spooned into the center of each dome, creating a spicy contrast to the egginess of the dish. To save time at breakfast, prepare the pear mixture the night before and refrigerate it. Reheat in the microwave or on the stovetop before use.

Individual Puff Pancakes with Pears

Pear Mixture

4 ripe pears, peeled, cored, cut crosswise into ¼-inch-thick slices

½ cup water

1 tablespoon sugar (see Cook's Note)

⅓ cup unsalted butter

1 teaspoon ground cinnamon

½ teaspoon ground cloves

1 teaspoon minced lemon zest (colored portion of peel)

½ teaspoon ground nutmeg

Egg Mixture

6 large eggs

1 cup all-purpose flour

1 cup whole milk

2 teaspoons vanilla

¼ cup (½ stick) unsalted butter, cut into 8 slices

Optional garnish: sprigs of fresh mint

1   Adjust oven rack to middle position. Preheat oven to 425°F.

2   Prepare pear mixture: Place pears in large, deep skillet with water, sugar, and butter; bring to boil on high heat. Reduce heat to medium and simmer until pears are softened, about 10 minutes. Stir in cinnamon, cloves, zest, and nutmeg; set aside.

2   Prepare egg mixture: Whisk together eggs, flour, milk, and vanilla in medium bowl; some small lumps may remain. Place 1 slice of butter in each of 8 (12-ounce) individual soufflé dishes or ramekins. Heat in oven until butter is melted and very hot, 10 to 12 minutes. Evenly divide batter between dishes.

3   Bake 10 minutes. Reduce heat to 400°F and bake 10 more minutes or until golden and puffy.

4   Remove from oven; spoon pear mixture into center of each puffed pancake. Garnish each with fresh mint, if desired. Serve immediately.

Nutritional information (per serving): Calories 310, fat calories 160; total fat 18 grams, sat fat 10 grams, cholesterol 200 milligrams; sodium 65 milligrams; total carbohydrates 29 grams, fiber 3 grams, sugars 12 grams; protein 8 grams; vitamin A IUs 15%; vitamin C 10%; calcium 10%; iron 8%.

Cook's Note: The sweetness of the pears will determine the need for sugar. If they are already sweet, you can omit the sugar. If they aren't very sweet, you may wish to increase the sugar to 1½ to 2 tablespoons. The pear mixture can also be used as a topping for French toast or waffles.

Grilled Pear Salad with Honey and Blue Cheese

YIELD: 4 SERVINGS

I f you like, infuse the vinaigrette with the scent and flavor of lavender. In a small saucepan combine ¼ cup honey and 10 sprigs of fresh lavender. Bring to a simmer on medium heat; remove from heat and set aside for 30 minutes. Strain and use 2 tablespoons in the dressing.

Vinaigrette

4 tablespoons honey, divided use

2 tablespoons sherry vinegar

1 teaspoon Dijon-style mustard

1 small shallot, finely minced

4 tablespoons extra-virgin olive oil

Salt and freshly ground black pepper

Salad

1 Belgian endive, cut into ½-inch-wide slices

1 small head curly endive or frisée, torn into bite-size pieces

½ small head butter lettuce, torn into bite-size pieces

2 ripe pears, red-skinned preferred

4 ounces crumbled blue cheese

1 Heat grill. Clean grates and brush with vegetable oil or canola oil.

2 Prepare vinaigrette: Combine 2 tablespoons honey with vinegar, mustard, shallot, and oil. Add salt and pepper to taste. Whisk to combine.

3 Prepare salad: Place endive, curly endive or frisée, and lettuce in large bowl. Stir vinaigrette and set aside 2 tablespoons for grilling pears. Toss remaining vinaigrette with endive mixture. Arrange salad on 4 plates.

4 Cut pears in quarters and core. Brush cut sides with reserved 2 tablespoons vinaigrette. Grill 2 minutes on each side. They should be warm but not mushy. Place pears atop each salad and top with cheese. Heat remaining 2 tablespoons honey and drizzle over the salads. Serve immediately.

Nutritional information (per serving): Calories 330, fat calories 200; total fat 22 grams, sat fat 7 grams, cholesterol 20 milligrams; sodium 420 milligrams; total carbohydrates 28 grams, fiber 5 grams, sugars 18 grams; protein 8 grams; vitamin A IUs 25%; vitamin C 8%; calcium 25%; iron 4%.

Chilled Pear and Wine Soup

YIELD: 6 SMALL FIRST-COURSE SERVINGS

S erve this easy-to-prepare soup chilled as a first course in small cups at picnics or backyard gatherings. The soup can be prepared one day in advance of serving and stored airtight in refrigerator.

1 cup dry red wine, such as Shiraz or Zinfandel

⅔ cup water

½ cup fresh orange juice

½ cup sugar

1 lemon

1¾ pounds ripe pears (about 5 medium pears), peeled, quartered, cored

Garnish: ½ cup sour cream or crème fraîche

1   In large nonreactive saucepan, combine wine, water, orange juice, and sugar; bring to boil on high heat, stirring frequently.

2   Using small knife or swivel-bladed vegetable peeler, remove 2 strips of lemon zest (colored portion of peel). Add zest to wine mixture along with 1 tablespoon of lemon juice. Add pears and bring to boil; reduce to medium-low and simmer until pears are tender, about 12 minutes. Remove and discard strips of zest.

3   Process in several batches in food processor fitted with metal blade. Place in bowl; cover and chill until very cold, at least 1½ hours.

4   Serve in small chilled cups, garnished with a spoonful of sour cream or crème fraîche.

Nutritional information (per serving without garnish): Calories 170, fat calories 35; total fat 3.5 grams, sat fat 2 grams, cholesterol 5 milligrams; sodium 10 milligrams; total carbohydrates 30 grams, fiber 3 grams, sugars 24 grams; protein 1 gram; vitamin A IUs 2%; vitamin C 20%; calcium 4%; iron 0%.

Poached Pears in Burgundy "Syrup"

YIELD: 4 SERVINGS

Dry red wine combined with sugar, zest, spices, and balsamic vinegar simmers into a mixture that perfectly complements fruit. In addition to whole pears, apples, apricots, peaches, cherries, and plums poach well in this wine-based concoction (poaching times will depend upon size and ripeness of fruit). Poached fruit can be made several days in advance and refrigerated. For best results, bring to room temperature before serving, about 1 hour.

3 cups Pinot Noir

1 cup water

1 cup sugar

Minced zest of ½ orange (colored portion of peel)

1 cinnamon stick

½ vanilla bean, split lengthwise

6 black peppercorns

1 tablespoon balsamic vinegar

4 ripe pears, peeled

Optional for serving: ice cream, frozen yogurt, or sweetened mascarpone cheese

1   Pour all ingredients except pears into large nonreactive saucepan or Dutch oven. Bring to a boil on high heat; reduce heat to medium and simmer 5 minutes.

2   Add pears to wine mixture and simmer gently on medium-low heat until fruit is fork-tender, about 15 to 25 minutes. Cool in liquid. (Poached pears will continue to cook a bit as they cool.)

3   Serve warm, cold, or at room temperature with about half of the poaching liquid. If desired, accompany with ice cream, frozen yogurt, or sweetened mascarpone cheese (see Grape Compote, page 149).

Nutritional information (per serving): Calories 240, fat calories 10; total fat 1 gram, sat fat 0 gram, cholesterol 0 milligrams; sodium 0 milligrams; total carbohydrates 54 grams, fiber 4 grams, sugars 43 grams; protein 1 gram; vitamin A IUs 0%; vitamin C 15%; calcium 2%; iron 0%.

Peas

Crescent-shaped sugar snap peas have a sweet flavor profile inside and out. The outside shell is just as delectable as the plump peas inside. Sno peas (also called snow peas, mange-tout, or Chinese snow peas), are so delectably delicate, you can detect the immature peas through the slender shell. Both maintain their bright green color and appealing crunch when cooked just until tender-crisp.

Organic growers face more challenges with sno peas than with sugar snap peas. Sno peas are very sensitive to changes in weather conditions, while sturdier sugar snap peas hold up better.

BUYING AND STORING: To test for freshness, snap a pea in half. It should make a nice crisp, crunching sound. Color should be bright green. Avoid any that are limp or have soft spots or discolorations. Store unwashed in perforated bag in crisper drawer up to 7 days for sno peas, or 10 days for sugar snap peas.

PREP AND USE: Some have strings that need removal, others don't. For sno peas, partially snap off stem end so string stays attached; pull toward opposite end to remove string. For sugar snap peas, there are often strings on both top and bottom. If blanching or steaming sugar snap peas, remove strings after peas are cool enough to handle.

Sno

Sugar Snap

Whether raw or cooked, to remove strings, snap off stem end, breaking it toward side of pea rather than bottom or top; pull in opposite directions to remove strings on both bottom and top.

Eat raw or cooked. Brief cooking is best. Stir-fry, blanch, or steam. Use hot, warm, or cold.

AVAILABLE:

Sno peas: December to March, June to July

Sugar snap peas: February to December

NUTRITIONAL INFORMATION (per 1 cup serving): Calories 117, fat calories 5; total fat 1 gram, sat fat 0 grams, cholesterol 0 milligrams; sodium 7 milligrams; total carbohydrates 21 grams, fiber 7 grams, sugars 8 grams; protein 8 grams; vitamin A IUs 22%; vitamin C 97%; calcium 4%; iron 12%.

SERVING SUGGESTIONS

New Look for Old-Fashioned Favorite

A classic pea salad is traditionally made with frozen peas. To give it a fresher taste, try using 1 pound fresh sugar snap peas instead of English peas; string sugar snap peas (if needed) and cut each into 3 pieces crosswise. Blanch until tender-crisp, drain, refresh with cold water, drain again, and chill. Combine with ½ cup minced green onions (including some of dark green stalks) and 1 cup peeled jicama cut into ¾-inch-long matchsticks. Toss with ¼ cup mayonnaise to lightly coat. Add 2 teaspoons lemon juice, and salt and freshly ground black pepper to taste. Serve chilled in lettuce cups.

Gremolata Topping

Blanch or steam sugar snap peas or sno peas until tender-crisp. Drain and remove strings if present. Toss with a smidgen of extra-virgin olive oil and orange gremolata to taste. To make gremolata, combine minced zest of 1 large orange (colored portion of peel), 1 medium clove garlic (minced), 3 tablespoons minced fresh basil leaves, and 1 tablespoon minced fresh Italian parsley.

Snappy Crudités

Along with traditional carrots and celery served with dips or spreads, include peas, either raw or quickly blanched tender-crisp, refreshed with cold water, and patted dry.

Greek-Style Salad

Blanch or steam 3 cups sugar snap peas until tender-crisp. Drain and refresh with cold water. Remove strings, if present, and cool peas. Place in bowl with 1 cup halved cherry tomatoes, 2 tablespoons chopped fresh parsley or mint, leaves from 2 sprigs fresh thyme, 2 tablespoons fresh lemon juice, ⅓ cup extra-virgin olive oil, 4 ounces crumbled feta cheese, and salt and freshly ground black pepper to taste. Gently toss and taste. Adjust seasoning if needed.

Risotto with Sugar Snap Peas

YIELD: 4 TO 6 SERVINGS AS SIDE DISH OR FIRST COURSE

No doubt this classic Italian rice dish is beautiful augmented with bright green sugar snaps, but those tender-crisp peas also offer a nice contrast in texture. If available, sugar snap peas' leaves and tendrils can make a showy garnish.

4 cups low-fat chicken broth or vegetable broth

1 tablespoon unsalted butter

1 tablespoon extra-virgin olive oil

2 medium cloves garlic, minced

1 cup Arborio rice

½ cup dry white wine

2 cups sugar snap peas, strings removed

¼ cup freshly grated Parmesan cheese

Salt and freshly ground black pepper

1   In medium saucepan, bring chicken broth or vegetable broth to simmer on medium heat.

2   Meanwhile, heat butter and oil in large, deep skillet on medium-high heat. Add garlic and cook 30 seconds. Add rice and toss to coat with oil. Cook 1 minute, stirring frequently. Do *not* brown rice or garlic.

3   Add wine and cook until most of wine is absorbed. Add hot broth, ½ cup at a time, stirring frequently, waiting to add another ½ cup broth when most of liquid is absorbed. When only about 1 cup of broth remains to be added, add sugar snap peas to rice and continue to cook, adding remaining broth ½ cup at a time.

4   Rice should be creamy, but each kernel should be a little firm at the center. Remove from heat and add cheese, and salt and pepper to taste. Taste and adjust seasoning as needed. Spoon into shallow bowls and serve.

Nutritional information (per serving, using 6 servings): Calories 230, fat calories 60; total fat 6 grams, sat fat 2.5 grams, cholesterol 10 milligrams; sodium 550 milligrams; total carbohydrates 33 grams, fiber 3 grams, sugars 3 grams; protein 7 grams; vitamin A IUs 10%; vitamin C 20%; calcium 8%; iron 6%.

Risotto with Sugar Snap Peas

Mélange of Baby Artichokes, Favas, and Sugar Snap Peas

YIELD: 8 FIRST-COURSE OR SIDE-DISH SERVINGS

Start by prepping the fava beans. It's a time-consuming task, but the color, flavor, and texture is a really nice addition to this dish. If you want to take a shortcut, instead of fava beans use store-bought, already-shelled-cooked soybeans (edamame). If you like, pass a bowl of freshly grated Parmesan cheese for optional topping.

1 lemon, halved

12 baby artichokes

3 tablespoons extra-virgin olive oil

4 large shallots, coarsely chopped

¼ cup water or vegetable broth plus 3 tablespoons, divided use

2 large cloves garlic, thinly sliced

¾ pound fresh sugar snap peas, strings removed

3 small carrots, peeled, cut into ¼-inch-thick diagonal crosswise slices

Salt

1 pound fresh fava beans, shelled, blanched, skinned (see page 53)

3 tablespoons minced fresh basil leaves

Freshly ground black pepper

1   Squeeze lemon juice into medium bowl filled two-thirds full with cold water; drop in lemon halves. To prepare baby artichokes, use sharp knife (not carbon steel) to cut off stem at base and cut off top ½ inch of leaves. Remove and discard outer leaves; bend them back until they snap and the edible portion at bottom will stay intact. Trim sides of base with paring knife as if peeling an apple. Cut in half lengthwise. Drop each into lemon water as soon as it is trimmed to prevent discoloration.

2   In large, deep skillet heat oil on medium-high heat. Add shallots and cook until starting to soften, about 1 minute. Drain artichokes and add to shallots. Add ¼ cup water or vegetable broth and garlic. Bring to boil on high heat; cover and reduce heat to medium-low. Simmer 5 minutes. Add peas, carrots, and 3 tablespoons water or vegetable broth. Season with salt to taste and simmer, covered, 5 minutes. Add fava beans, cover, and cook until vegetables are fork-tender, about 5 more minutes. Remove from heat and toss in basil. Taste; add salt and pepper as needed. Place in shallow bowls and serve.

Nutritional information (per serving): Calories 180, fat calories 50; total fat 5 grams, sat fat 0.5 grams, cholesterol 0 milligrams; sodium 210 milligrams; total carbohydrates 26 grams, fiber 6 grams, sugars 9 grams; protein 7 grams; vitamin A IUs 20%; vitamin C 30%; calcium 6%; iron 20%.

Fusilli with Peas and Sugar Snaps

YIELD: 6 SERVINGS

Appealing flavors along with refreshing colors make this pasta dish a favorite. Serve it as a main course teamed with crusty bread and a tomato salad. The salad can be as simple as thickly sliced tomatoes topped with vinaigrette and chopped fresh herbs.

3 tablespoons extra-virgin olive oil

6 ounces pancetta, finely chopped (see Meatless Tip)

3 medium shallots, finely chopped

1 large clove garlic, minced

1 pound sugar snap peas, strings removed, cut crosswise in thirds

2 medium carrots, peeled, cut into ¼-inch crosswise diagonal slices

1½ cups frozen peas, thawed

1 pound fusilli

¼ cup finely chopped fresh basil leaves

Pinch dried red chile flakes

Salt

For serving: freshly grated Parmesan cheese

1   Bring large pot of salted water to boil on high heat.

2   Meanwhile, place large, deep skillet on medium heat; add oil and pancetta. Cook, stirring frequently, until pancetta is browned and starting to get crisp, about 8 minutes. Stir in shallots and cook until softened, stirring frequently, about 1 to 2 minutes. Add garlic and cook 30 seconds. Remove from heat and set aside.

3   Add sugar snap peas and carrots to boiling salted water. Cook 1 minute. Add peas and cook 2 minutes or until tender-crisp. Keeping water in pot to use to cook pasta, use slotted spoon or slotted scoop to remove vegetables from water. Place in colander in sink and refresh vegetables with cold water.

4   Add fusilli to boiling water and cook according to package direction until al dente (tender but with a little bite). Reserve ⅔ cup pasta water. Drain pasta and add to skillet with pancetta-shallot mixture. Add cooked vegetables, basil, chile flakes, and half of reserved pasta water. Gently toss. Place on medium and cook until just heated through and creamy, and pasta water is absorbed. Add more reserved pasta water if necessary to reach a creamy consistency.

5   Taste and add salt if needed. Divide between 6 shallow bowls and top with cheese.

Nutritional information (per serving with 1 teaspoon grated Parmesan): Calories 480, fat calories 160; total fat 17 grams, sat fat 7 grams, cholesterol 40 milligrams; sodium 1870 milligrams; total carbohydrates 59 grams, fiber 6 grams, sugars 11 grams; protein 22 grams; vitamin A IUs 100%; vitamin C 35%; calcium 20%; iron 10%.

Meatless Tip: Omit pancetta. In step 2, cook shallots in oil and proceed with recipe. Pancetta delivers a peppery spiciness to the dish, so if omitting it, add a pinch more of chile flakes and just before serving, season to taste with freshly ground black pepper. If desired, instead of Parmesan cheese, use pecorino. It has a sharper, more pungent flavor.

Stir-Fried Sugar-Sno Showoffs

YIELD: 4 SERVINGS

Stir-fries are perfect for quick meals. This colorful blend of two pea varieties and slivers of bright red bell pepper is delicious spooned over cooked rice or farro. The peas are cut into pieces before cooking to speed up the cooking process.

1 tablespoon vegetable oil or canola oil

1 large clove garlic, minced

1 tablespoon finely chopped fresh ginger

¼ teaspoon dried red chile flakes

2½ cups sno peas, strings removed, cut diagonally into 1-inch pieces

2½ cups sugar snap peas, strings removed, cut diagonally into 1-inch pieces

1 medium red bell pepper, cored, seeded, cut into 1-inch-long matchsticks

1½ teaspoons soy sauce

1 tablespoon Lemon-Infused Olive Oil (page 191)

Salt

1 tablespoon toasted sesame seeds (see Cook's Note)

For serving: 4 cups cooked rice or farro

Optional topping: 1 thinly sliced green onion, including dark green stalks

1   Heat oil in large, deep skillet on medium-high heat. Add garlic, ginger, and red chile flakes; cook 45 seconds, stirring occasionally (do *not* brown garlic). Add sno peas, sugar snaps, and pepper. Stir-fry until tender-crisp, about 3 to 4 minutes.

2   Remove from heat. Stir in soy sauce and lemon olive oil. Add salt to taste. Sprinkle with sesame seeds and serve over rice. If desired, top with green onion slices.

Nutritional information (per serving without rice): Calories 100, fat calories 45; total fat 5 grams, sat fat 0.5 grams, cholesterol 0 milligrams; sodium 680 milligrams; total carbohydrates 11 grams, fiber 3 grams, sugars 5 grams; protein 4 grams; vitamin A IUs 30%; vitamin C 150%; calcium 6%; iron 10%.

Cook's Note: To toast sesame seeds, place in small skillet over medium-high heat. Shake handle to redistribute seeds and cook until lightly browned. Watch carefully because they burn easily. Cool.

Persimmon

Fall brings two luscious varieties of organic persimmons to the marketplace. One, the Hachiya, is heart-shaped and a vivid orange; it needs to be fully ripe with a water balloon–like consistency to be delectable. Underripe, it is unpleasantly astringent. The Fuyu variety is tomato-shaped and is a lighter orange color; it can be enjoyed when apple-like firm or slightly softened.

Unlike conventional fields where Hachiya persimmons are the dominant crop, the Fuyu persimmon is preferred by most organic persimmon farmers primarily because it has a longer shelf life.

The leaves at the stem end of the persimmon (the calyx) can harbor unwanted pests. Organic growers apply a soapy chlorine-based solution to the fruit as it matures to combat the problem. Note that in order for fruit to be labeled organic it cannot be dipped in a chlorine solution after it is harvested.

A natural powdery sheen on the persimmon's exterior is sometimes created by polishing with a cloth before organic persimmons are brought to market; nonorganic waxes or polishes cannot be used.

Hachiya

Fuyu

BUYING AND STORING: For Hachiya persimmons: The skin is the same vivid orange color whether at the highly astringent, unripe stage or fully ripened, luscious point. Touch them; they should feel like water balloons. Cut off the top and their pulp can be scooped from the skin like jam from a cup. They are seldom sold ripe because they are super-soft and fragile. Ripen at home, either at room temperature or place in loosely sealed paper bag with another fruit, such as apple or banana (see page 323). When ripe, store at room temperature up to 3 days, or refrigerate in plastic bag in crisper drawer up to 7 days. Freeze up to 3 months, either whole or just the pulp.

For Fuyu persimmons: They can be eaten when firm or slightly soft. Look for fruit with green (not brown) leaves. Skin should be a consistent light orange color, not yellow or green. Store at room temperature up to 7 days, or refrigerate in plastic bag in crisper drawer up to 12 days.

PREP AND USE: For Hachiya persimmons: Wash thoroughly with cold water. Cut top off ripe fruit and scoop out jelly-like pulp with spoon. Mash the pulp by pulsing in food processor fitted with metal blade, or press through a large-mesh strainer, or mash with tines of fork. Discard skin.

Incorporate pulp into jam, cookies, sorbet, pudding, smoothies, quick breads, and muffins.

For Fuyu persimmons: Wash thoroughly with cold water; remove calyx. If core is pulpy or hard, remove it. Peel if skin is thick. Eat fresh out of hand like an apple. Or cut into medium dice or thin wedges for salads or other cold dishes.

Use raw, diced or sliced, in salad or salsa, or cooked in cake, chutneys, or sauces.

AVAILABLE: October to December

NUTRITIONAL INFORMATION (per 1 ounce diced, raw): Calories 36, fat calories 1; total fat 0 gram, sat fat 0 grams, cholesterol 0 milligrams; sodium 0 milligrams; total carbohydrates 9 grams, fiber 0 grams, sugars 4 grams; protein 0 grams; vitamin A IUs 0%; vitamin C 31%; calcium 1%; iron 4%.

SERVING SUGGESTIONS

Persimmon Vinaigrette

This tasty vinaigrette is delicious drizzled over pear slices and baby greens. To make it, combine the pulp of 1 ripe Hachiya persimmon with 1 small minced shallot, 3 tablespoons white wine vinegar, and ⅓ cup extra-virgin olive oil; whisk in salt and freshly ground black pepper to taste.

Fuyu "Crackers"

Slice Fuyu into ⅛-inch-thick crosswise slices. Often a flower-like pattern is created when sliced this way. Serve instead of bread or crackers with assorted cheeses.

Couscous Muse

Peel a Fuyu persimmon if the skin is thick. Cut into ¼-inch-thick wedges and toss with cooked couscous (see Couscous with Plumcots and Mint, page 267).

Bacon and Fuyu Sandwich

Substitute a thin, peeled slice of Fuyu persimmon for the tomato in a sandwich. Or for a meatless delicacy, augment a grilled cheese sandwich with a thin, peeled slice of Fuyu.

Persimmon Cookies

YIELD: ABOUT 34 COOKIES

Aromatic Hachiya persimmons, mashed to produce an almost smooth pulp, add sweet fruitiness to these cookies. The spice trio of cinnamon, clove, and nutmeg provide the scent and flavor profile often associated with fall, making them a great treat for Halloween and Thanksgiving holidays.

- ½ cup (1 stick) unsalted butter, softened
- 1 cup sugar
- 1 egg
- 1½ cups all-purpose flour
- ½ teaspoon ground cinnamon
- ¼ teaspoon ground cloves
- ½ teaspoon ground nutmeg
- 1 teaspoon baking soda
- ¼ teaspoon salt
- 1 cup persimmon pulp, about 2 very ripe, large Hachiya persimmons (see Cook's Note)
- 1 cup raisins
- 1 cup chopped pecans

1 Adjust oven rack to middle position. Preheat the oven to 350°F. Line 2 baking sheets with parchment paper; set aside.

2 In large bowl of electric mixer, beat butter and sugar until creamy and light in color. Add egg and mix until well combined.

3 In separate medium bowl, combine flour, cinnamon, cloves, nutmeg, baking soda, and salt. Stir with whisk to combine. Add to butter mixture and mix to combine. Add persimmon pulp, raisins, and pecans; mix until combined.

4 Drop dough by rounded tablespoons onto lined baking sheets, leaving 1½ inches between each. Bake 12 to 15 minutes or until nicely browned. Place on wire rack to cool.

Nutritional information (per cookie): Calories 110, fat calories 50; total fat 5 grams, sat fat 2 grams, cholesterol 15 milligrams; sodium 60 milligrams; total carbohydrates 16 grams, fiber 1 gram, sugars 7 grams; protein 1 gram; vitamin A IUs 6%; vitamin C 2%; calcium 0%; iron 2%.

Cook's Note: If pulp is lumpy, mash with fork.

Persimmon Caprese Salad

YIELD: 6 TO 8 SERVINGS

The traditional caprese salad hails from the isle of Capri, the sun-splashed island off Italy's Amalfi Coast. This adaptation substitutes sliced Fuyu persimmons for tomatoes, and instead of spiking the vinaigrette with capers, it softens the flavor profile with a little honey or agave syrup. The vinaigrette can be made ahead and stored for several days in the refrigerator. For an additional splash of color, top the salad with a handful of microgreens.

- 1 teaspoon minced lemon zest (colored portion of peel)
- 2 tablespoons fresh lemon juice
- 1 teaspoon honey or agave syrup
- 1 tablespoon white wine vinegar
- ½ cup extra-virgin olive oil
- Garlic salt
- 6 Fuyu persimmons, trimmed, cut crosswise into ¼-inch-thick slices (see Cook's Note)
- 1 cup packed fresh basil leaves
- 12 ounces fresh mozzarella cheese, sliced
- 6 cherry tomatoes, halved
- Freshly ground black pepper

1   Prepare vinaigrette: Combine zest, juice, honey or agave syrup, and vinegar. Whisk in oil. Add garlic salt to taste; stir to combine. Taste and adjust seasoning as needed to suit your taste.

2   Arrange persimmon slices in a single layer on platter. Top each with basil leaf. Top with slices of cheese. Stir vinaigrette and spoon on top. Place cherry tomato halves randomly around edge of platter. Top all with pepper to taste and serve.

Nutritional information (per serving): Calories 340, fat calories 160; total fat 17 grams, sat fat 2 grams, cholesterol 0 milligrams; sodium 0 milligrams; total carbohydrates 37 grams, fiber 5 grams, sugars 17 grams; protein 13 grams; vitamin A IUs 45%; vitamin C 20%; calcium 2%; iron 2%.

Cook's Note: Before slicing, peel persimmons if skin is thick.

Persimmon and Strawberry Spinach Salad

YIELD: 8 SERVINGS

A salty, meaty garnish is a delicious option on this salad. So if you like, top each serving with a thin slice of prosciutto. Or sprinkle a little crumbled cooked vegetarian bacon.

2 tablespoons white wine vinegar

2 tablespoons raspberry jam

1 teaspoon salt

½ cup canola oil or extra-virgin olive oil

Freshly ground black pepper

2 Fuyu persimmons, trimmed, cut into ¼-inch-wide wedges

2 tablespoons finely chopped fresh basil leaves

8 ripe strawberries, hulled, quartered

8 cups baby spinach

½ cup coarsely chopped toasted walnuts (see Cook's Note)

1   In large bowl, combine vinegar, jam, and salt. Whisk to combine. Whisk in canola oil or extra-virgin oil in slow stream. Season to taste with pepper. Add persimmons and basil; toss to combine.

2   Add strawberries and spinach. Toss. Taste and adjust seasoning as needed. Divide between 8 salad plates and top with walnuts.

Nutritional information (per serving): Calories 220, fat calories 160; total fat 18 grams, sat fat 2 grams, cholesterol 0 milligrams; sodium 310 milligrams; total carbohydrates 14 grams, fiber 3 grams, sugars 9 grams; protein 3 grams; vitamin A IUs 45%; vitamin C 30%; calcium 4%; iron 6%.

Cook's Note: To toast walnuts, place in single layer on rimmed baking sheet. Toast in middle of 350°F oven for 3 to 5 minutes, until nicely browned. Watch carefully because nuts burn easily. Cool.

Cakey Persimmon Puddings

YIELD: ABOUT 10 SERVINGS

This dessert showcases the likable elements of fruitcake without the components that many find objectionable. The underlying sweetness of the persimmon shines through, augmented with the taste and texture of nuts and raisins, as well as chopped dried apricots. If you like, substitute dried cherries or dried cranberries for the raisins.

Nonstick vegetable oil spray

½ cup (1 stick) unsalted butter, softened

2 cups granulated sugar

2 eggs, well beaten

½ teaspoon vanilla

2 cups all-purpose flour

1 ¼ teaspoons ground cinnamon

4 teaspoons baking soda

½ teaspoon salt

2 cups persimmon pulp, 3 to 4 very ripe Hachiya persimmons (see Cook's Note)

¾ cup finely chopped dried apricots

¾ cup raisins

¼ cup finely chopped crystallized ginger, store-bought or homemade (page 146)

¼ cup chopped walnuts

⅓ cup chopped pecans

Garnish: 1 cup heavy whipping cream and powdered sugar.

Garnish: 2 tablespoons ground cinnamon

1 Adjust oven rack to middle position. Preheat oven to 350°F. Generously spray 10 (6-ounce) soufflé cups with nonstick spray; set aside.

2 In large bowl of electric mixer, cream butter and granulated sugar until smooth. Add eggs and vanilla; mix until well blended.

3 In separate medium bowl, combine flour, cinnamon, baking soda, and salt; stir with whisk to combine.

4 Add dry ingredients to butter mixture; mix until blended. Add persimmon pulp; mix until blended. Add raisins, ginger, and nuts; mix until blended.

5 Spoon into prepared cups, filling a little less than three-quarters full; smooth tops to make even, using back of large spoon or rubber spatula. Bake until toothpick inserted in center comes out clean, 40 to 50 minutes. Cool 15 minutes on wire rack before serving.

6 In large bowl of electric mixer, beat cream and powdered sugar until soft peaks form. Add a dollop of whipped cream to each cooled pudding and serve. Place remaining whipped cream in bowl and pass for optional topping.

Nutritional information (per serving, with 1 cup whipped cream): Calories 550, fat calories 180; total fat 20 grams, sat fat 9 grams, cholesterol 85 milligrams; sodium 650 milligrams; total carbohydrates 93 grams, fiber 5 grams, sugars 56 grams; protein 6 grams; vitamin A IUs 40%; vitamin C 8%; calcium 4%; iron 15%.

Cook's Note: If persimmon pulp is chunky, mash with fork.

Cakey Persimmon Puddings

Pineapple

Beneath pineapple's prickly peel, below those spirals of fibrous "eyes" is juicy, lush sweet-tart treasure. The fruit grows from a bromeliad, rising from the center of the plant on a single spike bordered with sword-like leaves. Fresh pineapple contains an enzyme that breaks down protein, making it very beneficial in marinades for meat, but unwelcome in gelatins because it interferes with the jelling process.

Grown in subtropical climes, rain acts as a natural pesticide for organic pineapples. Typically, conventionally grown pineapples are dipped in fungicidal chlorine baths after harvest to prevent mold. This process is forbidden with organic pineapples, which are wrapped at stem end in special paper-like tape where the fruit is most susceptible to mold.

BUYING AND STORING: Generally, skin color isn't an indication of ripeness. First look at leaves on crown; they should be bright green, not dried or brown. Fruit should yield to light pressure and smell fragrant. Firm fruit will soften when left at room temperature for 2 to 4 days. But sweetest fruit is picked when ripe; sugar content does not increase after harvest. Refrigerate ripe pineapples up to 5 days. Or peel and cut into chunks and freeze on baking sheet. Once frozen, store in airtight container; use frozen in smoothies and pureed cocktails.

PREP AND USE: Using a sharp, sturdy knife cut off crown and bottom. Place cut-side down on cutting board. Remove skin and "eyes" by cutting in strips from top to bottom, following the contour of the fruit. If cutting into chunks, cut into lengthwise quarters and remove core, cutting from top to bottom; cut quarters into chunks. If cutting whole crosswise slices, use a pineapple corer, a cylindrical device that cuts down through center of pineapple to extract the central core.

Eat raw out of hand or in salads, rice dishes, fritters, sorbets, salsas, and compotes. Do not use in gelatin because a natural enzyme in fresh pineapples prevents setting. Or use cooked, either sautéed, grilled, roasted, or broiled; or showcase in baked goods.

AVAILABLE: Year-round

NUTRITIONAL INFORMATION (per 1 cup chunks, raw): Calories 82, fat calories 2; total fat 0 grams, sat fat 0 grams, cholesterol 0 milligrams; sodium 2 milligrams; total carbohydrates 22 grams, fiber 2 grams, sugars 16 grams; protein 1 gram; vitamin A IUs 2%; vitamin C 131%; calcium 2%; iron 3%.

SERVING SUGGESTIONS

Spiced Pineapple

In large saucepan, combine 1 cup cider vinegar, 1¾ cups sugar, 2 teaspoons whole cloves, 1 tablespoon whole allspice, 1 cinnamon stick (broken into 4 pieces), and 1 cup water. Place on high heat and bring to boil; reduce heat and simmer 10 minutes. Add 6 cups fresh pineapple chunks; simmer 30 minutes. Cool and place in clean pint jars. Seal and refrigerate up to 3 weeks. Serve with ham, cold cuts, or grilled tofu.

Tropical Hot Chocolate Sundaes

For the sauce, place 1 cup semisweet chocolate chips and ¼ cup coconut milk in small, heavy-bottomed saucepan. Stir on medium-low heat until melted. Place large scoops of ice cream in 6 shallow bowls. Spoon hot sauce over ice cream. Top with fresh pineapple chunks and serve. If desired, top with whipped cream and toasted nuts.

Party Pineapple

Cut peeled ripe, medium pineapple in half lengthwise. In 9 × 13-inch baking dish, combine 3 tablespoons each of tequila, fresh lime juice, and sugar. Stir to dissolve sugar. Add pineapple, flat-side down, and spoon tequila mixture over fruit. Bake in 425°F oven until lightly caramelized, 35 to 40 minutes, basting with pan juices every 15 minutes. Cool 10 minutes. Cut in half or fourths lengthwise, then into crosswise slices. Remove core. Spoon pan juices over top of pineapple and then sprinkle with 3 tablespoons chopped fresh cilantro. Serve with grilled meat or tofu.

Island Kebabs

Thread sturdy chunks of pineapple on bamboo skewers that have been soaked in water for 30 minutes, alternating with chunks of well-seasoned pork shoulder or pork loin. Grill until meat is done, basting with your favorite sweet-and-sour sauce during the last 2 minutes of grilling.

Easy Pineapple Upside-Down Cake

YIELD: 12 SERVINGS

An upside-down cake sparkles with old-fashioned goodness. The butter, brown, sugar, and rum mixture combines with juices from the pineapple slices to create a glorious glaze under that cake batter, a presentation that is revealed when the treat is inverted after baking. A cake mix is used to save time, and is augmented with toasted macadamia nuts for added richness.

Nonstick vegetable oil spray

1 box (17.1-ounce) organic yellow or vanilla cake mix (see Cook's Notes)

¾ cup chopped, unsalted macadamia nuts, toasted (see Cook's Notes)

Ingredients listed on cake mix package, such as eggs, milk and oil

3 tablespoons unsalted butter

3 tablespoons dark rum

6 tablespoons light brown sugar

½ medium pineapple, peeled, cored, cut into ⅜-inch-thick slices

¼ cup dried cherries

Citrus Cream

¾ cup chilled heavy whipping cream

2 tablespoons powdered sugar

1 teaspoon grated fresh ginger

1½ teaspoons minced lemon zest (colored portion of peel)

1 Heat oven according to cake mix instructions. Lightly spray the sides of 9 × 13-inch baking pan with nonstick vegetable oil cooking spray; set aside.

2 Place cake mix in large bowl of electric mixer. Add nuts. Prepare batter according to cake mix instructions.

3 Melt butter in a saucepan over medium heat. Add rum and mix thoroughly. Pour mixture into prepared baking pan. Sprinkle brown sugar evenly on top of butter-rum mixture. Arrange pineapple slices evenly over the mixture, overlapping slices slightly if needed. Add cherries in the spaces between pineapple slices. Gently pour batter into pan and cautiously spread to even out the surface of the cake batter. Bake according to cake mix instructions.

4 Prepare citrus cream: Whip cream and sugar until soft peaks form. Fold in remaining ingredients. Cover and chill.

5 Remove cake from the oven and allow to cool on wire rack for 5 minutes. Run thin-bladed knife around edge of cake. Place platter over top. Wearing oven mitts or holding potholders, invert. Tap bottom of cake pan and lift pan off cake. If any pineapple slices stick to pan, pry them off and place on top of cake in appropriate spots. Allow cake to cool 20 minutes before cutting into squares. Serve warm or at room temperature with citrus cream on the side.

Nutritional information (per serving with citrus cream): Calories 470, fat calories 270; total fat 29 grams, sat fat 9 grams, cholesterol 90 milligrams; sodium 300 milligrams; total carbohydrates 45 grams, fiber 2 grams, sugars 6 grams; protein 6 grams; vitamin A IUs 10%; vitamin C 15%; calcium 10%; iron 8%.

Cook's Notes: This recipe was developed using the Dr. Oetker Organics Vanilla Cake Mix.

To toast macadamia nuts, place on rimmed baking sheet in single layer. Toast in middle of 350°F oven for about 7 minutes, or until lightly toasted. Watch carefully because they burn easily. Cool.

Pineapple and Spinach Salad

YIELD: 6 SERVINGS

Fresh ginger, rice vinegar, soy sauce, and sesame seeds produce an Asian-style dressing that tastes delicious with sweet, juicy pineapple chunks. The dressing can be prepared in advance without the sesame seeds and refrigerated in an airtight container (add sesame seeds just before serving). If you like, accompany the salad with some tasty potstickers (Asian dumplings) or Grilled Tofu with Asian-Style Marinade (page 321).

2 tablespoons rice vinegar

1 tablespoon honey or agave syrup

1 tablespoon soy sauce

2 teaspoons minced fresh ginger

¼ cup vegetable oil or canola oil

Salt

1 tablespoon toasted sesame seeds (see Cook's Note)

½ cup peeled, shredded carrots

4 cups baby spinach leaves

4 cups baby mixed greens

½ medium jicama, peeled, cut into 1-inch-long matchsticks

½ ripe medium pineapple, peeled, cored, cut into ½-inch chunks

1   In small bowl or glass measuring cup with handle, whisk vinegar, honey or agave syrup, soy sauce, and ginger. Whisk in vegetable oil or canola oil in thin stream. Taste and add salt if needed. Stir in sesame seeds.

2   In large bowl, toss carrots, spinach, mixed greens, jicama, and pineapple. Drizzle with dressing and toss. Divide between plates and serve.

Nutritional information (per serving without salt): Calories 150, fat calories 90; total fat 10 grams, sat fat 1 grams, cholesterol 0 milligrams; sodium 200 milligrams; total carbohydrates 13 grams, fiber 4 grams, sugars 7 grams; protein 2 grams; vitamin A IUs 70%; vitamin C 50%; calcium 6%; iron 10%.

Cook's Note: To toast sesame seeds, place in small skillet over medium-high heat. Shake handle to redistribute seeds as they toast to light brown. Watch carefully because they burn easily. Cool.

Jerk-Light Chicken with Pineapple Salsa

YIELD: 10 SERVINGS

Organic Scotch Bonnet or habanero chiles, the traditional fiery element in Jamaican jerk seasonings, are a challenge to find. This "light" version uses serrano chiles instead. They offer reduced spicy heat, although their heat level could hardly be described as sissy. The pineapple and cucumber in the cooling salsa offer a nice balance.

Marinade

4 large cloves garlic, chopped

3 green onions, chopped, including dark green stalks

4 serrano chiles, unseeded, chopped (see Cook's Note)

¼ cup fresh lime juice

2 tablespoons soy sauce

3 tablespoons extra-virgin olive oil

1½ tablespoons salt

2 tablespoons packed dark brown sugar

2 teaspoons ground allspice

½ teaspoon ground cinnamon

5 pounds skin-on, bone-in chicken breasts and thighs

Salsa

- 2 tablespoons honey
- 2 tablespoons fresh lime juice
- ½ cup peeled, seeded, finely diced cucumber
- 2 cups finely diced pineapple
- 2 tablespoons fresh mint

1   Place all marinade ingredients in blender; whirl until smooth. Place chicken in 2 large zipper-style plastic bags and place bags open side up in large bowl. Divide marinade between the bags. Press out air and seal. Refrigerate at least 8 hours or up to 24 hours, turning bags several times to redistribute marinade.

2   Prepare salsa: Combine all ingredients in nonreactive container (plastic, glass, or ceramic). Gently toss to combine and refrigerate well sealed up to 1 hour.

3   Take chicken out of refrigerator 30 minutes before cooking. Adjust 2 oven racks, one to upper third level, the other to lower third. Preheat oven to 400°F.

4   Arrange chicken in 2 large, shallow baking pans; discard marinade. Roast 25 minutes. Switch pan positions, placing the one on top on the bottom rack and vice versa. Roast an additional 20 to 25 minutes, or until chicken is thoroughly cooked. Serve chicken topped with salsa.

Nutritional information (per serving): Calories 400, fat calories 210; total fat 23 grams, sat fat 6 grams, cholesterol 130 milligrams; sodium 1380 milligrams; total carbohydrates 12 grams, fiber 1 gram, sugars 9 grams; protein 36 grams; vitamin A IUs 6%; vitamin C 40%; calcium 4%; iron 10%.

Cook's Note: Use caution when working with fresh chiles. Wash hands and work surface thoroughly upon completion and do *not* touch eyes or face.

Jerk-Light Chicken with Pineapple Salsa

Pineapple and Almond Pilaf

YIELD: 6 SIDE-DISH SERVINGS

Cooking pilaf begins by browning the rice before adding the broth or stock, a technique that improves both taste and texture. This pilaf shows off the sweet-tart taste of pineapple and the crunchy bite of toasted almond slivers. Serve it with grilled pork, chicken, or tofu.

1 tablespoon unsalted butter

1 tablespoon extra-virgin olive oil

1½ cups long-grain white rice

1 large clove garlic, minced

1 red bell pepper, cored, seeded, diced

3 cups vegetable broth or chicken broth

⅓ cup raisins or dried cranberries

¼ teaspoon salt

½ cup slivered almonds, toasted

1½ cups diced pineapple

⅓ cup chopped fresh cilantro

Garnish: 2 green onions, cut into ⅛-inch-thick diagonal slices (use half of dark green stalks)

1 In large saucepan, melt butter in oil on medium-high heat. Add rice and toss to coat grains with butter-oil mixture. Cook, stirring frequently, until rice is nicely browned, about 4 minutes. Add garlic and pepper; cook, stirring frequently, about 1 minute.

2 Add broth, raisins or dried cranberries, and salt; increase heat to high and bring to boil. Cover and reduce heat to medium-low. Gently simmer, covered, 18 minutes.

3 Remove from heat and fluff with fork. If some liquid remains, return to low heat and cook until all liquid is absorbed. Taste rice and adjust seasoning as needed. Add nuts, pineapple, and cilantro; toss. Garnish with green onions.

Nutritional information (per serving): Calories 330, fat calories 90; total fat 10 grams, sat fat 2 grams, cholesterol 5 milligrams; sodium 330 milligrams; total carbohydrates 56 grams, fiber 4 grams, sugars 12 grams; protein 7 grams; vitamin A IUs 15%; vitamin C 70%; calcium 8%; iron 20%.

Cook's Note: To toast slivered almonds, place on rimmed baking sheet in single layer. Toast in middle of 350°F oven for about 3 minutes, or until lightly toasted. Watch carefully because they burn easily. Cool.

Plum and Plumcot

Plums and plumcots are wrapped in eye-popping skin colors, some displaying solid hues; others are generously speckled with tiny yellow dots. Their juicy flesh is smooth-textured like deep-pile velvet, imbued with flowery fragrances. They are sweet but with an irresistibly tart edge.

Organic plumcots (sometimes labeled by the trademarked name pluot) are delectable apricot-plum hybrids. Although the ratios can vary, they are generally a 75 percent plum and 25 percent apricot cross.

Organic plum and plumcot farmers plant clover around the trees to attract beneficial insects. The organic fruit is often smaller than that grown conventionally, but is sweeter, usually with 4 to 5 percent higher Brix readings (see page 323). The yield is about 25 percent less than in conventional orchards.

The most commonly grown organic plum varieties are Casselman, Santa Rosa, and Grand Rosa. The most commonly grown organic plumcots include Dapple Dandy and Flavorosa.

BUYING AND STORING: Look for plump fruit that is relatively firm yet gives slightly to gentle pressure. If fruit is too soft, it can be mushy. Avoid those with shriveling or soft spots. Ripen using brown bag ripening technique (see page 323). Store ripe, unwashed fruit up to 3 days in cool location or refrigerate loose in crisper drawer up to 7 days.

PREP AND USE: Wash thoroughly with cold running water. Most are semi-freestone, meaning they can be cut in half from top to bottom, following suture (lengthwise seam). Twist halves in opposite directions and fruit will break in half. Pits cling more stubbornly in some varieties. If needed, release by prying pit with a teaspoon or small end of melon baller. Eat raw out of hand, or pit, slice, or dice, then use in fruit salad, green salad, salsa, fruit-based cold soup, or chicken salad. Or cook in poultry dishes or baked goods such as pies, tarts, cakes, or custards. Or use for jam, preserves, or as garnish.

AVAILABLE:

Plums: May to October

Plumcots: May to August

NUTRITIONAL INFORMATION (per 1 cup sliced, raw plums): Calories 76, fat calories 4; total fat 0 grams, sat fat 0 grams, cholesterol 0 milligrams; sodium 0 milligrams; total carbohydrates 19 grams, fiber 2 grams, sugars 16 grams; protein 1 gram; vitamin A IUs 11%; vitamin C 26%; calcium 1%; iron 2%.

SERVING SUGGESTIONS

Plum and Melon Compote

Combine 6 to 8 cups melon balls (watermelon, honeydew, and/or cantaloupe), and 4 plums or plumcots (pitted, cut in wedges) in large bowl. In small bowl, combine 2 tablespoons fresh lime juice, 1 tablespoon sugar, and a pinch of salt; stir until sugar dissolves. Pour over fruit; toss gently. Cover and refrigerate 6 to 8 hours. Add 1 teaspoon minced fresh mint. Toss and serve.

Plum Coulis, a Pureed Sauce

This topper is delicious over ice cream, angel food cake, or pudding. Cut 3 large pitted ripe plumcots or plums into small wedges. Place in blender with 2½ tablespoons water; whirl to puree. Strain into small bowl through medium sieve, pressing down on remnants in sieve with rubber spatula to extract as much as possible. Add 1½ tablespoons agave syrup or honey; stir to combine. Cover and chill.

Thyme-Scented Plum Side Dish

Preheat oven to 425°F. Cut 5 medium pitted plums or plumcots into ¾-inch wedges. In large ovenproof skillet combine plums or plumcots with 5 sprigs of fresh thyme, 3 tablespoons balsamic vinegar, ¾ teaspoon minced orange zest (colored portion of peel), and 1 tablespoon honey. Season to taste with coarse salt, such as kosher, and freshly ground black pepper; toss. Place on medium-high heat and bring to simmer. Place in oven and roast 8 to 10 minutes, or until plums are softened and beginning to fall apart. Allow to cool to room temperature. Remove thyme sprigs. Taste; adjust seasoning as needed and serve with pork, game, lamb, or Sautéed Breaded Tofu (page 320).

Plum-Tangy Salsa

This plum-based salsa is great spooned over grilled chicken or roast duck. To make it, combine 3 cups diced plums or plumcots, ¼ cup minced red onion, 1 tablespoon fresh lime juice, 1 tablespoon vegetable oil or canola oil, 1 teaspoon sugar, and 1 teaspoon minced seeded jalapeño chile. Stir; add ¼ cup chopped fresh mint or cilantro. Add salt and freshly ground black pepper to taste.

Couscous with Plumcots and Mint

YIELD: 13 CUPS

This salad is delicious on its own or as a side dish with grilled lamb or pork. The recipe yields about 10 to 12 servings, so it is an inviting party dish. If you like, substitute fresh apricots or plums for the plumcots.

Couscous

4½ cups water

¼ cup extra-virgin olive oil

1 teaspoon ground cumin

2 teaspoons salt

2 (10-ounce) packages couscous

½ cup dried currants or raisins

½ cup chopped dried apricots

Dressing

4 shallots, minced

½ cup rice vinegar

⅓ cup honey

½ cup extra-virgin olive oil

3 tablespoons chopped fresh mint

Garlic salt

1 bunch green onions, trimmed and thinly sliced, including ½ dark green stalks

Juice of 1 to 2 lemons

Freshly ground white pepper

1 cup shelled pistachios, coarsely chopped

4 plumcots or red-fleshed plums, pitted, cut into ½-inch dice

Garnish: chopped fresh mint and sprigs of fresh mint

1 Prepare couscous: In large saucepan, combine water, oil, cumin, and salt; bring to boil on high heat. Remove from heat and stir in couscous. Cover and let stand 5 minutes. Add raisins and apricots. Fluff with fork.

2 Prepare dressing: Combine shallots, vinegar, honey, and oil; stir vigorously to blend. Stir in mint and garlic salt to taste. Toss dressing with couscous. Add green onions and toss. Taste and adjust seasoning, adding lemon juice and pepper, and additional salt as needed. (Amount of lemon juice will vary depending on tartness of plumcots or plums.)

3 Add nuts and plumcots; toss. Garnish servings with chopped fresh mint, and if desired, a nice sprig of mint.

Nutritional information (per 1 cup): Calories 410, fat calories 160; total fat 18 grams, sat fat 2.5 grams, cholesterol 0 milligrams; sodium 410 milligrams; total carbohydrates 58 grams, fiber 8 grams, sugars 17 grams; protein 9 grams; vitamin A IUs 8%; vitamin C 10%; calcium 4%; iron 15%.

Easy Way Chocolate Spice Cake with Plums in Rum Syrup

YIELD: 12 SERVINGS

Cinnamon, allspice, and nutmeg are delectable spices to pair with plums. In this recipe, those lovely ground spices are used to accent a simple made-from-a-mix chocolate cake. Once baked and cooled, slices of the aromatic cake are topped with wedges of fresh plums that are soaked with rum syrup.

6 ripe plums or plumcots, pitted, cut into ⅜-inch wedges

2 tablespoons dark rum, divided use

1 tablespoon honey or agave syrup

Cake

    Nonstick vegetable oil cooking spray for greasing pan

    1 (17.1-ounce) organic chocolate cake mix (see Cook's Note)

    1⅓ cups heavy whipping cream

    1 teaspoon fresh lemon juice

    ⅓ cup vegetable oil or canola oil

    3 eggs, lightly beaten

    4 ounces semisweet chocolate, chopped, melted, but not hot

    1½ teaspoons ground cinnamon

    ½ teaspoon ground nutmeg

    ⅛ teaspoon ground allspice

Topping

    1 cup heavy whipping cream

    1 tablespoon powdered sugar

1 Combine plums, 1 tablespoon rum, and honey or agave syrup in ceramic or glass bowl. Toss. Cover and chill.

2 Adjust oven rack to middle position. Preheat oven to 350°F. Grease a 10-inch round cake pan (at least 2 inches deep) with nonstick spray. Line bottom of pan with parchment paper. Set aside.

3 In large bowl of electric mixer, combine cake mix, cream, lemon juice, oil, eggs, melted chocolate, and spices. Mix on low speed for 1 minute. Scrape down sides with rubber spatula. Increase speed to medium and beat 2 minutes. Pour batter into prepared pan. Bake until toothpick inserted in center comes out clean, about 35 to 45 minutes.

4 Cool 10 minutes on wire rack. Run knife around edge of cake and invert onto wire rack. Remove parchment. Cool.

5 In large bowl of electric mixer, beat cream and powdered sugar until stiff. Cut cake into 12 wedges and place on individual dessert plates. Top each serving with whipped cream, using a total of about half of whipped cream. Toss plum mixture, spoon on top, and pass remaining whipped cream for optional topping.

Nutritional information (per serving): Calories 500, fat calories 310; total fat 34 grams, sat fat 15 grams, cholesterol 115 milligrams; sodium 390 milligrams; total carbohydrates 47 grams, fiber 2 grams, sugars 28 grams; protein 6 grams; vitamin A IUs 15%; vitamin C 6%; calcium 10%; iron 15%.

Cook's Note: Recipe was developed using Dr. Oetker Organics Chocolate Cake Mix.

Leftover Pork, Wild Rice, and Plum Salad

YIELD: 6 SERVINGS

This is the kind of salad that makes great use of leftovers. Roast turkey, lamb, chicken, duck, ham, or sautéed tofu can easily be substituted for the pork. If you have 3 to 4 cups of cooked leftover brown or white rice, barley, wheat berries, or orzo, use it instead of wild rice, omitting Step 1.

    1½ cups uncooked wild rice

    3¾ cups vegetable broth or chicken broth

    Pinch of salt

    2 large ripe plumcots or plums, unpeeled, pitted, diced

    2 tablespoons vegetable oil or canola oil

    1½ tablespoons red wine vinegar

    2 teaspoons honey or agave syrup

    1 teaspoon minced orange zest (colored portion of peel)

    1 tablespoon fresh orange juice

    Salt and freshly ground black pepper

½ cup slivered almonds

3 cups diced roast pork (see Meatless Tip)

3 green onions, cut into ⅛-inch-wide diagonal slices (use ½ dark green stalks)

⅓ cup finely diced dried mango or raisins

¼ cup chopped fresh Italian parsley

1   In large saucepan, combine rice, vegetable broth or chicken broth and generous pinch of salt. Bring to boil on medium-high heat; cover and reduce to simmer on low heat. Cook 45 to 55 minutes (cooking time varies) or until liquid is absorbed and most grains have started to crack open to reveal white interior. Drain if necessary and set aside to cool.

2   In blender, puree plums, vegetable oil or canola oil, vinegar, honey or agave syrup, zest, and juice. You may need to stop the machine from time to time and redistribute contents. Season to taste with salt and pepper.

3   In large bowl, place cooled rice, almonds, pork, green onions, mango or raisins, and parsley. Toss. Add dressing and toss. Taste and adjust seasoning as needed. Serve at room temperature, or cover and refrigerate up to 1 hour.

Nutritional information (per serving): Calories 460, fat calories 170; total fat 19 grams, sat fat 4 grams, cholesterol 55 milligrams; sodium 370 milligrams; total carbohydrates 51 grams, fiber 6 grams, sugars 8 grams; protein 25 grams; vitamin A IUs 20%; vitamin C 15%; calcium 6%; iron 15%.

Meatless tip: Omit pork. Spoon salad over Quick Stir-Fried Tofu (page 322).

Cook's Note: To toast almonds, place on rimmed baking sheet in single layer. Toast in middle of 350°F oven for about 4 minutes, or until lightly toasted. Watch carefully because they burn easily. Cool.

Warm Plum-Plumcot Bleeding Heart "Pies"

YIELD: 8

These baked plums and plumcots are vibrantly flavored and delectably juicy. This simple presentation showcases small "pies" baked without bottom crusts. The fruit and heart-shaped top crusts bake separately. Once the filling is baked, each one is topped with a sugared crust and allowed to sit about twenty minutes before serving accompanied with sweetened whipped cream. To save time, prepared refrigerated crust can be substituted for the from-scratch dough.

Crust

1⅓ cups all-purpose flour, plus flour for dusting work surface

½ teaspoon salt

1 teaspoon sugar

½ cup (1 stick) cold unsalted butter, cut into 8 pieces

¼ cup ice water

Filling

¾ cup sugar plus 1 tablespoon, divided use

2 tablespoons instant tapioca

1 tablespoon cornstarch

½ teaspoon ground cinnamon

¼ teaspoon ground ginger

3 pounds plums or plumcots, pitted, cut in ⅜-inch wedges

Egg wash: 1 tablespoon cream or 1 egg yolk beaten with 1 teaspoon water

For serving: cold sweetened whipped cream

Warm Plum-Plumcot Bleeding Heart "Pies"

1 Adjust oven rack to middle position. Preheat oven to 375°F.

2 Prepare crust: In food processor fitted with metal blade, pulse flour, salt, and sugar 2 or 3 times. Add butter and pulse until mixture resembles coarse meal. With motor running, add ice water through feed tube, processing until mixture just barely comes together. Pat into disk shape; place in plastic bag and refrigerate for 1 hour.

3 Prepare filling: Whisk to combine ¾ cup sugar, tapioca, cornstarch, cinnamon, and ginger in large bowl. Add plums or plumcots; toss. Arrange 8 (6- or 8-ounce) soufflé cups or ramekins on rimmed baking sheet. Divide plum mixture between cups, filling each even with top (wipe rims clean).

4 Lightly flour clean, dry work surface, as well as a rolling pin. Place dough in center and roll to ¼-inch thickness. Use small sharp knife to cut out 8 hearts large enough to sit atop filling without touching sides of soufflé cup or ramekin (or if preferred use a heart-shaped cookie cutter). Place hearts in single layer on parchment paper–lined baking sheet; dip pastry brush in wash (either cream or egg mixture) and brush lightly on tops of hearts. Bake until cooked through and nicely browned, about 15 minutes. Remove from oven and sprinkle with 1 tablespoon sugar; set aside. Increase oven temperature to 450°F.

5 Place plum-filled cups on rimmed baking sheet. Bake 25 minutes in 450°F oven, or until plums are soft. Remove from oven. If tops look dry, carefully stir hot mixture to bring some juicy portion to top. Place a baked crust heart on top of each; press down gently to surround edges of heart with juice. Allow to cool at least 20 minutes. Serve warm with whipped cream.

Nutritional information (per serving without whipped cream): Calories 350, fat calories 110; total fat 12 grams, sat fat 7 grams, cholesterol 30 milligrams; sodium 150 milligrams; total carbohydrates 59 grams, fiber 3 grams, sugars 38 grams; protein 3 grams; vitamin A IUs 20%; vitamin C 25%; calcium 2%; iron 8%.

Pomegranate

Inside the leathery shell, clusters of pomegranate seeds shine like ruby prisms. Their visual appeal is matched by their seductive flavor, a perky sweet-tart blend edged with subtle notes of tannin.

Conventionally grown pomegranates are sprayed with fungicides and pesticides to treat the crown of the fruit, an area that can be prone to mold or insect invasion. With organic pomegranates those frilly calyx caps aren't sprayed, so growers are vigilant in their effort to protect the fruit.

Botanically speaking, pomegranate seeds are arils, edible juice sacs that contain a tiny seed. Most refer to them simply as "seeds." But whether you call them seeds or arils, if you know the underwater trick for removing those jewels, it's a mess-free way to enjoy them (see Prep and Use).

BUYING AND STORING: Fruit should be heavy for its size without soft spots or bruises. Generally skin color is not an indication of ripeness. Foothill variety, an early season variety that is less sweet, has skin that is pink to red. Wonderful variety has deep red skin and is sweeter. Store at room temperature up to 7 days, or refrigerate up to 2 weeks. Seeds can be refrigerated airtight up to 5 days or frozen up to 3 months.

PREP AND USE: The underwater technique is the easy, no-mess way to remove seeds. Place paper towel on work surface. Cut pomegranate into quarters over a paper towel. Fill a medium bowl with cold water. Hold a pomegranate quarter under the water, seed-side down. Pull edges back, exposing seeds. Run fingers over seeds to remove them. Turn over, still holding under water, and pick out remaining seeds. Seeds will sink to the bottom of the bowl and small membrane pieces will float to the top. Discard membranes (they're bitter) and drain seeds. Pat seeds dry with a paper towel. If you need a small amount of pomegranate juice, place pomegranate seeds in food processor fitted with metal blade or blender. Press though fine sieve (1 cup seeds will yield about ⅓ cup juice).

Eat seeds raw. Use for garnish on salads, vegetables, meat or desserts.

AVAILABLE: August to mid-December

NUTRITIONAL INFORMATION (per 1 large pomegranate, raw): Calories 105, fat calories 4; total fat 1 gram, sat fat 0 grams, cholesterol 0 milligrams; sodium 5 milligrams; total carbohydrates 26 grams, fiber 1 gram, sugars 26 grams; protein 2 grams; vitamin A IUs 3%; vitamin C 16%; calcium 0%; iron 3%.

SERVING SUGGESTIONS

Chocolate Ruby Slippers

Chocolate and pomegranate seeds make delectable partners; the chocolate is smooth and the seeds are both crunchy and juicy. To make this simple "candy," melt 1 cup of semisweet chocolate chips over simmering water in a double boiler. Stir frequently; the idea is to melt the chocolate without getting it hot (it will melt when it is just warm). Remove top part of double boiler and set on countertop. Stir in ½ cup pomegranate seeds. Using two teaspoons (one to scoop and the other to push mixture off), place 14 small mounds on baking sheet lined with wax paper. Chill. Serve within 24 hours for best flavor and texture.

PBP Sandwich

Omit the jelly on a peanut butter sandwich. Instead, top peanut butter with a layer of pomegranate seeds.

Pomegranate Vinaigrette with Mint

Make a mixed green salad topped with this easy dressing to accompany pork, chicken, lamb, or game. In small bowl or glass measuring cup, combine ½ cup extra-virgin olive oil, 3 tablespoons balsamic vinegar, 1 teaspoon cider vinegar, and ½ teaspoon salt. Stir to combine. Add ⅓ cup pomegranate seeds and 1 tablespoon minced fresh mint or 1 teaspoon dried mint; stir to combine. Use just enough dressing to lightly coat leaves.

Hummus Crown

Sprinkle a generous amount of pomegranate seeds on homemade or store-bought hummus. Serve with crackers, thinly sliced French bread, or toasted pita bread.

Rice Medley with Pomegranate

YIELD: 10 SERVINGS

The pomegranate topping on this tasty rice casserole makes it pretty enough for a buffet table. You can change the dried fruit to suit your taste; omit the dried cherries and add a handful of raisins or dried cranberries. Or augment the recipe by adding a ½ cup of chopped dried apricots. Use as a side dish with turkey, pork, or game. Chilled leftovers can be tossed with simple vinaigrette to make a colorful rice salad served on a bed of mixed baby greens (see page 325).

½ cup (1 stick) unsalted butter, divided use

1 large onion, chopped

1 medium clove garlic, minced

5 cups chicken broth or vegetable broth

3 tablespoons chopped fresh thyme leaves or 1 tablespoon dried thyme

1 teaspoon finely minced fresh or dried rosemary leaves

1¼ cups wild rice

1½ cups long-grain white rice, basmati preferred

1 cup dried cherries

1 cup toasted coarsely chopped pecans (see Cook's Note)

Salt and freshly ground black pepper

2 tablespoons minced fresh Italian parsley

1 pomegranate, seeded, about 1 cup seeds

1 Grease a 9 × 13-inch baking dish with 1 tablespoon butter.

2 In medium, deep skillet, melt remaining butter on medium-high heat. Add onion and garlic; cook, stirring occasionally, until softened, about 5 minutes. Set aside.

3 Place chicken broth or vegetable broth, thyme, and rosemary in large saucepan or Dutch oven on high heat. Add wild rice and bring to boil; reduce heat to medium-low, cover, and simmer 35 minutes. Add white rice, cover, and simmer until both rices are tender (some wild rice kernels will probably have burst) and most of liquid is absorbed, about about 15 minutes. Adjust oven rack to middle position. Preheat oven to 350°F.

4 Add cherries, pecans, and onion mixture to rices. Gently toss. Add salt and pepper to taste. Place in prepared baking dish and cover with aluminum foil. Bake 20 minutes.

5 Remove foil. Sprinkle parsley on rice. Top with pomegranate seeds.

Nutritional information (per serving): Calories 390, fat calories 160; total fat 18 grams, sat fat 7 grams, cholesterol 25 milligrams; sodium 230 milligrams; total carbohydrates 53 grams, fiber 4 grams, sugars 10 grams; protein 7 grams; vitamin A IUs 15%; vitamin C 4%; calcium 4%; iron 8%.

Cook's Note: To toast chopped pecans, place on rimmed baking sheet in single layer. Toast in middle of 350°F oven about 3 minutes, or until lightly toasted. Watch carefully because nuts burn easily.

Jeweled Chicken Salad

YIELD: 4 SERVINGS

This veggie-packed salad can be served over mixed baby greens or baby spinach. It is also delicious stuffed into hollowed-out heirloom tomatoes, or scooped over avocado slices. For a shortcut, use frozen peas and corn kernels, thawed and drained.

2 cups shredded cooked chicken (see Meatless Tip)

1 medium tomato, seeded, diced

½ red bell pepper, cored, seeded, finely diced

½ cup cooked corn kernels, drained, cooled

½ cup cooked peas, drained, cooled

Seeds from 1 pomegranate, about 1 cup

¼ red onion, minced

¾ cup mayonnaise

3 tablespoons fresh lemon juice

1 teaspoon Dijon-style mustard

½ teaspoon salt

1 teaspoon freshly ground black pepper

For serving: 3 cups baby spinach or mixed baby greens or 4 hollowed-out heirloom tomatoes or 2 medium avocados, pitted, peeled, sliced

1 In medium bowl, combine chicken, tomato, bell pepper, corn, peas, pomegranate seeds (reserving 1 tablespoon for garnish), and onion.

2   In small bowl, whisk mayonnaise, juice, mustard, salt, and black pepper. Pour over chicken mixture and gently toss to combine. Spoon over fresh spinach or your favorite leafy greens and serve. Or use to fill hollow heirloom tomatoes. Or arrange avocado slices in single layer on plates (like spokes of fan) and top with scoop of salad.

3   Garnish with reserved pomegranate seeds and serve.

Nutritional information (per serving with greens): Calories 340, fat calories 160; total fat 18 grams, sat fat 3 grams, cholesterol 65 milligrams; sodium 680 milligrams; total carbohydrates 25 grams, fiber 2 grams, sugars 9 grams; protein 21 grams; vitamin A IUs 25%; vitamin C 70%; calcium 4%; iron 8%.

Meatless Tip: Instead of chicken, use cubed soy chicken.

Quinoa Confetti

YIELD: 4 SERVINGS

Colorful and delicious, this quinoa-based dish can be a side dish or the main course. The tiny, bead-shaped quinoa is a high-protein grain and expands to four times its size when cooked. If you want to add meat to the menu, make a bed of the confetti on the plate and top with a grilled chop, baked chicken breast, or slices of cooked spicy sausage.

1¼ cups uncooked quinoa

2¾ cups water

3 tablespoons extra-virgin olive oil, divided use

1 small zucchini, diced

1 small yellow crookneck squash, diced

1 small carrot, peeled, diced

1 red bell pepper, cored, seeded, diced

1 medium sweet onion, minced

2 large cloves garlic, minced

1 teaspoon salt

1 teaspoon freshly ground black pepper

Seeds of 2 pomegranates, about 1 cup

1   Adjust oven rack to middle position. Preheat oven to 350°F. Place quinoa in large saucepan with water. Bring to boil on high heat; reduce heat to medium and cook 11 to 15 minutes, or until quinoa is tender but with a little chewy crunch and most of liquid is absorbed.

2   Heat 1 tablespoon oil in large, deep ovenproof skillet on medium-high heat. Add zucchini, crookneck squash, carrot, and bell pepper. Cook, stirring frequently, until softened, about 5 minutes. Set aside.

3   In a large saucepan, heat remaining 2 tablespoons oil over medium heat. Add onion, garlic, salt, and black pepper. Cook until onion starts to brown, stirring occasionally.

4   Add onion mixture and drained quinoa to squash mixture; gently toss. Bake for about 10 minutes or until heated through. Remove from oven and gently fold in pomegranate seeds. Serve hot or at room temperature.

Nutritional information (per serving): Calories 370, fat calories 120; total fat 13 grams, sat fat 1.5 grams, cholesterol 0 milligrams; sodium 610 milligrams; total carbohydrates 57 grams, fiber 5 grams, sugars 9 grams; protein 9 grams; vitamin A IUs 20%; vitamin C 110%; calcium 6%; iron 30%.

Pomegranate and Apple Cake

YIELD: 8 SERVINGS

Apples and pomegranates combine to make this lovely cake a symbol of autumn. The buttery cake is topped with overlapping apple slices before baking. Out of the oven, it's brushed with a pomegranate-jelly glaze. Before serving, a blanket of pomegranate seeds is added to the top of the cake.

Unsalted butter or margarine for greasing pan

½ cup (1 stick) unsalted butter, softened

¾ cup sugar plus 2 to 3 tablespoons sugar, divided use

Pomegranate and Apple Cake

1 teaspoon finely minced lemon zest or orange zest
(colored portion of peel)

2 large eggs

1 cup plus 2 tablespoons all-purpose flour

1 teaspoon baking powder

1 teaspoon salt

4 tablespoons milk

3 Granny Smith apples

2 tablespoons unsalted butter, melted

¼ cup currant jelly or strawberry jelly

2 tablespoons pomegranate juice

Seeds of 1 pomegranate, about 1 cup

Optional garnish: sprigs of fresh mint

For serving: vanilla ice cream or whipped cream

1   Adjust oven rack to middle position. Preheat oven to 400°F. Generously grease a 9-inch springform pan with butter. Set aside.

2   In food processor fitted with metal blade or in large bowl of an electric mixer, combine softened butter, ¾ cup sugar, and lemon zest or orange zest; process until blended. Add eggs 1 at a time, beating between additions.

3   In separate bowl, mix flour, baking powder, and salt. Add to butter mixture and beat until blended, stopping to scrape down sides with rubber spatula if needed. Add milk and beat until smooth. Spoon batter into prepared pan and smooth out top.

4   Peel, core, and thinly slice apples and arrange slices atop batter in pan, overlapping slices in concentric circles, starting at outside edge. Brush top with melted butter. Sprinkle 2 tablespoons sugar on top. If you prefer a sweeter dessert, you can add 1 additional tablespoon of sugar.

5   Place springform pan on rimmed baking sheet. Bake for 15 minutes. Reduce heat to 375°F and bake an additional 30 minutes or until a toothpick inserted in center comes out clean and apples are golden. Place on wire rack to cool 10 minutes.

6   Carefully remove rim from springform pan, running a sharp knife around the edge if necessary.

7   In small saucepan, combine currant jelly or strawberry jelly and pomegranate juice. Place on high heat and stir until melted. Remove from heat and brush on top and sides of warm cake. Cool cake.

8   Sprinkle pomegranate seeds on top of cake. Garnish with fresh mint, if desired. Serve warm or at room temperature accompanied by ice cream or whipped cream.

Nutritional information (per serving): Calories 330, fat calories 130; total fat 15 grams, sat fat 9 grams, cholesterol 40 milligrams; sodium 380 milligrams; total carbohydrates 1 gram, fiber 1 gram, sugars 31 grams; protein 3 grams; vitamin A IUs 8%; vitamin C 8%; calcium 6%; iron 6%.

Year-Round

Best Buy

Potato

 Baby, Creamer (Red, Purple, White, Yellow)

Fingerling (French, Russian Banana, Ruby Crescent, Purple Peruvian)

 Red

 Russet

Yukon Gold

Whether their texture is fluffy or waxy, whether petite or grand, potatoes may well be the ultimate comfort food. Heirloom fingerling varieties are often shaped like elongated, knobby digits and have flavors that range from chestnut to butter to slightly sweet. Baby or creamer potatoes can have red, purple, white, or yellow skin. Most have a waxy texture and slightly sweet flavor profile. Red potatoes have a waxy texture and buttery flavor. Russets have thick brown skin, flaky-fluffy texture and earthy aroma. Yukon Golds have yellow or tan skin and golden yellow flesh. They have an earthy-sweet flavor profile and a moderately flaky texture, a consistency that is somewhere between the russet and the red potato.

Russet

Purple Creamer (baby)

Russian Banana Fingerling

French Finger

Yukon Gold

Purple Peruvian Fingerling

Ruby Crescent Fingerling

Red Creamer (baby)

Organic potato growers use alfalfa and wheat as cover crops to maintain soil fertility. Weather with warm days and cool nights is ideal. Allowing the leaves and stems of the potato plants to dry naturally is key to producing potatoes with longer storage potential.

Organic potato yields are about 25 percent less those grown with conventional methods.

BUYING AND STORING: Look for wrinkle-free potatoes, without green tinges, sprouts, or cracks. Store in dark, airy, cool location. Place in open paper sack or basket, not a sealed plastic bag. Do not store in container with onions. Do not refrigerate for a long period of time because starch in potato will gradually convert to sugar, causing a disagreeable taste, especially in russets or Yukon Golds. Red potatoes and red creamers can be stored in refrigerator.

PREP AND USE: Wash thoroughly with cold water and dry. Solanine, green patches on skin or flesh, is a natural toxin that occurs when potatoes are exposed to bright light. Remove all green areas before cooking. Russets and Yukon Golds are generally peeled, except when baked. Use swivel-bladed vegetable peeler or paring knife. Most often other varieties are cooked skin on.

Use waxier potatoes when you want potato to retain shape when cooked. Use flakier potatoes when starchy taste is desired. For example, add waxy red potatoes to soup and they hold their shape. Add flakier potatoes such as russets to soup and they will fall apart and starch will thicken broth. Essentially, all potatoes can be baked, broiled, roasted, grilled, simmered, steamed, sautéed, or boiled.

AVAILABLE:

Baby (Creamer): September to May

Fingerling: September to March

Red, Russet, Yukon Gold: Year-round

NUTRITIONAL INFORMATION (per 148 grams fingerling potato, raw with skin): Calories 100, fat calories 0; total fat 0 grams, sat fat 0 grams, cholesterol 0 milligrams; sodium 0 milligrams; total carbohydrates 26 grams, fiber 3 grams, sugars 3 grams; protein 4 grams; vitamin A IUs 0%; vitamin C 45%; calcium 2%; iron 6%.

NUTRITIONAL INFORMATION (per 369 grams purple potato, raw with skin): Calories 131, fat calories 1; total fat 0 grams, sat fat 0 grams, cholesterol 0 milligrams; sodium 10 milligrams; total carbohydrates 30 grams, fiber 4 grams, sugars 1 gram; protein 3 grams; vitamin A IUs 0%; vitamin C 55%; calcium 2%; iron 7%.

NUTRITIONAL INFORMATION (per 369 grams red potato, raw with skin): Calories 258, fat calories 4; total fat 1 gram, sat fat 0 grams, cholesterol 0 milligrams; sodium 22 milligrams; total carbohydrates 59 grams, fiber 6 grams, sugars 4 grams; protein 7 grams; vitamin A IUs 1%; vitamin C 53%; calcium 4%; iron 15%.

NUTRITIONAL INFORMATION (per 170 grams russet potato, raw with skin): Calories 134, fat calories 1; total fat 0 grams, sat fat 0 grams, cholesterol 0 milligrams; sodium 9 milligrams; total carbohydrates 31 grams, fiber 2 grams, sugars 1 gram; protein 4 grams; vitamin A IUs 0%; vitamin C 16%; calcium 2%; iron 8%.

NUTRITIONAL INFORMATION (per 110 grams Yukon Gold potato, raw with skin): Calories 80, fat calories 0; total fat 0 grams, sat fat 0 grams, cholesterol 0 milligrams; sodium 35 milligrams; total carbohydrates 20 grams, fiber 2 grams, sugars 1 gram; protein 2 grams; vitamin A IUs 0%; vitamin C 6%; calcium 8%; iron 6%.

SERVING SUGGESTIONS

Chile Spuds

Line rimmed baking sheet with aluminum foil; preheat oven to 450°F. Wash and dry 3 medium russet potatoes; cut into 3-inch lengthwise skin-on wedges. Place in bowl and toss with 3 tablespoons extra-virgin olive oil. In small bowl, combine 1 teaspoon coarse salt, such as kosher, and 1 teaspoon chili powder; add to potatoes and toss. Place in single layer on prepared baking sheet. Bake 25 to 30 minutes or until potatoes are fork-tender and nicely browned. Sprinkle with 1 tablespoon minced fresh Italian parsley.

Potatoes Tapas-Style

Preheat oven to 475°F. Cut 2 pounds peeled Yukon Gold potatoes into ¼-inch slices; toss with 2 tablespoons extra-virgin olive oil, 2 large cloves garlic (thinly sliced), 2 teaspoons salt, and freshly ground black pepper. Place in 9 × 13-inch baking pan and cover with aluminum foil. Bake until tender, about 25 minutes. Remove foil, drizzle with 2 teaspoons extra-virgin olive oil; roast until lightly browned, about 10 minutes. Sprinkle with a little paprika, a smidgen of dried red chile flakes, 1 tablespoon minced fresh Italian parsley, and 2 thinly sliced green onions, including dark green stalks; toss. As an appetizer, serve in small bowls.

Fingerling Vino Braise Glaze

Preheat oven to 350°F. Cut 1½ pounds fingerling potatoes in half lengthwise if large, leave whole if small. In shallow roasting pan, toss spuds with 1 teaspoon coarse salt, such as kosher, 3 tablespoons dry white wine, and 4 tablespoons extra-virgin olive oil. Add 1 tablespoon fresh thyme leaves; toss. Potatoes should be crowded. Cover and bake in middle of oven 30 to 35 minutes or until very tender.

Fingerling Fondue Dippers

In addition to chunks of rustic bread and steamed broccoli florets, whole fingerlings make tempting scoops for cheese fondue. Boil them unpeeled until fork-tender and toss with a smidgen of olive oil, just enough oil so that they look irresistible. Provide fondue forks or bamboo skewers to aid dipping, and accompany fondue and dippers with bowls of pickled onions and olives tossed with orange zest (colored portion of peel) and ground fennel.

Yukon Gold O'Brien

YIELD: 6 SERVINGS

Yukon Gold potatoes have the perfect texture for this classic dish. They crisp to a golden brown without falling apart. Turn the side dish into a one-dish meal by topping each serving with a fried or poached egg.

- 4 slices thick-cut bacon (see Meatless Tip)
- 1 pound Yukon Gold potatoes, scrubbed, cut into ¼-inch dice
- ⅓ cup cored, seeded, diced green bell pepper
- ⅓ cup cored, seeded, diced red bell pepper
- ⅓ cup cored, seeded, diced yellow bell pepper
- 1 medium sweet onion, diced
- 2 medium cloves garlic, minced
- ⅛ teaspoon salt
- Freshly ground black pepper
- Optional garnish: minced fresh Italian parsley

1 Cook bacon in large, deep skillet until crisp; remove bacon from pan and drain on paper towels, reserving about 3 tablespoons bacon grease in pan (see Cook's Note).

2 Heat grease on medium-high heat. Add potatoes, bell peppers, onion, and garlic; reduce heat to medium. Cook, stirring occasionally, until potatoes are tender and nicely browned. Season with salt and black pepper.

3 Crumble bacon and add to potato mixture. Cook to heat bacon, about 1 minute. If desired, sprinkle with minced parsley.

Nutritional information (per serving): Calories 180, fat calories 100; total fat 12 grams, sat fat 4 grams, cholesterol 15 milligrams; sodium 260 milligrams; total carbohydrates 13 grams, fiber 2 grams, sugars 2 grams; protein 5 grams; vitamin A IUs 2%; vitamin C 60%; calcium 2%; iron 4%.

Cook's Note: If you prefer, use 1½ tablespoons bacon grease combined with 1½ tablespoons canola oil to sauté vegetables.

Meatless Tip: Omit bacon. Start with step 2, using 3 tablespoons canola oil instead of bacon grease; top dish with cooked and chopped vegetarian bacon.

Yukon Gold O'Brien

Warm Fingerling Potatoes, Cabbage, and Kielbasa with Mustard Dressing

YIELD: 8 SERVINGS

Potatoes braised with cabbage and sausage is a cold weather one-pot concoction that involves very little work. This recipes showcases fingerling potatoes, intriguing (and delicious) little potatoes that look something like endearing bloated fingers (varieties such as Ruby Crescent and Russian Banana). They have widths that are generally less than 1 inch and can be left whole. Other fingerling varieties are more blimp-shaped with waistlines that are greater than 1 inch; they should be cut in half lengthwise for this recipe.

- 2 tablespoons Dijon-style mustard
- ⅓ cup white wine vinegar
- 1 teaspoon salt
- 2 shallots, minced
- ¾ cup olive oil plus 1 tablespoon extra-virgin olive oil, divided use
- 1¼ pounds fingerling potatoes, cut in half if large
- 1 pound low-fat kielbasa, such as turkey kielbasa (see Meatless Tip)
- ½ large head of green cabbage, cut in half, cored, shredded
- 2 teaspoons caraway seeds
- 1 bunch green onions, thinly sliced, including ½ dark green stalks
- Salt and freshly ground black pepper
- Optional garnish: sprigs of fresh Italian parsley

1   In small bowl, combine mustard, vinegar, 1 teaspoon salt and shallots; stir to combine. Stirring constantly, add ¾ cup oil in a thin stream. Set aside.

2   Place potatoes in a large pot or Dutch oven and cover with water. Bring to boil on high heat. Reduce to simmer, cover, and simmer 10 minutes. Add kielbasa and cook until potatoes are just tender and sausage is heated through. Remove sausage and place on cutting surface. Drain potatoes and place in large bowl. Pour ½ cup of dressing on potatoes and gently toss.

3   Heat remaining 1 tablespoon oil on medium-high heat (use the same large pot or Dutch oven, wiped dry). Add cabbage. Stir and cook on medium-high heat until wilted, adding a little water if needed to prevent sticking and browning, about 4 to 5 minutes. Remove from heat and toss with remaining dressing and caraway seeds. Taste and add salt and pepper if needed.

4   Cut sausage into ¼-inch slices. Add sausage and green onions to potatoes. Gently toss. Taste; add salt and pepper as needed. Arrange cabbage around the edge of platter. Place potato-sausage mixture in center. Garnish with parsley.

Nutritional information (per serving): Calories 360, fat calories 240; total fat 27 grams, sat fat 4.5 grams, cholesterol 35 milligrams; sodium 870 milligrams; total carbohydrates 19 grams, fiber 4 grams, sugars 5 grams; protein 12 grams; vitamin A IUs 4%; vitamin C 110%; calcium 6%; iron 10%.

Meatless Tip: Omit sausage or use soy kielbasa sausage.

Spicy Potato Salad with Grainy Mustard Vinaigrette

YIELD: 8 SERVINGS

This tart, spicy potato salad is spiked with both dried red chile flakes and minced fresh jalapeño. The grown-up palate will appreciate the punch the chiles gives to the spuds. Yukon Gold potatoes are a good variety to use in potato salads because they absorb the vinaigrette but keep their shape.

3 pounds Yukon Gold potatoes, peeled, cut into 1-inch cubes

1 tablespoon salt

2 tablespoons extra-virgin olive oil

¼ cup rice vinegar

3 tablespoons coarse-grain mustard

1 teaspoon dried red chile flakes

1 jalapeño chile, seeded, finely minced (see Cook's Note)

1 teaspoon coarse salt, such as kosher

1 teaspoon freshly ground black pepper

1   Place potatoes in pot or Dutch oven; add enough water to cover potatoes by 2 inches. Add 1 tablespoon salt and bring to boil on high heat. Reduce heat and simmer potatoes until just barely fork tender. Drain and place potatoes in bowl.

2   In small bowl, whisk oil and vinegar; add mustard, chile flakes, jalapeño chile, coarse salt, and pepper and whisk to combine. Pour mixture over hot potatoes, toss gently. Let stand for 1 hour.

3   Toss and taste. Adjust seasoning if necessary with more salt, pepper, or chile flakes.

Nutritional information (per serving): Calories 180, fat calories 35; total fat 4 grams, sat fat 0.5 grams, cholesterol 0 milligrams; sodium 430 milligrams; total carbohydrates 31 grams, fiber 3 grams, sugars 0 grams; protein 4 grams; vitamin A IUs 2%; vitamin C 60%; calcium 0%; iron 10%.

Cook's Note: Use caution when working with fresh chiles. Wash hands and work surface upon completion; do *not* touch eyes or face.

Salt-Baked Potatoes with Sour Cream and Caramelized Onion

YIELD: 8 HALF-POTATO SERVINGS

Rubbing russet potatoes with a little oil and baking them at high heat on a thin bed of salt gives the spuds an appealing crunchy exterior. A topping of browned onions permeated with fresh thyme and sour cream makes them irresistible. If you like, add a pinch of chopped Italian parsley for a colorful garnish.

1 ¼ cups coarse salt, such as kosher

3 tablespoons extra-virgin olive oil, divided use

4 medium-large russet potatoes, scrubbed, dried, poked in 3 or 4 places with tines of fork

1 large yellow onion, halved lengthwise, cut into ¼-inch crosswise slices

Freshly ground black pepper

1 ½ teaspoons chopped fresh thyme leaves

½ cup sour cream

1 Adjust oven rack to middle position. Preheat oven to 400°F.

2 Place salt in large ovenproof skillet, preferably cast iron. Place 2 tablespoons oil in medium bowl. Roll potatoes in oil and place in single layer on the salt in the skillet. Roast in for 60 to 70 minutes or until fork-tender.

3 Meanwhile, caramelize the onion. Pour leftover oil from bowl plus remaining 1 tablespoon into medium-size skillet. Heat oil on medium-high heat; add onion and cook, tossing occasionally, until starting to brown, about 4 to 5 minutes. Add thyme; lower heat to medium-low and cook, stirring occasionally, until nicely browned, about 10 minutes. Season with freshly ground black pepper and, if desired, a smidgen of salt.

4 Remove skillet from oven (remember that the handle of the skillet will be very hot). Remove potatoes from salt (dust off any excess salt) and cautiously cut in half lengthwise (hold in place on cutting board with potholder or doubled kitchen towel). Place cut-side up on platter and squeeze to break up the potatoes' interior a little. Top each with onions and sour cream.

Nutritional information (per half potato serving): Calories 180, fat calories 70; total fat 8 grams, sat fat 2.5 grams, cholesterol 5 milligrams; sodium 15 milligrams; total carbohydrates 23 grams, fiber 3 grams, sugars 2 grams; protein 3 grams; vitamin A IUs 2%; vitamin C 25%; calcium 4%; iron 6%.

Radish

A radish resembles a small turnip, the plump round or oblong form topped with edible, peppery green leaves and a spindly rattail root dangling at the bottom.

They are crunchy like turnips, but their flavor profile can be much sharper. Some can have a downright fiery bite, while others are mild. The common red radish, sometimes labeled red globe, is the one that is most commonly grown organically. It is most often fairly small with thin, bright red skin and a dense, crisp white interior.

Organic growers compost the soil weeks before radishes are planted. Radishes flourish in an environment with warm days and cool nights. So do weeds, and all weeding is done by hand. Beneficial insects are used to control predatory pests such as aphids and flea beetles.

BUYING AND STORING: Look for radishes that are no larger than 1 inch in diameter to avoid pithy centers. Avoid those with cracks or soft spots. If purchasing radishes with leaves, leaves should be green and crisp without yellowing. To store, trim off leaves, leaving about ½ inch of stem intact. Refrigerate radishes in plastic bag up to 14 days. For greens, rinse in tub of cold water; repeat if necessary, until water is clear and free of grit. Shake off excess water or drain, wrap in clean kitchen cloth or paper towels, and place in plastic bag. Refrigerate up to 3 days in the crisper drawer.

PREP AND USE: Wash radishes thoroughly in cold running water. Trim and discard roots. Trim stem ends or leave a small portion of stem to use as a "handle" when serving raw as finger food. Serve whole, or slice, chop, or grate. Generally served raw, but can be delicious when cooked, either braised, sautéed, or simmered. Clean radish greens (see Buying and Storing) can be tossed with other milder greens in a salad. Or they can be simmered, blanched, sautéed, or steamed.

AVAILABLE: Year-round

NUTRITIONAL INFORMATION (per 1 cup sliced, raw): Calories 19, fat calories 1; total fat 0 grams, sat fat 0 grams, cholesterol 0 milligrams; sodium 45 milligrams; total carbohydrates 4 grams, fiber 2 grams, sugars 2 grams; protein 1 gram; vitamin A IUs 0%; vitamin C 29%; calcium 3%; iron 2%.

SERVING SUGGESTIONS

Salad Topper

Trim and slice 3 large radishes. Place radishes in bowl with 1 peeled, sliced medium carrot, 1 thinly sliced stalk celery, and 6 chives cut in ½-inch pieces. Add 1 tablespoon rice vinegar plus salt and freshly ground black pepper to taste. Toss. Spoon a generous portion on 4 to 6 servings of dressed green salad.

Radish Raita

A great sauce to serve with spicy curries. To make it combine ⅓ cup plain unsweetened yogurt, 2½ tablespoons finely chopped radish, ½ teaspoon fresh lime juice, and 1 teaspoon finely chopped red onion. Add salt and freshly ground black pepper to taste. Stir to combine.

Dip with Zip

In food processor fitted with metal blade, place cloves squeezed from 1 medium head roasted garlic (see page 139) and 8 sliced radishes; pulse to finely chop. Add 12 ounces room-temperature cream cheese; pulse to combine. Place in serving dish; top with generous amount of chopped chives. Serve with crackers and radishes for dipping.

Shred in Slaw

Add spiciness to coleslaw by augmenting the cabbage with shredded radishes

Chunky Radish Salad

YIELD: 4 SERVINGS

Crunchy and filled with lively flavors, this salad is delectable served atop toasted rustic bread. Make sure the slices are no thinner than ½ inch and bake them until they are nicely browned with a crisp exterior. Taste the salad mixture before placing it on the bread. If you want a little extra tartness, add a smidgen of cider vinegar and some finely minced lemon zest to the salad.

4 thick slices rustic whole wheat sourdough bread

3 tablespoons extra-virgin olive oil, divided use

Garlic salt

¼ cup rice vinegar

¾ teaspoon salt

¼ teaspoon freshly ground black pepper

1 large common cucumber, peeled, seeded, or 1 medium (hothouse) English cucumber

10 radishes, trimmed

1 cup crumbled feta cheese

1 cup halved cherry tomatoes

½ cup fresh basil leaves, cut into thin strips

1 Adjust oven rack to middle position. Preheat oven to 350°F. Brush bread on both sides with 1 tablespoon oil and sprinkle top with a little garlic salt. Place in single layer on rimmed baking sheet. Bake until nicely toasted, about 6 to 10 minutes. Cool.

2 In small bowl, combine remaining 2 tablespoons oil, vinegar, salt, and pepper; whisk to combine.

3 Cut cucumber in lengthwise quarters; cut into ½-inch-long pieces. Place in medium bowl. Trim radishes and cut into quarters; add to bowl. Add remaining ingredients and toss. Taste; adjust seasoning as needed.

4 Place toasted bread on 4 salad plates. Top each toast with salad. Serve immediately.

Nutritional information (per serving): Calories 320, fat calories 180; total fat 20 grams, sat fat 7 grams, cholesterol 35 milligrams; sodium 1060 milligrams; total carbohydrates 25 grams, fiber 3 grams, sugars 6 grams; protein 11 grams; vitamin A IUs 15%; vitamin C 25%; calcium 25%; iron 10%.

Tex-Mex Green Salad

YIELD: 4 TO 6 SERVINGS

A well-seasoned buttermilk dressing augmented with a little fiery hot sauce gives this salad a pleasant kick. Before adding red onion, taste a small piece. If it has an unpleasant amount of mouth burn, place the onion slices in a bowl of ice water and allow them to soak for 10 to 15 minutes; drain and pat dry before using. If desired, add fresh corn kernels or diced red bell pepper.

4 corn tortillas

Dressing

½ cup buttermilk

½ cup mayonnaise

3 tablespoons finely chopped fresh Italian parsley

3 tablespoons finely chopped fresh cilantro

½ teaspoon onion powder

¾ teaspoon garlic salt

½ teaspoon freshly ground black pepper

½ teaspoon hot sauce

Salad

1 large head romaine, torn into bite-size pieces

1½ cups cherry tomatoes, halved

2 ripe avocados, pitted, peeled, cut into chunks

1 (15-ounce) can black beans, drained, rinsed

1 cup sliced radishes

1 small red onion, cut in half, sliced crosswise

1 To make toasted tortilla strips, preheat oven to 375°F. Cut corn tortillas into ¼-inch-wide strips. Place on rimmed baking sheet in single layer. Bake in middle of preheated oven and bake until crisp and lightly browned, about 10 to 11 minutes. Set aside to cool.

2 Prepare dressing: Whisk all ingredients together in medium bowl. Taste and adjust seasoning if needed.

3 Prepare salad: Combine salad ingredients in large bowl. Add enough dressing to lightly coat leaves. Divide salad between 4 plates. Top with cooled tortilla strips and serve.

Nutritional information (per serving): Calories 340, fat calories 160; total fat 18 grams, sat fat 2.5 grams, cholesterol 5 milligrams; sodium 300 milligrams; total carbohydrates 40 grams, fiber 13 grams, sugars 6 grams; protein 9 grams; vitamin A IUs 35%; vitamin C 45%; calcium 15%; iron 15%.

Tex-Mex Green Salad

Yogurt Cheese with Radish-Apple Relish

YIELD: ABOUT 2 CUPS CHEESE, OR ABOUT 32 (1-TABLESPOON) SERVINGS

Yogurt cheese, sometimes labeled *lebne* or *lebni* at Middle Eastern markets, is easy to make at home. Its bright, no-nonsense tartness pairs beautifully with this radish-apple relish. Provide a spoon for guests to use to scoop cheese and relish onto small wedges of pita bread.

- 4 cups plain whole-milk yogurt
- 6 radishes, trimmed, halved lengthwise, sliced crosswise
- ¼ cup finely chopped red onion
- 1 Fuji or Gala or Ambrosia apple, seeded, finely diced
- 1½ tablespoons minced fresh mint
- 1 tablespoon extra-virgin olive oil
- 1 teaspoon fresh lemon juice
- Salt and freshly ground black pepper
- ⅔ cup coarsely chopped walnuts, toasted (see Cook's Note)
- For serving: about 32 wedges of pita bread

1   Line strainer with 3 layers of cheesecloth (allow 4 inches to extend over sides of strainer); suspend strainer over a bowl so that bottom of strainer is 4 inches above bottom of bowl. Spoon yogurt into strainer; gather ends of cheesecloth together and fold over top of yogurt. Refrigerate at least 8 hours; liquid will drain out and yogurt will thicken.

2   In medium bowl, combine radishes, onion, apple, mint, oil, and juice. Season with salt and pepper to taste and toss to combine.

3   Unwrap top portion of yogurt cheese and invert in middle of large shallow bowl. Remove cheesecloth. Spoon radish mixture around the cheese. Sprinkle with walnuts. Surround with wedges of pita bread and a spoon for scooping.

Nutritional information (per serving): Calories 40, fat calories 25; total fat 3 grams, sat fat 1 gram, cholesterol 5 milligrams; sodium 15 milligrams; total carbohydrates 3 grams, fiber 0 grams, sugars 2 grams; protein 2 grams; vitamin A IUs 0%; vitamin C 2%; calcium 4%; iron 0%.

Cook's Note: To toast walnuts, place on rimmed baking sheet in single layer. Toast in middle of 350°F oven for 4 minutes, or until lightly toasted. Watch carefully because they burn easily. Cool.

Roasted Red Radishes

YIELD 6 SIDE-DISH SERVINGS

Seldom does the humble radish come to mind when we think of roasted root vegetables. But these red-skinned wonders taste delicious cooked to tender delectability. Serve them with roast lamb, pork, or duck. Or for a vegetarian version, serve them with red cabbage braised with apples along with wild rice or brown rice on the side.

- ½ pound radishes, trimmed
- 3 tablespoons extra-virgin olive oil
- ½ teaspoon coarse salt, such as kosher

1   Adjust oven rack to middle position. Preheat oven to 450°F.

2   Cut radishes in half lengthwise. Toss with oil. Spread on rimmed baking sheet and sprinkle with salt.

3   Roast until cut sides begin to turn golden, about 15 minutes. Serve hot or at room temperature. If dry, drizzle with a little olive oil.

Nutritional information (per serving): Calories 70, fat calories 60; total fat 7 grams, sat fat 1 gram, cholesterol 0 milligrams; sodium 210 milligrams; total carbohydrates 1 gram, fiber 0 grams, sugars 1 gram; protein 0 grams; vitamin A IUs 0%; vitamin C 15%; calcium 0%; iron 0%.

Shallot

Paper-thin copper-colored skin encloses shallot's sweeter-than-onion flesh. A member of the *Allium* (onion) genus, shallots are formed something like garlic, but generally have only two large cloves that attach at root end. Recipes that call for one shallot generally mean one large clove.

Cold weather and heavy rain can be problematic for organic shallot growers. When planting organic shallot crops, they leave more empty space between each shallot to help prevent mildew. This method creates shallots with larger cloves, but lowers organic yields by about 15 percent. Shallots give off gasses that act as a natural insect repellent.

BUYING AND STORING: Look for dry, plump, firm bulbs free of wrinkles, sprouts, soft spots, or mold. Store in cool, well-ventilated area, out of direct sunlight for up to 3 weeks.

PREP AND USE: Cut off ends, making a very shallow cut at root end so layers stay intact. Cut in half lengthwise. Use paring knife to peel; catch end of papery brown skin with knife, then holding skin pull in opposite direction. Rinse with cold water and pat dry. Place cut-side down on work surface; slice, dice, or mince, as desired.

Substitute for onion when a subtler, sweeter flavor is preferred. Can be eaten raw and used in salads, relishes, salsas, and vinaigrettes. To cook, braise, sauté, simmer, or roast.

AVAILABLE: August to April

NUTRITIONAL INFORMATION (per 1 tablespoon chopped, raw): Calories 7, fat calories 0; total fat 0 grams, sat fat 0 grams, cholesterol 0 milligrams; sodium 1 milligram; total carbohydrates 2 grams, fiber 0 grams, sugars 0 grams; protein 0 grams; vitamin A IUs 2%; vitamin C 1%; calcium 0%; iron 1%.

SERVING SUGGESTIONS

Shallot Steak Sauce

Sauté 2 seasoned rib-eye steaks in lightly oiled large, heavy-bottomed skillet on medium-high heat, searing exteriors until crusty and cooking to desired doneness. Place on warm serving platter and cover with foil. Lower heat to medium and add 1 tablespoon unsalted butter and 8 thinly sliced shallots. Cook, stirring occasionally until softened but not browned, about 3 minutes. Increase heat to medium-high and add 2 tablespoons red wine vinegar; cook until almost entirely evaporated. Add ⅓ cup dry red wine; cook until reduced by half. Remove from heat and swirl in 4 teaspoons unsalted butter. Stir in 1 tablespoon minced fresh Italian parsley. Spoon over steaks.

Pickled Shallots

These tasty slivers are delicious in chicken salad, egg salad, or on turkey sandwiches. In a glass jar, combine 4 large shallots, thinly sliced, ½ cup water, ½ cup red wine vinegar, and 1½ tablespoons coarse salt, such as kosher. Cover and shake to combine. Refrigerate at least 1 day or up to 2 weeks.

Crisp-Fried Shallots

Vietnamese salads often are topped with fried-until-crispy shallots. They add a touch of sweetness along with an appealing texture. Cut 4 large shallots into ⅛-inch-thick crosswise slices. Heat ¼ inch canola oil or vegetable oil in medium, deep skillet or wok on medium-high heat. Add shallots and cook until golden brown. Drain on paper towels and season with coarse salt, such as kosher. Store at room temperature and use as garnish on green salads or casseroles within 8 hours.

Shallot Pasta Sauce

Cut 6 shallots into thin crosswise slices. Heat ⅛ inch vegetable oil in medium skillet on medium heat. Add shallots and cook until caramelized to golden brown, stirring occasionally. Add 1 large clove garlic (minced) and cook 20 seconds. Toss with 8 ounces hot cooked pasta. Season with seasoned salt and a generous amount of freshly ground black pepper. Add 2 teaspoons minced fresh Italian parsley and toss. Top each serving with grated Parmesan cheese.

Caramelized Shallot and Bacon Tart

YIELD: 8 SERVINGS

This showy tart makes a beautiful first course, whether served at a picnic or showy dinner party. If serving for an outdoor gathering, provide small plates or sturdy napkins and a sharp knife; place the tart on a rustic cutting board and let guests help themselves. The combination of sweet, caramelized shallots and onions, salty bacon, and creamy ricotta is a winning combination.

Easy Processor Pie Dough

1⅓ cups all-purpose flour plus flour for dusting work surface

½ teaspoon salt

1 teaspoon sugar

½ cup (1 stick) cold unsalted butter, cut into 8 pieces

¼ cup ice water

Filling

4 slices thick bacon (see Meatless Tip)

1 tablespoon canola oil

4 large shallots, cut crosswise into thin slices

1½ large yellow onions, cut in half top to bottom, thinly sliced crosswise

⅛ teaspoon sugar

1½ tablespoons chopped fresh thyme leaves

Salt and freshly ground black pepper

1 cup whole-milk ricotta cheese

1 egg yolk

¼ cup grated Parmesan cheese

Egg wash: 1 egg yolk beaten with ½ teaspoon water

1   Prepare pie dough: In food processor fitted with metal blade, pulse flour, ½ teaspoon salt and 1 teaspoon sugar 2 or 3 times. Add butter and pulse until mixture resembles coarse meal. With motor running add ice water through feed tube, processing just until mixture just barely comes together. Pat into disk shape; place in plastic bag and refrigerate 1 hour.

2   Adjust oven rack to middle position. Preheat to 350°F. On lightly floured work surface, roll dough into a circle roughly 11 inches in diameter, using a floured rolling pin. Place dough in 9½-inch tart pan with removable bottom. Use top of bent finger to press dough into fluted sides of pan. To create a double layer of dough on sides of crust, trim dough ¼ inch above top of pan; fold overhanging dough over so top of fold is even with top of pan to reinforce sides; press with top of bent finger to seal sides. Roll rolling pin over top of tart pan to make top of dough even all the way around. Poke dough at 1-inch intervals with tines of fork (bottom and sides). Line dough with sheet of aluminum foil. Add about 1 cup dry beans, raw rice, or pie weights. Bake 15 minutes. Remove from oven; remove foil and beans, rice, or weights. Set aside.

3   Prepare filling: In large, deep skillet, cook bacon until crisp; remove bacon from pan and drain on paper towels, reserving 1 tablespoon bacon grease in pan. Add oil and heat on medium-high heat. Add shallots and onions; cook, stirring occasionally, until soft and starting to brown, about 9 minutes.

4   Reduce heat to medium to medium-low. Add sugar, thyme, and salt and pepper to taste; stir to combine. Cook until onions are golden, stirring occasionally, about 20 additional minutes.

5   In small bowl, combine ricotta, egg yolk, cheese, and salt and pepper to taste.

6   Cautiously spread ricotta mixture on bottom of tart shell. Top with shallot mixture, spreading out in an even layer. Crumble bacon and sprinkle on top of shallot mixture. Brush top edge of crust lightly with egg wash. Place on rimmed baking sheet and bake until golden brown and heated through, 35 to 45 minutes. Allow to cool 15 minutes before cutting into wedges and serving.

Nutritional information (per serving): Calories 380, fat calories 250; total fat 27 grams, sat fat 13 grams, cholesterol 85 milligrams; sodium 520 milligrams; total carbohydrates 24 grams, fiber 1 gram, sugars 2 grams; protein 10 grams; vitamin A IUs 15%; vitamin C 6%; calcium 10%; iron 10%.

Meatless Tip: Omit bacon. If desired, substitute cooked and crumbled vegetarian bacon.

Caramelized Shallot and Bacon Tart

Pasta Salad with Shallot Dressing

YIELD: 12 SERVINGS

This salad tastes like cold antipasti in a bowl, pairing salami, cold green beans, bell pepper, celery, tomato, olives, and corkscrew pasta with a shallot-filled vinaigrette.

2 cups 1-inch pieces trimmed fresh green beans

12 ounces small spiral pasta, such as rotini or gemelli, or small shells

Dressing

¼ cup red wine vinegar

3 tablespoons Dijon-style mustard

2 large cloves garlic, minced

4 tablespoons minced fresh Italian parsley

4 tablespoons minced shallots

2 teaspoons agave syrup or honey

½ teaspoon dried oregano or 1½ teaspoons minced fresh oregano leaves

Salt and freshly ground black pepper

¾ cup extra-virgin olive oil

Salad

1 cup sliced green onions, including dark green stalks

1½ cups diced salami (see Meatless Tip)

1 cup diced red bell pepper or yellow bell pepper, or a combination

1½ cups sliced celery

2 Roma tomatoes, diced

Garnish: ¾ cup grated Parmesan cheese

Optional garnish: pitted kalamata olives

1   Bring a large pot of water to boil on high heat. Add green bean pieces and cook until tender-crisp, about 3 to 4 minutes. Remove with slotted spoon. Place in colander and refresh with cold water. Set aside.

2   In same pot of boiling salted water, add pasta and cook according to package directions until al dente (tender but with a little bite). Drain. Set aside.

3   In large bowl, combine all dressing ingredients except oil; whisk to combine. Whisk in oil. Add pasta to bowl and toss. Add all salad ingredients except cheese and olives. Add green beans. Gently toss. Taste and adjust seasoning. Serve immediately or cover and refrigerate up to 6 hours.

4   Top each serving with cheese and, if desired, additional pepper. If desired, garnish with olives.

Nutritional information (per serving without olives): Calories 420, fat calories 290; total fat 32 grams, sat fat 5 grams, cholesterol 15 milligrams; sodium 390 milligrams; total carbohydrates 27 grams, fiber 2 grams, sugars 3 grams; protein 9 grams; vitamin A IUs 10%; vitamin C 30%; calcium 10%; iron 10%.

Meatless Tip: Omit salami and, if desired, add a pinch of dried red chile flakes to the dressing to give it a flavor boost.

Caramelized Shallot and Blue Cheese Dip

YIELD: 2 ¼ CUPS

Surround this luscious dip with a variety of dippers such as raw vegetables, crackers, or toasted slices of baguette. The dip can be prepared two days in advance of serving and stored airtight in the refrigerator. If you like, top the dip with a little minced fresh tarragon or crumbled bacon.

- 1 tablespoon vegetable oil
- 1 ¼ cups sliced shallots
- ¾ cup mayonnaise
- ¾ cup sour cream
- 4 ounces crumbled blue cheese, room temperature
- Seasoned salt and freshly ground black pepper
- For serving: raw vegetables or crackers or toasted baguette slices

1   Heat oil in medium, heavy-bottomed saucepan on medium-low heat. Add shallots. Cover and cook until shallots are deep golden brown, stirring occasionally, about 20 minutes. Cool completely.

2   In medium bowl, combine mayonnaise and sour cream; stir to combine. Add blue cheese and mash into mayonnaise mixture with fork. Stir in caramelized shallots. Season with seasoned salt and pepper to taste. Cover and refrigerate at least 2 hours or up to 2 days.

3   Serve with assorted raw vegetables, such as carrots, turnips, jicama, celery, radish, and red bell pepper. Crackers or toasted baguette slices are also delicious dippers.

Nutritional information (per tablespoon of dip, without dippers): Calories 50, fat calories 35; total fat 4 grams, sat fat 1.5 grams, cholesterol 5 milligrams; sodium 80 milligrams; total carbohydrates 2 grams, fiber 0 grams, sugars 1 gram; protein 1 gram; vitamin A IUs 2%; vitamin C 0%; calcium 2%; iron 0%.

Chicken with Blueberries and Shallots

YIELD: 4 SERVINGS

Blueberries may seem like a surprising ingredient to pair with sautéed chicken breasts. But the sweet-tart flavor of the berries tastes delicious with the chicken, or if you prefer, substitute Sautéed Breaded Tofu (page 320) for the meat. Either way, serve the dish with brown rice or orzo and a crisp green salad.

- ¼ cup all-purpose flour
- Salt and freshly ground black pepper
- 4 (6-ounce) skinless, boneless chicken breasts (see Meatless Tip)
- 1 ½ tablespoons extra-virgin olive oil, plus additional oil if needed
- ½ medium yellow onion, coarsely chopped
- 4 shallots, cut in half lengthwise or quartered if large
- 3 medium cloves garlic, chopped
- ½ cup dry red wine
- ¼ cup vegetable broth or chicken broth
- 1 tablespoon cold unsalted butter, cut into quarters
- ¼ teaspoon Italian herb seasoning (mixture of dry herbs such as basil, oregano, rosemary, thyme, and marjoram)
- 2 cups blueberries
- ¼ teaspoons fresh lemon juice

1   In plastic bag or bowl, combine flour and salt and pepper to taste. Add chicken and toss to lightly coat.

2   In large, deep skillet, heat oil on medium-high heat. Add chicken and cook, browning well on both sides, about 4 to 6 minutes per side. Reduce heat if necessary to prevent over-browning. Remove chicken from pan. Check to make sure that it is completely cooked. Place on plate and cover with aluminum foil.

3   Add onion and shallots to pan; cook until softened and starting to brown, about 4 to 5 minutes; add additional oil if pan is dry. Add garlic and cook 20 seconds. Add wine and cook until most of wine evaporates, scraping up any browned bits in bottom of pan. Add vegetable broth or chicken broth and return to a boil. Reduce to medium heat; add butter and herb seasoning. Add blueberries and juice; stir to combine. Simmer 5 minutes. Add salt and pepper to taste. Spoon sauce over chicken.

Nutritional information (per serving with chicken): Calories 330, fat calories 110; total fat 12 grams, sat fat 3.5 grams, cholesterol 75 milligrams; sodium 95 milligrams; total carbohydrates 23 grams, fiber 2 grams, sugars 9 grams; protein 26 grams; vitamin A IUs 8%; vitamin C 4%; calcium 4%; iron 10%.

Meatless Tip: Omit chicken, instead use Sautéed Breaded Tofu (see page 320). Start with step 3. Place 1½ tablespoons extra-virgin olive oil in large, deep skillet. Heat oil on medium-high heat and proceed to cook onions and shallots. Proceed with recipe. Spoon sauce over tofu.

Squash

SUMMER SQUASH:

Crookneck

Zucchini

WINTER SQUASH:

Acorn

Butternut

Kabocha

Spaghetti

Summer squash are harvested when their seeds and skins are still tender. Firm exteriors and hard seeds (that need toasting to be edible) are the trademarks of winter squash. They are harvested when fully mature, and some varieties require a heavy-duty cleaver or sturdy chef's knife to cut their rigid rinds.

Organic growers report that they often use plastic mulch to help prevent weeds and hold in moisture on their summer squash crops. They compost the soil well before seeding and use crop rotation to nourish the soil.

For winter squash, organic growers often rotate corn and squash crops. Weeding is done by hand and most is harvested before the fall frost, typically in early October. Organic wax is sometimes used on the exterior of acorn squash due to a light powder that forms naturally on the rind. Farmers report that organic winter squash crops yield about 10 percent less than conventionally farmed fields.

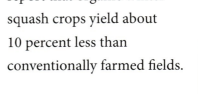

Butternut

Kabocha

Acorn

Spaghetti

BUYING AND STORING FOR SUMMER SQUASH:
Exteriors should be free of soft spots, nicks, or shriveling. Smaller, less mature squash will have fewer seeds and more delicate flavor. Large overmature specimens can be woody and bitter. Store unwashed, in plastic bag in crisper drawer of refrigerator up to 4 days.

BUYING AND STORING FOR WINTER SQUASH:
Rind should be intact with no signs of decay or soft spots. Avoid squash with cracks or nicks. Choose squash that seem heavy for their size; a heavier squash contains more edible flesh. If buying precut winter squash, look for brightly colored and fresh-looking flesh; avoid discolored pieces; refrigerate in plastic bags up to 5 days.

Uncut, their thick, hard rinds form a protective barrier around flesh so they can be kept in a cool, dark, well-ventilated location between 30 and 180 days. Do not refrigerate uncooked, uncut winter squash. If cut, refrigerate. Cooked, pureed squash freezes well up to 3 months.

PREP AND USE FOR SUMMER SQUASH: Just before using, wash thoroughly with cold water and trim ends. Eat raw in salads, or grill, blanch, microwave, roast, or sauté. Use in soups, stews, or casseroles. Stuff and bake, or dredge in seasoned breadcrumbs, fry, and top with grated Parmesan cheese. Garlic, basil, and tomatoes can add a perky edge to cooked summer squash. Cook slices with canned stewed tomatoes and top with grated Parmesan.

PREP AND USE FOR WINTER SQUASH: Wash with cold water before using. All winter squash must be cooked. Can be steamed, baked, roasted, microwaved, or blanched (but boiling can make it watery and diminish flavor).

Acorn squash and kabocha need to be cut in half and seeded before cooking; use a cleaver or hefty chef's knife to cut in half. Easier-to-cut butternut squash and spaghetti squash also need to be cut in half lengthwise and seeded before baking.

To bake winter squash (except spaghetti squash), brush either rimmed baking sheet or squash cut side with either vegetable oil or olive oil. Place flesh-side down on rimmed baking sheet. Bake in 375°F oven until fork-tender, about 30 to 45 minutes; baking times vary depending on size and shape. Spaghetti squash is an exception: Place cut-side down in baking pan with ¼ inch water; bake about 35 minutes. When cool enough to handle, scrape out interior with a fork and separate into strands.

AVAILABLE: Year-round

Crookneck

Zucchini

NUTRITIONAL INFORMATION (per 1 cup cubed raw acorn squash): Calories 56, fat calories 1; total fat 0 grams, sat fat 0 grams, cholesterol 0 milligrams; sodium 4 milligrams; total carbohydrates 15 grams, fiber 2 grams, sugars 0; protein 1 gram; vitamin A IUs 10%; vitamin C 26%; calcium 5%; iron 5%.

NUTRITIONAL INFORMATION (per 1 cup cubed raw butternut squash): Calories 63, fat calories 1; total fat 0 grams, sat fat 0 grams, cholesterol 0 milligrams; sodium 6 milligrams; total carbohydrates 16 grams, fiber 3 grams, sugars 3 grams; protein 1 gram; vitamin A IUs 298%; vitamin C 49%; calcium 7%; iron 5%.

NUTRITIONAL INFORMATION (per 1 cup sliced raw crookneck squash): Calories 25, fat calories 3; total fat 0 grams, sat fat 0 grams, cholesterol 0 milligrams; sodium 3 milligrams; total carbohydrates 5 grams, fiber 2 grams, sugars 2 grams; protein 1 gram; vitamin A IUs 4%; vitamin C 18%; calcium 3%; iron 3%.

NUTRITIONAL INFORMATION (per ¾ cup cubed raw kabocha squash): Calories 30, fat calories 0; total fat 0; sat fat 0 grams, cholesterol 0 milligrams; sodium 0 milligrams; total carbohydrates 7 grams, fiber 1 gram, sugars 3 grams; protein 1 gram; vitamin A IUs 70%; vitamin C 15%; calcium 2%; iron 2%.

NUTRITIONAL INFORMATION (per 1 cup raw spaghetti squash): Calories 31, fat calories 5; total fat 1 gram, sat fat 0 grams, cholesterol 0 milligrams; sodium 17 milligrams; total carbohydrates 7 grams, fiber 0 grams, sugars 0; protein 1 gram; vitamin A IUs 1%; vitamin C 4%; calcium 2%; iron 2%.

NUTRITIONAL INFORMATION (per 1 cup chopped raw zucchini): Calories 20, fat calories 2; total fat 0 grams, sat fat 0 grams, cholesterol 0 milligrams; sodium 12 milligrams; total carbohydrates 4 grams, fiber 1 gram, sugars 2 grams; protein 2 grams; vitamin A IUs 5%; vitamin C 35%; calcium 2%; iron 2%.

SERVING SUGGESTIONS

Acorn Squash Rings with Rice

Cut 2 acorn squash horizontally into ⅝-inch-wide rings. Remove seeds and place in single layer (unpeeled) on oiled rimmed baking sheet. You can add the end cuts (that are solid, not rings), too; cut off the pointed ends so they will lie flat. Drizzle squash with a little maple syrup and bake in 375°F oven until fork-tender, 20 to 25 minutes. Transfer to plates and season with salt and freshly ground black pepper. Place a scoop of a favorite pilaf in center of each (or use Brown Rice with Corn and Cheese, page 111).

Pickled Zukes

Wash 4 medium zucchini and cut into thin slices. Place in bowl with 1 tablespoon coarse salt, such as kosher; toss with hands, lightly rubbing salt into squash. Place in colander in sink; set aside for 25 minutes, tossing 2 or 3 times. Rinse with cold running water. Place in nonreactive bowl (such as glass or ceramic) with 2 teaspoons sugar or agave syrup, 2 tablespoons minced fresh dill and 1½ tablespoons distilled white vinegar. Set aside for 30 to 60 minutes and serve.

No-Spaghetti Spaghetti with Pesto

Bake spaghetti squash (see Prep and Use). When cool enough to handle, scrape out interior and separate into strands dragging a fork through the flesh. Toss warm strands with your favorite pesto sauce or use Basil-Parsley Pesto, page 167.

Roasted Zucchini Slices

Preheat oven to 375°F. Trim 10 zucchini and cut into ½-inch-wide crosswise slices. Place in large, ovenproof skillet and toss with 6 tablespoons extra-virgin olive oil and 1 teaspoon coarse salt, such as kosher. Spread out slices so they are in a fairly even double layer and roast 30 to 40 minutes, gently tossing every 15 minutes (remember handle of skillet is hot). Toss with 2 tablespoons chopped fresh tarragon leaves and sprinkle with grated Parmesan cheese to taste.

Summer Squash Orzo Salad

YIELD: 6 SERVINGS

Olives make a great garnish for this colorful salad. Their salty brininess adds an appealing contrast. Olives with their pits still in place taste better than pitted, but if using the unpitted beauties, be sure to put them off to the side rather than atop each serving so guests have a better visual clue that they aren't pitted.

8 ounces orzo (rice-shaped pasta)

1 teaspoon salt

3 tablespoons extra-virgin olive oil plus 1 teaspoon extra-virgin olive oil, divided use

2 medium yellow crookneck squash, trimmed, diced

2 medium zucchini, trimmed, diced

½ large red onion, finely diced

1 red bell pepper, cored, seeded, diced

1 cup grape or cherry tomatoes, halved lengthwise

Minced zest of 1 lemon (colored portion of peel)

2 tablespoons fresh lemon juice

2 teaspoons salt

Freshly ground black pepper

1 tablespoon chopped fresh Italian parsley

4 cups baby spinach or mixed baby greens

1 ounce salami, cut into ⅛-inch dice (see Meatless Tip)

½ cup crumbled feta cheese

Garnish: ½ cup unpitted olives, such as kalamata or Niçoise

Optional garnish: microgreens

1 Bring large pot of salted water to boil on high heat. Add orzo and cook according to package directions until al dente (tender but with a little bite). Drain, refresh with cold water. Drain and toss with 1 teaspoon oil. Set aside.

2 Place zucchini, crookneck squash, onion, bell pepper, and tomatoes in large bowl. Gently toss. In small bowl or glass measuring cup with handle, combine zest, juice, 3 tablespoons oil, salt, black pepper to taste, and parsley. Stir to thoroughly combine. Pour on vegetables and toss. Add orzo and toss. Taste and adjust seasoning.

3 Divide spinach between 6 small plates. Top with vegetable-orzo mixture. Sprinkle each serving with diced salami and crumble cheese on top. Place a small pile of olives off to the side of each salad. If desired, scatter some microgreens (tiny immature greens) on top of salad.

Nutritional information (per serving without salami): Calories 310, fat calories 120; total fat 13 grams, sat fat 4 grams, cholesterol 15 milligrams; sodium 1100 milligrams; total carbohydrates 39 grams, fiber 4 grams, sugars 7 grams; protein 11 grams; vitamin A IUs 45%; vitamin C 120%; calcium 10%; iron 15%.

Meatless Tip: Omit salami. If desired, use 1 cup pitted olives in the salad instead of ½ cup as a garnish.

Summer Squash Orzo Salad

Vegetable Soup

YIELD: 6 SERVINGS

A blueprint for a simple vegetable soup such as this cries out for adaptations. If you like, add some cooked rice or canned beans. If you like a brothy soup, add more broth. If you like it herbal, add more Italian seasoning. If you like garnishes, top each serving with a Roasted Garlic Crostini (page 139). Or omit the final addition of fresh parsley and top each serving with a dollop of pesto.

2 tablespoons extra-virgin olive oil

2 tablespoons unsalted butter

1 large yellow onion, diced

3 medium carrots, peeled, diced

2 large or 4 small stalks celery, diced

3 medium cloves garlic, minced

Salt and freshly ground black pepper

2 teaspoons Italian herb seasoning (mixture of dry herbs such as basil, oregano, rosemary, thyme and marjoram)

6 cups chicken broth or vegetable broth

6 ripe Roma tomatoes, seeded, chopped

1½ cups diced zucchini

1½ cups diced yellow crookneck squash

Leaves from large sprig fresh thyme

4 tablespoons chopped fresh Italian parsley or 3 tablespoons chopped fresh basil leaves

1 In large saucepan or Dutch oven, heat oil and butter on medium-high heat. Add onion and lower heat to medium. Cook, stirring occasionally, until onion starts to soften, about 5 minutes. Add carrots and celery and cook, stirring occasionally, about 5 minutes. Add garlic, salt and pepper to taste, and Italian seasoning; toss to combine.

2 Add chicken broth or vegetable broth, tomatoes, zucchini, crookneck squash, and thyme; increase heat to high. Bring to boil; reduce heat to medium. Partially cover and simmer 30 minutes. Add parsley or basil and stir. Remove from heat and serve.

Nutritional information (per serving): Calories 140, fat calories 80; total fat 9 grams, sat fat 3 grams, cholesterol 0 milligrams; sodium 530 milligrams; total carbohydrates 13 grams, fiber 4 grams, sugars 5 grams; protein 3 grams; vitamin A IUs 120%; vitamin C 35%; calcium 4%; iron 6%.

Pasta with Butternut Squash, Fingerlings, and Lima Beans

YIELD: 6 SERVINGS

T he earthy-sweet flavor profile of butternut squash makes it a perfect partner with neutral starches such as pasta or rice. In this recipe, penne pasta and butternut squash team with chunks of fingerling potato and lima beans.

2 tablespoons extra-virgin olive oil

1 large sweet onion, cut in half lengthwise, cut into thin crosswise slices

2 large cloves garlic, minced

1 tablespoon chopped fresh thyme leaves

¼ teaspoon dried red chile flakes

3 cups ½-inch cubes of peeled butternut squash

6 fingerling potatoes, cut into ¾-inch crosswise slices

¾ cup thawed frozen lima beans, baby lima beans preferred

2 cups vegetable broth

10 ounces penne

Salt and freshly ground black pepper

¼ cup grated Parmesan cheese

1   Heat oil in large, deep skillet over medium-high heat. Add onion and cook until tender and golden, about 10 minutes. Add garlic, thyme, and chile flakes; cook 30 seconds. Add squash and potatoes; toss to coat. Add broth and bring to boil. Add lima beans. Cover and reduce heat to medium-low. Simmer until vegetables are tender, about 8 minutes.

2   Meanwhile, bring a large pot of salted water to boil on high heat. Cook penne according to package directions until al dente (just tender but with a little bite). Drain, reserving about ½ cup of pasta cooking water. Add pasta to vegetables. Toss. If needed, stir in enough pasta cooking water to make the mixture creamy, cooking and stirring mixture over heat about 1 minute. Season with salt and pepper to taste. Serve in shallow bowls, topped with cheese.

Nutritional information (per serving): Calories 320, fat calories 60; total fat 6 grams, sat fat 1.5 grams, cholesterol 5 milligrams; sodium 200 milligrams; total carbohydrates 57 grams, fiber 7 grams, sugars 6 grams; protein 11 grams; vitamin A IUs 230%; vitamin C 40%; calcium 10%; iron 15%.

Baked Kabocha with Toasted Buttery Breadcrumbs

YIELD: 6 SERVINGS

Kabocha is a variety of Japanese pumpkin. It has a deep green rind that is mottled with pale green splotches. Round but flattened at top and bottom, its flesh is a beautiful deep yellow-orange. In this recipe, the kabocha is halved, seeded, and roasted, then cut into smaller servings. Each piece of kabocha is topped with a coarse breadcrumb mixture and toasted under the broiler.

Extra-virgin olive oil or nonstick vegetable oil spray or olive oil spray for greasing pan

1 medium kabocha squash, 3 to 3½ pounds, halved, seeded

Salt and freshly ground black pepper

1½ cups coarse fresh breadcrumbs, such as sourdough or rustic whole wheat baguette (see Cook's Note)

3 tablespoons unsalted butter, melted

1½ teaspoons finely chopped fresh rosemary leaves or fresh thyme leaves

1   Adjust oven rack to lower third of oven. Preheat oven to 375°F. Brush rimmed baking sheet with oil or coat with nonstick spray. Place kabocha halves cut-side down. Roast until fork-tender, about 40 to 45 minutes (roasting times vary). Remove baking sheet from oven. Move oven rack to 8 inches below broiler element and preheat broiler.

2   Wearing oven mitts, remove squash from sheet and place flesh-side up on cutting board. Cut each half into thirds. Return squash, flesh-side up, to baking sheet. Season with salt and pepper to taste.

3   In medium bowl, toss breadcrumbs with butter and rosemary or thyme. Add salt and pepper to taste; toss. Spoon mixture on top of squash. Broil until breadcrumb mixture is nicely browned, about 1 to 3 minutes. Watch carefully because broiling times vary and breadcrumbs burn easily. Serve hot.

Nutritional information (per serving): Calories 180, fat calories 70; total fat 8 grams, sat fat 4 grams, cholesterol 15 milligrams; sodium 75 milligrams; total carbohydrates 24 grams, fiber 3 grams, sugars 8 grams; protein 4 grams; vitamin A IUs 190%; vitamin C 40%; calcium 8%; iron 9%.

Cook's Note: To make fresh breadcrumbs, tear untrimmed bread into 1-inch pieces and place in food processor fitted with metal blade. Pulse machine on and off until coarse crumbs form, the largest about the size of peas. Crumbs will be irregular in size, some much smaller than that.

Sweet Potato

Sweet potatoes aren't just for Thanksgiving. These delectable root vegetables have a natural sweetness that adds flavor (as well as appealing color and texture) to everyday dishes, from casseroles to desserts, soups to stews.

They fall into two main categories: those with light tan skin and those with dark, red-brown skin. Tan-skinned varieties generally have white to light yellow flesh and have a dry, flaky texture when cooked, much like a russet baking potato.

The flesh of dark-skinned varieties is orange to red-orange inside. It is very moist and sweet. Often this variety is labeled yam. But in fact, true yams are from a different botanical group.

Sweet potatoes are planted in springtime and often the soil is covered with a "hot bed," a layer of cotton topped with a plastic sheet, to increase humidity. Harvested in August, they are stored in temperature-controlled rooms for year-round availability.

BUYING AND STORING: Choose those that are heavy for their size and free of bruises or soft spots. Store unwashed in cool, dark location up to 7 days. Do not refrigerate.

PREP AND USE: Wash well before cooking with cold water. If baking with skin on, thoroughly pat dry with clean kitchen towel or paper towel. If peeling, use stainless-steel knife or swivel-bladed vegetable peeler to prevent discoloration. Once cut, if not using immediately, submerge in cold water to prevent discoloration.

Bake, boil, sauté, steam, or deep-fry. To bake, wash, dry, and pierce skin in several places with fork tines. Place on rimmed baking sheet lined with parchment paper and bake in 400°F oven for 45 to 60 minutes or until fork-tender. Serve in the jacket as with baked potatoes; skin is edible and contains many nutrients. To boil sweet potatoes, peel and cut into ¾-inch dice. Add to large pot of boiling, salted water and cook until tender, about 4 to 5 minutes. Or to sauté, boil about 3 minutes, then drain, rinse with cold water, and pat dry. In large nonstick skillet, sauté partially cooked cubes in a little olive oil on medium-high heat, tossing frequently until nicely browned. Gently toss with chopped parsley, salt, and freshly ground black pepper.

AVAILABLE: Year-round (peak is September to February)

NUTRITIONAL INFORMATION (per 1 medium with skin): Calories 110, fat calories 0; total fat 0 grams, sat fat 0 grams, cholesterol 0 milligrams; sodium 40 milligrams; total carbohydrates 27 grams, fiber 4 grams, sugars 9 grams; protein 2 grams; vitamin A IUs 480%; vitamin C 30%; calcium 4%; iron 6%.

SERVING SUGGESTIONS

Tangerine Mash
Prick 2 sweet potatoes with tines of fork on all sides. Place on rimmed baking sheet lined with parchment paper and bake in 400°F oven 45 to 60 minutes, or until fork-tender. When cool enough to handle, cut in half lengthwise and scoop out flesh with spoon and place in bowl. Season with salt to taste. Add 2 tablespoons fresh tangerine juice and mash with fork or potato masher.

Sweet Oven Fries
Preheat oven to 400°F. Peel 2 sweet potatoes and cut into ¼-inch-wide sticks. Spray rimmed baking sheet generously with nonstick olive oil spray. Place "sticks" on sprayed sheet and top with seasoned salt; toss and arrange in single layer. Spray with additional nonstick spray and bake 25 to 30 minutes, turning after 15 minutes. If desired, sprinkle with a little grated Parmesan cheese.

Chili, but Better
Add cubes of peeled sweet potatoes to chili and cook until tender.

Marinated Slices
Preheat oven to 400°F. Peel 3 sweet potatoes and cut into 1-inch slices. Place in single layer on rimmed baking sheet lined with parchment paper. Drizzle with 3 tablespoons extra-virgin olive oil and season with salt and freshly ground black pepper. Roast until fork-tender, about 20 to 25 minutes. In small bowl, combine 3 tablespoons extra-virgin olive oil, 3 tablespoons red wine vinegar, 3 tablespoons finely diced red onion or shallot, pinch dried red chile flakes, 1 tablespoon minced fresh basil leaves, and 1 tablespoon minced fresh Italian parsley. Cool sweet potatoes for 15 minutes. Place in single layer on rimmed platter, turning slices over so that caramelized side is on top. Spoon olive oil mixture over slices; marinate at room temperature 1 hour. If desired, sprinkle with microgreens or surround with baby lettuces before serving as a side dish.

Sweet Potato Casserole

YIELD: 12 SERVINGS

Fresh cranberries bring a welcome tart edge to the sweet topping on this mashed sweet potato dish. Piping hot, it is delicious served with ham, turkey or game. If making ahead, prepare mashed sweet potatoes through step 2; cover and refrigerate up to two days. Topping can be prepared in advance as well; seal airtight and refrigerate separately. Allow the components to set for 20 minutes at room temperature before assembling. Break up topping with spoon and sprinkle over potatoes; bake as directed.

- 4 medium-large sweet potatoes, scrubbed
- ½ cup light brown sugar
- ⅓ cup milk
- 2 eggs, lightly beaten
- 1 teaspoon vanilla
- ½ cup (1 stick) unsalted butter, melted
- Vegetable oil, canola oil, or olive oil nonstick spray

Topping

- 1 cup light brown sugar
- ⅓ cup all-purpose flour
- ⅓ cup unsalted butter, melted
- 1 cup coarsely chopped pecans
- 2 cups fresh cranberries

1 Adjust oven rack to middle position. Preheat oven to 400°F. Using tines of fork poke holes in potatoes on all sides. Place on rimmed baking sheet lined with parchment paper and bake until fork tender, 45 to 60 minutes depending on size of sweet potatoes. Remove from oven. When cool enough to handle, cut in half and scoop out flesh and mash. Add ½ cup sugar, milk, eggs, vanilla, and butter; stir to combine. You should have 3 to 4 cups of mashed sweet potatoes. Reduce oven temperature to 350°F.

2 Spray 8-inch square baking dish with nonstick spray. Place potatoes in prepared dish.

3 In small bowl, combine topping ingredients; spoon topping over potato mixture. Bake 30 to 40 minutes or until bubbling and topping is crisp.

Nutritional information (per serving): Calories 350, fat calories 190; total fat 21 grams, sat fat 9 grams, cholesterol 70 milligrams; sodium 45 milligrams; total carbohydrates 37 grams, fiber 3 grams, sugars 22 grams; protein 4 grams; vitamin A IUs 190%; vitamin C 15%; calcium 6%; iron 6%.

Sweet Potato Muffins

YIELD: 24 MUFFINS

Serve these muffins at breakfast or brunch, especially if ham or bacon is on the menu. If desired, accompany them with honey butter or apple butter.

- 2½ pounds sweet potatoes, scrubbed
- 2 cups cake flour
- 2 teaspoons baking powder
- 1 teaspoon salt
- 1 tablespoon ground cinnamon
- 4 large eggs
- 1½ cups sugar
- 1 cup vegetable oil
- 2 teaspoons vanilla
- 3 tablespoons orange liqueur
- 1 cup coarsely chopped toasted pistachio nuts (see Cook's Note)

1   Preheat oven to 400°F. Line rimmed baking sheet with parchment paper. Line two standard-size 12-cup muffin pans with paper liners.

2   Use tines of fork to prick potatoes on all sides. Place on rimmed baking sheet lined with parchment paper. Bake until tender, about 45 to 60 minutes. Remove from oven and reduce oven temperature to 350°F. When sweet potatoes are cool enough to handle, cut in half and scoop out flesh. Puree in food processor fitted with metal blade or mash until lump-free with potato masher.

3   Place flour, baking powder, salt, and cinnamon into medium bowl; stir with whisk to combine.

4   In large bowl of electric mixer, mix eggs and sugar until light yellow and smooth, about 5 to 7 minutes on medium-high speed. Add oil, vanilla, and liqueur; mix on medium speed to combine, scraping down sides and bottom with rubber spatula as needed. Add 3 cups mashed sweet potatoes and combine on low speed.

5   Remove bowl from mixer. Add dry ingredients and nuts to batter and combine with sturdy rubber spatula until just combined. Do not overmix. Spoon the batter into paper-lined cups, filling almost to the top. Bake 30 minutes or until toothpick inserted in center comes out clean. Once cooled, the muffins may feel moist on the bottom, but be confident that they are done. Cool on wire rack.

Nutritional information (per muffin): Calories 240, fat calories 110; total fat 12 grams, sat fat 1.5 grams, cholesterol 35 milligrams; sodium 150 milligrams; total carbohydrates 29 grams, fiber 2 grams, sugars 17 grams; protein 4 grams; vitamin A IUs 130%; vitamin C 4%; calcium 4%; iron 10%.

Cook's Note: To toast pistachios, place in single layer on rimmed baking sheet. Toast in middle of 350°F oven for about 3 minutes or until nicely browned. Watch carefully because nuts burn easily.

Sweet Potato and Chicken Stew

YIELD: 6 TO 8 SERVINGS

A classic Moroccan tomato-based stew is a perfect dish to showcase colorful chunks of sweet potatoes. Although this recipe includes chicken, the vegetarian version is also delicious (see Meatless Tip). With or without chicken, serve it over rice, and top with toasted slivered almonds.

- 2 tablespoons vegetable oil or canola oil
- 5 skin-on, bone-in chicken thighs, skin trimmed so it covers center portion of meat in a 1-inch strip (see Meatless Tip)
- 4 skin-on, bone-in chicken breasts, cut in half crosswise (see Meatless Tip)
- 2 large yellow onions, chopped
- 2 large cloves garlic, minced
- 2 large red bell peppers, cored, seeded, diced
- 2 teaspoons ground turmeric
- ½ teaspoon ground cinnamon
- ⅛ teaspoon dried red chile flakes
- 3 large sweet potatoes, peeled, cut into 1-inch cubes
- 3 cups chicken broth or vegetable broth, low-sodium preferred
- 1 (15-ounce) can diced tomatoes with juice
- ½ cup raisins
- 1 teaspoon minced fresh ginger
- Salt and freshly ground black pepper
- Optional for serving: 6 to 8 cups cooked brown rice or white rice
- Garnish: minced fresh Italian parsley
- Garnish: ½ cup toasted slivered almonds (see Cook's Note, page 302)

1   In large pot or Dutch oven, heat oil on medium-high heat. Brown chicken on both sides, about 4 minutes per side. This may need to be accomplished in two or three batches. Set chicken aside and remove all but about 1½ tablespoons of fat from the pot.

2   Add onions, garlic, and bell peppers; cook, stirring frequently until onions are softened, about 5 minutes. Stir in turmeric, cinnamon, and chile flakes.

3   Add chicken to onion mixture along with any accumulated juices. Add potatoes, chicken broth or vegetable broth, tomatoes with juice, and raisins. Bring to boil on high heat; reduce to medium low and simmer, stirring occasionally, about 40 minutes or until sweet potatoes are fork-tender. Stir in ginger and season with salt and pepper to taste.

4   If using rice, divide it between shallow bowls. Spoon stew on top of rice. Garnish with parsley and almonds.

Nutritional information (per serving with chicken): Calories 400, fat calories 130; total fat 14 grams, sat fat 3.5 grams, cholesterol 90 milligrams; sodium 230 milligrams; total carbohydrates 40 grams, fiber 6 grams, sugars 12 grams; protein 230 grams; vitamin A IUs 430%; vitamin C 90%; calcium 8%; iron 15%.

Cook's Note: To toast slivered almonds, place on rimmed baking sheet in single layer. Toast in middle of 350°F oven for 3 to 5 minutes, or until golden. Watch nuts carefully because they can burn easily.

Meatless Tip: Omit chicken. Skip step 1. Heat oil on medium-high heat and proceed with step 2.

Sweet Potato and Bean Soup

YIELD: 12 SERVINGS

Serve this hearty soup in mugs at informal gatherings. If desired, accompany it with toasted baguette slices topped with grated Parmesan cheese.

- 2½ tablespoons extra-virgin olive oil
- 12 ounces fully-cooked sausage, such as kielbasa or smoked chicken sausage, cut into ¼-inch slices (see Meatless Tip)
- 1 large yellow onion, chopped
- 2 large cloves garlic, minced
- ½ pound fingerling potatoes, unpeeled, scrubbed, cut into ½-inch wide slices
- 1 pound sweet potatoes, peeled, cut into ½-inch cubes
- 8 cups chicken broth or vegetable broth
- 1 large bunch kale or chard, trimmed, roughly chopped
- 2 (15-ounce) cans cannellini beans or white beans, drained, rinsed
- Salt and freshly ground black pepper
- Optional: pinch dried red chile flakes (see Cook's Note)
- Garnish: minced fresh Italian parsley

1   Line a plate with paper towels and set next to stove. Heat oil in large pot or Dutch oven on medium-high heat. Add sausage slices and brown on both sides, about 6 minutes. Remove sausage and drain on paper towels; do not clean pot.

2   Add onion; cook until softened, stirring occasionally, about 4 minutes. Add garlic and potatoes; reduce heat to medium; cook, stirring occasionally, until potatoes start to soften slightly, about 10 minutes.

3   Add chicken broth or vegetable broth and scrape up any brown bits on bottom of pot. Increase heat to high and bring to boil. Reduce heat to medium-low, cover and simmer 5 to 10 minutes, or until potatoes are tender enough to mash. Use potato masher to mash a few potatoes.

4   Add sausage, kale or chard, and beans; simmer, partially covered, about 6 minutes, or until kale softens. Add salt and black pepper to taste and dried red chile pepper flakes, if using.

5   Ladle into bowls and top each serving with a pinch of parsley.

Nutritional information (per serving with sausage): Calories 210, fat calories 60; total fat 7 grams, sat fat 2.5 grams, cholesterol 35 milligrams; sodium 120 milligrams; total carbohydrates 22 grams, fiber 6 grams, sugars 2 grams; protein 14 grams; vitamin A IUs 130%; vitamin C 40%; calcium 6%; iron 10%.

Cook's Note: If sausage is spicy, you probably won't need to add chile flakes.

Meatless Tip: Omit sausage; the soup is delicious without it. Start with step 2, heating 1 tablespoon vegetable oil or canola oil before adding onion. Cook onion until starting to soften, about 3 to 4 minutes, then add garlic and proceed with recipe.

Sweet Potato and Bean Soup

Tangerine, Mandarin

Clementine

Honey

Lee

Minneola Tangelo

Orlando Tangelo

Page

Satsuma

Tangerines are a subclass of mandarins, fruit that has been grown in China for thousands of years. Tangerines may have gotten their name when mandarins were introduced to Europe via Tangiers (Morocco), hence the title "native of Tangiers." An increasing number of growers are labeling their fruit mandarins rather than tangerines.

Juicy, brightly colored segments are only a gentle tug away. Most have loose skin that separates easily, revealing segments packed with fragrant sweetness edged with subtle tartness.

BUYING AND STORING: Look for fruit that is heavy for its size and fragrant, without soft spots or bruises. Green skin is indication that fruit was picked too early. Store at room temperature up to 1 week, or refrigerate wrapped in plastic bag up to 10 to 12 days. Juice can be frozen. If desired freeze juice in ice cube trays and use cubes to chill iced tea or punch.

PREP AND USE: Peel skin with fingers and separate segments. If seeds are present, remove with tip of paring knife. Eat raw out of hand or in fruit salads or Chinese chicken salad; stir into yogurt or pudding, or dip in chocolate fondue. Use juice in dressings or marinades. Use zest in sauces, desserts, and marinades.

VARIETIES

Clementine: Many say this is the crown jewel of the mandarin family. Easy to peel and extremely juicy with a perky, sweet tang. Generally seedless.

Honey: Dark orange skin that is easy to peel. Tastes lemony-orange. Few or no seeds.

Lee: A cross between clementines and Orlando tangelos. Deep, fiery-orange flesh with smooth skin and sweet juice. Often harvested with stem and a leaf or two attached. May contain a few seeds.

Minneola tangelo: Cross between a tangerine and grapefruit. Looks like an orange with thick, deep red-orange skin that is easy to peel. Juice is sweet-tart with a honey-like note. Typically seedless.

Orlando tangelo: Looks like an orange, but has a sweet tangerine flavor profile. It is a cross between a mandarin and a pomelo. Typically no seeds.

Page: A cross between clementines and Minneola tangelos. Tender and juicy with rich, sweet flavor. Generally seedless.

Satsuma: Sweet and juicy. Most widely available tangerine and, seasonally, the first one to market. Most often harvested with part of stem intact, often with leaves as well. Very, very easy to peel. Generally seedless.

AVAILABLE:

Clementine: November to January

Honey: February

Lee: January to February

Minneola tangelo: February to April

Orlando tangelo: November to January

Page: December to January

Satsuma: November to January

NUTRITIONAL INFORMATION (per 1 medium peeled tangerine, raw): Calories 50, fat calories 5; total fat 0.5 grams, sat fat 0 grams, cholesterol 0 milligrams; sodium 0 milligrams; total carbohydrates 13 grams, fiber 3 grams, sugars 8 grams; protein 1 gram; vitamin A IUs 0%; vitamin C 50%; calcium 4%; iron 0%.

SERVING SUGGESTIONS

Perky Citrus Glaze

A tangerine-based glaze gives an irresistible sweet-sour finish to banana bread, cupcakes, coffee cake, or pound cake. To make it, place 1 cup powdered sugar in food processor fitted with metal blade. Add 1 tablespoon soft unsalted butter and juice of 1 tangerine (about 2½ to 3 tablespoons). Process until completely blended. If mixture is too thick, add more tangerine juice.

Tangerine Pancakes

Add tangerine zest to batter. For the topping, heat maple syrup in small saucepan; remove from heat and stir in handful of tangerine sections, and spoon over servings of hot pancakes.

Citrus Sugar

Tangerine-scented sugar is delicious used in pastry or pudding. Use to sweeten hot or iced tea or lemonade. Or use it to rim glass for a tropical cocktail, dipping lip of glass first in tangerine juice to moisten, then in tangerine sugar. To make it, combine 1 cup granulated sugar and 2 tablespoons minced tangerine zest (colored portion of peel; see Glossary, page 325) in food processor fitted with metal blade; pulse 5 times.

Frisky Grill Sauce

Brush on chicken or pork the last 2 minutes of grilling (or spoon over Sautéed Breaded Tofu (see page 320). Place 1 cup fresh tangerine juice in small saucepan and boil on high heat until reduced by half. Stir in 2 tablespoons honey, 2 tablespoons soy sauce, 1 tablespoon minced tangerine zest (colored portion of peel), and ½ teaspoon hot sauce.

Page

Satsuma

Clementine

Tangerine Coconut Rice

YIELD: 6 SERVINGS

Although it's delicious on its own, this rice is a great team player. Serve it as a side dish with pork, poultry, or roasted winter squash, such as butternut or acorn. If desired, it can be prepared several hours in advance up to step 3. Reheat covered in microwave and fluff with a fork; add fruit and cilantro as directed.

- 1 tablespoon extra-virgin olive oil
- 1 medium shallot, minced
- 1 cup basmati rice
- 1½ cups vegetable broth or chicken broth
- ½ cup coconut milk
- 3 small tangerines, peeled, sectioned, seeded if necessary (see Cook's Note)
- ¼ cup fresh cilantro, finely minced
- Optional: salt

1   Heat oil in large saucepan on medium heat. Add shallot and cook until tender, but not transparent, about 1 minute, stirring occasionally (do not brown). Add rice and stir to coat evenly with oil. Add vegetable broth or chicken broth and coconut milk; increase heat to high and stir to combine. Bring to boil.

2   Cover and reduce heat to medium-low; simmer 20 minutes or until all liquid has evaporated. Gently stir rice to fluff and separate grains.

3   Add tangerine sections and cilantro; gently fold. Taste and adjust seasoning, adding a little salt if needed.

Nutritional information (per serving): Calories 200, fat calories 60; total fat 7 grams, sat fat 4 grams, cholesterol 0 milligrams; sodium 100 milligrams; total carbohydrates 35 grams, fiber 2 grams, sugars 4 grams; protein 3 grams; vitamin A IUs 2%; vitamin C 25%; calcium 4%; iron 6%.

Cook's Note: To save time, choose a tangerine variety that has few or no seeds, such as clementine, Fairchild, satsuma, or Page.

Grilled Chicken Breasts with Tangerine Vinaigrette and Black Bean Salsa

YIELD: 6

Sweet-tart tangerine juice is the delectable backdrop that puts this dish over the top. The juice is reduced to intensify its brillant flavor profile. It's showcased in a sweet-hot-tart vinaigrette that tops grilled chicken breast and black bean salsa. If you're looking for a shortcut, instead of making the salsa, buy a fresh tomato salsa and toss with black beans and a little extra-virgin olive oil.

Salsa

- 1½ cups canned black beans, drained, rinsed
- ½ cup finely diced red bell pepper or yellow bell pepper, or some of each
- 1 medium shallot, minced
- 1 teaspoon seeded, minced fresh jalapeño chile (see Cook's Note)
- 1 teaspoon chopped fresh cilantro or fresh Italian parsley
- ½ cup diced seeded Roma tomatoes
- 1 teaspoon chopped garlic
- 2 tablespoons fresh lime juice
- 1½ tablespoons raspberry vinegar or sherry vinegar
- 2 tablespoons extra-virgin olive oil
- Salt and freshly ground black pepper

Tangerine Vinaigrette

- 1¼ cups fresh tangerine juice
- 2 teaspoons minced tangerine zest (colored portion of peel)

1 teaspoon hot sauce

⅓ cup extra-virgin olive oil, plus more for brushing on chicken

1 teaspoon grated lime zest (colored portion of peel)

1 tablespoon fresh lime juice

1 teaspoon rice vinegar

2 teaspoons honey or agave syrup

1½ teaspoons minced fresh oregano leaves or ½ teaspoon dried oregano

1 teaspoon ground cumin

Chicken

6 (6-ounce) skin-on, boneless chicken breasts

1 tablespoon extra-virgin olive oil

Salt and freshly ground black pepper

Optional garnish: sprigs of fresh cilantro

1 Prepare salsa: Combine all salsa ingredients in nonreactive bowl; gently toss. Taste and adjust seasoning as needed; set aside.

2 Prepare vinaigrette: In small saucepan on medium heat, cook tangerine juice until reduced to about ¾ cup. Cool. Place in blender. Add tangerine zest and remaining vinaigrette ingredients. Blend until smooth. Set aside.

3 Heat grill. Clean grates. Brush chicken on both sides with oil; sprinkle with salt and pepper to taste. Grill chicken just until cooked through, about 7 to 8 minutes on each side. Or if preferred, cook in hot, well-seasoned grill pan with ridges, covered, over medium-high heat about 5 minutes on each side (a panini machine can be used instead of grill pan if desired). Remove chicken from heat and allow to rest for a few minutes. Cut into ½-inch-wide diagonal slices.

4 Fan slices on plates and top each serving with salsa. Stir vinaigrette and spoon on top. If desired, garnish with sprigs of fresh cilantro.

Nutritional information (per serving with chicken): Calories 440, fat calories 230; total fat 26 grams, sat fat 5 grams, cholesterol 95 milligrams; sodium 85 milligrams; total carbohydrates 15 grams, fiber 4 grams, sugars 2 grams; protein 38 grams; vitamin A IUs 6%; vitamin C 25%; calcium 4%; iron 15%.

Cook's Note: Use caution when working with fresh chiles. Wash work surface and hands thoroughly upon completion and do *not* touch eyes or face.

Meatless Tip: Omit step 3 and substitute Sautéed Breaded Tofu for chicken (page 320).

Grilled Chicken Breasts with Tangerine Vinaigrette and Black Bean Salsa

Tangerine and Spinach Salad

YIELD: 8 FIRST-COURSE SERVINGS

A touch of Asian-style dressing balances nicely with the grassy taste of crisp baby spinach and the sweet-tart pizzazz of fresh tangerine segments. Toast the slivered almonds or sesame seeds that are used for a garnish in advance to give them time to cool. If desired, the dressing can be made in advance and refrigerated.

- 9 cups baby spinach
- 12 tangerines, peeled, sectioned, seeded if necessary
- ½ medium jicama, peeled, cut into ¼-inch cubes
- 1 bunch green onions, trimmed, sliced, including ½ dark green stalks
- 2 tablespoons soy sauce
- 1 tablespoon hoisin sauce
- 1 tablespoon toasted sesame oil
- ½ teaspoon ground mustard
- ½ cup shelled unsalted sunflower seeds
- Salt and freshly ground black pepper
- Garnish: ½ cup slivered toasted almonds or ¼ cup toasted sesame seeds (see Cook's Notes)

1 Place spinach, tangerines, jicama, and green onions in large bowl. Gently toss.

2 In small bowl, combine soy sauce, hoisin sauce, oil, and mustard; stir to combine. Add to spinach mixture and top with sunflower seeds; toss. Add salt and pepper to taste.

3 Divide between 8 plates. Garnish with slivered almonds or sesame seeds. Serve.

Nutritional information (per serving): Calories 220, fat calories 90; total fat 11 grams, sat fat 1 gram, cholesterol 0 milligrams; sodium 310 milligrams; total carbohydrates 32 grams, fiber 9 grams, sugars 20 grams; protein 7 grams; vitamin A IUs 40%; vitamin C 110%; calcium 15%; iron 15%.

Cook's Notes: To toast slivered almonds, place on rimmed baking sheet in single layer. Toast in middle of 350°F oven until golden brown about 5 minutes. Watch nuts carefully because they can burn easily. Cool.

To toast sesame seeds, place in small skillet on medium heat. Shake handle to redistribute seeds as they toast to light brown. Watch carefully because they burn easily. Cool.

Wheat Berry and Tangerine Salad

YIELD: 8 TO 10 SERVINGS

Cooked wheat berries (sometimes labeled wheat kernels or whole grain wheat) add appealing chewy texture and nutty taste to this grain-based salad. They are sold at natural food stores and many supermarkets. In this dish, the tangerine-based vinaigrette complements the tender, almost crunchy berries, but it isn't absorbed by them. So serve the salad in small bowls, or over a bed of raw baby spinach.

Vinaigrette

- 1 tablespoon minced tangerine zest (colored portion of peel)
- 4 shallots, minced
- ½ cup rice vinegar
- 2 tablespoons tangerine juice
- ⅓ cup honey
- Salt and freshly ground black pepper
- ½ cup extra-virgin olive oil
- 3 tablespoons chopped fresh mint

Salad

- 2½ cups cooked, drained wheat berries (see Cook's Notes)

- 4 small tangerines or 3 large, peeled, sectioned, seeded if necessary

- ½ cup coarsely chopped salted pistachio nuts or toasted slivered almonds (see Cook's Notes) or salted pumpkin seeds, or a combination

- Optional for serving: 8 cups baby spinach

1   Place all vinaigrette ingredients except oil and mint in small bowl or glass measuring cup with handle; stir to combine. Whisk in oil. Stir in mint.

2   In medium-large bowl, combine wheat berries and vinaigrette; set aside for 10 minutes. Add tangerine sections and pistachio nuts or almonds or pumpkin seeds; toss. Allow to rest at room temperature for 10 to 15 minutes. Toss again and taste; adjust seasoning as needed. Serve in small cups or over baby spinach.

Nutritional information (per serving, using 10 servings): Calories 250, fat calories 130; total fat 14 grams, sat fat 2 grams, cholesterol 0 milligrams; sodium 30 milligrams; total carbohydrates 29 grams, fiber 3 grams, sugars 14 grams; protein 5 grams; vitamin A IUs 6%; vitamin C 15%; calcium 4%; iron 6%.

Cook's Notes: To cook wheat berries, place 1 cup in medium saucepan and cover with 3 cups water. Bring to boil on high heat; cover and reduce heat to medium-low. Simmer, covered, 50 to 60 minutes, or until a few berries have burst and grains are tender. During cooking process, check from time to time to make sure there is water in the pan; add more water if needed. Drain. Allow to cool 10 minutes. Yield is 2½ cups.

To toast nuts, place on rimmed baking sheet in single layer. Toast in middle of 350°F oven for 3 to 5 minutes, or until lightly toasted. Watch carefully because they burn easily. Cool.

Tomato

Baby Heirloom

 Cherry

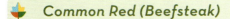 Common Red (Beefsteak)

 Grape

Heirloom

Red (Cluster, On-the-Vine)

Roma (Plum)

Teardrop (Red, Yellow)

Some store-bought tomatoes

used to be troublesome. They lacked flavor, juiciness, and aroma. They were as different from vine-ripened tomatoes as show dogs are from donkeys. Picked prematurely, they were exposed to ethylene gas to accelerate ripening after shipping.

But organic tomatoes have a "no-gas" restriction. Whether they are grown in fields or greenhouses, certified organic tomatoes are left on the vines long enough to ripen. The results are tomatoes that taste better, tomatoes with an alluring sweetness balanced with appealing acidity.

Heirloom

Heirloom

Roma

Baby Heirloom

Heirloom

Red (on-the-vine)

Baby Heirloom

Teardrop

Cherry

BUYING AND STORING: Look for plump, heavy-for-their-size tomatoes without bruises or soft spots. Never buy from refrigerated case and store at room temperature. Do not refrigerate tomatoes unless they are very ripe.

PREP AND USE: Gently wash in cold water. To slice for sandwiches, some like to cut from top to bottom; these slices tend to hold together better than when cut from side to side.

To remove seeds and juice, cut in half crosswise at the "waistline." Turn cut-side down and gently squeeze.

AVAILABLE:

Baby Heirloom: July to August

Cherry, Common, Grape, Heirloom, Red (Cluster, On-the Vine), Roma, Teardrop (Red or Yellow): Year-round

NUTRITIONAL INFORMATION (per 1 cup chopped, raw): Calories 32, fat calories 3; total fat 0 grams, sat fat 0 grams, cholesterol 0 milligrams; sodium 9 milligrams; total carbohydrates 7 grams, fiber 2 grams, sugars 5 grams; protein 2 grams; vitamin A IUs 30%; vitamin C 38%; calcium 2%; iron 3%.

SERVING SUGGESTIONS

Tomato Dress-up Dressing

Stir together ⅓ cup tomato juice, 1 clove garlic (minced), pinch sugar, 1 teaspoon balsamic vinegar, and 2 teaspoons minced fresh basil leaves or mint or tarragon leaves; gradually add ⅓ cup extra-virgin olive oil, stirring constantly. Add 1 medium tomato (diced), and salt and freshly ground black pepper to taste. Spoon over grilled fish, chicken, or pork; green beans, roasted vegetables, or grilled eggplant.

Vodka Dip

Arrange sweet cherry tomatoes or tiny teardrops on platter. Combine ¼ cup coarse salt, such as kosher, and 2 teaspoons finely minced fresh basil leaves in small bowl. Place about ¼ cup premium vodka in another small bowl. To serve as appetizer, have guests dip tomatoes in vodka, then in a smidgen of salt.

Bruschetta Topping

Combine 3 medium diced tomatoes with 2 tablespoons extra-virgin olive oil, 1 tablespoon minced red onion, ½ cup crumbled feta cheese, 2 tablespoons minced fresh basil leaves, and 1 teaspoon red wine vinegar. Toss and season with salt and freshly ground black pepper. Use on top of crackers or toasted baguette slices (see Roasted Garlic Crostini, page 139). Or spoon on cooked brown rice or pasta.

Tomato, Corn, and Olive Salad

In large bowl, 2 tablespoons extra-virgin olive oil, 1 clove garlic (minced), 1½ tablespoons balsamic vinegar; stir and add salt and freshly ground black pepper to taste. Add 2 cups corn kernels, ½ cup pitted cured black olives, and ¼ cup shredded fresh basil leaves. Gently toss and spoon over 3 large, thick-sliced tomatoes.

Heirloom Tomato Salad with Mangoes and Blue Cheese

YIELD: 8 GENEROUS SERVINGS

Heirloom tomatoes should taste like you just picked them from your grandmother's garden. They should have a sweet edge combined with a leafy green smell. This salad shows off their irresistible side by combining them with sweet-tart mangoes and herbaceous torn basil. Blue cheese adds a just-right salty element that balances the dish to perfection.

Dressing

½ cup safflower oil or extra-virgin olive oil

½ cup crumbled blue cheese

3 tablespoons balsamic vinegar

1 teaspoon cider vinegar

1 teaspoon salt

1 large shallot, minced

Salad

2 to 3 cups mixed baby greens

4 heirloom tomatoes, sliced or cut into large wedges (see Cook's Note)

3 mangoes, peeled, seeded, diced

10 large, fresh basil leaves, torn into pieces

Garnish: 1 sprig basil

Optional garnish: ½ cup mixed microgreens

1   In glass measuring cup with handle or in small bowl, combine safflower oil or extra-virgin olive oil and blue cheese. Using tines of fork, press some of the cheese against side of container to mash it into the oil. Stir in vinegars, salt, and shallot. Set aside.

2   Line platter or individual shallow bowls with baby greens. Top with tomatoes. Add mangoes, placing some on top of tomatoes and some along the edges. Top with torn basil leaves. Stir dressing and spoon over tomatoes and mangoes. Any leftover dressing can be refrigerated and used for another salad, either with assorted greens or sliced fruit (such as apples or tangerines) atop mixed lettuces.

3   If desired, scatter microgreens on top of salad.

Nutritional information (per serving): Calories 230, fat calories 150; total fat 16 grams, sat fat 3.5 grams, cholesterol 5 milligrams; sodium 420 milligrams; total carbohydrates 19 grams, fiber 3 grams, sugars 15 grams; protein 3 grams; vitamin A IUs 35%; vitamin C 60%; calcium 8%; iron 4%.

Cook's Note: You can use any variety of full-flavored, ripe tomatoes in this recipe. A mixture of uncut tiny cherry tomatoes mixed with small teardrop tomatoes works beautifully. The dressing can be prepared two days in advance and refrigerated airtight; stir before using.

Heirloom Tomato Salad with Mangoes and Blue Cheese

Taco Salad with Grape Tomatoes, Chicken, and Avocado

YIELD: 6 SERVINGS

A tangy salad that showcases grape tomatoes, black beans, and avocado is a great way to use leftover cooked chicken breast. Bake strips of corn tortillas to use as a crunchy garnish. The baked tortilla strips can be prepared 1 day in advance. Cool completely and store in airtight container at room temperature.

4 (6-inch) corn tortillas

3 tablespoons extra-virgin olive oil

3 tablespoons fresh lime juice

½ teaspoon salt

Optional: pinch dried red chile flakes

1½ cups grape tomatoes, halved lengthwise

1 cup diced cooked chicken breast (see Meatless Tip)

2 (15-ounce) cans black beans, drained, rinsed

1 ripe avocado, pitted, peeled, diced

4 cups mixed baby greens

1   Adjust oven rack to middle position. Preheat oven to 350°F. Cut tortillas into ¼-inch-wide strips. Place on rimmed baking sheets and bake until crisp, about 10 to 11 minutes. Cool.

2   In large bowl, combine oil, juice, salt and, if using, chile flakes. Stir to combine.

3   Add tomatoes and chicken; toss. Add black beans and avocado; gently toss. Line 6 salad plates with greens. Spoon tomato mixture on top of greens. Top with baked tortilla strips.

Nutritional information (per serving with chicken): Calories 310, fat calories 130; total fat 14 grams, sat fat 2 grams, cholesterol 20 milligrams; sodium 230 milligrams; total carbohydrates 33 grams, fiber 11 grams, sugars 2 grams; protein 16 grams; vitamin A IUs 25%; vitamin C 25%; calcium 6%; iron 15%.

Meatless Tip: Instead of chicken, substitute 4 ounces chopped tempeh that has been cooked until crisp in a little canola oil on medium-high heat. Or use Grilled Tofu with Mediterranean-Style Marinade (page 321), cut into cubes.

Mediterranean Salsa

YIELD: 2 ½ CUPS

Mediterranean Salsa gives a delectable boost to bland food. Spoon it on grilled chicken, fish or pork. Ladle it over grilled veggie burgers, vegetables, or roasted slices of russet potato. Or serve accompanied with crackers for an appetizer. Can be prepared 2 days in advance and stored airtight in refrigerator.

1 large clove garlic, minced

12 large fresh basil leaves

1 fresh jalapeño chile, seeded, minced (see Cook's Notes, page 314)

4 sun-dried tomatoes, drained if packed in oil

¼ cup chopped red onion

¼ cup extra-virgin olive oil

1 tablespoon balsamic vinegar

1 tablespoon red wine vinegar

Salt and freshly ground black pepper

1 large red bell pepper, roasted, chopped

2 large ripe fresh tomatoes, seeded, diced

10 pitted cured black olives, coarsely chopped

1   With machine running, drop garlic into food processor fitted with metal blade; mince garlic. Add basil and chile; pulse until finely minced.

2   Add sun-dried tomatoes and pulse until coarsely chopped.

3   Add onion, oil, vinegars, and salt and black pepper to taste; process about 5 seconds. Stir in bell pepper, fresh tomatoes, and olives. Refrigerate in airtight container if not using immediately.

Nutritional information (per serving): Calories 70, fat calories 60; total fat 6 grams, sat fat 1 gram, cholesterol 0 milligrams; sodium 220 milligrams; total carbohydrates 5 grams, fiber 1 gram, sugars 3 grams; protein 1 gram; vitamin A IUs 8%; vitamin C 35%; calcium 2%; iron 4%.

Cook's Notes: To roast pepper, place broiler rack 6 to 8 inches below broiler element. Preheat broiler. Line bottom portion of broiler pan with aluminum foil. Place pepper on foil and broil on each side until charred, turning with tongs. Remove from oven and pull up sides of foil to enclose pepper; let it sit 5 minutes. Open foil. When cool enough to handle, peel, seed, and dice.

Use caution when working with fresh chiles. Wash work surface and hands thoroughly upon completion and do *not* touch face or eyes.

Marinated Fresh Mozzarella or Goat Cheese with Fresh Tomatoes

YIELD: 10 SERVINGS

Marinated cheese is a mouthwatering treat served on slices of vine-ripened tomatoes. If desired, instead of fresh mozzarella, use ½-inch slices of cold, soft goat cheese (the easiest way to slice goat cheese is with dental floss). If using goat cheese, only marinate up to 3 days.

8 ounces small balls fresh mozzarella cheese (bocconcini)

3 sprigs fresh thyme

5 fresh basil leaves

½ teaspoon freshly ground black pepper

Pinch dried red chile flakes

About 2 tablespoons extra-virgin olive oil

For serving: 10 thick slices rustic bread, toasted

For serving: 5 heirloom tomatoes, seeded, cut into ½-inch slices

1   Place cheese in clean, 1-pint canning jar, separating it by placing herbs between cheese spheres. Add black pepper and chile flakes. Add enough oil to cover contents. Cover and refrigerate up to 1 week.

2   Place 1 slice of toasted bread on 10 salad plates. Top with sliced tomatoes. Top with cheese and a little of the marinade.

Nutritional information (per serving): Calories 160, fat calories 50; total fat 5 grams, sat fat 0.5 grams, cholesterol 18 milligrams; sodium 120 milligrams; total carbohydrates 19 grams, fiber 1 gram, sugars 2 grams; protein 9 grams; vitamin A IUs 10%; vitamin C 15%; calcium 2%; iron 4%.

Cook's Note: Since cheese can be stored for several days, you can make fewer servings if you like, then use leftover cheese for appetizers or snacks. If desired, garnish salad plates with mixed baby greens. For best flavor, allow time for cheese to marinate, at least 1 hour or refrigerated airtight up to 7 days.

Turnip

With a gentle hint of mustardy heat, these jolly roots add a just-right spark to everything from roasted vegetables to au gratin potatoes. Large turnips have more pronounced peppery flavor profiles, especially if they have spent a long time in cold storage. Atop the bulb, tender green leaves stand ready for steaming or sautéing after a good bath in cold water. They have a perky, mustard-edged taste that teams well with bacon, white beans, duck, or roast pork. The general rule is the younger (smaller) the leaves, the milder the taste.

BUYING AND STORING: Choose those with firm, smooth skin. If large, select a turnip that is heavy for its size. Overly large turnips may have woody cores. Green tops, if present, should look green and have a fresh scent. If greens are attached, twist them off. Store root portion, unwashed, in plastic bag in crisper drawer up to 5 days. For greens, rinse in tub of cold water; repeat if necessary, until water is clear and free of grit. Shake off excess water or drain, wrap in clean kitchen cloth or paper towels, and place in plastic bag. Refrigerate up to 3 days.

PREP AND USE: Peel root; slice or dice. If turnip is over 3 inches in diameter, cut ⅛ inch off outer portion because it may be tough. Eat raw or cooked. Raw sliced turnip makes a great dipper served with hummus or creamy vegetable dips. To cook tender-crisp, boil, simmer, roast, or steam. Clean turnip greens (see Buying and Storing) can be tossed with other milder greens in a salad. Or they can be simmered, blanched, or steamed.

AVAILABLE: Year-round

NUTRITIONAL INFORMATION (per 1 cup chopped, raw): Calories 18, fat calories 1; total fat 0 grams, sat fat 0 grams, cholesterol 0 milligrams; sodium 22 milligrams; total carbohydrates 4 grams, fiber 2 grams, sugars 0 grams; protein 1 gram; vitamin A IUs 127%; vitamin C 55%; calcium 10%; iron 3%.

SERVING SUGGESTIONS

Taco Filling with Turnip

In large, deep skillet, combine 8 ounces lean ground beef with ½ cup peeled and finely chopped turnip. Cook on medium-high heat until no pink color remains in meat, breaking up meat with spatula as it cooks. Reduce heat to medium; add ⅓ cup finely diced sweet onion, 1½ teaspoons chili powder, ½ teaspoon ground cumin, and ½ teaspoon dried oregano. Cook, stirring occasionally, until onion softens, about 5 minutes. Spoon into warm corn tortillas; fold and top with shredded lettuce or cabbage, chopped tomatoes, and grated cheese, such as Jack or cheddar.

Turnip and Cucumber Salad

Peel 1 turnip; cut in half and thinly slice. Place in bowl with ½ hothouse (English) cucumber or 1 common cucumber (peeled, seeded), thinly sliced. Add 2 teaspoons rice vinegar and ½ teaspoon cider vinegar; toss. Cover and refrigerate 2 hours. Sprinkle with coarse salt, such as kosher, and top with toasted sesame seeds.

Mash with Apple

Trim and peel 2 medium turnips; cut into ½-inch slices. Place in large saucepan and add just barely enough water to cover. Bring to boil on high heat; cover and reduce heat to low. Simmer 10 minutes. Add 1 tart apple, such as Granny Smith (peeled, cored, cut into ¼-inch wedges). Cover and cook until tender, about 10 minutes. Drain and reserve cooking water. Add 2 tablespoons unsalted butter, 1 teaspoon light brown sugar, and 1 teaspoon finely chopped fresh sage leaves. Mash with potato masher, adding a little cooking liquid if necessary to make creamy consistency. Season to taste with salt and freshly ground black pepper.

Braised in Broth

Place 1½ tablespoons extra-virgin olive oil and ⅔ cup vegetable broth in medium, heavy-bottomed skillet. Add 3 medium turnips (peeled, halved, cut into ½-inch slices). Bring to boil on high heat; cover and reduce heat to medium-low. Simmer 15 minutes. Remove cover and season with salt and freshly ground black pepper. Increase heat to high and cook until liquid in pan reduces to about 1½ tablespoons. Drizzle with ¼ cup heavy whipping cream and heat through. Garnish with 1 tablespoon finely chopped fresh Italian parsley.

Roasted Root Vegetables

YIELD: 8 SERVINGS

Roasted vegetables can be a meal or a side dish. After tossing with salt and pepper in the last step, taste the mixture. If desired, drizzle a little freshly-squeezed lemon juice over the vegetables and toss. Or instead of plain salt, season to taste with Lemon-Rosemary Salt (page 191).

3 medium beets, unpeeled, with 1-inch stem attached

3 tablespoons extra-virgin olive oil

2 medium turnips, peeled, halved lengthwise, cut into ¼-inch slices

4 medium carrots, peeled, cut into ¾-inch pieces

2 parsnips, peeled, cut into ¾-inch pieces

1 large sweet potato, peeled, halved lengthwise, cut into ¼-inch slices, light tan variety preferred

1 large yellow onion, cut into 1-inch-wide wedges

3 tablespoons honey

1½ tablespoons fresh thyme leaves

2 medium cloves garlic, peeled, cut in half lengthwise

Salt and freshly ground black pepper

1 Adjust oven rack to middle position. Preheat oven to 400°F. To bake beets, scrub beets and wrap (still wet) in heavy-duty aluminum foil. Bake in preheated oven until fork-tender, 45 to 60 minutes, depending on size. When cool enough to handle, slip off peel.

2 Place oil in large roasting pan; place in oven until oil is hot, about 4 minutes. Cautiously add all vegetables except beets and toss to coat. Roast 15 minutes. Add honey and thyme; toss to coat. Roast 60 to 65 minutes, or until vegetables are tender and nicely browned, tossing vegetables every 15 minutes.

3 Cut beets half from top to bottom; cut ⅜-inch wedges and add to roasted vegetables. Season to taste with salt and pepper. Gently toss.

Nutritional information (per serving): Calories 190, fat calories 50; total fat 5 grams, sat fat 1 gram, cholesterol 0 milligrams; sodium 90 milligrams; total carbohydrates 35 grams, fiber 6 grams, sugars 17 grams; protein 3 grams; vitamin A IUs 200%; vitamin C 35%; calcium 6%; iron 6%.

Carrot, Turnip, and Lentil Soup

YIELD: 8 SERVINGS

Red lentils give this pureed soup an inviting rich taste and texture. These reddish-orange lentils are sometimes labeled Egyptian. They are smaller than French lentils and do not have a seed coat. Larger portions of this hearty soup could serve as a main course for a simple weeknight meal.

2 tablespoons unsalted butter

2 tablespoons vegetable oil

2 medium yellow onions, chopped

5 medium carrots, peeled, chopped

1 medium turnip, peeled, chopped

½ cup raw red lentils

1 large clove garlic, chopped

5 cups vegetable broth

Salt and freshly ground black pepper

1 tablespoon minced fresh Italian parsley

Garnish: sour cream

Optional garnish: crumbled cooked bacon or crumbled cooked vegetarian bacon

1 Melt butter in oil in large saucepan or Dutch oven on medium-high heat. Add onions and cook, stirring occasionally, until softened, about 4 to 5 minutes. Add carrots, turnip, and lentils; stir to combine.

2 Add broth and bring to boil on high heat. Add garlic and reduce heat to low. Partially cover and gently simmer 35 to 45 minutes or until vegetables and lentils are tender.

3 Remove from heat. Cautiously puree in 2 or 3 batches in food processor. Return to pan and heat. Add salt and pepper to taste and parsley. Ladle into soup bowls. Garnish each serving with a small dollop of sour cream; and, if desired, add a smidgen of cooked crumbled bacon or meatless bacon.

Nutritional information (per serving without garnish): Calories 140, fat calories 60; total fat 7 grams, sat fat 2.5 grams, cholesterol 10 milligrams; sodium 430 milligrams; total carbohydrates 17 grams, fiber 4 grams, sugars 4 grams; protein 4 grams; vitamin A IUs 130%; vitamin C 15%; calcium 4%; iron 6%.

Potato-Turnip Au Gratin

YIELD: 6 SERVINGS

Turnips offer a taste bud tickle to this potato au gratin, adding a peppery hint to the rich blend of potatoes, cheese, and cream. Each serving is baked in an individual ramekin so the blanket of golden brown crust stays perfectly intact for a glamorous presentation.

1 tablespoon unsalted butter for greasing ramekins

1½ cups heavy whipping cream

2 medium turnips, peeled, sliced ⅛-inch thick

1 large Yukon Gold potato, peeled, sliced ⅛-inch thick

2 medium cloves garlic, minced

3 cups grated Swiss cheese

Salt and freshly ground black pepper

1   Adjust oven rack to middle position. Preheat oven to 350°F. Grease 6 (10-ounce) round ramekins or soufflé cups with butter.

2   Pour a little cream in the bottom of each ramekin. Layer in each: turnip slice, potato slice, a tiny bit of garlic, enough cheese to cover surface, salt and pepper to taste, a little more cream. Repeat this sequence until ramekins are full, ending with a little cheese. Place ramekins on rimmed baking sheet and bake 60 minutes or until vegetables are tender. Allow to rest 10 minutes before serving. Serve in ramekins.

Nutritional information (per serving): Calories 280, fat calories 220; total fat 25 grams, sat fat 16 grams, cholesterol 90 milligrams; sodium 260 milligrams; total carbohydrates 12 grams, fiber 1 gram, sugars 2 grams; protein 4 grams; vitamin A IUs 30%; vitamin C 30%; calcium 8%; iron 2%.

Potato and Turnip Curry

YIELD: 6 SERVINGS

Turnips bring a lot of flavor personality to this vegetarian potato curry dish, but the essential flavor base is a curry-like blend of spices and herbs. Curry powder is a blend of ground dried spices and herbs; often as many as 20 are used to make the concoction. This recipe, rather than using a store-bought curry powder, utilizes its own signature blend, combining ground cardamom, cinnamon, chili powder, cumin, ginger, pepper, and turmeric. Serve the dish over brown rice and, if desired, top each serving with a generous amount of chopped cilantro.

4 tablespoons vegetable oil or canola oil

2 medium yellow onions, halved lengthwise, cut into ¼-inch-wide slices

1 large clove garlic, minced

2 large russet potatoes, peeled, cut into ⅜-inch cubes

3 medium turnips, peeled, cut into ⅜-inch cubes

1 cup vegetable broth

1 (14.5-ounce) can diced tomatoes, drained, juice reserved

1 cup coconut milk

¾ teaspoon ground turmeric

1 teaspoon ground cinnamon

¾ teaspoon ground cardamom

¾ teaspoon freshly ground black pepper

¾ teaspoon ground cumin

1 teaspoon minced fresh ginger

2 teaspoons sugar

1 teaspoon chili powder

1 teaspoon salt

½ cup dried cranberries

For serving: cooked brown rice

Optional garnish: chopped fresh cilantro

1 Heat vegetable oil or canola oil in large, deep skillet on medium-high heat. Add onions; cook, stirring occasionally, until onions soften, about 5 minutes. Add garlic, potatoes, and turnips; cook 2 minutes, stirring frequently. Add all remaining ingredients except cranberries, rice, and cilantro. Stir and bring to boil on high heat. Reduce heat to medium-low and gently simmer until potatoes and turnips are tender, 20 to 30 minutes. If mixture gets too thick, add reserved tomato juice.

2 Taste and adjust seasoning as needed. Add dried cranberries and gently toss. Serve in bowls over rice. If desired, garnish with cilantro.

Nutritional information (per serving): Calories 310, fat calories 160; total fat 17 grams, sat fat 8 grams, cholesterol 0 milligrams; sodium 550 milligrams; total carbohydrates 37 grams, fiber 6 grams, sugars 9 grams; protein 5 grams; vitamin A IUs 10%; vitamin C 60%; calcium 8%; iron 20%.

Potato and Turnip Curry

Meatless Options

When meat is used in this book, Meatless Tips are noted at the end of the recipes. Many of those tips refer readers to the meat-free recipes in the Meatless Options section. Enjoy these tofu-based recipes as meat substitutes in our recipes, or in your own cooking.

Sautéed Breaded Tofu

YIELD: 7 SERVINGS

1 (14-ounce) block firm tofu, cut into ½-inch slices (see Cook's Note)

½ cup fresh breadcrumbs

¼ cup grated Parmesan cheese

1 teaspoon dried thyme or minced fresh thyme leaves

1 tablespoon minced fresh Italian parsley

Optional: 1 ½ teaspoons finely minced lemon zest or tangerine zest (colored portion of peel)

1 egg

2 teaspoons milk or soymilk

Canola oil or olive oil for frying

1 Place tofu on paper towels to drain.

2 In shallow bowl or pie pan, combine breadcrumbs, cheese, thyme, parsley, and zest, if using.

3 In another shallow bowl or pie pan, beat egg and milk.

4 Dip each tofu slice on both sides in egg mixture, then in breadcrumb mixture.

5 In large skillet add enough oil to cover bottom of pan. Heat on medium-high and when hot, add breaded tofu slices in single layer (you may need to work in batches depending on side of skillet). Reduce heat to medium and sauté on both sides until nicely browned, about 10 minutes total.

Nutritional information (per serving, using 2 tablespoons oil for sautéing): Calories 120, fat calories 80; total fat 9 grams, sat fat 2 grams, cholesterol 30 milligrams; sodium 75 milligrams; total carbohydrates 3 grams, fiber 1 gram, sugars 0 grams; protein 9 grams; vitamin A IUs 2%; vitamin C 2%; calcium 10%; iron 8%.

Cook's Note: If you would like tofu to have a meatier texture, slice tofu into ½-inch slices and place in single layer on rimmed baking sheet lined with parchment paper. Place in freezer and freeze thoroughly. Place on paper towels and defrost, pat dry, and use.

Grilled Tofu with Asian-Style or Mediterranean-Style Marinade

YIELD: 4 SERVINGS

mprove tofu's texture, as well as its ability to absorb marinade, by layering it between paper towels and placing it under a weighted baking sheet. Here are two marinade styles, one with Asian flavors, the other with Mediterranean.

2 (14-ounce) blocks firm tofu, drained

Asian-Style Marinade

½ cup low-sodium soy sauce

1 tablespoon minced fresh ginger

2 teaspoons toasted sesame oil

2 teaspoons packed dark brown sugar

¼ teaspoon dried red chile flakes

¼ cup vegetable oil or canola oil, plus oil for brushing grill pan

Mediterranean-Style Marinade

¼ cup fresh lemon juice

½ cup extra-virgin olive oil, plus oil for brushing grill pan

1 teaspoon packed dark brown sugar

¼ teaspoon dried red chile flakes

1 teaspoon dried oregano

1 teaspoon dried thyme

1 teaspoon seasoned salt

1 large clove garlic, minced

1 Weight tofu to remove excess moisture: Cut each block of tofu into 6 crosswise slices. Layer several paper towels on rimmed baking sheet and arrange tofu slices in single layer. Top tofu with 3 layers of paper towels and arrange a second baking sheet on top; set aside for 5 minutes. Repeat 2 more times.

2 Place marinade ingredients in 9 × 13-inch glass baking pan; stir to combine. Add tofu and marinate 20 minutes, turning occasionally.

3 Heat a lightly oiled well-seasoned ridged grill pan over moderately high heat until hot but not smoking. Use a slotted spoon or slotted spatula to lift tofu from marinade and place on grill pan. Grill until heated through and grill marks appear, cautiously turning once, about 3 minutes on each side.

Nutritional information (per serving with Asian-Style Marinade): Calories 250, fat calories 150; total fat 17 grams, sat fat 1 gram, cholesterol 0 milligrams; sodium 800 milligrams; total carbohydrates 7 grams, fiber 0 grams, sugars 0 grams; protein 15 grams; vitamin A IUs 0%; vitamin C 0%; calcium 6%; iron 10%.

Nutritional information (per serving with Mediterranean-Style Marinade): Calories 310, fat calories 220; total fat 24 grams, sat fat 2.5 grams, cholesterol 0 milligrams; sodium 450 milligrams; total carbohydrates 8 grams, fiber 0 grams, sugars 1 gram; protein 14 grams; vitamin A IUs 2%; vitamin C 15%; calcium 6%; iron 15%.

Quick Stir-Fried Tofu

YIELD: 4 SERVINGS

2½ tablespoons peanut oil or vegetable oil, divided use

1 (8-ounce) package extra-firm tofu, drained, patted dry, cut into 1-inch cubes

2 large cloves garlic, minced

5 green onions, thinly sliced, including ⅓ dark green stalks

Salt and freshly ground black pepper

1   Place wok or large, deep nonstick skillet on medium-high heat. Add 2 tablespoons peanut oil or vegetable oil. When hot but not smoking, add tofu; sauté until nicely browned on all sides, stirring every couple of minutes. Remove tofu from pan.

2   Heat remaining ½ tablespoon oil and add garlic and onions; cook, stirring frequently, about 1 minute (do *not* brown garlic). Return tofu to pan and toss. Remove from heat and season with salt and pepper.

Nutritional information (per serving): Calories 140, fat calories 110; total fat 12 grams, sat fat 2 grams, cholesterol 0 milligrams; sodium 300 milligrams; total carbohydrates 3 grams, fiber 1 gram, sugars 0 grams; protein 7 grams; vitamin A IUs 4%; vitamin C 6%; calcium 8%; iron 8%.

Glossary and Prep Help

Acidulated water: Cold water augmented with either lemon juice, lime juice, or distilled white vinegar is used to prevent discoloration of some cut fruit and vegetables (such as apples and artichokes). Generally the cut produce is soaked in the acidulated water, but it can also be used as a cooking medium.

Agave syrup: Organic agave syrup is a sweetener that is extracted from the agave plant. Sometimes labeled agave nectar, it has a relatively low glycemic index due to its proportion of fructose to glucose.

Blanch: This is a cooking technique in which food is submerged in boiling water. After the food has reached the desired degree of doneness, it is often drained and submerged in ice water to stop the cooking and brighten the color. Rather than an ice-water bath, a quicker technique is to drain the food in a colander in the sink and quickly run cold water over the contents. This method is best used for firm, nonporous vegetables such as asparagus, broccoli stalks, green beans, or sugar snap peas.

Brix levels: Brix levels (measured with a device called a refractometer) are used to measure the specific amount of sugar in fruits, vegetables and wines. The following examples show Brix levels for some fruits:

FRUIT	Poor	Average	Good	Excellent
APPLE	6	10	14	18
AVOCADO	4	6	8	10
BANANA	8	10	12	16
CANTALOUPE	8	10	12	14
CHERRIE	6	8	14	16
GRAPE	8	12	16	20
GRAPEFRUIT	6	10	14	18
HONEYDEW	8	10	12	14
KUMQUAT	4	6	8	10
LEMON	4	6	8	12
LIME	4	6	10	14
ORANGE	6	10	16	20
PAPAYA	6	10	18	20
PEACH	6	10	12	14
PINEAPPLE	12	14	20	22
STRAWBERRY	6	10	14	16
TOMATO	4	6	8	12
WATERMELON	8	12	14	16

Brown-bag ripening: To ripen some firm fruit, place in paper bag (check Buying and Storing information for specific fruit to see if it's appropriate). Loosely close top of bag and store at room temperature out of direct sunlight. The paper bag traps ethylene while allowing for exchange of air into and out of the bag. Check fruit daily; once it gives to gentle pressure, refrigerate.

Cutting citrus into supremes (peeled segments): Cut top and bottom off citrus, making those 2 cuts parallel to each other and cutting just below white pith. Place cut-side down on work surface. Cut off peel and pith in strips about 1 inch wide, starting at the top of the fruit and cutting down (following contour of fruit). Working over bowl to collect juice, use a sharp small knife to cut parallel to one section's membrane, cut to center; turn knife and cut along the membrane on the other side of that section to remove it. Repeat until all sections are removed and cut from their membranes.

Organic versus conventional: Organic farming maintains and replenishes soil fertility without the use of toxic and persistent pesticides and fertilizers (persistent, meaning that they do not break down chemically, or break down very slowly, and remain in the environment after a growing season). Organic foods are minimally processed without artificial ingredients, preservatives, or irradiation. Prevention is one of the organic farmer's primary strategies for disease, weed, and insect control. By building healthy soil, organic farms find that healthy plants are better able to resist disease and insects. When pest populations get out of balance, growers will try various options like insect predators, mating disruption, traps, and barriers. If these techniques fail, permission may be granted by the certifier to apply botanical or other nonpersistent pest conrols under restricted conditions. Botanicals are derived from plants and are broken down quickly by oxygen and sunlight.

Conventional farming methods may employ some of the same practices used in organic farming, but are under no obligation or regulation to do so.

Puree: To grind or mash food until it is smooth.

Sauté: This is a cooking technique in which the food is quickly cooked or browned in a little oil (or a combination or oil and butter) in a hot pan over high heat. This method allows cooks to season during the cooking process, augmenting with flavor enhancers such as garlic, herbs, or spices.

Steam: This is a cooking technique in which the food is placed on a rack or steamer basket over boiling or simmering water in a covered pan. This method works best with small portions.

Toasting Nuts: Nuts acquire irresistible flavor and texture when toasted until lightly browned. The flavors are rounder, mellower, and a little sweeter. The texture is crunchier. Place shelled nuts in a single layer on a rimmed baking sheet and toast in the middle of a 350°F oven, between 3 and 10 minutes. Toasting times vary depending on size of nuts and the fat content of nut variety. If they are chopped, for example, they will toast more quickly than if they are in large pieces or whole. Nuts burn easily. Turn on the oven light and watch them carefully. They can quickly go from toasty to over-toasted black.

Vinaigrette: To prepare a basic dressing, combine 2 tablespoons red wine vinegar, 2 tablespoons sherry vinegar, and ½ teaspoon kosher salt or fine sea salt in small bowl or 4-cup glass measuring cup with a handle. Whisk to dissolve salt. Whisk in ¾ cup extra-virgin olive oil. Taste and adjust seasoning as needed. If desired, lemon juice can be substituted for all or part of the vinegar. If a mustardy edge is preferred, add 1 teaspoon Dijon-style mustard. Proportions of oil to lemon juice or vinegar can be adjusted to suit individual taste.

Zest and zesters: Zesters are handy gadgets designed to remove outer colored portion of citrus peel (called zest). Some zesters have a curved metal bar attached to a handle; the bar has several tiny holes. When drawn lengthwise down the peel, thin ribbons of zest erupt. Another style, called a Microplane, is a long, stainless steel rasp; some have rubber handles, others don't. To use, swipe the citrus down the length of the rasp. Tiny, lace-like shards fall from the blade.

Index